D1448383

Institutional Work

The "institutional" approach to organizational research has shown how enduring features of social life – such as marriage and bureaucracy – act as mechanisms of social control. Such approaches have traditionally focused attention on the relationships between organizations and the fields in which they operate, providing strong accounts of the processes through which institutions govern action. In contrast, the study of institutional work reorients these traditional concerns, shifting the focus to understanding how action affects institutions. This book sets a new research agenda for institutional studies of organization by analyzing the ways in which individuals, groups, and organizations work to create, maintain, and disrupt the institutions that structure their lives. Through a series of essays and case studies, it explores the conceptual core of institutional work, identifies institutional work strategies, provides exemplars for future empirical research, and embeds the concept within broader sociological debates and ideas.

THOMAS B. LAWRENCE is the Weyerhaeuser Professor of Change Management and Director of the CMA Centre for Strategic Change and Performance Measurement in the Faculty of Business Administration at Simon Fraser University in Vancouver, Canada.

ROY SUDDABY is Professor of Management and Rice Faculty Fellow at the Alberta School of Business, University of Alberta, Canada.

BERNARD LECA is Assistant Professor in the Department of Management and Strategy at Groupe ESC Rouen, France.

Institutional Work

Actors and Agency in Institutional Studies
of Organizations

Edited by
THOMAS B. LAWRENCE
ROY SUDDABY
AND
BERNARD LECA

CAMBRIDGE
UNIVERSITY PRESS

CAMBRIDGE UNIVERSITY PRESS
Cambridge, New York, Melbourne, Madrid, Cape Town,
Singapore, São Paulo, Delhi, Tokyo, Mexico City

Cambridge University Press
The Edinburgh Building, Cambridge CB2 8RU, UK

Published in the United States of America by Cambridge University Press, New York

www.cambridge.org
Information on this title: www.cambridge.org/9780521178525

© Cambridge University Press 2009

First published 2009
First paperback edition 2010

A catalogue record for this publication is available from the British Library

Library of Congress Cataloguing in Publication Data
Institutional work : actors and agency in institutional studies of organization / edited by
Thomas B. Lawrence, Roy Suddaby, Bernard Leca.
    p. cm.
ISBN 978-0-521-51855-0
1. Social institutions. 2. Organizational sociology. I. Lawrence, Thomas B.,
1964– II. Suddaby, Roy. III. Leca, Bernard. IV. Title.
HM826.I556   2009
306.01-dc22

                                                        2009019280

ISBN 978-0-521-51855-0 Hardback
ISBN 978-0-521-17852-5 Paperback

Contents

Figures

Tables

Contributors

Julie Battilana, Harvard Business School

Y. Sekou Bermiss, Kellogg School of Management, Northwestern University

Eva Boxenbaum, Copenhagen Business School

Thomas D'Aunno, INSEAD

Timothy J. Hargrave, University of Washington, Bothell

Paul M. Hirsch, Kellogg School of Management, Northwestern University

Paula Jarzabkowski, Aston Business School, Aston University

Matthew S. Kraatz, University of Illinois at Urbana-Champaign

Thomas B. Lawrence, Simon Fraser University

Bernard Leca, Groupe ESC Rouen

Johanna Mair, IESE Business School

Ignasi Martí, EM Lyon

Jane Matthiesen, Aston Business School, Aston University

Brent McKnight, Richard Ivey School of Business, University of Western Ontario

Jesper Strandgaard Pedersen, Copenhagen Business School

Roy Suddaby, University of Alberta

Christine Quinn Trank, Rawls College of Business, Texas Tech University

Andrew H. Van de Ven, Carlson School of Management, University of Minnesota

Marvin Washington, University of Alberta

Charlene Zietsma, Richard Ivey School of Business, University of Western Ontario

Tammar B. Zilber, The Hebrew University of Jerusalem

1 | Introduction: theorizing and studying institutional work

THOMAS B. LAWRENCE, ROY SUDDABY, AND
BERNARD LECA

T H E concept of institutional work describes "the purposive action of individuals and organizations aimed at creating, maintaining and disrupting institutions" (Lawrence & Suddaby, 2006: 215). Institutional work represents an exciting direction for institutional studies of organization, not because it represents a "new" idea, but because it connects a set of previously disparate ideas, and in doing so points to new questions and opens up space for new conversations. Institutional approaches to organization theory have traditionally focused attention on the relationships among organizations and the fields in which they operate, providing strong accounts of the processes through which institutions govern action. The study of institutional work reorients these traditional concerns, shifting the focus to understanding how action affects institutions. Connecting, bridging, and extending work on institutional entrepreneurship, institutional change and innovation, and deinstitutionalization, the study of institutional work is concerned with the practical actions through which institutions are created, maintained, and disrupted. The concept of institutional work highlights the intentional actions taken in relation to institutions, some highly visible and dramatic, as often illustrated in research on institutional entrepreneurship, but much of it nearly invisible and often mundane, as in the day-to-day adjustments, adaptations, and compromises of actors attempting to maintain institutional arrangements. Thus, a significant part of the promise of institutional work as a research area is to establish a broader vision of agency in relationship to institutions, one that avoids depicting actors either as "cultural dopes" trapped by institutional arrangements, or as hypermuscular institutional entrepreneurs.

The overarching aim of this book is to present a series of chapters which will collectively articulate a research agenda for the study of institutional work. We approach that aim in two main ways. First, the chapters in this book explore both the conceptual core and the

1

boundaries of the idea of institutional work. Through both theoretical discussions and empirical research, the authors in this volume provide explicit and implicit articulations of these issues, revealing both considerable agreement and significant conflict especially with respect to the term's conceptual boundaries. Second, the book provides a set of empirical works that can serve as exemplars for scholars undertaking the study of institutional work. The research described in this volume demonstrates the importance of rich, detailed case studies in understanding the practical actions of individual and organizational actors attempting to create, maintain, and disrupt institutions, as well as showing the value of examining a wide range of empirical contexts, across sectors, geopolitical boundaries, and time frames.

The study of institutional work has the potential not only to positively affect scholarly discussions within the institutional community, but also to generate conversations which might bridge the interests of those who study institutions and organizations, and those who work in them. Although institutional theory has become a standard point of reference in contemporary textbooks of organization theory (Greenwood, Oliver, Sahlin & Suddaby, 2008), it has largely failed to affect the practical discussions of organizational managers and members outside the academy (Miner, 2003). We believe this is a shame and a waste; much of the appeal of an institutional perspective is its "realistic" treatment of organizations – as more than production machines or economic actors. The institutional perspective has brought to organization theory a sophisticated understanding of symbols and language, of myths and ceremony, of decoupling, of the interplay of social and cognitive processes, of the impact of organizational fields, of the potential for individuals and groups to shape their environments, and of the processes through which those environments shape individual and collective behavior and belief. These are critically important issues for those working in organizations to understand, and yet these issues have for the most part remained trapped within the confines of academic text and talk. Our hope is that shifting the focus to the practical work of actors in relation to institutions will help lead to an easier and more compelling translation of institutional ideas into non-academic discourses.

In this introductory chapter, our aim is to examine some key issues with respect to the concept of institutional work, both in terms of how we might usefully elaborate and refine our conception of it, and how it relates to broader issues in institutional studies of organization. In first proposing the concept (Lawrence & Suddaby, 2006), our primary goal was to develop an inductive, empirically grounded understanding of the terrain that might be mapped using the concept of institutional work. With that accomplished, we now turn to developing a more systematic, theoretical exploration, in order to provide a more nuanced and detailed description of the concept. We present this chapter in four main sections. First, we review the role of actors, agency, and institutions in institutional studies of organization. Second, we elaborate the concept of institutional work. Third, we theorize the notion of institutional work by situating it in terms of a set of key issues and concepts. Finally, we provide an overview of the book; for each chapter, we discuss the main issue it addresses, and the perspective it adopts on that issue.

Actors, agency, and institutions

The interplay of actors, agency, and institutions has come to occupy a dominant place in institutional studies of organization (see Battilana & D'Aunno in this volume for an excellent discussion of the evolution of these issues). Although neo-institutional writing on organizations began with a strong emphasis on the cultural processes through which institutions affected organizational practices and structures (Hinings & Greenwood, 1988; Meyer & Rowan, 1977) and led to patterns of isomorphism within fields of activity (DiMaggio & Powell, 1983; Tolbert & Zucker, 1983), more recent work has focused significantly on the processes through which actors affect the institutional arrangements within which they operate (Beckert, 1999; DiMaggio, 1988; Greenwood & Suddaby, 2006; Hensmans, 2003; Lawrence, 1999; Suddaby & Greenwood, 2005). We believe that these two orientations have each been associated with somewhat stylized representations of the relationships among actors, agency, and institutions: early work suggested a dominant impact of institutions on organizational structure and practice, and a limited role for agency; in contrast, more recent work, organized significantly under the rubric of institutional entrepreneurship, has portrayed some actors as powerful, heroic figures able to dramatically shape institutions. In this section, we discuss these approaches to the relationship between actors, agency, and institutions, and explore the potential for the concept of institutional work to provide an alternative approach that draws on the strengths of the traditional views without suffering from their overstated positions.

The initial concern of neo-institutionalism was to explain organizational isomorphism that could not be explained by competitive pressures or efficiency motives (DiMaggio & Powell, 1983; Meyer & Rowan, 1977; Tolbert & Zucker, 1983). Consequentially, researchers focused on the ways in which institutions shape the behavior of organizational actors. From this perspective, agency was a secondary consideration, understood either as a reaction to institutional pressures (and thus seen in processes of adoption, decoupling, and ceremonial display), or not seriously considered at all. Where it was considered explicitly, the scope and extent of agency was understood as dependent on the influence of the social context and the interactions among organizational actors. In work that has extended this approach to the global level, Meyer and his colleagues have documented how agency as a social construction developed in contemporary societies (e.g. Frank & Meyer, 2002; Meyer & Jepperson, 2000). Frank and Meyer argue that the decline of the nation state, and economic and cultural changes in post-war societies led to the rise of generalized actorhood of individuals and the increase of specializing identities claims. Both the profusion of individual roles and identities are viewed as special cases of common underlying institutional processes (2002: 90). In this view, institutions not only influence how agents will act, but which collective or individual actor in a society will be considered to have agency and what such agents can legitimately do. In this regard, those works might be considered as belonging to a form of radical constructivism as agency had no ontological status by itself.

The neo-institutional approach came under increasing criticism on several fronts for developing an oversocialized view of agency. Perrow (1985) argued that institutional authors ignored power relations and had gone "overboard" with their emphasis on myths and symbols. DiMaggio (1988: 3) criticized institutional research as being "frequently laden with 'metaphysical pathos' – specifically, a rhetorical defocalization of interest and agency," and called for the explicit incorporation of agency into institutional theory, and the study of how actors pursue their interests in the face of institutions. Oliver offered a syncretic approach, combining strategic approaches with new institutionalism to analyze how actors develop specific strategies depending on their institutional environment (Oliver, 1990) or react to institutional pressures (Oliver, 1991). Other authors joined the chorus, calling for the injection of agency into institutional theory (Beckert, 1999; Hoffman &

Ventresca, 2002; Hirsch, 1997; Hirsch & Lounsbury, 1997a, 1997b; Lawrence, 1999).

Partly in response to these calls, a body of literature has emerged that examines "institutional entrepreneurs" – organized actors "who leverage resources to create new institutions or to transform existing ones" (Maguire, Hardy & Lawrence, 2004: 657). The focus of this literature has been primarily on the strategies used by actors to change institutional arrangements rather than just comply with them. While this research has provided valuable insights, such work tends to overemphasize the rational and "heroic" dimension of institutional entrepreneurship while ignoring the fact that all actors, even entrepreneurs, are embedded in an institutionally defined context. Institutional entrepreneurship has thus been criticized as a *deus ex machina* within institutional theory, used to explain institutional change as the outcome of attempts by a few rational and powerful actors (Delmestri, 2006: 1536–1537). Meyer (2006: 732) even suggests that such a view of institutional entrepreneurship as belonging to a particular "species" of actors more rational than others, and downplaying their institutional embeddedness, is unable to offer a viable endogenous explanation of institutional change within the tenets of institutional theory.

DiMaggio and Powell (1991: 23–24) suggest that one way to develop a more balanced view of the relationship between actors and institutions would be to draw from the practice approach that has emerged since the 1970s. A significant focus of research and writing in this tradition is on explaining the relationship between human action and the cultures/structures in which actors are embedded (Bourdieu, 1993; Giddens, 1984). A practice perspective contrasts with both structuralist views derived from Parsons and Saussure, in which human action is limited to an enactment, or execution, of rules and norms, and a voluntaristic view of agency whereby actors have unlimited freedom and capacity to invent new arrangements (Ortner, 1984). In their exploration of practice as a micro-foundation for institutional research, DiMaggio and Powell (1991) provide detailed analyses of how such a perspective might apply.

Despite the power of their analysis, however, relatively little work has taken up its call. We suggest this may be for two reasons. First, the focus of their analysis, and indeed of most practice-oriented writing, is on the micro/individual level. In contrast, institutional studies of organization have tended to accentuate the role of collective actors, and interactions among actors, especially in terms of creating and transforming institutional arrangements (Garud, Jain & Kumaraswamy, 2002; Greenwood, Suddaby & Hinings, 2002; Suddaby & Greenwood, 2005). Second, the temporal orientation of action in practice-oriented writing tends toward either relatively short term "moves" that fulfill "practical functions" in everyday life (e.g. Bourdieu, 1977, 1990; de Certeau, 2002), or longer term but stereotyped forms (Ortner, 1984: 150). Again, this contrasts with institutional approaches, in which the temporality in question tends to be of an intermediate nature – long enough for social action to influence institutional structure or for institutional structures to change and thus affect social action, but short enough for those rhythms of change not to be overwritten by the *longue durée* of history.

Thus, in looking across the relatively brief history of neo-institutionalism, we see two key tensions with respect to the issue of agency, one concerned with the degree of agency attributed to organizational actors, and one concerned with the degree to which a practice approach can adequately describe the relationship between agency and institutions. We introduced the notion of institutional work in an effort to help overcome these tensions by defining an area of institutional research that highlights the middle ground of agency and connects the insights of practice theory with institutionalists' traditional concerns for collective action and social change (Lawrence & Suddaby, 2006). The concept of institutional work is based on a growing awareness of institutions as products of human action and reaction, motivated by both idiosyncratic personal interests and agendas for institutional change or preservation. The aspiration of the concept of institutional work is that, through detailed analyses of these complex motivations, interests, and efforts, institutional research will be able to better understand the broad patterns of intent and capacity to create, maintain, and alter institutions.

Conceptualizing institutional work

In our original discussion of institutional work (Lawrence & Suddaby, 2006: 215), our aim was to provide a starting point for understanding the connections among a broad range of studies and to point toward some significant gaps in our understanding of how actors and institutions interact with each other. Most central to our definition of institutional work is its "direction." If one thinks of institutions and action as existing in a recursive relationship (Archer, 1995; Barley & Tolbert,

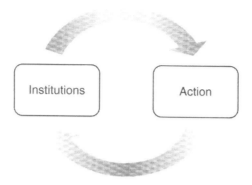

Figure 1.1 The recursive relationship between institutions and action

1997; Fairclough, 1992; Phillips, Lawrence & Hardy, 2004), in which institutions provide templates for action, as well as regulative mechanisms that enforce those templates, and action affects those templates and regulative mechanisms (see Figure 1.1), then we are centrally concerned in the study of institutional work with the second arrow, that from action to institutions. We neither deny nor ignore the effect of institutions on action, and indeed those effects are crucial to understanding the nature of institutional work, but our analytical focus in the study of institutional work, unlike most institutional studies of organization, is on how action and actors affect institutions.

Our interest in developing an institutionally situated understanding of the effect of actions on institutions led us to argue that the study of institutional work should be oriented around three key elements (Lawrence & Suddaby, 2006): (1) it would "highlight the awareness, skill and reflexivity of individual and collective actors" (219); (2) it would generate "an understanding of institutions as constituted in the more and less conscious action of individual and collective actors" (219); and (3) it would identify an approach that suggests "we cannot step outside of action as practice – even action which is aimed at changing the institutional order of an organizational field occurs within sets of institutionalized rules" (220).

We went on to propose three broad categories of institutional work: creating, maintaining, and disrupting institutions. Based on a review of institutional studies published in *Organization Studies*, *Administrative Science Quarterly*, and *Academy of Management Journal*, over a fifteen-year period, we identified forms of institutional work that had been examined empirically for each of those three categories. As we discussed at the time,

[a]lthough relatively few articles within the now voluminous body of empirical research in neo-institutional theory focus solely on institutional work, a significant number of them provide descriptions of institutional work, some directly as they examine the rise and fall of various institutional arrangements, and others in the context of background empirical material intended. (Lawrence & Suddaby, 2006: 220)

Based on this survey, we argued that the practices associated with creating institutions represent the category of institutional work most extensively examined in the literature. This work builds primarily on the notion of institutional entrepreneurship (DiMaggio, 1988; Eisenstadt, 1980), to explore the kinds of actors who attempt to create new institutions, the conditions under which they do so, and the strategies they employ (Garud *et al.*, 2002; Greenwood *et al.*, 2002; Hargadon & Douglas, 2001; Lawrence, 1999; Lounsbury, 2001; Maguire, Hardy & Lawrence, 2004). We identified ten forms of institutional work associated with creating institutions, which broke roughly into three types: "overtly political work in which actors reconstruct rules, property rights and boundaries that define access to material resources"; "actions in which actors' belief systems are reconfigured"; and "actions designed to alter abstract categorizations in which the boundaries of meaning systems are altered" (Lawrence & Suddaby, 2006: 221).

The second category of institutional work that we proposed – maintaining institutions – has received relatively little empirical or theoretical attention. Although institutions are often defined as phenomena which are self-reproducing, either because of their taken-for-granted status (Phillips & Malhotra, 2008; Scott, 2001), or because of their association with regulative mechanisms which ensure their survival (Jepperson, 1991; Lawrence, Winn & Jennings, 2001), we argue that the institutional work of maintaining institutions is both necessary and overlooked. As demonstrated in this volume (Hirsch & Bermiss, this volume; Trank & Washington, this volume; Zilber, this volume), even powerful institutions require maintenance so that those institutions remain relevant and effective. In our previous survey of the empirical literature, we found six forms of institutional work, three that "primarily address the maintenance of institutions through ensuring adherence to rules systems," and three that "focus efforts to maintain institutions on reproducing existing norms and belief systems" (Lawrence & Suddaby, 2006: 230).

Our third category of institutional work – disrupting institutions – has been the subject of institutional concern since the early work of Selznick, and gained significant attention following Oliver's (1992) discussion of deinstitutionalization. Despite this long history, however, the practices associated with actors attempting to undermine institutional arrangements is not well documented, outside the indirect processes associated with creating institutions. In our survey of empirical work in the area, we found relatively little in terms of concrete descriptions of actors disrupting institutions. What we did find fell into three forms: "work in which state and non-state actors worked through state apparatus to disconnect rewards and sanctions from some sets of practices, technologies or rules"; attempts to "disrupt institutions by disassociating the practice, rule or technology from its moral foundation"; and "undermining core assumptions and beliefs" which stabilize institutions (Lawrence & Suddaby, 2006: 235–237).

Theorizing institutional work

We believe that our original definition and categories of institutional work provide a broad but useful direction for studying and further theorizing this concept. At the same time, however, they leave several key issues unexamined and others underspecified. In this section, we aim to refine our understanding of institutional work by exploring its relationship to several important issues – accomplishment and unintended consequences, intentionality, and effort. In doing so, we seek to strike a balance. On the one hand, we want to specify the concept so that its core meaning and boundaries are clear and distinguishable. For the study of institutional work to advance, construct definition and clarity are important so that its meaning does not diffuse to the point of uselessness. On the other hand, the community of scholars interested in the concept of institutional work is broad, with a range of interests and approaches, as shown in the chapters contained in this volume. Within this community, there is significant diversity with respect to the questions we ask, and consequently the aspects of institutional work that we highlight. Thus, our aim in trying to refine the concept is to narrow the notion of institutional work, so that it more clearly points at specific phenomena, while at the same time ensuring that the definition includes important forms of institutional agency that the previous definition may have excluded (or at least steered us away from considering).

Institutional work, accomplishment, and unintended consequences

A critical issue for the study of institutional work is the distinction between "creating, maintaining, and disrupting institutions" and the "creation, maintenance, and disruption of institutions." The former describe a set of activities, whereas the latter describe a set of accomplishments. Either set could be (and often is) the focus of institutional studies of organization, but we argue that it is the former set which is at the core of the study of institutional work. This distinction is important for at least two reasons. First, exploring a set of activities leads to a very different set of questions and answers than does exploring a set of accomplishments. Why, how, when, and where actors *work at creating* institutions, for instance, describes a distinctly different (and we would suggest broader) arena of inquiry than does asking those questions about the *creation* of institutions. Studying the institutional work of creating institutions could, of course, include the investigation of the forms of institutional work and the supporting factors that are likely to lead to successfully creating new institutions (Garud *et al.*, 2002; Maguire *et al.*, 2004), but this is only one potential issue that could be examined within the domain of institutional work aimed at creating institutions. Other, relatively neglected issues include understanding which actors are more likely to engage in institutional work, what factors might support or hinder that work (independent of its success or failure), why certain actors engage in institutional work while others in similar contexts do not, and what practices constitute the range of ways in which actors work to create institutions. Such questions push us toward the examination of institutional work as practice rather than as part of a linear process (with the tendency to see such a process as a continuum of steps and stages). This is an important shift for institutional studies of organization because, despite the injection of actors and agency that we have suggested marks a major stream of work in this area, relatively little is still known about the concrete practices employed by actors in relation to institutions.

The second implication of focusing on the activities rather than the accomplishments is that it brings back into focus some important ideas that have largely disappeared from most institutionalist discourse. One of these is "unintended consequences." Particularly notable is this concept's relative neglect in research on actors' effects on institutions (Beckert, 1999; DiMaggio, 1988; Greenwood *et al.*, 2002; Greenwood & Suddaby, 2006; Lawrence, 1999; Maguire *et al.*, 2004). Although there are occasional admissions of unintended consequences in these studies, the general image of institutionally oriented action that emerges is highly successful with respect to creating intended institutional effects. We suggest that this tendency stems from a focus on charting processes that connect action to institutional effects, rather than on understanding the sets of practices that connect actors to institutions and have variably intended and unintended results with respect to those institutions. Institutional work aimed at creating institutions may create institutions, but it might also fail to do so; it might affect unanticipated institutions in unintended ways, including disrupting those institutions or creating ones very different from those originally conceived of by the actors involved.

Thus, we argue that a focus on activities allows for an account of the relationship between institutions and action that is well suited to the "muddles, misunderstanding, false starts and loose ends" (Blackler & Regan, 2006: 1843) that often characterize this relationship. Consistently with recent research on institutional change (Blackler & Regan, 2006) and organizational fields (Meyer, Gaba & Colwell, 2005), the study of institutional work offers an invitation to move beyond a linear view of institutional processes – to account for, and reflect on, the discontinuous and non-linear processes that take place (see Zietsma & McKnight, this volume, for an empirical illustration of this). Because it points to the study of activities rather than accomplishment, success as well as failure, acts of resistance and of transformation, the concept of institutional work may contribute to a move away from a concentrated, heroic, and successful conception of institutional agency.

Institutional work and intentionality

Focusing on activity, rather than accomplishment, pushes us to consider the issue of intentionality in the study of institutional work. Our original definition of institutional work included the phrase "purposive action," which suggests a high degree of conscious intentionality. This relatively simple association, however, may belie a significant complexity. Here, we first consider the meaning of intentionality, broadening our understanding of it based on a relational understanding of agency, and then examine the role of this broader conception of intentionality in identifying and understanding institutional work.

At a fundamental level, the question is whether conscious intentionality exists or not. Two antinomic approaches are often opposed (e.g. Emirbayer, 1997; Bourdieu & Wacquant, 1992). On the one hand, objectivists and structuralists suggest that actors' actions follow predefined models and relations they might not be aware of, thus denying any "real" intentionality and possible deviance (Wrong, 1961). On the other hand, subjectivists and constructivists insist that social reality is a contingent and ongoing achievement of actors who constantly construct their world in interested and strategic ways. From a practice perspective, however, there is a desire to move beyond this objective/subjective divide in social sciences (Bourdieu, 1977, 1990; Giddens, 1979, 1984; Ortner, 1984; Schatzki, Knorr Cetina & von Savigny, 2001). The work of Emirbayer and Mische (1998) presents a relational view of agency (see Battilana & D'Aunno, this volume, for a more complete and nuanced account of this perspective), which usefully complicates simplistic notions of intentionality by suggesting three sets of cognitive processes that describe distinct modes of intentionality, each of which is associated with a different temporal orientation. One form of intentionality, they argue, can be associated with the past, and is "manifested in actors' abilities to recall, to select, and to appropriately apply the more or less tacit and taken-for-granted schemas of action that they have developed through past interactions" (Emirbayer & Mische, 1998: 975). Thus, even habitual action can be understood as intentional, since there are always multiple habits and routines from which to choose at any given moment. The second form of intentionality they articulate is present-oriented, and "lies in the contextualization of social experience," which involves deliberation with others (or sometimes, self-reflexively, with oneself) about the pragmatic and normative exigencies of lived situations (Emirbayer & Mische, 1998: 994). In contrast, future-oriented intentionality involves "the hypothesization of experience, as actors attempt to reconfigure received schemas by generating alternative possible responses to the problematic situations they confront" (Emirbayer & Mische, 1998: 984). Clearly, the notion of hypothesization is closest to traditional understandings of intention, with its goal-directed, future orientation. We argue, however, that each of these processes – schematization, contextualization, hypothesization – describes a kind of intentionality, where actors relate their actions to their situations. Together, these forms of intentionality provide a useful range of images to consider with respect to the intentionality of institutional work. They suggest that what the intentions of those engaged in institutional work might look like will vary significantly depending on their temporal orientation.

This broader understanding of intentionality encourages us to consider what role actors' intentions play in institutional work. To do so, we build on our discussion of activities and accomplishments to consider two potential ways of defining the boundaries of institutional work, each with distinctive implications for the role of intentionality. The first approach defines institutional work as work that is motivated significantly by its potentially institutional effects. This would describe the efforts of actors to create, maintain, and disrupt institutions. From this perspective, intentionality is central to the determination of what constitutes institutional work: without intentionality, actions may have profound institutional effects but still not be institutional work. An alternative reading of institutional work includes all human action that has institutional effects. At the extreme, such an understanding would support the notion that the speaking of the English language in a predominantly English-language country would constitute institutional work, since it serves to reproduce the dominance of that language, and may through cumulative effects also serve to transform the language over time. More subtle examples of this conception of institutional work, however, include the activities of scientists who, through their curiosity-driven, basic research, establish the processes or materials which later innovators use to develop commercial products that go on to topple existing institutionalized designs, and establish new market leaders.

The choice among these approaches has significant implications for how one studies institutional work and the potential impacts of the concept for institutional theory. We argue that the latter approach – defining the scope of institutional work based on its effects – is the more conservative: it aligns well with traditional institutional approaches and concerns, but shifts their scope and orientation by highlighting the role of relatively less visible micro-processes, relationships, and action. Such an approach may be particularly appropriate if one is primarily interested in explaining the evolution of institutions, since it highlights the role of action in those processes, regardless of whether that action was intended, or even remotely conceived of, as having those effects. Perhaps the easiest way to understand this is by looking back at Figure 1.1: if one's scholarly spotlight is on the "Institutions" box, and "Action" is intended as an explanation (or partial explanation), and/or a consequence, then one might not care so much about the intentionality of actors (or adopt the perspective that intentionality is unknowable and consequently irrelevant to scientific study).

In contrast, including intentionality in the definition of institutional work aims may push us toward a more radical shift in our approach to understanding institutions and organizations. This approach points to a focus on institutional work itself as the primary object of analysis. So, looking back again at Figure 1.1, if one's research focuses on the "Action" box, then one is likely to be interested in the intentionality of that action, both the degree to which it is connected to the institutions in which it is embedded, and the degree to which it is motivated to affect those same or other institutions. Most studies of institutional entrepreneurship, for instance, have been relatively institution-centric: they have tended to make the focus of their inquiry the explanation of institutional change, with human action being the primary explanatory factor. In contrast, a work-centric approach to institutional entrepreneurship would still focus on the arrow running from action to institutions, but might begin with a set of actions or practices which were "aimed" at creating or transforming some set of institutions, and then explore them as interesting social phenomena in and of themselves (why and how they occurred), along with their potential impacts or lack of impacts on institutions (see Martí & Mair, this volume, for an extensive discussion of a work-centric approach to institutional entrepreneurship). Such an approach is hardly free from problems, of course – assessing and inferring intentionality raises a host of complex and potentially problematic issues. So, while we believe that addressing the issue of intentionality is critical to the advancement of institutional work as a research area, we do not expect consensus in this domain.

Institutional work and effort

The third issue we address here is the relationship between institutional work and "effort." Although not generally a central issue for institutional, or even organizational, studies, the concept of effort might provide a useful dimension along which to characterize potential instances of institutional work, and perhaps to discriminate between them and other forms of institutionally related action. Our interest in the idea of effort comes from our desire to explore the notion of "work" from an institutional perspective. The notion of work can be understood to have quite different connotations from action, which is generally used as a broader, more inclusive term. In particular, there is a connotative connection between work and effort. Dictionary definitions of work make this clear, defining work as "activity involving mental or physical effort done in order to achieve a result" (*OED*, 2007). Moreover, as this definition makes clear, the notion of work connects effort to a goal, and thus institutional work can be understood as physical or mental effort done in order to achieve an effect on an institution or institutions. Effort varies, of course, in both degree and kind, and so suggests a range of forms of action we might recognize as institutional work.

For instance, we can draw on Scott's three pillars of institutionalization to point to a variety of kinds of effort associated with institutional work. Institutions embodied in routines rely on automatic cognition and uncritical processing of existing schemata, and privilege consistency with stereotypes and speed over accuracy (Berger & Luckmann, 1967; DiMaggio, 1997; Scott, 2001). Actors can routinely enforce institutions without being aware that they are socially constructed. Thus, moving beyond the automatic cognition associated with these kinds of institutions involves a level of cognitive effort as actors shift, even subtly, toward a more complex, reflexive, slow, and self-controlled form of thought (Metcalfe & Mischel, 1999). This effort is necessary for agents to see information that contradicts the existing schemata and become aware that institutions are not natural and "taken for granted" but are social constructions. This kind of effort can also imply the potential for questioning the taken-for-grantedness of routines and assumptions, and thus the possibility of institutional change. In contrast, institutions supported by regulative and normative mechanisms involve more or less well-established laws, rules, or codes of conduct. Institutional work aimed at these kinds of institutions requires of actors not only a personal effort to move beyond taken-for-granted routines, but also an involvement in political and/or cultural action (Fligstein, 1997; Greenwood *et al.*, 2002; Rao, 1998). The effort suggested in such cases relates to forms of social action necessary to create, maintain or disrupt the regulative or normative bases of institutions (Lawrence et al., 2001).

Variation in degrees of effort also points to a way of understanding the range of actions which might be considered institutional work. This may be clarified by focusing on a single institution, and exploring the various forms of action which may be involved in maintaining it. The institution of marriage in the United States and Canada has undergone significant transformation over the past decade, with the local legalization of same-sex marriages occurring in several jurisdictions (sometimes temporarily so), and the threat of legal challenges to the ban on polyamorous marriage. Within this context, we can compare two sets of practices, both of which serve to maintain the institution of heterosexual marriage: the wedding of a man and a woman; and the operation of a "pro-family" group, such as the Institute of Marriage and Family Canada or Abiding Truth Ministries. Clearly, the institution of heterosexual marriage is fundamentally dependent for its maintenance on male–female couples getting married to each other. And, clearly, getting married is not a trivial exercise – indeed weddings can be expensive, stressful, highly effortful events. The effort associated with a wedding, however, has relatively little to do with the institution of marriage (stemming instead from institutionalized ideas of what constitutes a proper, contemporary wedding). The more the idea of marriage is cognitively institutionalized for actors, the more their actions are likely to be defined by a sphere of taken-for-granted routines (Berger & Kellner, 1964). People might just get married because that is the way it should be done and consider the related effort as necessary and a taken-for-granted obligation. In contrast, the operation of a pro-family organization is a complex, effortful affair, which is made so directly by its relationship to the institution of marriage and its aim of maintaining that institution in its "traditional" form. The effort performed by a "pro-family" group, such as the Institute of Marriage and Family Canada or Abiding Truth Ministries, implies that its members have moved beyond considering marriage as "just" taken for granted and are aware of the fragility of it as an institution, and the need to act to maintain and, possibly, reinforce it. If we were to take the relationship between institutional work and effort seriously, it would seem that the managers of pro-family organizations are working significantly "harder" to maintain the institution of marriage than is the typical male–female couple planning and executing their wedding.

Our point here, as with intentionality, is not to declare one set of activities institutional work and the other not, but to point out the implications of considering effort when examining institutional work. And, as with intentionality, we believe that the potential importance of considering effort as a dimension of institutional work may depend significantly on one's focus, either on institutions (in relationship to action) or on actions (in relationship to institutions). We argue that the notion of effort is particularly important for studies in which the point of departure is institutional work itself – understanding the conditions and motivations that lead to it, the practices and strategies that constitute it, and its effects, intended and otherwise. In such studies, the effort associated with institutional work might help to clarify its relationship to the institutions at which it is aimed, as well as its relationship to the institutional context within which it occurs.

Considering effort also opens new perspectives for connections between research on institutional work and critical research on emancipation. Emancipation – i.e. "the process through which individuals and groups become freed from repressive social and ideological conditions" (Alvesson & Willmott, 1992: 432) – is one of the main topics of the critical management agenda which "seeks to probe taken-for-granted assumptions for their ideological underpinnings and restore meaningful participation in arenas subject to systematic distortion of communication" (Levy, Alvesson & Willmott, 2003: 93). In a critical view, this implies informing individuals of the institutionalized mechanisms of domination, helping them to reflect on those mechanisms and eventually develop the capability of changing those institutions. In other words, it aims at helping individuals to become able to perform institutional work. Critical authors also acknowledge that emancipation comes at a cost and that effort is necessary (Alvesson & Willmott, 1992). All this suggests potential avenues of collaboration between critical research and works on institutional work to understand better the forms of this effort, its origins and mechanisms.

Institutional work: theorizing and studying

The chapters in this book offer exemplars of how management scholarship can creatively engage with and illuminate the construct of institutional work. The chapters are organized in two broad parts. The first part is comprised of four chapters (Battilana & D'Aunno; Kraatz; Martí &

Mair; and Hargrave & Van de Ven), each of which addresses a distinct element of institutional work and, at the same time, raises important questions about how future research might further reveal the construct. The second part consists of six empirical applications of institutional work. The empirical chapters reflect the temporal stages of institutional work; two chapters (Zietsma & McKnight and Boxenbaum & Strandgaard Pedersen) examine the work associated with creating institutions, two chapters (Zilber and Trank & Washington) analyze the work of actors engaged in maintaining institutions, and two chapters (Hirsch & Bermiss and Jarzabkowski, Matthiesen & Van de Ven) examine the interplay of creating, maintaining, and disrupting institutions.

Essays on institutional work

Battilana and D'Aunno offer an in-depth analysis of an issue central to institutional analysis, and of particular importance for the institutional work project: the paradox of embedded agency. They situate it within the larger debate about dualism between agency and structure in social sciences and review the existing works addressing the paradox in institutional theory. In particular, they show that research on the enabling conditions in institutional theory accounts for field-level and organization-level conditions but does not address the central issue of the individual-level enabling conditions for strategic action despite institutional pressures, and thus the central paradox of embedded agency. Battilana and D'Aunno address this issue and set foundations for a theory of human agency consistent with the institutional work project. They draw from the works by Emirbayer (1997) and Emirbayer and Mische (1998) to develop a relational perspective. In this view, agency has three dimensions – iteration (habit), projection (imagination), and practical evaluation (judgment). Battilana and D'Aunno show how those three dimensions articulate with the different types of institutional work: creating, maintaining, and disrupting institutions. Thus, they show that institutional work may involve a wide range of levels of self-consciousness and reflexivity, as well as a wide range of temporal orientations.

Kraatz examines the institutional work of leadership. Drawing from institutional theory's historical roots, Kraatz's chapter reminds us of Selznick's core contribution to institutional theory – that organizations become institutionalized and leaders are the key agents of that process. Kraatz skillfully reviews Selznick's work to identify the institutional work of organizational leadership. He identifies seven categories of institutional work: symbolic manipulation, creating formal structures, making value commitments, creating coherence, maintaining integrity, making character-defining choices, and self-transformation. Embedded throughout the chapter is the core understanding that organizations are inherently political structures and that, in order to enact institutional work, leaders must transcend their narrow administrative role and technical functions to see organizations as underpinned by core-value structures. Perhaps the key insight of Kraatz's chapter is the observation that organizations are the often forgotten sites of institutional action.

The location of institutional work is also an important aspect of Martí and Mair's chapter on institutional change in the developing world. These authors challenge the dominant view of agency in institutional theory by shifting the focus away from powerful, centrally positioned actors to those on the margins of industrialized society. Concentrating instead on the perspective of marginal actors, Martí and Mair expose us to what are for most of us invisible elements of institutions and institutional work. Martí and Mair introduce the term "provisional institutions" to capture the clearly instrumental view of institutions shared by actors who use established institutional structures to alleviate institutionalized outcomes, such as poverty. Such actors, Martí and Mair observe, engage in institutional work in a relatively experimental manner and adopt strategies of institutional work that are more minimalist, incremental, and delicate than the existing literature on institutional change would suggest. This chapter usefully challenges our taken-for-granted assumptions about the nature of institutional change and sensitizes the researcher to the importance of perspective and context in fully understanding how institutions are created, maintained, and changed.

Hargrave and Van de Ven also challenge traditional assumptions concerning the relationship between agency and institutions in their examination of institutional work. Most critically, they explore the issues of contradiction and dialectics in relation to institutional work, and offer an image of institutional work as the creative embrace of contradiction. They argue that the relationships among categories of institutional work and institutional actors which have been presented as primarily oppositional – creating and disrupting institutions, incumbents, and challengers – are never so simple. Drawing on the writing of Saul Alinsky, the famous Chicago community organizer, Hargrave and Van de Ven argue that effective institutional work often involves the skillful combination of creating, maintaining, and disrupting institutions, and that the strategies of different institutional actors are often highly interdependent. Full of insight, this chapter offers significant value to those interested in how skilled institutional actors effect change and stability. With their focus on dialectics, contradiction, and innovation, Hargrave and Van de Ven open up the study of institutional work to a much broader range of images and actors.

Studies of institutional work

Creating institutions

Zietsma and McKnight explore the episodic, temporal nature of institutional work in the formative stages of an emerging organizational field. Through a longitudinal study of Canadian forestry, Zietsma and McKnight systematically analyze the ongoing interaction of established forestry corporations and environmental activist groups. Their key finding is twofold; first, they observe that institutional work involves iterative phases of conflict and cooperation, which they term "collaborative co-creation" and "competitive convergence." Like Martí and Mair, above, the authors in this study view institutions as both relatively instrumental and provisional structures. A second key finding is that the iterative nature of institutional work means that the outcomes of these efforts are rarely unilateral. Rather, institutions are the compromised product of the "detritus" of episodic bouts of conflict and compromise. Zietsma and McKnight's study skillfully exposes the process by which purposive action produces unintended consequences. Their results, however, suggest that the end product still strongly reflects the key values and interests of the dominant players. Significantly, they also observe that moments of institutional creation, maintenance, and change, while theoretically distinct, are empirically coterminous and, during the term of their study, they observe instances of each category of institutional work.

Boxenbaum and Strandgaard Pedersen account for what could be termed "Scandinavian institutionalism" and characterize its main features. Their chapter contributes to the advance of research on institutional work in two regards. First, with an ironic twist they document the birth and development of Scandinavian institutionalism as an illustrative case of institutional work. In doing so, they account for the creation and development of the SCANCOR institution, a unique transnational initiative to exchange and confront ideas between North American and Scandinavian scholars. Second, they present the main characteristics of Scandinavian institutionalism and the potentially important contribution it can bring to research on institutional work. They indicate that Scandinavian institutionalism has analyzed how agents respond to institutional pressures and adapt and mediate them through loose coupling, sense-making, and modification of ideas when implemented in specific settings (translation). The authors demonstrate that Scandinavian research has already developed a tradition to analyze agency in institutional theory, actors' responses to institutional pressures, as well as empirical methods to conduct intensive, rich, process-oriented, and qualitative approaches. Thus, as the authors point out, Scandinavian institutionalism can make a very strong contribution to research on institutional work. This chapter is also a call to build bridges between different research traditions as much can be learned by doing so. Scandinavian institutionalism is a good example as it appears to have developed powerful analysis in relative isolation, probably due to language as Boxenbaum and Strandgaard Pedersen suggest, since research in this tradition is often published in Scandinavian languages.

Maintaining institutions

Zilber's study investigates how elite agents use stories to ensure the diffusion and maintenance of organizational values by building on her celebrated study of a rape crisis center in Israel. She makes several important contributions. First, she offers researchers a detailed framework to analyze the articulation between meta-narratives at the societal level, their translation into more local versions by the organizational elite, and the appropriation of both meta-narratives and organizational stories by individual organizational members to construct their own personal life stories. She develops a rich, multi-level framework to analyze narratives at different levels, distinguish, and connect them. While she uses this framework empirically to investigate institutional maintenance, it opens avenues for new research on other kinds of institutional work as well. Second, she goes into much detail about her research method. She gives very clear indications in what is already considered an exemplary piece of qualitative research, thus providing guidelines for researchers willing to follow the same approach. In particular she discusses how researchers can collect "life stories" and use them as very rich material for analysis. Finally, she shows in a very clear and subtle way how the organizational elite translate meta-narratives as well as the political aspects of such a translation. She thus provides a clear link between narrative analysis and institutional work, and makes a strong case for the political use of narratives in institutional work.

Trank and Washington present a multiperspectival investigation of the institutional work of legitimating organizations, such as accreditation bodies and professional associations, to maintain their own legitimacy and that of the institutional arrangements for which they are responsible. In this case, the authors explore the work of the AACSB in maintaining the legitimacy of university business school accreditation, as well as the work of a range of different university business schools in response to this institution. This study provides a transparent and important example of how the study of institutional work can intersect with traditional institutional concerns for the structuration of organizational fields and the institutionalization of language and practice across organizations. It goes beyond traditional images of diffusion and isomorphism, however, by revealing the practices through which central agents work to maintain the impact of institutions in the face of competing sources of social and cultural capital, and the various responses by field members to that work. Trank and Washington also demonstrate the importance of attending to field-level heterogeneity in order to understand the interplay of different institutional strategies and organizational identities: they show how the AACSB recognized the diverse audiences for its work, including not only universities, but employers, students, and the media, and how the differential resources available to different business schools led to their adopting or failing to adopt AACSB materials.

Creating, maintaining, and disrupting institutions

Hirsch and Bermiss describe what they refer to as "institutional 'dirty' work" that is aimed at preserving institutions through strategic decoupling. Drawing on the fascinating case of the transformation of the Czech Republic from a communist to a capitalist state, Hirsch and Bermiss show how central actors engaged in a wide range of creative forms of institutional work to both transform and maintain key institutions. Several contributions emerge from their study. Hirsch and Bermiss propose a novel form of institutional work – the preserving of institutions, which they argue "entails the actions undertaken by actors searching for ways to carry over norms from the previous regime into the construction of the new institutional order." This concept bridges across previously conceived of categories of institutional work, to show the links among the forms of action associated with creating, maintaining, and disrupting institutions. Hirsch and Bermiss also connect the work of preserving institutions to the notion of decoupling. This chapter also points the way to work that integrates the material and symbolic in studies of institutional work – they show how the transformation (and maintenance) of the Czech Republic depended on the skillful combination of financial and cultural resources. Critically, Hirsch and Bermiss point to the importance of cultural and historical sensitivity in examining institutional work – theirs is a study that shines a light on the backstage work of skilled and interested actors to explain the drama that unfolded on the global political stage.

Jarzabkowski, Matthiesen, and Van de Ven conclude the book with a study which provides an integrated view of institutional work in the face of institutional pluralism. The authors draw on a real-time, longitudinal case study of a utility company to examine the creating, maintaining, and disrupting of institutions that occur in response to opposing market and regulatory logics. This chapter draws on an explicit consideration of a practice-theoretic approach to institutional work which provides the foundation for several significant contributions. First, it contributes to our understanding of how actors work to maintain institutions, particularly in organizations operating in pluralistic environments which energize the internal institutional politics, and where maintaining institutions may demand creatively combining strategies for creating and disrupting institutions. Their chapter also adds significantly to our understanding of the dynamics of institutional pluralism: focusing on the practical work of organizational actors points to the complex moves associated with creating, maintaining, and disrupting institutions in pluralistic environments, where creating institutions may be a means of establishing space for action, and mutual adjustment between logics is a key coping strategy.

References

Alvesson, M. & Willmott, H. (1992) On the idea of emancipation in management and organization studies. *Academy of Management Review*, 17(3): 432–464.

Archer, M. S. (1995) *Realist Social Theory: The Morphogenetic Approach*. Cambridge: Cambridge University Press.

Barley, S. R. & Tolbert, P. S. (1997) Institutionalization and structuration: studying the links between action and institution. *Organization Studies*, 18: 93–117.

Beckert, J. (1999) Agency, entrepreneurs, and institutional change: the role of strategic choice and institutionalized practices in organizations. *Organization Studies*, 20(5): 777–799.

(2003) Economic sociology and embeddedness: how shall we conceptualize economic action? *Journal of Economic Issues*, 37: 769–787.

Berger, P. & Kellner, H. (1964) Marriage and the construction of reality: an exercise in the microsociology of knowledge. *Diogenes*, 12: 1–24.

Berger, T. & Luckmann, P. (1967) *The Social Construction of Reality*. New York: Doubleday Anchor.

Blackler, F. & Regan, S. (2006) Institutional reform and the reorganization of family support services. *Organization Studies*, 27(12): 1843–1861.

Bourdieu, P. (1977) *Outline of a Theory of Practice*. Cambridge: Cambridge University Press.

(1990) *The Logic of Practice*. Stanford, CA: Stanford University Press.

(1993) *The Field of Cultural Production: Essays on Art and Literature*. Cambridge: Polity Press.

Bourdieu, P. & Wacquant, J. D. (1992) *An Invitation to Reflexive Sociology*. Chicago: University of Chicago Press.

de Certeau, M. (2002) *The Practice of Everyday Life*. Berkeley: University of California Press.

Chang, M. H. (2004) *Falun Gong: The End of Days*. New Haven, CT: Yale University Press.

Cookson, P. W. (1994) *School Choice: The Struggle for the Soul of American Education*. New Haven, CT: Yale University Press.

Delmestri, G. (2006) Streams of inconsistent institutional influences: middle managers as carriers of multiple identities. *Human Relations*, 59(11): 1515–1541.

DiMaggio, P. J. (1988) Interest and agency in institutional theory. In L. G. Zucker (ed.), *Institutional Patterns and Organizations: Culture and Environment*, pp. 3–22. Cambridge, MA: Ballinger.

(1997) Culture and cognition. *Annual Review of Sociology*, 23: 263–287.

DiMaggio, P. J. & Powell, W. W. (1983) The iron cage revisited: institutional isomorphism and collective rationality in organizational fields. *American Sociological Review*, 48: 147–160.

(1991) Introduction. In W. W. Powell & P. J. DiMaggio (eds.), *The New Institutionalism in Organizational Analysis*, pp. 1–38. Chicago: University of Chicago Press.

Eisenstadt, S. N. (1980) Cultural orientation, institutional entrepreneurs and social change: comparative analysis of traditional civilizations. *American Journal of Sociology*, 85(4): 840–869.

Emirbayer, M. (1997) Manifesto for a relational sociology. *American Journal of Sociology*, 103(2): 281–317.

Emirbayer, M. & Mische, A. (1998) What is agency? *American Journal of Sociology*, 103: 962–1023.

Fairclough, N. (1992) *Discourse and Social Change*. Cambridge: Polity Press.

Fligstein, N. (1997) Social skill and institutional theory. *American Behavioral Scientist*, 40(4): 397–405.

Frank, D. J. & Meyer, J. W. (2002) The profusion of individual roles and identities in the postwar period. *Sociological Theory*, 20(1): 86–105.

Garud, R., Jain, S. & Kumaraswamy, A. (2002) Institutional entrepreneurship in the sponsorship of common technological standards: the case of Sun Microsystems and Java. *Academy of Management Journal*, 45(1): 196–214.

Giddens, A. (1979) *Central Problems in Social Theory*. Berkeley: University of California Press.

(1984) *The Constitution of Society: Outline of the Theory of Structuration*. Cambridge: Polity Press.

Greenwood, R., Oliver, C., Sahlin, K. & Suddaby, R. (2008) Introduction. In R. Greenwood, C. Oliver, K. Sahlin & R. Suddaby (eds.), *Handbook of Organizational Institutionalism*, pp. 1–46. London: Sage.

Greenwood, R., Suddaby, R. & Hinings, C. R. (2002) Theorizing change: the role of professional associations in the transformation of institutional fields. *Academy of Management Journal*, 45(1): 58–80.

Greenwood, R. & Suddaby, R. (2006) Institutional entrepreneurship in mature fields: the big five accounting firms. *Academy of Management Journal*, 49: 27–48.

Hargadon, A. B. & Douglas, J. Y. (2001) When innovations meet institutions: Edison and the design of the electric light. *Administrative Science Quarterly*, 46: 476–501.

Hensmans, M. (2003) Social movement organizations: a metaphor for strategic actors in institutional fields. *Organization Studies*, 24(3): 355–381.

Hinings, C. R. & Greenwood, R. (1988) *The Dynamics of Strategic Change*. Oxford: Basil Blackwell.

Hirsch, P. M. (1997) Sociology without social structure: neo-institutional theory meets brave new world. *American Journal of Sociology*, 102(6): 1702–1723.

Hirsch, P. M. & Lounsbury, M. D. (1997a) Putting the organization back into organization theory. *Journal of Management Inquiry*, 6(1): 79–89.

(1997b) Ending the family quarrel: towards a reconciliation of "old" and "new" institutionalism. *American Behavioral Scientist*, 40: 406–418.

Hoffman, A. J. & Ventresca, M. J. (2002) Introduction. In A. J. Hoffman & M. J. Ventresca (eds.), *Organizations, Policy and the Natural Environment: Institutional and Strategic Perspectives*, pp. 1–38. Stanford: Stanford University Press.

Hwang, H. & Powell, W. W. (2005) Institutions and entrepreneurship. In S. A. Alvarez, R. Agarwal & O. Sorenson (eds.), *Handbook of Entrepreneurship Research*, pp. 179–210. Dordrecht: Kluwer Publishers.

Jepperson, R. L. (1991) Institutions, institutional effects, and institutionalization. In W. W. Powell & P. J. DiMaggio (eds.), *The New Institutionalism in Organizational Analysis*, pp. 143–163. Chicago: University of Chicago Press.

Joas, H. (1996) *The Creativity of Action*. Chicago: University of Chicago Press.

Lawrence, T. B. (1999) Institutional strategy. *Journal of Management*, 25: 161–187.

Lawrence, T. & Suddaby, R. (2006) Institutions and institutional work. In S. Clegg, C. Hardy, T. B. Lawrence & W. R. Nord (eds.), *Handbook of Organization Studies*, 2nd edn., pp. 215–254. London: Sage.

Lawrence, T. B., Winn, M. & Jennings, P. D. (2001) The temporal dynamics of institutionalization. *Academy of Management Review*, 26: 624–644.

Levy, D. L., Alvesson, M. & Willmott, H. (2003) Critical approaches to strategic management. In M. Alvesson & H. Willmott (eds.), *Studying Management Critically*, pp. 92–110. Newbury Park, CA: Sage.

Lounsbury, M. (2001) Institutional sources of practice variation: staffing college and university recycling programs. *Administrative Science Quarterly*, 46: 29–56.

Maguire, S., Hardy, C. & Lawrence, T. B. (2004) Institutional entrepreneurship in emerging fields: HIV/AIDS treatment advocacy in Canada. *Academy of Management Journal*, 47: 657–69.

Metcalfe, J. & Mischel, W. (1999) A hot-cool system analysis of delay of gratification: dynamics of willpower. *Psychological Review*, 106(1): 3–19.

Meyer, A. D., Gaba, V. & Colwell, K. A. (2005) Organizing far from equilibrium: non-linear change in organizational fields. *Organization Science*, 16(5): 456–473.

Meyer, J. W. & Jepperson, R. (2000) The "actors" of modern society: the cultural construction of social agency. *Sociological Theory*, 18(1): 100–120.

Meyer, J. W. & Rowan, B. (1977) Institutionalized organizations: formal structure as myth and ceremony. *American Journal of Sociology*, 83: 440–463.

Meyer, R. E. (2006) Visiting relatives: current development in the sociology of knowledge. *Organization*, 13(5): 725–738.

Miner, J. B. (2003) The rated importance, scientific validity, and practical usefulness of organizational behavior theories: a quantitative view. *Academy of Management Learning and Education*, 2(3): 250–268.

Nussbaum, M. C. (1986) *The Fragility of Goodness*. Cambridge: Cambridge University Press.

Oliver, C. (1990) Determinants of interorganizational relationships: integration and future directions. *Academy of Management Review*, 15(2): 241–265.

(1991) Strategic responses to institutional processes. *Academy of Management Review*, 16: 145–179.

(1992) The antecedents of deinstitutionalization. *Organization Studies*, 13: 563–588.

OED. 2007. work n. In *The Concise Oxford English Dictionary*, 11th edn. revised, ed. C. Soanes and A. Stevenson. Oxford: Oxford University Press. Accessed online, June 11, 2007. www.oxfordreference.com

Ortner, S. B. (1984) Theory in anthropology since the sixties. *Comparative Studies in Society and History*, 26(1): 126–166.

Perrow, C. (1985) Review essay: overboard with myth and symbols. *American Journal of Sociology*, 91(1): 151–155.

Phillips, N. & Malhotra, N. (2008) Taking social construction seriously: extending the discursive approach in institutional theory. In R. Greenwood, C. Oliver, K. Sahlin & R. Suddaby (eds.), *Handbook of Organizational Institutionalism*, pp. 702–720. London: Sage.

Phillips, N., Lawrence, T. B. & Hardy, C. (2004) Discourse and institutions. *Academy of Management Review*, 29(4): 635–652.

Rao, H. (1998) Caveat emptor: the construction of non-profit watchdog organizations. *American Journal of Sociology*, 103: 912–961.

Schatzki, T. R., Cetina, K. K. & von Savigny, E. (2001) *The Practical Turn in Contemporary Theory*. London: Routledge.

Scott, R. W. (2001) *Institutions and Organizations*, 2nd edn. Thousand Oaks, CA: Sage.

Suddaby, R. & Greenwood, R. (2005) Rhetorical strategies of legitimacy. *Administrative Science Quarterly*, 50: 35–67.

Tolbert, P. S. & Zucker, L. G. (1983) Institutional sources of change in the formal structure of organizations: the diffusion of civil service reform, 1880–1935. *Administrative Science Quarterly*, 30: 22–39.

Wrong, D. (1961) The oversocialized conception of man in modern sociology. *American Sociological Review*, 26: 183–196.

Essays on institutional work

2 | *Institutional work and the paradox of embedded agency*

JULIE BATTILANA AND THOMAS D'AUNNO

Introduction

Institutions are social structures that are characterized by a high degree of resilience (Scott, 2001). They have a self-activating nature (Lawrence, Hardy & Phillips, 2002; Jepperson, 1991). Actors tend to reproduce institutions in a given field of activity without requiring either repeated authoritative intervention or collective mobilization (Clemens & Cook, 1999: 445). Early neo-institutional studies emphasized ways that institutions constrained organizational structures and activities, and thereby explained the convergence of organizational practices within institutional environments. They proposed that actors' need to be regarded as legitimate in their institutional environment determined their behavior. This work implicitly assumed that individuals and organizations tend to comply, at least in appearance, with institutional pressures. In fact, actors were often implicitly assumed to have a limited degree of agency.

Such a conception of agency was problematic when institutional theorists started tackling the issue of institutional change. While early neo-institutional studies accounted for organizational isomorphism and for the reproduction of institutionalized practices, they did not account well for the possibility of change. Even though institutions are characterized by their self-activating nature, we know that they do change (e.g. Fligstein, 1991). Since the late 1980s, institutional theorists have started addressing the issue of institutional change. They have highlighted the role that organizations and/or individuals play in institutional change.

Studies that account for the role of organizations and/or individuals in institutional change, however, face a paradox. Indeed, if we assume that institutional environments shape individuals and organizations who have a very limited degree of agency, the question to ask is: "How can actors change institutions if their actions, intentions, and rationality are all conditioned by the very institution they wish to change?" (Holm, 1995). Seo and Creed (2002) label this paradox between institutional determinism and agency as the "paradox of embedded agency." It corresponds to the agency vs. structure debate in the framework of institutional theory.

The concept of institutional work, which refers to "the purposive action of individuals and organizations aimed at creating, maintaining and disrupting institutions" (Lawrence & Suddaby, 2006: 215), deals with the relationship between agency and institutions. This concept assumes that actors can purposively behave either to maintain or transform existing institutions. For the concept of institutional work to hold, it is thus necessary to address the paradox of embedded agency, or the contradiction between actors' agency and institutional determinism.

While a number of studies have explained how field-level and organization-level conditions enable agency despite the existence of institutional pressures toward stasis, we still know little about potential individual-level enabling conditions for agency. In fact, recent work in institutional theory has tended to neglect the individual level of analysis (Reay, Golden-Biddle & Germann, 2006). To address the paradox of embedded agency and thereby set up theoretical foundations for the concept of institutional work, it is, however, necessary to account for the individual level of analysis and to tackle the issue of human agency.

In this chapter, we first situate the paradox of embedded agency within the ongoing structure vs. agency debate in the field of organizational studies. We then highlight the necessity to address the paradox of embedded agency and we review studies that have done so. This enables us to highlight different categories of enabling conditions (i.e. field-level and organization-level enabling conditions) for agency and thereby institutional work. Finally, we propose to adopt a relational perspective (Emirbayer, 1997) that accounts for the ongoing interactions between individual actors and the institutional environment in which they are embedded. Relying on this relational perspective and on a multidimensional view of agency (Emirbayer & Mische, 1998), we distinguish between different types of institutional work.

Institutional theory and the agency versus structure debate

The agency versus structure debate in the field of organization studies

The agency versus structure debate is ongoing in the social sciences. This debate stems from assumptions about relationships between actors (be they individuals or organizations) and their environments (Burrell & Morgan, 1979; Astley & Van de Ven, 1983). One can distinguish two extreme perspectives. The first perspective argues that actors' environments determine their responses to situations they encounter in the external world. In this view, individuals and their experiences are products of external environments that condition them. There is little room for human agency. As a result, the determinist orientation focuses not on action, but on the structural properties of the context within which action unfolds, and on structural constraints that shape individual or organizational behavior and provide organizational life with overall stability and control (Astley & Van de Ven, 1983).

We can contrast this perspective with a voluntarist orientation. The voluntarist perspective attributes to actors a much more creative role: they have free will and are autonomous, pro-active, and self-directed (Burrell & Morgan, 1979). Actors are seen as the basic unit of analysis and source of change in social life (Astley & Van de Ven, 1983).

The debate about the role of agency versus structure in social life has touched all areas of the social sciences (Archer, 1982). It has been used as a device to categorize theories and to examine the evolution of fields. For example, the field of sociology is characterized by a number of dualisms (Dawe, 1970), such as methodological individualism versus holism or macro- versus micro-sociology, that stem from the tension between structure and agency in explaining social life. Based on the importance of this tension, it might be tempting to classify any socio-logical theory in one of two categories, i.e. sociology of social system or sociology of social action (Dawe, 1970).

The former views individual actions as derivative of social systems, while the latter views social systems as derivative of individual action (Astley & Van de Ven, 1983). The dichotomy between these two types of sociology is fostered by the fact that the different schools of thought often tend to caricature themselves and each other in conferences and review papers and books, shaped by a logic of both dialogue and polemic (Aron, 1967). However, such manichean classification (Archer, 1982) of existing sociological research is simplistic and does not do justice to the complexity of most existing theories. Indeed, much sociological research is neither clearly in one camp nor in the other, and can be seen as part of a continuing debate over the relationship between agency and structure.

There is a sharper contrast between most sociological research and neoclassical economics when it comes to their respective views of human agency. The rational actor model – also referred to as the model of the *homo economicus* – that is used in neoclassical economics holds an extreme view of human agency. Indeed, it assumes that agents always select the most efficient alternative, that is, the alternative that maximizes output for a given input or minimizes input for a given output under a specified set of financial constraints. Further, the rational actor model assumes that agents' preferences are ordered and stable. Rational consumers purchase the amount of goods that maximizes their utility, by choosing the basket of goods on the highest possible indifference curve. Rational firms produce at a point that maximizes profits, by setting marginal cost equal to marginal revenue. Actually, the rational actor model ignores the impact that the agents' environment may have on their preferences, on their decisions, and on their behaviors. As Granovetter (1985) emphasized, it is based on an undersocialized view of action.

The field of organization studies is at the frontier of a number of disciplines, including, among others, sociology and economics (Scott, 1996). As a result, the agency versus structure debate is particularly salient in the field of organization studies. It has been used to classify organization theories depending on whether they tilt more toward structure or agency (Crozier & Friedberg, 1980; Astley & Van de Ven, 1983).

In the late 1960s, 1970s, and early 1980s, a number of organization theories, including the collective-action view and the strategic-choice view (for a review see Astley & Van de Ven, 1983), tilted more toward agency. In addition, the rational actor model influenced the development of economic theories of organization, such as public-choice theory, agency theory, and the new institutional economics. While most of these theories recognize the importance of bounded rationality (Simon, [1947] 1997), they still rely on an economic model of organizational behavior (Argyris, 1973; Pfeffer, 1997). As a result, they tend to isolate organizations from their societal context and to focus on the analysis of the decisions of "the instrumental, rational individual, whose choices in myriad exchanges are seen as the primary cause of societal arrangements" (Friedland & Alford, 1991: 232). Such theories tilt more toward agency.

All theoretical developments in the field of organization studies did not have a voluntarist perspective. Contingency theories (Woodward, 1958; Lawrence & Lorsch, 1967; Thompson, 1967) took into account the role of the environment and had a more deterministic orientation

(Astley & Van de Ven, 1983). However, they did not focus on how social structure shaped organization, but rather identified optimal structure–context congruence that would enable managers to enhance the performance of their organizations (Lounsbury & Ventresca, 2003).

The late 1970s and early 1980s marked a turning point in the evolution of the field of organization studies both in North America and in Europe, as a number of scholars were driven to better account for the interaction between an organization and the environment (Thoenig, 1998). Institutional theory, as well as a number of other theoretical perspectives, such as population ecology (Hannan & Freeman, 1977), contributed to this evolution of the field of organization studies.

The contribution of institutional theory to the agency versus structure debate

Institutional theory suggests that institutions shape patterns of action and organization rather than instrumental calculations aimed solely at maximizing profit or utility (Meyer & Rowan, 1977; DiMaggio & Powell, 1983). As opposed to theories of organization that are based on the rational actor model, institutional theory posits that broader social and cultural processes shape organizational action (Lounsbury & Ventresca, 2003). It proposes that agents' behaviors are determined by their need to be regarded as legitimate in their institutional environment.

The key difference between institutional theory and rational actor models that characterize economic theories concerns the role that is assigned to the environment in which actors are embedded. While rational actor models tend to neglect environmental influences on actors' decisions, institutional theory takes into account these external influences by assigning a key role to legitimacy considerations in actors' decision processes.

Indeed, institutional theory is based on the notion that, to survive, organizations must convince larger publics that they are legitimate entities worthy of support (Meyer & Rowan, 1977). To do so, they must conform – at least in appearance – to the institutional norms of their environment. In institutional environments, organizations are rewarded for using acceptable structures and practices, not the quantity, quality, and efficiency of their output (Meyer & Scott, 1983). Therefore, legitimacy has a central role in neo-institutional theory as a force that constrains change and pressures organizations to act alike (DiMaggio & Powell, 1983).

Concerns over legitimacy force organizations to adopt managerial practices or organizational forms that are widely used in their fields. These practices and organizational forms may or may not enable organizations to maximize the quality and/or quantity of their outputs. As Oliver (1991: 148) explains, in neo-institutional theory "when external norms or practices obtain the status of a social fact, organizations may engage in activities that are not so much calculative and self-interested as obvious or proper." On the whole, institutional theory argues that agents' preferences, decisions, and behaviors are influenced by the institutional environment in which they are embedded (Dacin, Ventresca & Beal, 1999).

But before being "objectivated" (i.e. experienced as an objective reality that is taken for granted) by human beings, institutions are first produced by them (Berger & Luckmann, 1967: 60; DiMaggio & Powell, 1991). Thus, institutional theory is inherently characterized by the tension between agency and institutions (structure).

The paradox of embedded agency in institutional theory

While studies that have been referred to as "old institutionalism" accounted for the role of agency in institution building and transformation in the 1950s and 1960s (e.g. Selznick, 1949), in the late 1970s and the 1980s, institutional theory (often referred to as neo-institutional theory) focused primarily on explaining organizational homogeneity within organizational fields (e.g. DiMaggio & Powell, 1983; Tolbert & Zucker, 1983). These studies emphasized increasing isomorphism among organizations subject to similar institutional pressures. These early studies (e.g. Meyer, Scott & Deal, 1983; Tolbert & Zucker, 1983; Zucker, 1983; Tolbert, 1985) often implicitly assumed that organizations and individuals passively adapt to institutions. Human agency was implicitly viewed as habitual and repetitive. Institutional theorists emphasized the taken-for-granted quality of knowledge and action that makes organizations relatively stable and resistant to change, once their members have adopted institutionalized organizational forms and practices. In short, early neo-institutional studies viewed institutions as external constraints on organizational and human agency. They have been criticized for relying on an oversocialized view of action (Hirsch & Lounsbury, 1997).

As long as institutional theorists mainly concentrated on explaining organizational conformity, the issue of agency was not a central one.

Now that institutional theorists have begun to tackle the issue of change, the question of organizational and human agency has become central. Since the 1990s, new institutionalists have focused more on the ways in which both individuals and organizations innovate, act strategically, and contribute to institutional change (e.g. DiMaggio, 1988; Leblebici, Salancik, Copay & King, 1991; Greenwood & Hinings, 1996; Kraatz & Zajac, 1996; Barley & Tolbert, 1997; Fligstein, 1997; Karnoe, 1997; Kondra & Hinings, 1998). The special research forum on institutional theory and institutional change, published by the *Academy of Management Journal* in February 2002, gathered contributions that analyze the role of individual or organizational agents in institutional change.

Addressing the issue of institutional change, DiMaggio (1988) introduced the notion of institutional entrepreneurship, which he borrowed from Eisenstadt's (1964, 1980) work. Analyzing patterns of social change within different historical contexts and the conditions that gave rise to the variations among these patterns, Eisenstadt (1980: 848) proposed that institutional entrepreneurs were one variable – among a "constellation" of others – that was relevant to the process of social change. In Eisenstadt's work, institutional entrepreneurs are those individuals and groups who adopt leadership roles in episodes of institution building (Colomy, 1998).

By introducing the notion of institutional entrepreneurship in the framework of neo-institutional theory, DiMaggio (1988) put more emphasis on the role of actors and agency in institutional change processes: "New institutions arise when organized actors with sufficient resources (*institutional entrepreneurs*) see in them an opportunity to realize interests that they value highly" (DiMaggio, 1988: 14, emphasis in original). He thus revived dimensions of "old institutionalism" (Selznick, 1949, 1956) that early neo-institutional studies had de-emphasized (e.g. DiMaggio & Powell, 1983; Meyer *et al.*, 1983; Tolbert & Zucker, 1983; Zucker, 1983; Tolbert, 1985). DiMaggio also revived the debate about the place of agency versus structure within the framework of neo-institutional theory. Because they diverge from the existing institutions by proposing alternative rules and practices, institutional entrepreneurs appear to display a high level of agency. How can actors who are embedded in the institutional environment display such a high level of agency?

Two decades after the publication of DiMaggio's (1988) seminal contribution, more than fifty papers have been published about institutional entrepreneurship in peer-reviewed journals (Leca, Battilana & Boxenbaum, 2008). Examining the evolution of the field of institutional studies, Lawrence and Suddaby (2006: 215) noticed that the role of actors in the transformation of existing institutions has "risen in prominence within institutional research." In an effort to organize existing institutional research on the role of actors in institutional change under a common umbrella, Lawrence and Suddaby (2006) introduced the concept of "institutional work." But, for the concept of institutional work to hold, it is necessary to address the paradox of embedded agency.

Enabling conditions for agency

One might argue that the paradox of embedded agency is a straw man argument. It would be so, for example, if, in fact, it didn't exist, if it corresponded to the fantasy of scholars whose reading of institutional theory was simplistic. The tension between agency and structure (institutions) is, however, undeniably inherent in institutional theory (Berger & Luckmann, 1967; DiMaggio & Powell, 1991), and indeed, in any theory that originates in the social sciences.

Alternatively, one could argue that the paradox of embedded agency has become a straw man argument because studies have tackled – and resolved – it. Evidence from a number of studies of institutional change conducted over the past decade indicates that actors are not always prisoners of the "iron cage" of existing institutions: is the paradox of embedded agency outdated? Has neo-institutional theory resolved it? To answer these questions, we must review the studies that have addressed this problem. A number of studies have accounted for the fact that enabling conditions often usher institutional entrepreneurs onto the stage (Strang & Sine, 2002). Two categories of enabling conditions for agency and thereby institutional work have so far received a great deal of attention, namely, field-level and organization-level conditions.

Field-level enabling conditions

Results from several studies show that certain field-level conditions are correlated with agency, and, far from being mutually exclusive, these conditions and agency often are interrelated (Leca *et al.*, 2008). One is a jolt or crisis that precipitates action that diverges from a field's existing institutions (Oliver, 1991; Holm, 1995; Clemens & Cook, 1999; Fligstein & Mara-Drita, 1996; Fligstein, 2001; Greenwood, Suddaby & Hinings, 2002). Oliver (1992) and Greenwood *et al.* (2002) posit that such jolts might take the form of social upheaval, competitive discontinuities, technological disruption, or regulatory changes that disturb the socially constructed field-level consensus and thereby contribute to agency in the form of the introduction of new ideas. An acute, field-level problem that spawns a crisis might also be a field-level enabling condition for institutional work to occur (Fligstein & Mara-Drita, 1996; Phillips, Lawrence & Hardy, 2000; Wade-Benzoni, Hoffman, Thompson *et al.*, 2002). Phillips *et al.* (2000) suggest, for example, that the existence of complex, multifaceted problems such as environmental issues and workplace diversity can spur individuals engaged in inter-organizational collaboration to engage in institutional work.

Finally, scholars have emphasized the enabling role of the degree of heterogeneity and incomplete institutionalization of practices, values, and norms. Both heterogeneity (Sewell, 1992; Whittington, 1992; Clemens & Cook, 1999; D'Aunno, Succi & Alexander, 2000; Seo & Creed, 2002; Schneiberg & Soule, 2005; Lounsbury, 2007) and incomplete institutionalization (Tolbert & Zucker, 1996) have the potential to affect actors' agency and thereby their likelihood to engage in institutional work. The heterogeneity of institutional arrangements, that is, variance in the characteristics of different institutional arrangements, may facilitate agency because to the extent that there are heterogeneous institutional arrangements in a given organizational field, institutional incompatibilities are more likely to emerge. Such incompatibilities are a source of internal contradictions (Jepperson, 1991). In turn, the ongoing experience of contradictory institutional arrangements is likely to trigger actors' reflective capacity (Emirbayer & Mische, 1998; Seo & Creed, 2002; Sewell, 1992) and thereby enable them to take some critical distance from the existing institutional arrangements.

Tolbert and Zucker (1996) argue that the degree to which practices, norms, and values are institutionalized (widely accepted, used, and taken for granted) affects actors' agency as well. To the extent that institutions are not widely used, accepted, and taken for granted, there is room for individuals and organizations to act independently. But the impact of incomplete institutionalization on agency is a subject of debate. Beckert (1999) suggests that strategic action is more likely to occur in relatively highly institutionalized organizational fields because uncertainty is reduced in such fields and, concomitantly, the reduced need for security, stability, and predictability, with respect to the persistence of institutionalized rules and norms, gives actors more freedom to engage in strategic behavior.

Dorado (2005) developed a typology to facilitate this analysis of field characteristics on actors' agency, taking into account degrees of both heterogeneity and institutionalization. She describes three dominant forms. "Opportunity opaque" fields are highly institutionalized and/ or isolated from the potential influence of other fields and, therefore, less likely to promote new ideas. These field characteristics do not provide opportunities for action. "Opportunity transparent" fields offer considerable opportunity for action: the coexistence of both heterogeneous institutional arrangements and a substantial level of institutionalization characterize these fields. Finally, fields characterized by minimal institutionalization and many heterogeneous models of practices make it difficult for agents to grasp opportunities for action because they must deal with a highly unpredictable environment; Dorado terms these fields "opportunity hazy."

Based on the work noted above, we know something about how field-level conditions enable agency and thereby institutional work. But, at least two questions remain unanswered. First, how can actors engage in institutional work in environments whose characteristics seem not to enable agency? Second, why are actors who are facing similar field-level conditions not equally likely to engage in institutional work?

Organization-level enabling conditions

Organizational-level factors may explain why actors who face the same field conditions are not equally likely to engage in institutional work. A host of researchers have weighed in on the role of organizational characteristics as enablers of agency (see, for example, Leblebici *et al.*, 1991; Kraatz & Zajac, 1996; Rao, Morrill & Zald, 2000; Garud, Jain & Kumaraswamy, 2002; Greenwood & Suddaby, 2006). Most have emphasized a particular organizational characteristic, namely, position in the organizational field, or, more broadly, in the institutional environment.

Results from several studies suggest that organizations and social movements at the margins of an organizational field (Leblebici *et al.*, 1991; Haveman & Rao, 1997; Garud *et al.*, 2002) or at the interstices of different organizational fields (Rao *et al.*, 2000; Levy & Egan, 2003) are more likely to act as institutional entrepreneurs. Leblebici *et al.*'s (1991) study of the US commercial radio broadcasting industry between 1920 and 1965, for example, found that organizations at the periphery of the field are more likely to break with existing institutions. Most new practices, they found, were introduced by peripheral, lower-status, organizations such as "shady traders, small independent stations, rene-gade record producers, weaker networks, or enterprising advertising agencies" (Leblebici *et al.*, 1991: 358). Higher-status organizations, in contrast, mobilized resources to maintain the status quo.

These studies help to explain part of the variance observed in actors' likelihood to engage in institutional work by showing that there is a relationship between actors' agency and the characteristics of the orga-nizations in which they are embedded. But even individual actors embedded in the same organization in the same organizational field are not all equally likely to engage in institutional work (Clemens & Cook, 1999). There must be other conditions that facilitate human agency and thereby institutional work.

What about individual-level enabling conditions?

Organizations and social movements are not the only actors that may engage in institutional work. Individuals or groups of individuals may also do so (e.g. Fligstein, 1997; Maguire, Hardy & Lawrence, 2004). For example, individuals who undertake divergent organizational changes, i.e. changes that break with the dominant institutional logic(s) in a given organizational field, may be regarded as institutional entre-preneurs (Battilana, 2006). However, most studies of institutional work to date have focused on the organizational field and organizational levels of analysis, neglecting the individual level of analysis (Reay *et al.*, 2006). As a result, scholars have tended to neglect the study of individual-level enabling conditions for engaging in institutional work, that is, for diverging from dominant institutions as well as for acting strategically to maintain the status quo. The question of how individual actors are enabled to engage in institutional work remains largely unanswered. To resolve the paradox of embedded agency and thereby set up theoretical foundations for the concept of institutional work, it is, however, necessary to account for the individual level of analysis and to tackle the issue of human agency.

The paradox of embedded agency is still a central issue in institutional theory because institutional theorists have never explicitly tackled the issue of human agency, sometimes arguing that institutional theory is not about individual behavior. In contrast, we argue that, to the extent possible, social theories should consider three levels of analysis, i.e. the individual, the organizational, and the societal levels of analysis (Friedland & Alford, 1991).

These three levels of analysis are nested. Individual, organizational, and organizational field dynamics are interrelated. Organizations and institutions specify progressively higher levels of constraint, as well as opportunities for individual action (Friedland & Alford, 1991). New institutionalists too often regard attempts at analyzing the role played by individuals in institutional phenomena as reductionist. But, as Hirsch and Lounsbury (1997) suggest, uncertainty about actors' agency raises serious questions about how macro-level phenomena change. A weakness of institutional theory is that it offers organizational-level and organizational-field-level explanations for phenomena that implicitly involve individual behavior without providing a basis for constructing a theory of individual behavior. Without solid micro-foundations, institutional theorists risk not accounting for institutionalization processes (Zucker, 1991).

Some institutional theorists (e.g. DiMaggio, 1988; Fligstein, 1997; Barley & Tolbert, 1997; Zilber, 2002; Seo & Creed, 2002) have analyzed human agency, and this work has contributed to the development of a theory of action. But there are still many questions that remain unanswered, especially regarding the role of individuals in institutional change. In particular, we need to know more about the mechanisms that enable some individuals to engage in institutional work. What are the individual-level enabling conditions for strategic action despite institutional pressures toward stasis?

Focusing on the enabling role of individual characteristics without accounting for the fact that actors are embedded in organizations, that are themselves embedded in organizational fields, would be equivalent to ignoring the influence of institutions and thereby would do little to resolve the paradox of embedded human agency. Relying on sociologists, such as Giddens (1976, 1979, 1984) and Bourdieu (1977, 1984), whose work aims to transcend the agency versus structure dichotomy, and on the work of Emirbayer (1997) and Emirbayer and Mische (1998), we propose to adopt a relational approach to account for three levels of analysis: the individual, organizational, and organizational field.

Setting up foundations for the concept of institutional work

To address the issue of human agency in institutional theory and set up theoretical foundations for the concept of institutional work, we suggest that it is necessary to adopt a relational perspective, which we present below. Relying on a multidimensional view of agency, we then further explore the link between the concepts of agency and institutional work. We suggest that different forms of agency might be associated with different forms of institutional work. Finally, we highlight new research directions to examine the enabling conditions for individual actors to engage in these different forms of institutional work.

Adopting a relational perspective

To resolve the paradox of embedded agency, it is necessary to take into account the interrelationships between individuals and their institutional environments. To conceptualize these interrelationships, many scholars (e.g. Beckert, 1999; DiMaggio & Powell, 1991; Hirsch & Lounsbury, 1997; Oakes, Townley & Cooper, 1998; Ranson, Hinings & Greenwood, 1980; Schmidt, 1997; Whittington, 1992) have proposed using the theoretical frameworks that Giddens (1976, 1979, 1984) and Bourdieu (1977, 1984) developed. Both Giddens' theory of structuration and Bourdieu's theory of practice view agency and structure as inextricably linked. Both theories are practice-based approaches, which, as Lawrence and Suddaby (2006: 19) underscore, can "contribute substantially to institutional research."

Structuration theory (Giddens, 1976, 1979, 1984) can be used to conceptualize the interrelationships between actors and their institutional environments. Giddens' structuration theory is a process-oriented theory that views structure as both a product of, and a constraint on, human action. For this reason, Giddens (1976, 1979, 1984) regards structures as "dual." The notion of "duality of structure" can be applied to institutions. Institutions shape people's practices, but it is also people's practices that constitute (and reproduce) institutions (see also Berger & Luckmann, 1967). From this perspective, agency and institutions, far from being opposed, presuppose each other. According to Giddens, "knowledgeable" human agents enact structures (i.e. people who know what they are doing and how to do it), and agents act by putting into practice their necessarily structured knowledge. Hence, "structures must not be conceptualized as simply placing constraints on human agency but as enabling" (Giddens, 1976: 161). This conception of human agents as "knowledgeable" and "enabled" implies that these agents are capable of putting their structurally formed capacities to work in creative or innovative ways (Sewell, 1992: 4).

Despite its contribution to the study of the interaction between actors and their institutional environments, Giddens' structuration theory has been criticized for its excessive subjectivism (e.g. Callinicos, 1985; Clegg, 1989) and its inability to transcend the agency versus structure dichotomy. As Archer (1982) summarizes, Giddens' "insistence on the simultaneity of transformative capacity and chronic recursiveness inhibits any theoretical formulation of the conditions under which either will predominate."

Similar to Giddens' structuration theory, Bourdieu's theory of practice can be used to conceptualize the relation between actors and their institutional environments as well. It rests on two main related notions: "field" and "habitus." Fields are "game spaces that offer stakes" (Bourdieu, 1984: 34). They are structured systems of social position within which struggles take place between individuals over resources, stakes, and access. Each field is characterized by specific social relations, stakes, and resources that are different from other fields.

The concept of habitus links macro-processes occurring at the field level with micro-level processes occurring at the individual level. Habitus is a system of temporally durable dispositions, predisposed to function as frameworks that generate and regulate practices and ideas (Bourdieu, 1977). Habitus is acquired through a relationship to a certain field. Through habitus, social structures are imprinted in an individual's mind and body. Accordingly, Bourdieu regards individuals as "agents" as opposed to "biological individuals, actors or subjects" (Bourdieu & Wacquant, 1992: 107) to convey that they are both socially constituted as active and acting on their own in the field.

Similar to Giddens' structuration theory, Bourdieu's theory of practice has been criticized for its ambiguity. The notion of habitus, in particular, has been criticized for being ambiguous (DiMaggio, 1979) and for leaving almost no room for agency, and thereby for social change (Sewell, 1992; Fowler, 1997; Boyer, 2003; Mutch, 2003). Certain definitions of habitus that Bourdieu himself has proposed make his theory of practice tilt toward structure. In *Questions de sociologie* (Bourdieu, 1984: 75), for example, he compares habitus to "computer programs" and thereby implies that individual actions are socially determined. In another instance, talking about his "theory of practice," Bourdieu (1984: 75) states, "All the dimensions of individual history, even the most singular ones, are socially determined." Such statements may suggest that, instead of transcending the agency versus structure dichotomy, the notion of habitus retains an "agent-proof quality" (Sewell, 1992: 15).

Despite these limitations, Giddens and Bourdieu, in taking into account agents' relation to their environments, have contributed to the development of a relational perspective in the field of social sciences (Emirbayer & Mische, 1998; Emirbayer, 1997); we argue that this perspective can be applied to the field of organization studies (Emirbayer & Johnson, 2008) and, more specifically, to institutional theory. Rather than considering that human agents pursue lines of conduct in a solipsistic manner or that institutional pressures largely determine their line of conduct, such a relational perspective views individuals as being embedded in a social context and as responding to the situations that they encounter in this context (Emirbayer, 1997). This conception of agency accounts for the fact that individual actors are not only shaped by the existing institutions, but that, by engaging in institutional work, individuals also may shape those institutions, at least in certain situations (Berger & Luckmann, 1967; DiMaggio & Powell, 1991).

A multidimensional view of agency

We now need to explore further the conceptual link between agency and institutional work. Can one distinguish different forms of agency that might be associated with different forms of institutional work? If so, what are the conditions that promote these different forms of agency?

The concept of agency is associated with terms such as motivation, will, intentionality, interest, choice, autonomy, and freedom. Agency is often referred to as actors' ability to operate somewhat independently of the determining constraints of social structure (Calhoun, 2002). There is, however, a range of possible interpretations of this rather vague definition. One view is that actors may be said to display agency when they make choices that go against the constraints of social structure, regardless of whether or not they then alter social structure. In contrast, another view is that actors display agency only when they alter rules that govern behavior or the distribution of resources (Scott, 2001), thereby altering some dimension(s) of the social structure. One problem with such an approach to the definition of agency is that it does not account for situations in which institutional work involves the reproduction of social structure (Oliver, 1992; Lawrence & Suddaby, 2006), as is the case, for example, when high-status actors take action to maintain the status quo in a sector of activity (Starr, 1982; Abbott, 1988; Fligstein, 1997; Hensmans, 2003).

One could consider that actors display different levels of agency on a continuum ranging from the ability to make choices independently of existing social structures to the ability to take strategic action either to transform social structure or maintain the status quo. This approach views agency as a unidimensional concept that can be represented on a continuum whose extremes correspond, respectively, to the highest level of agency possible (active agency) and to the lowest level of agency possible (passive agency) (Oliver, 1991).

A problem with such linear approaches, however, is that they do not clearly specify the extent to which an individual should be able to affect the social world for him/her to be regarded as having a high versus a low level of agency. In addition, relying on a unidimensional view of agency, one might be tempted to regard agency as an individual attribute that does not evolve: some people would have a high level of agency whereas others would not. Such a conception of agency is quite a simplistic one and neglects the relational dimension of agency that we presented above. Individuals' level of agency is not a constant attribute. It may vary depending on the context in which these individuals are embedded, and it may evolve through time, accordingly.

Instead of viewing agency as a unidimensional concept, we suggest that we should view it as a multidimensional concept. Following Emirbayer and Mische (1998), we define agency as an actor's engagement with the social world that, through the interplay of habit, imagination, and judgment, can both reproduce and transform an environment's structures. Emirbayer and Mische (1998) also argue that agency consists of three different elements: iteration, projectivity, and practical evaluation.

The first – iteration – is oriented toward the past, and describes the "selective reactivation by actors of past patterns of thought and action." Though such reactivation is often overlooked as a form of agency, Emirbayer and Mische (1998: 975) argue that agency is present in "how actors selectively recognize, locate, and implement such schemas in their ongoing and situated transactions," and that "[w]hile this may take place at a low level of conscious reflection, it still requires attention and engagement on the part of actors."

Emirbayer and Mische's (1998: 984) second dimension of agency is "projective" and involves "an imaginative engagement of the future." It encompasses the imaginative generation by actors of possible future trajectories of action, in which received structures of thought and action may be creatively reconfigured in relation to actors' hopes, fears, and desires for the future. Emirbayer and Mische (1998: 984) argue that such a form of agency need be "neither radically voluntarist nor narrowly instrumentalist; the formation of projects is always an interactive, culturally embedded process by which social actors negotiate their paths toward the future." Faced with problems that taken-for-granted habits cannot solve, actors adopt a reflexive stance and project themselves into the future.

The third dimension of agency is oriented to the present and described as "practical-evaluative" (Emirbayer & Mische, 1998: 994). This dimension of agency "responds to the demands and contingencies of the present," and is made necessary by "the exigencies of changing situations." It corresponds to actors' capacity to make practical and normative judgments among alternative possible trajectories of action, in response to emerging demands, dilemmas, and ambiguities of presently evolving situations (Emirbayer & Mische, 1998: 970–971).

In sum, we conceptualize agency as a temporally embedded process of social engagement, informed by the past (in its habitual aspect), but also oriented toward the future (as a capacity to imagine alternative possibilities) and toward the present (as a capacity to contextualize past habits and future projects within the contingencies of the moment). This view of agency challenges the notion of institutions as cognitively "totalizing" structures. We agree with Emirbayer and Mische (1998), who argue that even when actors are subject to institutional influences, they can develop a "practical consciousness." Though actors may participate in the habitualized routines and practices that reproduce institutions, they often do so with awareness and purpose, rather than simply acting as institutional automatons.

Linking agency to institutional work

We argue that the three dimensions of agency – iteration (habit), projection (imagination), and practical evaluation (judgment) – enable the

Table 2.1. Dimensions of agency and forms of institutional work

	Iterative agency	Practical-evaluative agency	Projective agency
Creating institutions	• Improvising • Modifying	• Translation • Bricolage • Reacting to shocks	• Inventing • Creating proto-institutions • Establishing institutional mechanisms • Advocating diffusion
Maintaining institutions	• Enacting institutionalized practices • Selecting one legitimate, institutionalized practice over another	• Adapting institutionalized practices • Bolstering regulative mechanisms	• Repairing • Defending
Disrupting institutions	• Failing to enact an institutionalized practice • Institutional forgetting	• Avoiding institutional monitoring and sanction • Not selecting institutional practices / selecting others	• Attacking the legitimacy or taken-for-grantedness of an institution • Undermining institutional mechanisms

three different types of institutional work: creating, maintaining, and disrupting institutions. Table 2.1 shows examples of action that might fall into the intersections of the dimensions of agency and the forms of institutional work.[1]

---

[1] We thank the editors of the book as well as the participants to the workshop about institutional work in Vancouver in May 2007 for their help in developing this table. We are particularly thankful to Tom Lawrence who directly participated in its development.

We want to emphasize that institutional work may involve a wide range of levels of self-consciousness and reflexivity, as well as a wide range of temporal orientations. Thus, we consider institutional work as intentional in its nature, but drawing on Emirbayer and Mische (1998), we argue that what those "intentions" might look like will vary considerably depending on the dimension of agency that dominates the instances of institutional work one considers. Indeed, we argue that all three of these constitutive dimensions of agency can be found, in varying degrees, within any empirical instance of action. The metaphor of the chordal triad can be used to illustrate this multidimensional view of agency: all three dimensions of agency resonate as separate, but not always harmonious, tones (Emirbayer & Mische, 1998: 971–972) and, depending on the situation, one dimension might dominate the others.

This view moves the concept of institutional work significantly beyond most analyses of agency in institutional studies of organizations, which have focused heavily on the projective agency associated with creating new institutions and occasionally with disrupting institutions (Beckert, 1999; DiMaggio, 1988; Greenwood & Suddaby, 2006; Hensmans, 2003; Lawrence, 1999; Maguire *et al.*, 2004; Suddaby & Greenwood, 2005; D'Aunno *et al.*, 2000). Not only has the agency associated with maintaining institutions been overlooked (Scott, 2001), but so have the iterative and practical-evaluative dimensions of agency that can be critical to institutional work.

Taking into account the different dimensions of agency and their associated forms of institutional work opens two new broad sets of research questions. First, under what conditions do different forms of agency predominate (and thus lead to institutional work)? In other words, what factors cause individuals to be more or less oriented to the past, present, or future? Similarly, what factors cause individuals to be more or less intentional and self-conscious? Seo and Creed (2002) argue, for example, that individuals become more intentional and self-conscious when faced with institutional practices that contradict or conflict with each other. In turn, raised consciousness enables individuals to change or drop institutions. Adopting the multidimensional view of agency discussed above is likely to stimulate similar theorizing because it emphasizes that individuals are capable of different levels and types of awareness that, in turn, prompt them to engage in institutional work.

Other than the experience of contradictory institutional arrangements, individual actors' social position might also influence their temporal orientation toward the past, present, or future (Battilana, 2006). Similarly, other individual-level conditions, such as psychological factors, may affect actors' temporal orientation. But, analyzing the impact of psychological factors without accounting for the fact that actors are institutionally embedded would contradict the premises of institutional theory and thereby do little to address the paradox of embedded human agency (Schneiberg & Clemens, 2006).

Adopting a relational approach, we argue that researchers should give priority to examining the influence of actors' social position on their temporal orientation because social position mediates actors' relationship with their institutional environment (Rousseau, 1978). Future research may then explore the influence of other individual factors, including individual psychological factors, for example. Such a line of inquiry, although promising, is highly demanding because it will require researchers to control for the impact of other identified factors. One way to avoid traps in such studies is to examine the role of psychological factors in relation to actors' social position, taking into account interaction between the individual, organizational, and organizational field levels of analysis (Rousseau, 1978).

Finally, taking into account the different dimensions of agency and their associated forms of institutional work opens a second set of research questions. To what extent are different types of agency associated with different types of institutional work? The examples in Table 2.1 suggest that each type of agency can be linked to each type of institutional work. Nonetheless, empirical work may show that some types of agency are more likely than others to promote a particular type of institutional work. For example, it may be the case that iterative agency, because it is oriented to the past, is less likely than practical-evaluative or projective agency to promote action that creates or disrupts institutions. In contrast, projective agency, because it is future-oriented, may be a strong predictor of individual efforts to create new institutions. A related research agenda is to examine the ways that different combinations of agency may be involved in institutional work over time, especially in the institutionalization of new practices. For example, under certain circumstances, projective agency may promote initial work on creating new institutions, while iterative agency may play a more important role in promoting institutionalization in later phases of the diffusion of a new practice.

Conclusion

Though a number of studies have started to identify conditions that enable actors to engage in institutional work despite institutional pressures towards stasis, the paradox of embedded agency has not yet been adequately resolved. In this chapter, we examined a multidimensional definition of agency that, we argue, promotes understanding of how individuals can both reproduce and challenge institutions.

We also want to emphasize that our focus on agency does not imply that individual agents' actions are the only sources of institutional change. In contrast, we attempt to account for the fact that institutional processes are complex processes, in which different types of forces and agents are involved, including individual agents (Jepperson, 1991). Indeed, we believe that there is a need for more multilevel studies to account for field-level, organization-level, as well as individual-level, enabling conditions for the different forms of institutional work. Such multilevel research has been suggested as a promising avenue of research within the framework of institutional theory (Friedland & Alford, 1991; Ocasio, 2002; Palmer & Biggart, 2002; Strang & Sine, 2002; Reay *et al.*, 2006).

It is well worth investing time and energy in multilevel research. If one considers that organizational theory has a mandate to account for the impact of organizations on contemporary societies (Stern & Barley, 1996; Scott, 1996; Davis & Marquis, 2005), it is then crucial to understand when and how individual agents embedded in organizations, which are themselves embedded in fields, can engage in different forms of institutional work and possibly influence institutions that have for long been dominant in our societies.

References

Abbott, A. (1988) *The System of Professions*. Chicago: University of Chicago Press.

Archer, M. (1982) Morphogenesis versus structuration: on combining structure and action. *The British Journal of Sociology*, 33(4): 455–483.

Argyris, C. (1973) The CEOs' behavior – key to organizational development. *Harvard Business Review*, 51(2): 55.

Aron, R. (1967) *Les étapes de la pensée sociologique*. Paris: Gallimard.

Astley, W. G. & Van de Ven, A. H. (1983) Central perspectives and debates in organization theory. *Administrative Science Quarterly*, 28: 245–273.

Barley, S. R. & Tolbert, P. S. (1997) Institutionalization and structuration: studying the links between action and institution. *Organization Studies*, 18(1): 93–117.

Battilana, J. (2006) Agency and institutions: the enabling role of individuals' social position. *Organization*, 13(5): 653–676.

Beckert, J. (1999) Agency, entrepreneurs, and institutional change: the role of strategic choice and institutionalized practices in organizations. *Organization Studies*, 20: 777–799.

Berger, P. & Luckmann, T. (1967) *The Social Construction of Reality*. Garden City, NY: Doubleday.

Bourdieu, P. (1977) *Outline of a Theory of Practice*. Cambridge: Cambridge University Press.

(1984) *Distinction: A Social Critique of the Judgement of Taste*. Cambridge, MA: Harvard University Press.

Bourdieu, P. & Wacquant, L. J. D. (1992) *An Invitation to Reflexive Sociology*. Chicago: University of Chicago Press.

Boyer, R. (2003) L'anthropologie économique de Pierre Bourdieu. *Actes de la Recherche en Sciences Sociales*, 150: 65–78.

Burrell, G. & Morgan, G. (1979) *Sociological Paradigms and Organizational Analysis*. London: Heinemann.

Calhoun, C. (ed.) (2002) *Dictionary of the Social Sciences*. Oxford: Oxford University Press.

Callinicos, A. (1985) A. Giddens: a contemporary critique. *Theory & Society*, 14: 133–166.

Clegg, S. (1989) *Frameworks of Power*. London: Sage.

Clemens, E. S. & Cook, J. M. (1999) Politics and institutionalism: explaining durability and change. *Annual Review of Sociology*, 25: 441–466.

Colomy, P. (1998) Neo-functionalism and neo-institutionalism: human agency and interest in institutional change. *Sociological Forum*, 13(2): 265–300.

Crozier, M. & Friedberg, E. (1980) *Actors and Systems: The Politics of Collective Action*. Chicago: University of Chicago Press.

Dacin, M. T., Ventresca, M. & Beal, B. (1999) The embeddedness of organizations: debates, dialogue and directions. *Journal of Management*, 25(3): 317–356.

D'Aunno, T., Succi, M. & Alexander, J. (2000) The role of institutional and market forces in divergent organizational change. *Administrative Science Quarterly*, 45: 679–703.

Davis, G. F. & Marquis, C. (2005) Prospects for organization theory in the early twenty-first century: institutional fields and mechanisms. *Organization Science*, 16(4): 332–343.

Dawe, A. (1970) The two sociologies. *The British Journal of Sociology*, 21(2): 207–218.

DiMaggio, P. (1979) Review essay: on Pierre Bourdieu. *American Journal of Sociology*, 84: 1460–1474.

　(1988) Interest and agency in institutional theory. In L. Zucker (ed.), *Institutional Patterns and Organizations*, pp. 3–22. Cambridge, MA: Ballinger.

DiMaggio, P. & Powell, W. (1983) The iron cage revisited: institutional isomorphism and collective rationality in organizational fields. *American Sociological Review*, 48: 147–160.

　(1991) Introduction. In W. Powell & P. DiMaggio (eds.), *The New Institutionalism in Organizational Analysis*, pp. 1–38. Chicago: Chicago University Press.

Dorado, S. (2005) Institutional entrepreneurship, partaking, and convening. *Organization Studies*, 26(3): 383–413.

Eisenstadt, S. N. (1964) Institutionalization and change. *American Sociological Review*, 29(2): 235–247.

　(1980) Cultural orientations, institutional entrepreneurs, and social change: comparative analysis of traditional civilizations. *American Journal of Sociology*, 85(4): 840–869.

Emirbayer, M. (1997) Manifesto for a relational sociology. *American Journal of Sociology*, 103: 281–317.

Emirbayer, M. & Johnson, V. S. (2008) Bourdieu and organizational analysis. *Theory and Society*, 37(1): 1–44.

Emirbayer, M. & Mische, A. (1998) What is agency? *American Journal of Sociology*, 103(4): 962–1023.

Fligstein, N. (1991) The structural transformation of American industry: an institutional account of the causes of diversification in the largest firms, 1919–1979. In W. Powell & P. DiMaggio (eds.), *The New Institutionalism in Organizational Analysis*, pp. 311–336. Chicago: University of Chicago Press.

　(1997) Social skill and institutional theory. *American Behavioral Scientist*, 40(4): 397.

　(2001) Social skills and the theory of fields. *Sociological Theory*, 19(2): 105–125.

Fligstein, N. & Mara-Drita, I. (1996) How to make a market: reflections on the attempt to create a single market in the European Union. *American Journal of Sociology*, 102(1): 1–33.

Fowler, B. (1997) *Pierre Bourdieu and Cultural Theory: Critical Investigations*. London: Sage.

Friedland, R. & Alford, R. R. (1991) Bringing society back in: symbols, practice, and institutional contradictions. In W. Powell & P. DiMaggio (eds.), *The New Institutionalism in Organizational Analysis*, pp. 232–263. Chicago: University of Chicago Press.

Garud, R., Jain, S. & Kumaraswamy, A. (2002) Institutional entrepreneurship in the sponsorship of common technological standards: the case of Sun Microsystems and Java. *Academy of Management Journal*, 45(1): 196–214.

Giddens, A. (1976) *New Rules for Sociological Method*. New York: Basic.
   (1979) *Central Problems in Social Theory*. Berkeley and Los Angeles: University of California Press.
   (1984) *The Constitution of Society*. Berkeley and Los Angeles: University of California Press.

Granovetter, M. (1985) Economic action and social structure: the problem of embeddedness. *American Journal of Sociology*, 91(3): 481–510.

Greenwood, R. & Hinings, C. R. (1996) Understanding radical organizational change: bringing together the old and the new institutionalism. *Academy of Management Review*, 21(4): 1022.

Greenwood, R. & Suddaby, R. (2006) Institutional entrepreneurship by elite firms in mature fields: the big five accounting firms. *Academy of Management Journal*, 49(1): 27–48.

Greenwood, R., Suddaby, R. & Hinings, C. R. (2002) Theorizing change: the role of professional associations in the transformation of institutionalized fields. *Academy of Management Journal*, 45(1): 58–80.

Hannan, M. T. & Freeman, J. (1977) The population ecology of organizations. *American Journal of Sociology*, 82: 929–964.

Haveman, H. A. & Rao, H. (1997) Structuring a theory of moral sentiments: institutional and organizational coevolution in the early thrift industry. *American Journal of Sociology*, 102(6): 1606–1651.

Hensmans, M. (2003) Social movement organizations: a metaphor for strategic actors in institutional fields. *Organization Studies*, 24(3): 355–381.

Hirsch, P. M. & Lounsbury, M. (1997) Putting the organization back into organization theory. *Journal of Management Inquiry*, 6(1): 79.

Holm, P. (1995) The dynamics of institutionalization: transformation processes in Norwegian fisheries. *Administrative Science Quarterly*, 40: 398–422.

Jepperson, R. (1991) Institutions, institutional effects, and institutionalism. In W. Powell & P. DiMaggio (eds.), *The New Institutionalism in Organizational Analysis*, pp. 143–163. Chicago: University of Chicago Press.

Karnoe, P. (1997) Only in social action. *American Behavioral Scientist*, 40: 419–430.

Kondra, A. Z. & Hinings, C. R. (1998) Organizational diversity and change in institutional theory. *Organization Studies*, 19(5): 743–767.

Kraatz, M. S. & Zajac, E. J. (1996) Exploring the limits of the new institutionalism: the causes and consequences of illegitimate organizational change. *American Sociological Review*, 61: 812–836.

Lawrence, P. R. & Lorsch, J. W. (1967) Differentiation and integration in complex organizations. *Administrative Science Quarterly*, 12(1): 1–47.

Lawrence, T. B. (1999) Institutional strategy. *Journal of Management*, 25: 161–187.

Lawrence, T. B., Hardy, C. & Phillips, N. (2002) Institutional effects of inter-organizational collaboration: the emergence of proto-institutions. *Academy of Management Journal*, 45(1): 281–290.

Lawrence, T. B. & Suddaby, R. (2006) Institutions and institutional work. In S. R. Clegg, C. Hardy, T. B. Lawrence & W. R. Nord (eds.), *Handbook of Organization Studies*, pp. 215–254. London: Sage.

Leblebici, H., Salancik, G., Copay, A. & King, T. (1991) Institutional change and the transformation of interorganizational fields: an organizational history of the US radio broadcasting industry. *Administrative Science Quarterly*, 36(3): 333–363.

Leca, B., Battilana, J. & Boxenbaum, E. (2008) Agency and institutions: a review of institutional entrepreneurship. Harvard Business School Working Paper 08-096. Cambridge, MA.

Levy, D. L. & Egan, D. (2003) A neo-Gramscian approach to corporate political strategy: conflict and accommodation in the climate change negotiations. *Journal of Management Studies*, 40(4): 803–829.

Lounsbury, M. (2007) A tale of two cities: competing logics and practice variation in the professionalizing of mutual funds. *Academy of Management Journal*, 50(2): 289–307.

Lounsbury, M. & Ventresca, M. (2003) The new structuralism in organizational theory. *Organization*, 10(3): 457–480.

Maguire, S., Hardy, C. & Lawrence, T. B. (2004) Institutional entrepreneurship in emerging fields: HIV/AIDS treatment advocacy in Canada. *Academy of Management Journal*, 47(5): 657–679.

Meyer, J. & Rowan, B. (1977) Institutionalized organizations: formal structure as myth and ceremony. *American Journal of Sociology*, 83: 340–363.

Meyer, J. & Scott, W. (1983) Centralization and the legitimacy problems of local government. In J. Meyer & W. Scott (eds.), *Organizational Environments: Ritual and Rationality*, pp. 199–251. Beverly Hills, CA: Sage.

Meyer, J., Scott, W. & Deal, T. E. (1983) Institutional and technical sources of organizational structure: explaining the structure of educational organizations. In J. Meyer & W. Scott (eds.), *Organizational Environments: Ritual and Rationality*, pp. 45–67. Beverly Hills, CA: Sage.

Mutch, A. (2003) Communities of practice and habitus: a critique. *Organization Studies*. 24(3): 383–401.

Oakes, L., Townley, B. & Cooper, D. (1998) Business planning as pedagogy: language and control in a changing institutional field. *Administrative Science Quarterly*, 43(2): 257–292.

Ocasio, W. (2002) Organizational power and dependence. In J. A. C. Baum (ed.), *Companion to Organizations*, pp. 363–385. Oxford: Blackwell.

Oliver, C. (1991) Strategic responses to institutional processes. *Academy of Management Review*, 16: 145–179.

(1992) The antecedents of deinstitutionalization. *Organization Studies*, 13(4): 563–588.

Palmer, D. & Biggart, N. W. (2002) Organizational institutions. In J. A. C. Baum (ed.), *Companion to Organization*, pp. 259–280. Oxford: Blackwell.

Pfeffer, J. (1997) *New Directions for Organization Theory: Problems and Prospects*. Oxford: Oxford University Press.

Phillips, N., Lawrence, T. & Hardy, C. (2000) Inter-organizational collaboration and the dynamics of institutional fields. *Journal of Management Studies*, 37(1): 23–45.

Ranson, S., Hinings, B. & Greenwood, R. (1980) The structuring of organizational structures. *Administrative Science Quarterly*, 25(1): 1–17.

Rao, H., Morrill, C. & Zald, N. (2000) Power plays: how social movements and collective action create new organizational forms. *Research in Organizational Behavior*, 22: 239–282.

Reay, T., Golden-Biddle, K. & Germann, K. (2006) Legitimizing a new role: small wins and microprocesses of change. *Academy of Management Journal*, 49(5): 977–998.

Rousseau, D. M. (1978) Characteristics of departments, positions, and individuals: contexts for attitudes and behaviour. *Administrative Science Quarterly*, 23: 521–540.

Schmidt, M. (1997) Habitus revisited. *American Behavioral Scientist*, 40(4): 444–453.

Schneiberg, M. & Clemens, E. (2006) The typical tools for the job: research strategies in institutional analysis. *Sociological Theory*, 3: 195–227.

Schneiberg, M. & Soule, S. (2005) Institutionalization as a contested, multilevel process: politics, social movements and rate regulation in American fire insurance. In G. Davis, D. McAdam, W. R. Scott & M. Zald (eds.), *Social Movements and Organizations*, pp. 122–160. Cambridge: Cambridge University Press.

Scott, W. R. (1996) The mandate is still being honored: in defense of Weber's disciples. *Administrative Science Quarterly*, 41(1): 163–171.

(2001) *Institutions and Organizations*, 2nd edn. Thousand Oaks, CA: Sage.

Selznick, P. (1949) *TVA and the Grass Roots*. Berkeley: University of California Press.

(1956) *Leadership in Administration: A Sociological Interpretation.* Berkeley: University of California Press.

Seo, M. G. & Creed, W. E. D. (2002) Institutional contradictions, praxis, and institutional change: a dialectical perspective. *Academy of Management Review*, 27(2): 222–247.

Sewell, W. H. (1992) A theory of structure: duality, agency, and transformation. *American Journal of Sociology*, 98(1): 1–29.

Simon, H. A. (1997) Administrative behaviour: a study of decision-making processes. *Administrative Organization*, 4th edn. New York: Free Press.

Starr, P. (1982) *The Social Transformation of American Medicine.* New York: Basic Books.

Stern, R. N. & Barley, S. R. (1996) Organizations and social systems: organization theory's neglected mandate. *Administrative Science Quarterly*, 41: 146–162.

Strang, D. & Sine, W. D. (2002) Inter-organizational institutions. In J. Baum (ed.), *Companion to Organizations*, pp. 497–519. Oxford: Blackwell.

Suddaby, R. & Greenwood, R. (2005) Rhetorical strategies of legitimacy. *Administrative Science Quarterly*, 50(1): 35–67.

Thoenig, J. C. (1998) Essai: how far is a sociology of organizations still needed? *Organization Studies*, 19(2): 307–320.

Thompson, J. D. (1967) *Organizations in Action: Social Science Bases of Administrative Theory.* New York: McGraw-Hill.

Tolbert, P. S. (1985) Resource dependence and institutional environments: sources of administrative structure in institutions of higher education. *Administrative Science Quarterly*, 20: 229–249.

Tolbert, P. S. & Zucker, L. G. (1983) Institutional sources of change in the formal structure of organizations: the diffusion of civil service reform 1880–1935. *Administrative Science Quarterly*, 28(1): 22–39.

(1996) The institutionalization of institutional theory. In S. R. Clegg, C. Hardy & W. R. Nord (eds.), *Handbook of Organization Studies*, pp. 175–190. London: Sage.

Wade-Benzoni, K. A., Hoffman, A. J., Thompson, L. L., Moore, D. A., Gillespie, J. J. & Bazerman, M. H. (2002) Barriers to resolution in ideologically based negotiations: the role of values and institutions. *Academy of Management Review*, 27(1): 41–58.

Whittington, R. (1992) Putting Giddens into action: social systems and managerial agency. *Journal of Management Studies*, 29(6): 693–712.

Woodward, J. (1958) *Management and Technology.* London: HMSO.

Zilber, T. B. (2002) Institutionalization as an interplay between actions, meanings, and actors: the case of a rape crisis center in Israel. *Academy of Management Journal*, 45(1): 234–254.

Zucker, L. (1983) Organizations as institutions. In S. B. Bacharach (ed.), *Research in the Sociology of Organizations*, 2: 1–47. Greenwich, CT: JAI Press.

   (1991) Postscript: microfoundations of institutional thought. In W. Powell & P. DiMaggio (eds.), *The New Institutionalism in Organizational Analysis*, pp. 103–106. Chicago: University of Chicago Press.

3 | *Leadership as institutional work: a bridge to the other side*

MATTHEW S. KRAATZ

> The great deed of the supreme hero is to come to the knowledge of this unity in multiplicity and then to make it known.
>
> – Joseph Campbell, *The Hero with a Thousand Faces*

> The most important thing is integrity. Once you figure out how to fake that you've got it made.
>
> – Variously attributed

Current interest in the phenomenon of institutional work was seemingly foreshadowed by Selznick (1957) in his *Leadership in Administration*. Therein, he developed a powerful theory of the institution which granted a central role to a particular type of institutional worker: the leader or "statesman." He saw leaders as playing an essential part in institutionalization processes, and focused in particular on the ways in which they help institutions develop, adapt, and endure. Selznick's concept of institutional leadership would thus appear to link quite well with the more contemporary concept of institutional work, which Lawrence and Suddaby (2006: 215) have defined as "purposive action of individuals and organizations aimed at creating, maintaining and disrupting institutions." However, this linkage remains a latent and largely undeveloped one. Lawrence and Suddaby's (2006) exhaustive review of the burgeoning literature on institutional work cited no studies of institutional leadership and made no explicit reference to Selznick's concept or his 1957 book. While this omission may reflect an oversight on those authors' part, it also says something about the current state of the field. Contemporary institutionalists have become increasingly interested in agency, practice, power, entrepreneurship, and like issues. But they have remained largely silent about the nature or existence of institutional leadership. Even those scholars who have made efforts to recover aspects of Selznick's theory and commensurate it with the more cognitive and cultural neo-institutionalism have made little use of his ideas about leadership (Oliver, 1991; Greenwood & Hinings, 1996; Hirsch & Lounsbury, 1997). Thus, while Selznick's "old institutionalism" seems to be newly alive and well, the same cannot be said for its leading actor, who appears to remain frozen in the 1950s. Washington, Boal, and Davis (2008) have recently made similar observations, and have also called for a renewed focus on institutional leadership in the Selznickian sense.

My purpose in this chapter is to revisit Selznick's perspective, recover some key ideas from it, and elaborate some specific ways in which these ideas can contribute to the contemporary study of institutional work. Following Selznick, I will emphasize the continuing (and renewed) need to study individual organizations as institutions in their own right. Though organizations are deeply embedded in institutional environments and are powerfully affected by cultural forces operating at the field level, I will show that these forces need not (and cannot) wholly trump or negate the organization-level institutionalization processes that Selznick theorized. Indeed, I will suggest that Selznickian organizational institutions actually emerge as adaptive responses to the field-level cultural forces that have preoccupied most contemporary scholars (Glynn, 2008; Kraatz & Block, 2008; Strandgaard Pedersen & Dobbin, 2006). I will further, and consistently, identify a continuing need for the type of "leadership work" that Selznick discussed *within* these organizations. Specifically, I will argue that institutional work researchers need to give more attention to the work involved in *governing*, *adapting*, and *reforming* organizational institutions.

Such research may help fill an apparent void in the institutional work literature, and not only because of its organization-level focus. Lawrence and Suddaby (2006) have noted a paucity of research examining institutional maintenance work relative to that focusing on institutional creation and disruption. Selznick's theory, which is all about the work of leading institutions that have become "going concerns" and taken on "lives of their own," appears quite germane to this neglected topic. A renewed focus on leadership may also help make the emerging literature on institutional work relevant to a broader range of constituencies (e.g. to those who hold positions of power in existing institutions in addition to would-be entrepreneurs and revolutionaries). An additional benefit might be to productively stretch scholars' conceptions of institutions themselves. Not all theories lead us to see institutions as entities that *require* governance, are *capable* of adaptation, or are *worthy* of reform. Selznick's does, and this may be a difference worth reflecting on. Some interparadigmatic tensions will, predictably, surface as the chapter unfolds. There appear to be some good reasons why contemporary scholars have thus far failed to pick up on Selznick's ideas about leadership. I will not try to minimize or eliminate these tensions. But I will try to build a sort of bridge between the paradigms, hopefully creating a place from which scholars might simultaneously see their respective truths and incorporate these into their empirical research. I will also argue that the study of institutional work (as an empirical phenomenon) might be productively expanded to accommodate more than one paradigm and more than one accompanying set of pragmatic concerns.

My chapter is similar to Washington, Boal, and Davis (2008) in several specific ways, beyond the shared argument for a renewed focus on institutional leadership. Among the most important of these is its parallel emphasis on the leader's role in both integrating the organization (internally) and legitimating it (with respect to external audiences). My chapter focuses somewhat more upon the political dimension of leadership, and particularly upon the subtle distinction between statesmanship and "mere politics." This distinction appears to be all-important to Selznick's theory. It also makes much more of the paradigmatic divide that appears to separate Selznick's perspective from contemporary institutional work research. I spend substantial time grappling with the question of how Selznickian organizational institutions and leadership are theoretically *possible* within the world as seen through the neo-institutional lens, and try to reach some resolution to this question as part of my recovery effort. These are merely distinguishing attributes of my chapter, and not necessarily relative strengths. Washington *et al.*'s study provides many more examples and much better links to the vast leadership literature than mine does. The two studies may be best read as complements for these reasons, among others.

Selznick on institutionalization and leadership

Institutionalization

In order to understand what Selznick meant by institutional leadership, it is first necessary to thoroughly understand what he meant by institutionalization. He saw the former as a type of work that occurred in response to particular problems that arose in the context of the latter sociological process (1957: 22). He portrayed the leader as both an "agent of institutionalization" (27) and a defender and steward of the living social entity that ultimately emerged from this process. The two concepts are thus inextricably linked in his thinking. They cannot be discussed in isolation from one another.

Selznick tried to explain the institutionalization process by contrasting two archetypal forms, which might be thought of as its input and output (1957: 5–22). He began with the "organization," a formally structured association of individuals that could be understood in narrowly technical terms. It was a socially engineered device that was rationally designed in order to achieve particular, limited objectives, and it operated in a rather machine-like fashion. When its goals were achieved or its function became obsolete, it was likely to be disassembled. He used this ideal-type as a sort of literary foil that allowed him to reveal the character of the "institution" that was his true concern. Where the organization had clear and fixed goals, the institution had contested and shifting ones. Where the organization appeared unitary, the institution was at best politically plural (and at worst deeply fragmented). Where the organization was essentially a formal administrative structure, the institution was also (and perhaps more essentially) an informal one, made up of interpersonal relationships, interest groups, norms, shared beliefs, etc. Where the organization was composed of jobholders who filled formal positions, the institution was composed of whole persons, who often broke out of their roles, to both good and ill effect. Where the organization justified its existence and its decisions on technical grounds (e.g. in terms of efficiency), the institution developed and espoused an ideology or mission that guided (or at least covered) its actions. Finally, where the organization was presumed to be independent, the institution was deeply affected by its external context. It was a path-dependent entity that could only be understood as the historical product of a series of "character-forming" adaptations and compromises. Selznick thus emphasized the need for a "developmental" and *diachronic* approach to the analyses of organizational institutions (Knudsen, 1995).

In making these contrasts, Selznick introduced a significant dose of sociological and political realism (and perhaps skepticism) into organization theory. He exposed a sort of hidden world within organizations, and showed that they were recalcitrant tools that often failed to fulfill their official purposes or serve their intended constituencies. These were the themes that he had developed earlier in *TVA and the Grass Roots*

(Selznick, 1949), and some have taken them to be the essential ones in his institutionalism (Gouldner, 1955; Perrow, 1986). However, Selznick did not see institutionalization as a process that was merely or inevitably negative.

The institution he described was certainly different from the organization and perhaps less attractive in the sense of being less orderly, less efficient, more political, and more subject to co-optation and goal-displacement. But it was also more "human" in all the positive senses of this term, and thus enjoyed a number of qualitative advantages. Chief among these was the fact that it was apt to have developed some unique and socially integrating *identity* (1957: 40) and some accompanying *distinctive competence* (42) as a result of the institutionalization process that left the aforementioned scars on its character. Selznick also suggested that organizations often became "value-infused" (17) and non-expendable (18) entities as they emerged from the transformative crucible of institutionalization. He argued that they took on lives of their own and became subjects of genuine moral concern for their constituencies. These groups came to see the institution as a "vehicle" for the realization of their own values and identities and were reluctant to let it perish for this reason (17). While these "dynamic adaptations" (e.g. from mechanical tool to living entity, means to end, unity to plurality, object to subject, etc.) exerted significant constraints on the institution (31), they also provided it with remarkable adaptive powers and a capacity for self-governance, self-direction, and self-perpetuation that the monolithic, limited-purpose organization lacked. Selznick's theory implies that these positive and integrative capacities emerge as a natural (if not inevitable) response to the divisive political processes mentioned just above. Thus, he portrayed institutionalization as very much a "bad news / good news" story for the organization. Its polarities are deeply involved with each other.

The leader

Selznick's leader is in large part just an administrator who understands the sociological and political complexities of the institution and acts accordingly. He is a realist, and a sentient and self-aware participant in an ongoing process that is likely to confuse and perhaps victimize others. Imagine, as one example, a savvy manager who doesn't rely naively upon his limited formal authority, and who understands the informal power structure, history, and built-in limitations of his organization. This hypothetical manager is capable of speaking to subordinates' values and ideals, as well as their interests, and is wise to the importance of rhetoric, culture, and symbols. He is, necessarily, adept at building coalitions, cutting deals, and other forms of pragmatic action. He is, in short – and at minimum – an effective organizational politician. This is the kind of work that the realities of institutional life demand of him. Selznick (1957: 61) says as much: *"These men are called leaders. Their profession is politics"* (italics added).

However, Selznick obviously saw a larger and more important function for the would-be leader, just as he saw a higher potentiality in the organizational institution itself. The better part of *Leadership in Administration* is concerned with understanding this function (which he also called "statesmanship"). "The argument of this essay is quite simply stated," he avers in his introduction (1957: 4). *"The executive becomes a statesman as he makes the transition from administrative management to institutional leadership"* (italics in original). He uses this same statement as the book's closing sentence, underscoring its felt importance (154). The leader/statesman, Selznick suggested, rose not only above his narrow and formal role as administrator, but also – *and much more remarkably* – above the organization's factional politics, or "rivalries" as he called them. He did this, apparently, by assuming personal responsibility for the well-being of the organizational "whole," identifying himself with it, and reconceptualizing himself as its steward. This is, seemingly, the substance of the aforementioned "transition."[1]

---

[1] In retrospect, it would have been helpful if Selznick had separated and elaborated the stages of this transition (first from role-bound administrator to knowing political actor, and from there onward to the role of principled and willfully committed statesman). The term politician obviously carries negative connotations which need to be surfaced and discussed. Many people seem to think of politics as the opposite of leadership, or as proof against its very possibility. Perhaps politics did not carry this connotation in the idealized world of the 1950s. Or perhaps Selznick just did not wish to make too much of this complexity in his short and normatively focused book. Selznick might also have done us a favor by drawing out the parallel transformation of the organizational institution (first from rational and unified system to divided and political one, and then onward to something more like a community or democratic polity wherein statesmanship can actually occur). Many contemporary institutionalists seem preoccupied with the study of boundaries and conflicts, neglecting the possibility that some form of social integration can (or must) emerge on the other side of them. Ironically, other more managerially inclined scholars who have been influenced by Selznick seem to miss these inevitable and necessary tensions altogether. That is, they seem to advocate integration without differentiation and mere consensus rather than the symbiosis or community that Selznick saw and advocated.

Whether Selznick was referring primarily to an outward and strictly behavioral transformation or to an intrapersonal one as well is not entirely clear based on what he says in the book itself.[2] I will return to this important question later. In any event, he argued that the administrator/politician becomes a leader as he begins to concern himself (at least outwardly) with defining the institution's mission and values, with creating structures that "embody" these values, and with ensuring the institution's adaptation to changing circumstances (1957: 62). In all of these matters, Selznick suggests, the leader needs to give foremost attention to the institution's *integrity*, and to protect it as if it was his own (63, 119). If the institution actually is (or is at least productively thought of as) a "subject," a "self," or a social "whole," it follows that it has an identity of its own and thus a potential for integrity (as well as integrity loss). Selznick argued that institutional integrity was at risk in any number of organizational decisions, particularly those he labeled as "critical" ones (29). He also said that maintaining integrity was very important from an instrumental standpoint, as it was the cornerstone of the organization's distinctive competence (139). To the extent that he offers anything like an "acid test" of leadership, it is found in the consequences that an executive's decisions (including his "default" choices) have upon the integrity of the institution. Selznick's theory implies that this integrity is thoroughly intertwined with the integrity of the leader himself, given the latter's deep personal identification with the organization (143).

Selznick set a very high bar for the would-be leader, and he provided many more examples of leadership failure than of success (so many that his book might have been more appropriately titled *Absence of Leadership in Administration*). He referred to such failures as the "Default of Leadership" (25), and he identified some common patterns of thought and behavior that appeared to contribute to this default (e.g. in his discussions of "utopianism" (147), "opportunism" (146), and the "retreat to technology" (74)). The integrating theme in these discussions was that would-be leaders defaulted when they failed to think holistically and did not consider the long term or potential

---

[2] Selznick's other writings reveal a deep and overt concern with the individual person's adaptation to society, and also emphasize the practical consequences of this highly variable process. See, for example, chapter 8 of his *Moral Commonwealth* ("The Responsible Self"). These themes are less explicit in *Leadership in Administration*.

unintended consequences of their actions (i.e. when they chose political expediency over statesmanship). Despite these sober warnings, Selznick remained very positive concerning the possibilities for leadership, and for institutions more generally. His thinking, both in *Leadership in Administration* and in his subsequent works, reflects a peculiar combination of pessimism and optimism, realism and romanticism, resignation and hopefulness. Krygier (2002: 25) has characterized it as "Hobbesian Idealism." An appreciation for this unique sensibility is key to understanding both what Selznick had to say about leadership fifty years ago and the potential contemporary uses of his ideas.

It is also important to understand something about Selznick's unique motivations for studying leadership, as these have some bearing on the transferability and contemporary relevance of his ideas. Like virtually all authors who invoke this value-laden term, he was concerned with providing practical and moral guidance to powerholders and with promoting the responsible use of power. Like most leadership writers, he also held out hope that moral behavior would translate into practical benefits (i.e. that idealism could actually pay). He argued, for example, that honoring commitments, developing principles, and protecting organizational integrity were essential to developing distinctive competence, creating social integration, and ensuring long-term success. Such arguments are, at least now, widespread in the vast academic and popular literature on organizational leadership. However, Selznick's perspective remains highly distinctive and interesting for at least two reasons.

First, he expressed a much more complex understanding of the moral and the practical than do most leadership writers. This understanding was grounded in the pragmatism of John Dewey and William James, and in his own empirical studies of organizational institutionalization processes (Selznick, 1949, 1952). These studies had revealed deep and abiding tensions between different conceptions of the good (a key pragmatist theme). They had also uncovered the complex interplay of morality and politics (as when noble ideologies are used as public rationalizations for ignoble actions, or when the sincere pursuit of high ideals has unintended and tragic consequences). As noted, Selznick's institution is no utopia, and its leader is no simple-minded moralist or Boy Scout. The institution is at least a political arena, and its leader is at least a politician. He may succeed in rising above this game (the very mark of statesmanship), but he must remain fully in it at the same time. This is a difficult (some would say impossible) trick.

Second, Selznick was not only interested in studying leadership in the prescriptive and idealized (i.e. *connotative*) sense of the term. He was also (and actually first) interested in scientifically cataloging and analyzing the behaviors of those people who might be called *denotative* leaders (i.e. those who were merely in charge, and were thus mired in ongoing institutionalization processes whether they wanted to be or not). Selznick's moralism and pragmatism led him to focus on translating his backward-looking knowledge of what various denotative leaders *had done* (often in error or by "default") into forward-looking knowledge about what other executives *should do* or could *reasonably hope to do* in the future (Selznick, 1996, 2000; Heclo, 2002). He did this by invoking the concept of leadership in the connotative sense. In other words, he introduced leadership as an ideal to which the ordinary organizational administrator/politician might realistically aspire (and perhaps also as a standard to which the organizational analyst could hold that same administrator).[3]

In the chapter's conclusion, I will say some words in support of Selznick's pragmatic approach toward leadership and organizational studies more generally. I will specifically emphasize the benefits of simultaneous realism and idealism, of equal concern with the true and the useful, and of developing a processual, developmental perspective that is both backward and forward looking. However, I will also

---

[3] The distinction between connotative and denotative meanings of the term leadership is essential, and it is one that I will use throughout the chapter. Leadership is, generally speaking, a connotative and *normative* concept. Leadership scholars and laypersons most often use the term to describe an *ideal* (though this ideal varies quite substantially across different accounts and is not always identified as such) (cf. Burns, 1978). Individuals are typically labeled as leaders when they appear to embody the ideal(s) in question, and denied this mantle when their actions, values, motives, or achievements fail to rise to the necessary connotative heights (cf. Rost, 1991). Selznick's use of the term leadership is quite conventional in this basic regard. (Recall as examples his aforementioned discussion of the "Default of Leadership" and his exhortation for the executive to rise to statesmanship.) Selznick's use of the leadership concept is also consistent with his larger body of work, which is notable for its focus on developing normative theories and "taking ideals seriously" (see Krygier, 2002; Lacey, 2002; Jaeger & Selznick, 1964; Selznick, 1992). My aim in introducing the concept of denotative leadership here is to partially detach the actual work of organizational leaders from the normative framework(s) that often envelop it. My hope is that this will help break down barriers and encourage empirical inquiry. I *do not* aim to delegitimate these normative frameworks or to reduce leadership to something less than it is.

emphasize throughout the chapter that scholars need not assume Selznick's overall orientation in order to make productive use of his ideas. Institutional work scholars might fruitfully import them on a retail basis rather than a wholesale one. They might focus, for instance, upon the work of denotative leaders in "merely political" organizations while maintaining some skepticism about whether either the person or his/her organization can actually make the parallel transitions that Selznick emphasized. Scholars might also focus upon the tactics that denotative leaders use in creating *the appearance* that they and their organizations are something more than political entities. As we shall see, the line separating such behaviors from genuine leadership is not an especially bright one.

Leadership as institutional work: building a bridge

As noted above, my aim in this chapter is to persuade other institutional work scholars to pick up on Selznick's neglected ideas about leadership and to show some specific ways that this can be done. My presumption is that many researchers would be interested in using these ideas, given their resonance and enduring influence, given their apparent (if thus far elusive) link to the emerging institutional work literature, and given the more general and persistent interest in the topic of leadership. Leadership simply *seems* like a topic that institutional theory should encompass (or at least inform), and it certainly seems like one that should have a place under the banner of institutional work. However, my suspicion is that this "bridge" has remained unbuilt because of the wide gap that still separates Selznick's perspective on institutions and leadership from the neo-institutional perspective that frames most contemporary research.

The gap to be crossed

The gap that I refer to exists partly because of Selznick's organization-level focus, partly because of his assumptions about organizational pluralism and dynamism, partly because of his emphasis on the organizational institution's socially integrating function, and partly because of his claim that (at least some) organizations can become autonomous, self-governing entities with distinctive identities and purposes that are uniquely their own (i.e. connotative institutions). These ideas are very difficult to hold on to when one wades across the gap into the neo-institutional "world." Within that world, institutions generally appear as cultural/cognitive control structures, and are most often seen to operate at the field level of analysis (DiMaggio & Powell, 1991; Scott, 2001; Schneiberg & Clemens, 2006). The individual organization is more apt to be seen as an institutional product than as an autonomous institution in its own right. Its identity appears to be ascribed and imposed by the overarching culture, rather than developing internally and being self-possessed (Glynn & Abzug, 2002; Zuckerman, 1999). This identity is thus a source of constraint and homogeneity, rather than a resource for change, differentiation, and competence development as Selznick theorized.

Further, in most neo-institutional research, the organization appears as a *synchronic* entity, rather than a *diachronic* one. Studies often examine how categorically similar organizations are collectively shaped and homogenized by their shared cultural and historical experiences (and by their interactions with each other). But they generally give little attention to an organization's unique, developmental history (e.g. the formative or "critical" decisions it has made, its espoused and rejected commitments, its past successes and failures, etc.). Extracted from this diachronic history, the individual organization has no possibility of developing a Selznickian character or distinctive competence, and no apparent integrity to be won or lost. It appears mainly as a "unit" of some larger institutional system, and it often seems to dissolve into the culture that surrounds it. The neo-institutional preoccupation with decoupling and field-level diffusion and legitimation processes also serves to further defocalize and decenter the organizational subject.

Many scholars have, of course, identified ways in which individual organizations might fight back against overarching institutional forces or find wiggle room while remaining within their grasp (Oliver, 1991; Scott, 2001: 171–175; Weber & Glynn, 2006). Selznick's ideas about internal politics and value conflicts have also served as the centerpiece of Greenwood and Hinings' (1996) influential account of "radical change" at the organizational level. However, none of these previous integrative efforts leaves us with a theoretical picture of an organization that is an institution in Selznick's connotative sense (i.e. one that is distinctive, purposive, autonomous, pluralistic, integrative, dynamic and evolving, etc.), or which is seemingly capable of developing such characteristics. Most efforts appear to introduce his theory around the margins of neo-institutionalism, thus assimilating it into the newer paradigm in one way or the other. It is for this main reason, I think, that Selznick's leader remains "frozen in the 1950s." As I noted at the outset, his theory of leadership and his theory of the organizational institution are inseparably joined. The former (a particular type of work) can only occur in a particular type of social situation, and in direct response to the opportunities and imperatives which that context creates. Such social contexts do not appear to exist within the organizational world as neo-institutionalists have constituted it.

Institutional pluralism as infrastructure

Given this deep tension, institutional work scholars appear to face a stark choice. One can either accept neo-institutionalism and forsake the ability to take organizational-institutionalization processes and leadership seriously, or one can embrace the latter phenomena and reject the former theoretical perspective (e.g. by ignoring field-level institutions and denying the constitutive role of culture, etc.). Most contemporary students of institutional work appear (quite understandably) to have opted for the former choice. Thus, while they have embraced agency, conflict, and change, they have focused most of their attention on the "purposive action" of entrepreneurs and revolutionaries who are involved in the episodic construction and dismantling of field-level control structures. The neo-institutional perspective directs scholarly attention to this type of work, this type of institution, and this level of analysis, at the same time that it defocalizes individual organizations and the developmental, adaptive, and integrative work that needs to be done by their existing elites.

While this interparadigmatic divide cannot be eliminated, Kraatz and Block (2008) have recently identified at least one way in which it might be spanned. They suggest that it is possible to recover Selznick's organizational institution (and perhaps his leader) without eschewing neo-institutionalism – and indeed by building on its core tenets. They try to do this by focusing attention on *institutional pluralism*, which is the situation faced by organizations that operate in multiple institutional spheres. Such organizations, Kraatz and Block suggest, are *multiply constituted* in the sense that they have more than one institutionally ascribed identity and more than one societally sanctioned purpose.

Kraatz and Block explore institutional pluralism's implications for organizational legitimacy, governance, and change, and also consider its implications for institutional theory, more generally. However, the phenomenon is also germane to the topic of institutional leadership, and for a very simple reason. Specifically, pluralism in the institutional environment has the effect of creating *persistent internal tensions* within the individual organization itself. Contending logics interpenetrate the pluralistic organization, and different people within its boundaries project different identities and purposes upon it. As a result, the organization confronting institutional pluralism appears to be a Selznickian institution in at least his minimal sense (i.e. in terms of being a divided entity with multiple shifting objectives that are politically determined by the pulling and hauling of its rival constituencies). Its administrators also appear to be leaders in at least Selznick's minimal sense of being political players whose actions and choices (including their "default choices") ultimately shape the organization's evolution and character development. The basic sources of these internal tensions are somewhat different than those which Selznick emphasized, but their effects are largely the same.[4]

Organizations that are built directly on the fault lines which separate different segments of society and their respective institutional logics from one another provide the most obvious and striking examples of institutional pluralism. The American university is an ideal-typical example. It is a vehicle of the academic profession, a branch of the government (or of the church), and, increasingly, a capitalist implement, as well. It is also a quasi-professional football team, among its many other institutionally ascribed identities. This organization enjoys a truly remarkable degree of societal support, but its legitimacy rests upon a number of distinct macro-institutional foundations. Different segments of society tolerate and support it for very different reasons, and its constituencies infuse it with a wide variety of different values and logics. Similar, if less extreme, instances of institutional pluralism abound. For-profit hospitals and other organizations with both professional and

---

[4] It is worth noting that Selznick himself recognized that overarching cultural divisions helped create the local tensions featured in his theory of institutionalization, even though he did not explore these in depth. Consider the following: "although organizational controversy may be directly motivated by narrow personal and group aims, the contending programs usually reflect ideological differences in the larger arena. In this way, the internal struggle for power becomes a channel through which external environmental forces make themselves felt" (1957: 20).

market identities are ready examples. Corporations also appear to be multiply constituted in the sense that they have institutionally ascribed identities as producers (product market identities), as employers (labor market identities), and as stocks (capital market identities), among others (e.g. legal identities, technological identities, etc.).

Kraatz and Block follow Selznick in arguing that pluralistic organizations have the opportunity and ability to develop a unique and distinctive diachronic character as they attempt to work out their (externally produced) internal tensions. They also invoke Mead (1934) and other scholars in his symbolic interactionist tradition by introducing the notion of an "organizational self." They conceptualize this self as the "whole" entity that both encompasses and directs the organization's various socially ascribed identities. They suggest that organizational selves are constructed using "raw materials" that organizations take from their pluralistic institutional environments (Glynn, 2008). Kraatz and Block also follow Selznick in arguing that organizations face an "integrity imperative" in addition to the legitimacy or conformity imperative which is featured in most neo-institutional accounts. Though they are politically divided and multiplicitous entities (and indeed *because of this*), organizations still have a need to create the appearance of self-consistency, integration, coherence, and reliability. They are evaluated as integrated subjects and as selves who are responsible for their own actions, at the same time that they are evaluated as externally controlled objects with socially given roles to play. Kraatz and Block suggest that leadership may play a critical role in helping the organization manage these dual imperatives, though they do not develop this argument in depth.

The basic nature of the work

In light of the preceding arguments, the institutional work done by an organization's administrators (i.e. its denotative leaders) might be seen as falling into two basic categories. The first consists of *legitimacy-seeking* behaviors. This work entails ongoing efforts to win the support of diverse constituencies and to symbolically demonstrate the organization's cultural fitness to different elements of its institutional environment. The pluralistic organization needs to be "multiple things to multiple people," and part of the leader's job is to convey that the organization is indeed each of these things. This work arises because the organization is a synchronic entity that is situated in a heteroge-neous institutional environment and has socially ascribed roles to play therein. It is thus essentially neo-institutional in nature, though the need to placate multiple constituencies also lends it a distinctly political flavor (Stryker, 2000).

The second type of work involves the *creation and maintenance of organizational integrity*. This work is more obviously Selznickian, and it more closely approximates the behavior that is traditionally asso-ciated with the concept of leadership. Specifically, it entails efforts to knit together diverse constituencies and purposes, to engender coopera-tion and win consent, and to create a "whole" entity that is at least minimally coherent, integrated, and self-consistent. This work is required because the organization is a diachronic entity, as well as a synchronic one (and is evaluated as such). It has a unique developmental history to which it is in some important sense a "hostage" (Selznick, 1996). It also has a projected future, and it must make certain commit-ments to its various constituencies in the here and now if it is to win and sustain their support as it moves forward (Knudsen, 1995). Selznick's exhortations concerning the making of commitments and the protection of organizational integrity thus remain remarkably insightful, even though they appear incomplete in light of current knowledge about the cultural bases of legitimacy and the dynamics of organizational fields.

The preceding discussion should help clarify Selznick's arguments and at least partially square them with the neo-institutional perspective. Accepting the reality of pluralism, it is apparent that the individual organization is an institution in at least some minimum sense and that its administrators have much important institutional work to do. My chapter's main aim is to focus research attention on that work and to begin to elaborate its complex, dual nature (e.g. the simultaneous need to pursue legitimacy and maintain integrity). But I also hope to make both the phenomenon and the idea of leadership somewhat more acces-sible and comprehensible to contemporary institutional scholars. As noted earlier, Selznick romanticizes and idealizes both the work of the leader and the organizational institution itself in *Leadership in Administration*. He "infuses value" into both of these things, even as he describes how this evaluation process often occurs in the empirical world (Heclo, 2002). Through his use of connotative, idealistic, and holistic concepts, he makes them both into something more than they necessarily are. This is a characteristic strategy in normative discussions of leadership (though Selznick's is particularly masterful and original). While this approach is a legitimate and valuable one, it also has the effect of blocking communication and inquiry. Selznick's powerful insights about the actual work that denotative leaders must do have been unavailable to those who are unable or unwilling to assume the larger perspective from which they derive. This need not be the case.

Leadership as institutional work: some sights seen from the bridge

In the pages that follow, I will identify seven related types of institutional work that the denotative leaders of pluralistic organizations appear to perform. I do this with an eye toward stimulating future empirical research on this work. These behaviors have all been observed, analyzed, and dissected before. Selznick and other leadership scholars have talked about many of them, and neo-institutionalists have discussed others. However, I hope that these ordinary and familiar actions may appear differently and take on new and interesting meanings when viewed from the interparadigmatic position that I have begun to develop here. I also hope that my metaphorical bridge will come to seem increasingly real and sturdy as we consider some of the specific empirical "sights" that are visible from it.

Sight 1: Denotative leaders engaging in ongoing and highly consequential symbolic exchanges with different elements of their organization's heterogeneous institutional environment

Both neo-institutionalists and leadership scholars have emphasized the important role of symbolism in organizations' (and leaders') relationships with their environments (Meyer & Rowan, 1977; Rao, 1994; Glynn, 2000; Westphal & Zajac, 1994; Pfeffer, 1981; Pondy, 1983; Zott & Huy, 2007). As such, the overt use of symbols is one of the first and most striking things researchers might expect to see as they focus their attention upon the work done by top administrators of institutionally plural organizations. These persons are likely to spend much of their time engaged in an institutionally informed brand of intra-organizational politics (Heimer, 1999; Stryker, 2000). They have a need to tell different institutional constituencies what they want to hear in order to maintain their support. They likely choose to discuss issues that are of known importance to a particular identity group and employ rhetoric ("institutional vocabulary") that is tailored to fit that crowd's values and constitutive beliefs (Suddaby & Greenwood, 2005).

Aware of the fact that their organization has multiple identities and distinct cultural bases of support, these administrators are also apt to develop an awareness of the different symbols that are totemic within its various sub-communities (Pratt & Foreman, 2000). Clark Kerr, as one example, once quipped that his job as chancellor of the University of California was to provide "parking for faculty, football for alumni, and sex for undergraduates." While this comment was surely a joke, it is resonant and enduring because it demonstrates the pluralism of the university and the way that this pluralism shapes the nature of the leader's work. One can imagine that the leaders of other pluralistic organizations might develop similar institutional maps. One example would be CEOs' understandings of the symbols that are revered by investors, employees, and government regulators, respectively. These executives' strategic decisions are also likely to be deeply influenced by these symbolic mappings.

While a focus on executives' symbolic actions and understandings is by no means novel, a specific focus on the symbols used by would-be leaders in institutionally plural organizations seems more so. This work also takes on new and different connotations when we hold the Selznickian and neo-institutional perspectives in tension as we observe it. One thing that becomes apparent about this work is that it is *ongoing* and seemingly quite central to the individual organization's success (and very existence). Institutional pluralism makes it necessary for the managers of individual organizations to build and sustain what Fligstein (2001) calls "local social orders." This is an integrative and unending task that requires the symbolic capacity he calls "social skill." A second notable fact is that this work cannot be neatly classified either as institutional rule-following on the one hand or as strategic and instrumental on the other. The boundaries between these types of actions seem to disappear, even as the importance of each is affirmed. The work is both completely institutional and completely strategic in its nature. A final observation is that this work might be quite perilous. Organizational leaders, like politicians, can get into much trouble by offering the right symbol to the wrong audience, by sending inconsistent symbols, and/or by making a gesture that commits the organization to an unwanted course of action over the long term. For these reasons, a facility with robust symbols may be of particular value to the denotative leader aspiring toward the connotative label – an idea I will return to shortly (Padgett & Ansell, 1993; Ansell, 1997).

Research focusing on the rhetoric and symbolism that existing elites use in the effort to hold together multiply constituted organizations might also be a nice complement to the larger body of recent research which has focused on the ways that rhetoric and symbols operate in overturning existing institutional orders and starting new ones (e.g. Suddaby & Greenwood, 2005; Hargrave & Van de Ven, 2006). It might also complement research that has examined the role of rhetoric in organization-level transformation processes (Heracleous & Barrett, 2001; Oakes, Townley & Cooper, 1998).

Sight 2: Denotative leaders creating formal structures in order to avoid co-optation and balance competing institutional demands against one another

While denotative leaders clearly have a need to get support from different institutional constituencies and surely do use symbolism toward that end, they have a simultaneous (and potentially complementary) need to avoid letting any one constituency take over (i.e. "co-opt") the organization. Selznick (1949, 1957, 1969) and contemporary theorists (e.g. Oliver, 1991) have both recognized this emergent need. Responding to this imperative entails a different type of institutional work. Some of this autonomy-maintaining work may involve openly confrontational and oppositional "legitimacy politics," as when a leader wholly rejects the claims of some group. But much of it is likely to be structural and quasi-integrative in nature. In this work, the leader acts as an architect, creating structures that grant various constituencies sufficient influence to secure their support, while simultaneously limiting their power over the whole organization. Part of this process entails placing constituent groups with divergent goals in dynamic tension with one another, through the creation of a constitutional system of checks and balances (Knudsen, 1995). While an organization's early leaders are charged with much of this work, it is likely to be an ongoing and evolutionary process, as Selznick theorized. That is, it likely involves "remodeling" as well as initial construction. It also involves the creation of informal constitutions, as well as formal ones.

While the existence of this work (basically the design and modification of organizational governance arrangements) is old news, it also takes on a new and different appearance when we view it from our metaphorical bridge. What is perhaps most striking about it is the fact that it is done in response to potentially fragmenting and controlling institutions which operate at the field level, but also involves the creation of integrative and autonomy-creating organization-level ones. The two processes seem to be mutually implicated and neither is clearly prior to the other.

Sight 3: Denotative leaders making value commitments in order to win trust and sustain cooperation among institutional constituencies

A third type of institutional work that we might expect to see from the leaders of organizations facing institutional pluralism involves making commitments in order to gain the trust and cooperation of particular institutional constituencies. Selznick emphasized that commitment was the price that institutional leaders had to pay for trust and reciprocal commitment from different interest groups. He thus counseled leaders to (carefully) make irreversible, character-defining commitments and to willfully give up certain freedoms in the interest of developing relationships that would be advantageous over the long run. His espoused concern with integrity is largely a reflection of this underlying core theme.

This message is not featured in neo-institutional accounts. Trust is not necessary to gain support (or compliance) in social settings that are typified by pervasive and deeply held cultural understandings. Indeed, it is not clear that people are *capable* of granting consent to the cultural and cognitive control structures that neo-institutionalists most often discuss. However, winning trust and cooperation seems considerably more important in pluralistic institutional contexts, wherein taken-for-granted beliefs and values are not widely shared (and wherein competition between internal constituencies is real) (Fligstein, 2001). Leaders may have a genuine need to make moral and emotional displays of commitment in order to create social cohesion and solve the collective action problems that exist in such settings.

Selznick's emphasis on the importance of espoused values, commitment, and integrity is also supported by research outside the domain of institutionalism. Evolutionary psychology, for instance, indicates that people respond to displays of commitment (and apparent opportunism) at a deeply emotional and preconscious level (Frank, 1988; Haidt, 2007; Hauser, 2006; Nesse, 2001). These evaluations may work at cross-purposes with the cognitive and culturally determined evaluation processes emphasized in neo-institutionalism.[5]

Sight 4: Denotative leaders trying to create the appearance of organizational coherence, wholeness, and purposiveness in the face of institutional fragmentation

A fourth related category of institutional leadership work involves creating (at least) the appearance of organizational integration, coherence, and shared purpose. As with the prior three types of work, this one is also seemingly compelled by the potentially fragmenting and controlling forces that operate in the organization's pluralistic cultural milieu. The same heterogeneous society that imposes divergent institutional identities on the organization, and demands that it "conform" to those roles, also demands (perhaps less perceptibly) that the entity be self-consistent, integrated, autonomous, and responsible for its own actions. It must, as previously explained, form some type of "organizational self" that can integrate, direct, and account for the things that "it" does under the auspices of "its" distinct institutionally given identities (Mead, 1934; Selznick, 1957; Kraatz & Block, 2008).

Some of Selznick's most recognizable leadership insights also appear to involve this type of integrative work. When he speaks of the leader's need to define an overall mission and purpose for the organization, he is offering a solution to a political and cultural problem (the need to project an image of integration to internal and external constituencies). When he writes about the need to develop an integrative identity and organizational mythology he is doing the same thing, in a way that is perhaps even more striking. "Mythology" is a word that has disparate connotations. In all of these instances, the leader's need is to create an imagery that makes sense out of an entity that is, in the best-case scenario, less than fully sensible. Forces in the environment, inside the

---

[5] Kraatz and Block (2008) suggest that organizations and their leaders often face what they call the "Politician's Dilemma." This conundrum results from the conjoint operation of the neo-institutional imperative for cultural conformity and the Selznickian imperative for self-consistency and integrity. They note that organizational leaders (like politicians) may ironically lose public support when their strategic efforts to cater to their constituencies send negative signals about their own character, commitment, and trustworthiness. Symbols offered in one spirit may often be received in a very different one. Love and Kraatz (2008) provide some empirical support for this proposition.

organization, and even inside the head of the individual leader (i.e. cognitive dissonance reduction) appear to compel this integrative work, however. Leaders may, in fact, be unable to control much of what happens in their organizations, and their organizations may, in fact, be very loosely coupled (March & Olsen, 1976; Weick, 1976). But, this is not generally a story that the public (or the legal system or the financial markets) is willing to accept. Leaders need to be able to talk about the organization as if it were an integrated whole even when it isn't (and perhaps especially when it isn't). The organizational governance structures seen in sight 2 may also help serve this coherence-creating role (as might bureaucracy more generally).

Sight 5: Denotative leaders trying to control ongoing, emergent, and evolutionary processes of organizational change and maintain the (apparent) integrity of their organizations

The multiply constituted, institutionally plural organization is dynamic and fluid. It is a *relational* entity and a *processual* one (Emirbayer, 1997; Tsoukas & Chia, 2002). It joins together distinct parts and unites them in an ongoing process with an indeterminate endpoint. For these reasons, it operates much like Selznick's organizational institution with respect to the problem of change. This means, among other things, that it is subject to goal displacement and other forms of accidental transformation (i.e. as a result of the unintended consequences of its actions). The effort to solve a particular problem and achieve a specific local goal can cause other unforeseen problems and undermine broader or parallel goals. These processes cannot occur in monistic organizations that have only one institutionally given objective and are thoroughly infused with a single constitutive logic.

There is important leadership work to be done in preventing and limiting such change processes in the plural organization, however (Selznick, 1957; March, 1981; Tsoukas & Chia, 2002). There is also important work to be done in guiding the ongoing evolution of this dynamic entity. This leadership work is also institutional in two different senses. First, it involves adapting to emergent problems and demands in the organization's broader institutional context. Second, it involves integrating these new changes in such a way that they do not disrupt the "whole" organization or damage its diachronic character (upon which its competence and public support may depend). Selznick talked about this integrity-maintaining work as "steering a course between

opportunism and utopianism," and he saw it as the very essence of
"responsible leadership" (1957: 149).[6]

Neo-institutionalism can contribute to our understanding of organizational integrity in at least two important ways. The first is by drawing attention to field-level forces that threaten it. Overarching institutional forces can disrupt organizational institutions. The second is by focusing upon the rhetorical (in addition to structural) ways in which it is maintained. Leaders are likely to attempt to maintain the appearance of cross-temporal consistency by strategically describing their present decisions in a way that makes them appear consistent with past actions and commitments (and by strategically reinterpreting the past). The integrity that they maintain may thus be mostly of the "narrative" variety. This makes it no less consequential, however.

Sight 6: Denotative leaders making existential, character-defining choices in response to competing demands of their pluralistic institutional environment

Organizations may prosper when they figure out how to operate at the intersection of overlapping institutional systems. Our pluralistic society may allow organizations and leaders much room to maneuver between institutional spheres, and may even reward and encourage such maneuvering. See, for example, the public admiration that is often bestowed upon profitable businesses that also take on social and environmental responsibilities. See also the remarkable legitimacy and support enjoyed by the seemingly schizophrenic research university. However, this latitude is not always granted and it clearly has limits. Organizations cannot be all things to all people and they are, at least occasionally, confronted with stark choices as a result of directly competing institutional demands. These choices are especially likely early on in an organization's developmental history. The neo-institutional perspective allows us to see the ultimate cultural and societal sources of these tensions. But organizational powerholders (sometimes even single individuals) must still make existential choices for their organizations in the face of these divergent social pressures and opportunities. These are the

---

[6] March (1999) seems to be saying much the same thing when he writes about the elusive quality of "organizational intelligence," defining it as the optimal mix of explorative and exploitative learning. He presents organizational intelligence as an ideal state, much like Selznick's ideal of integrity.

"critical" and "character-defining" decisions that Selznick referred to. March has also reflected upon their importance and their inescapability (March & Weil, 2005). Nothing we have seen thus far makes these existential choices seem any less critical or alleviates the leader's responsibility for making them.

Sight 7: Denotative leaders working on themselves in the effort to adapt to the demands of their pluralistic institutional context

A final type of work that we can see from our metaphorical bridge is the work that denotative leaders do in the effort to transform themselves (or at least their appearance). Here we return to Selznick's mysterious "executive to statesman" transition. We also enter (somewhat hesitantly) the territory of the "leadership industry," which largely traffics in the currency of personal transformation (Kellerman, 2004). The cynically inclined are likely to dismiss all talk of intrapersonal change out of hand, especially when it regards powerful persons and may have the effect of lending their power undue respect. Those who are merely sociological in their orientation (minus the cynicism) are also probably most comfortable focusing on outward behaviors, while bracketing the intrapersonal changes that may possibly accompany them. This is what I have tried to do up to this point.

But it might also be permissible (and perhaps useful) for institutional researchers to examine organizational leaders as if they were themselves multiply constituted, sociological entities; ones who are more or less well adapted to their pluralistic institutional environment and more or less at ease with the divergent identities and roles that it imposes upon them. Maybe some people do undergo "dynamic adaptations" when confronted with such complex, paradoxical, and "anxiety-laden" social situations, just as Selznick theorized. Maybe they come to terms with their context, make existential choices, and offer up "irreversible commitments" that enable and empower them even as they bind and constrain. Maybe these persons become autonomous, responsible, self-aware, purposive, and distinctively competent "selves" as a result of this transformative process. Maybe they become self-governing subjects rather than socially controlled objects, and integrated wholes rather than fragmented nonentities. Perhaps it is also the case that these positive personal transformations, being essentially sociological in character, can spill over and wash through networks of relationships, thus positively affecting entire organizations (or societies). In other words, maybe if we look hard enough from our bridge, we can see *denotative leaders actually becoming connotative leaders* (i.e. executives *really* making the transition to statesmanship).

Or maybe this is just a mirage. Perhaps what we really see is only powerful people faking integrity in the effort to buy political support and effectively mask their wholly selfish agendas.[7]

In either case, an empirical focus on the ways in which actual people adapt (more or less successfully) to the sociological demands of leading complex and plural organizations might be interesting. Individual leaders seem to face the same apparent dilemma confronted by organizations (in terms of the countervailing pressures for conformity to the environment on the one hand and self-consistency and coherence on the other). People (like organizations) cope with these demands differently and with varying degrees of grace and effectiveness. Much of the normative literature on leadership might be reinterpreted (and newly appreciated) in light of these sociological realities.

Sights not seen

I have focused here on the behaviors of powerholders who are assumed to be well intentioned, though by no means saintly. All of the above "sights" represent types of work that we might expect ordinary managers to do in the face of pluralistic institutional demands. Guileful and opportunistic persons who find themselves in the same situations may behave in radically different ways (e.g. by exploiting their institutionally central location for personal gain). Other people may enter leadership positions with high principles but become compromised or inverted by the experience of moral relativity and ambiguity that institutional pluralism ushers in. These less attractive sights can certainly be seen from the

---

[7] Cynics will particularly appreciate Machiavelli's observations on this point: "*Thus, it is not necessary for a prince to have all the above-mentioned qualities in fact, but it is indeed necessary to appear to have them. Nay, I dare say this, that by having them and always observing them, they are harmful; and by appearing to have them, they are useful, as it is to appear merciful, faithful, humane, honest, and religious, and to be so; but to remain with a spirit built so that, if you need not to be those things, you are able and know how to change to the contrary ... A prince should thus take great care that nothing escape his mouth that is not full of the above-mentioned five qualities and that, to see him and hear him, he should appear all mercy, all faith, all honesty, all humanity, all religion. And nothing is more necessary to appear to have than this last quality*" (1985: 70).

same bridge. Institutional scholars with a more critical bent may be more inclined to focus on them and can certainly do this legitimately. I am much more taken in by the difficulty, complexity, and tremendous human importance of the work itself.

I have also excluded a great many of the sights that are visible only from the Selznickian shore in my effort to build a bridge across the leadership gap. *Leadership in Administration* is merely one piece of a larger and remarkably well-integrated theoretical and philosophical vision that Selznick has developed across his long career. This vision is brilliantly articulated in his 1992 *Moral Commonwealth*. It is also elegantly summarized by Krygier (2002). I have not begun to do it justice in this chapter. I have, however, tried to make some important parts of it more broadly accessible, and perhaps sparked some interest in the larger picture in so doing.

Discussion

I began this chapter by noting that Selznick's concept of institutional leadership appeared to have no home within the burgeoning body of research on institutional work. Resolved to address this incongruity, I revisited *Leadership in Administration*, extracted some of its central ideas, and identified some particular ways in which these ideas might inform contemporary research.

Selznick's perspective exposes the political nature of all organizational institutions and, thus, the political nature of all organizational leadership work. But, it also highlights the organizational politician's apparent ability to transcend the realm of the merely political. He suggests that individual powerholders can assume a posture of statesmanship, and (seemingly) transform their organizations in a parallel transition process. I introduced the ideas of connotative and denotative leadership in the effort to clarify the two sides of this theoretical divide. The connotative leader governs an organization that is, while still political, also an integrative, purposive, autonomous, and distinctive social whole. This person's identity is deeply intertwined with that of the organization. The denotative leader exercises power within a system that lacks these qualities and has no necessary personal tie with it.

I then identified a paradigmatic gap separating the Selznickian perspective from contemporary scholarship on institutional work (with its attendant neo-institutional frame). While respecting this gap, I nevertheless tried to build a metaphorical "bridge" between the paradigms; a place where the two perspectives might be held in productive tension with one another, and from which the empirical world might be more fully observed. My key move in building this bridge was to highlight the empirical phenomenon of institutional pluralism; the situation faced by organizations that possess multiple institutionally ascribed identities and dwell in multiple institutional "worlds." Such organizations are, obviously, deeply affected by their overarching institutional environments. But they also appear to be sites where Selznickian institutionalization processes can occur. Indeed, I suggested that these latter processes (ones that create organizational autonomy, distinctiveness, and integration) appear to arise in direct response to the controlling, homogenizing, and/ or fragmenting influences that emanate from the broader institutional environment.

Building upon these observations, I went on to make the chapter's core argument: that *individual organizations are important venues for institutional work*. I more specifically argued that we could and should study the work that is done by these organizations' *denotative leaders*. I suggested that their work was often "institutional" in both the Selznickian (integrity-seeking) and neo-institutional (legitimacy-seeking) senses. I then identified seven related types of leadership work that appeared to be promising subjects for future empirical research. I indicated that scholars might view these actions from a romantic/connotative perspective (i.e. as efforts to find the "unity in multiplicity"), or in more critical and cynical terms (i.e. as "faking integrity"). Some combination of these perspectives is also possible and perhaps more desirable (though there appears to be a strong ideological pull toward the polar formulations).

I do not know whether my metaphorical bridge will carry much traffic, or reveal "sights" that others find to be compelling. It is possible that I have overestimated the size of the gap to be crossed, based upon my own idiosyncratic reading of the literature. Or perhaps I have tried to bring together two ways of thinking that are best left apart. I could be guilty of trying to explain the sacred in terms of the profane (or vice versa). It is also possible that I have tried to build a "bridge too far," one that tries to escape necessary and inevitable paradigmatic boundaries and ends up offering a "view from nowhere" (Nagel, 1986). I hope not.

The upshot of the chapter for empirical research is, I hope, much more clear. I have identified some particular, empirically observable behaviors that organizational leaders commonly perform and provided some different and expanded ways to think about these actions (i.e. new reasons to study old things). Neo-institutionalists might study such behaviors with a new appreciation for their integrative, local, and personal dimension. Selznickians and other leadership scholars might see these same tasks with a greater appreciation of their symbolic, cultural, and global meaning (Glynn, 2008; Weber & Glynn, 2006). Organizations are both synchronic and diachronic entities. They clearly do act out cultural scripts and perform institutionally given identities and roles. But they have to simultaneously act out multiple identities, find ways to make these identities fit together, and do all this with knowledge of their own (unique) history and the constraints and opportunities that it imposes. Their denotative leaders have important work to do in making these different institutional things happen. These persons also appear to face the same challenges in the interpersonal (and perhaps intrapersonal) realm. What they need to do for their organizations, they also need to do for themselves. To the extent that they can perform this multilevel work effectively and over an extended period, they are likely to be *perceived* as leaders in the connotative sense. Whether this perception is really correct is hard to know. It is perhaps the wrong question to ask.

This takes me to my closing point, which concerns how institutional work scholars should orient themselves with respect to normative and idealized notions of leadership (these being the ones that are most closely associated with the word and those which its very utterance will surely continue to conjure up). It also raises the parallel issue of what posture institutionalists, more generally, should take with respect to integrative, cooperative, and subject-centered theories of the organization like Selznick's. The question, more pointedly, is whether we should actually *believe* in leadership and in the forms of social organization that make such a thing theoretically possible. Even more sharply, should we encourage others to believe in these idealistic and hopeful notions? Or, should we instead devote our efforts to building an organizational science that serves to deflate such ideals and further disenchant the organizational world?

I think it is fair to say that neo-institutionalism, in general, has served the latter purpose. It is primarily a critical perspective. While I am hesitant to make any attributions regarding its practitioners' *intentions* (which are likely to be quite varied), the general *effect* of the perspective is to delegitimate power, to expose hidden forms of domination, and to reveal fragmentation and hypocrisy in the actions of organizations and their elites. It says very little about how to govern, reform, or productively improve any given existing social institution. But these issues are mostly beside the point. Neo-institutionalists generally take a societal perspective on organizations, and seek to understand the ways in which they affect (or more often "infect") the larger world of which they are a part (Scott & Davis, 2007: 1). The perspective is at least a-managerial, if not "anti-managerial" as Donaldson (1995) has charged. It is, likewise, at least indifferent to the well-being of established organizations if not overtly misarchistic. This same general sensibility has been carried over into the emerging literature on institutional work. Lawrence and Suddaby characterize institutional work as a "critical approach," and the literature's emphasis on the construction and dismantling of institutions (to the exclusion of their governance and reform) is consistent with this characterization.

I have done nothing in this chapter to deflate or delegitimate this sort of critical orientation, nor have I tried to force the acceptance of a managerial or socially integrative perspective. Indeed, I have gone so far as to build a bridge which invites the critically minded to transgress well-established boundaries and shows exactly how this might be done. I anticipate that scholars on the critical side of the bridge might have great success exposing managers' cynical attempts to "fake integrity," just as they have cynically exposed previous efforts at faking conformity. Countless examples of such behavior are readily apparent. Exposing them should not be hard work and it could add substantially to the neo-institutional catalogue of organizational foibles.

However, I also hope that at least some institutional work scholars might take on a more appreciative, empathetic, and nuanced sensibility in response to some of the complexities that I have revealed here. Maybe they will find it harder to criticize leaders and more difficult to reduce the concept of leadership to mere power. Perhaps they will be more appreciative of those who can pull the task off effectively, and more interested in understanding how this work can be done. No one, of course, can be forced to believe in leadership (or cooperation, or social integration, or free will, or any of the other ideals that typically accompany discussions of the concept). We are probably better off as a field if we have committed skeptics and critics, in addition to committed idealists. If my chapter accomplishes nothing else, it at least reveals that institutionalists have a choice to make in this matter. I hope that my bridge will prove to be a viable platform for research and theorizing that embodies Selznick's "Hobbesian idealism." But, at the very least, it should make it possible to walk from one paradigm to the other.

The great promise of the concept of institutional work, in my view, is that it puts people back into the institutional picture and provides a way to make institutions (once again) into vehicles for the realization of human purposes, rather than alien devices of social control. It suggests that institutions might serve people, rather than the other way around. The literature on institutional work can increase the chances of this happening by showing people how to erect and tear down institutions. Entrepreneurship and revolutionary activity are certainly important phenomena to understand and they are certainly institutional in nature. But it is also important to remember that the newly formed institution becomes a "going-concern" approximately five minutes after the revolution. At that same moment, the entrepreneur/revolutionary becomes an administrator and is then confronted by all of the knotty questions that Selznick sought to work out in *Leadership in Administration*. This suggests that the basic concerns that animate researchers on both sides of the metaphorical divide may not be nearly so great as they seem.

References

Ansell, C. A. (1997) Symbolic networks: the realignment of the French working class, 1887–1894. *American Journal of Sociology*, 103(2): 359–390.

Burns, J. M. (1978) *Leadership*. New York: Harper & Row.

Campbell, J. (1949) *The Hero with a Thousand Faces*. Princeton, NJ: Princeton University Press.

DiMaggio, P. J. & Powell, W. W. (1991) Introduction. In W. W. Powell & P. J. DiMaggio (eds.), *The New Institutionalism in Organizational Analysis*, pp. 1–38. Chicago: University of Chicago Press.

Donaldson, L. (1995) *American Anti-Management Theories of Organization: A Critique of Paradigm Proliferation*. Cambridge: Cambridge University Press.

Emirbayer, M. (1997) Manifesto for a relational sociology. *American Journal of Sociology*, 103(2): 281–317.

Fligstein, N. (2001) Social skill and the theory of fields. *Sociological Theory*, 19(2): 105–125.

Frank, R. H. (1988) *Passions within Reason: The Strategic Role of Emotions*. New York: W. W. Norton.

Glynn, M. A. (2000) When cymbals become symbols: conflict over organizational identity within a symphony orchestra. *Organization Science*, 11(3): 285–298.

    (2008) Beyond constraint: how institutions enable identities. In R. Greenwood, C. Oliver, R. Suddaby & K. Sahlin-Andersson (eds.), *Handbook of Organizational Institutionalism*, pp. 413–440. London: Sage.

Glynn, M. A. & Abzug, R. (2002) Institutionalizing identity: symbolic isomorphism and organizational names. *Academy of Management Journal*, 45: 267–280.

Gouldner, A. W. (1955) Metaphysical pathos and the theory of bureaucracy. *American Political Science Review*, 49: 496–507.

Greenwood, R. & Hinings, C. R. (1996) Understanding radical organizational change: bringing together the old and the new institutionalism. *Academy of Management Review*, 21: 1022–1054.

Haidt, J. (2007) The new synthesis in moral psychology. *Science*, 316(5827): 998.

Hargrave, T. & Van de Ven, A. (2006) A collective action model of institutional innovation. *Academy of Management Review*, 31(4): 864–888.

Hauser, M. D. (2006) *Moral Minds: How Nature Designed Our Universal Sense of Right and Wrong.* New York: HarperCollins.

Heclo, H. (2002) The statesman: revisiting leadership in administration. In R. A. Kagan, M. Krygier & K. Winston (eds.), *Legality and Community: On the Intellectual Legacy of Philip Selznick*, pp. 295–310. New York: Rowman & Littlefield.

Heimer, C. A. (1999) Competing institutions: law, medicine, and family in neonatal intensive care. *Law & Society Review*, 33(1): 17–66.

Heracleous, L. & Barrett, M. (2001) Organizational change as discourse: communicative actions and deep structures in the context of IT implementation. *Academy of Management Journal*, 44(4): 755–778.

Hirsch, P. M. & Lounsbury, M. (1997) Putting the organization back into organization theory. *Journal of Management Inquiry*, 6(1): 79–88.

Jaeger, G. & Selznick, P. (1964) A normative theory of culture. *American Sociological Review*, 29: 653–669.

Kellerman, B. (2004) *Bad Leadership.* Boston: Harvard Business School Publishing.

Knudsen, C. (1995) The competence view of the firm: what can modern economists learn from Philip Selznick's sociological theory of leadership? In W. R. Scott & S. Christensen (eds.), *The Institutional Construction of Organizations: International and Longitudinal Studies*, pp. 135–163. Thousand Oaks, CA: Sage.

Kraatz, M. S. & Block, E. S. (2008) Organizational implications of institutional pluralism. In R. Greenwood, C. Oliver, R. Suddaby & K. Sahlin-Andersson (eds.), *Handbook of Organizational Institutionalism*, pp. 243–276. London: Sage.

Krygier, M. E. (2002) Philip Selznick, normative theory and the rule of law. In R. A. Kagan, M. Krygier & K. Winston (eds.), *Legality and Community: On the Intellectual Legacy of Philip Selznick*, pp. 19–49. New York: Rowman & Littlefield.

Lacey, M. (2002) Taking ideals seriously. In R. Kagan, M. Krygier & K. Winston (eds.), *Legality and Community*, pp. 67–81. New York: Rowman & Littlefield.

Lawrence, T. & Suddaby, R. (2006) Institutions and institutional work. In S. Clegg, C. Hardy, W. R. Nord & T. Lawrence (eds.), *Handbook of Organization Studies*, pp. 215–254. London: Sage.

Love, E. G. & Kraatz, M. S. (2008) Character, conformity or the bottom line? How and why downsizing affected corporate reputation. *Academy of Management Journal*, forthcoming.

Machiavelli, N. (1998) *The Prince*, trans. H. C. Mansfield. Chicago: University of Chicago Press.

March, J. G. (1981) Footnotes to organizational change. *Administrative Science Quarterly*, 26(4): 563–577.

(1999) *The Pursuit of Organizational Intelligence*. Malden, MA: Blackwell.

March, J. G. & Olsen, J. P. (1976) *Ambiguity and Choice in Organizations*, 2nd edn. Bergen: Universitetsforlaget.

March, J. G. & Weil, T. (2005) *On Leadership*. New York: Blackwell.

Mead, G. H. (1934) *Mind, Self, and Society*. Chicago: University of Chicago Press.

Meyer, J. W. & Rowan, B. (1977) Institutionalized organizations: formal structure as myth and ceremony. *American Journal of Sociology*, 83: 340.

Nagel, T. (1986) *The View from Nowhere*. New York: Oxford University Press.

Nesse, R. M. (2001) Natural selection and the capacity for subjective commitment. In R. M. Nesse (ed.), *Evolution and the Capacity for Commitment*. New York: Sage.

Oakes, L. S., Townley, B. & Cooper, D. J. (1998) Business planning as pedagogy: language and control in a changing institutional field. *Administrative Science Quarterly*, 43: 257–292.

Oliver, C. (1991) Strategic responses to institutional processes. *Academy of Management Review*, 16(1): 145–179.

Padgett, J. F. & Ansell, C. K. (1993) Robust action and the rise of the Medici, 1400–1434. *American Journal of Sociology*, 98: 1259.

Perrow, C. (1986) *Complex Organizations: A Critical Essay*, 3rd edn. New York: Random House.

Pfeffer, J. (1981) Management as symbolic action: the creation and maintenance of organizational paradigms. In L. L. Cummings & B. M. Shaw (eds.), *Research in Organizational Behavior*, 3: 1–52. Greenwich, CT: JAI Press.

Pondy, L. (1983) The role of metaphors and myths in organizations and in the facilitation of change. In L. R. Pondy, P. J. Frost, G. Morgan & T. C. Dandridge (eds.), *Organization Symbolism*, pp. 157–166. Greenwich, CT: JAI Press.

Pratt, M. G. & Foreman, P. O. (2000) Classifying managerial responses to multiple organizational identities. *Academy of Management Review*, 25: 18–42.

Rao, H. (1994) The social construction of reputation – certification contests, legitimation, and the survival of organizations in the American automobile-industry – 1895–1912. *Strategic Management Journal*, 15: 29–44.

Rost, J. C. (1991) *Leadership for the Twenty-First Century*. New York: Praeger.

Schneiberg, M. & Clemens, E. (2006) The typical roots for the job: research strategies in institutional analysis. *Sociological Theory*, 24:3.

Scott, W. R. (2001) *Institutions and Organizations*, 2nd edn. Thousand Oaks, CA: Sage.

Scott, W. R. & Davis, G. F. (2007) *Organizations and Organizing: Rational, Natural and Open System Perspectives*. Upper Saddle River, NJ: Prentice Hall.

Selznick, P. (1949) *TVA and the Grass Roots*. Berkeley: University of California Press.

(1952) *The Organizational Weapon*. New York: McGraw-Hill.

(1957) *Leadership in Administration*. New York: Harper & Row.

(1969) *Law, Society and Industrial Justice*. New York: Russell Sage Foundation.

(1992) *The Moral Commonwealth: Social Theory and the Promise of Community*. Berkeley: University of California Press.

(1996) Institutionalism "old" and "new." *Administrative Science Quarterly*, 41.

(2000) On sustaining research agendas – their moral and scientific basis: an address to the Western Academy of Management. *Journal of Management Inquiry*, 9(3): 277–282.

Strandgaard Pedersen, J. & Dobbin, F. (2006) In search of identity and legitimation. *American Behavioral Scientist*, 49: 897–907.

Stryker, R. (2000) Legitimacy processes as institutional politics: implications for theory and research in the sociology of organizations. *Organizational Politics: Research in the Sociology of Organizations*, 17: 179–223.

Suddaby, R. & Greenwood, R. (2005) Rhetorical strategies of legitimacy. *Administrative Science Quarterly*, 50(1): 35–67.

Tsoukas, H. & Chia, R. (2002) On organizational becoming: rethinking organizational change. *Organization Science*, 13(5): 567–582.

Washington, M., Boal, K. B. & Davis, J. N. (2008) Institutional leadership: past, present and future. In R. Greenwood, C. Oliver, R. Suddaby & K. Sahlin-Andersson (eds.), *Handbook of Organizational Institutionalism*, pp. 721–737. London: Sage.

Weber, K. & Glynn, M. A. (2006) Making sense with institutions: the role of context in Karl Weick's sensemaking perspective. *Organization Studies*, special issue in Honor of Karl Weick, 27: 1639–1660.

Weick, K. (1976) Educational organizations as loosely-coupled systems. *Administrative Science Quarterly*, 21: 1–21.

Westphal, J. D. & Zajac, E. J. (1994) Substance and symbolism in CEOs' long-term incentive plans. *Administrative Science Quarterly*, 39: 367–390.

Zott, C. & Huy, Q. N. (2007) How entrepreneurs use symbolic management to acquire resources. *Administrative Science Quarterly*, 52(1): 70–105.

Zuckerman, E. W. (1999) The categorical imperative: securities analysts and the illegitimacy discount. *American Journal of Sociology*, 104(5): 1398–1438.

4 Bringing change into the lives of the poor: entrepreneurship outside traditional boundaries

IGNASI MARTÍ AND JOHANNA MAIR

Introduction

The powerful imagery of entrepreneurship as a means to induce and explain institutional change is gaining momentum (Greenwood & Suddaby, 2006; Lawrence & Suddaby, 2006). In response to criticisms that institutional theory was chiefly being used to explain homogeneity and persistence, important efforts have been devoted to restoring human agency in explanations of endogenous institutional change (DiMaggio, 1988; Sewell, 1992; Emirbayer & Mische, 1998). However, the image of the entrepreneur as institutional change agent has also been a source of controversy among institutional theorists, especially when accompanied by voluntarist, un-embedded conceptions of individual action (Holm, 1995; Leca & Naccache, 2006). As a result we observe vivid scholarly discussions on how to solve the "paradox of embedded agency" – i.e. on explaining how institutional change is possible if actors are fully conditioned by the institutions that they wish to change (Holm, 1995; Seo & Creed, 2002; Greenwood & Suddaby, 2006).

The current debate is important and we welcome more agent-oriented views on institutions. The purpose of this chapter is to advance institutional theory by rethinking various aspects of institutional work (Lawrence & Suddaby, 2006; DiMaggio, 1988) and thereby to contribute new insights into the paradox of embedded agency. We do so by challenging and breaking dominant patterns in current empirical research. While previous research on institutional entrepreneurship has predominantly looked at elite and/or powerful actors (DiMaggio, 1988; Fligstein & Mara-Drita, 1996) who assume either peripheral (Leblebici, Salancik, Copay & King, 1991) or central (Greenwood & Suddaby, 2006) positions, we focus instead on institutional work carried out by actors with limited power and very few resources. In addition, whereas existing research has largely centered on the study of institutional work in the developed world, favouring well-known settings, we advocate an approach that emphasizes attempts to create, transform, and maintain institutions in the developing world. By focusing on actors with little power and limited resources, we are able to elaborate on features of institutional work rarely explored in existing empirical studies. More specifically, we question the common assumption that the work of marginalized actors is aggressive in style; we point towards the experimental and developmental nature of institutional work; we (re)emphasize the importance of challenging cultural beliefs, myths, and traditions; and we introduce the notion of provisional institutions. Finally, we call for more empirical work on how actors navigate across different institutional logics.

Ultimately we challenge traditional approaches that place institutional work on a continuum of greater and lesser degrees of agency. The relationship between the powerful and the powerless, between elites and subordinates, is extremely complex (Gaventa, 1982; Lawrence, 2008; Scott, 1990). Thus it would be too simplistic to categorize agency in this setting according to a continuum or according to agency vs. no agency. Rather than quantitative differences grounded in a material view of agency, our research suggests qualitative differences between categories, grounded in an emancipatory view of agency. Agency in these "unusual" settings goes beyond new ways of *doing* things and implies new ways of *seeing* things.[1]

Context and actors in research on institutional work

Lawrence and Suddaby refer to institutional work as "the purposive action of individuals and organizations aimed at creating, maintaining and disrupting institutions" (2006: 215). An important contribution of the concept of institutional work is that it defies the dominant heroic view of agency in much research on institutional entrepreneurship and encompasses a broader spectrum of actors and activities.

In their comprehensive review of research on institutional work, Lawrence and Suddaby also briefly elaborate on the theoretical foundations of the concept: the work of DiMaggio (1988) and Oliver (1991, 1992); and research on the sociology of practice (Bourdieu, 1977; De Certeau, 1984; Giddens, 1984). Interestingly these seminal studies

[1] We thank Roy Suddaby for pushing us in our thinking on forms of agency.

emphasize the importance of power in discussions of agency. We argue in this chapter that, while efforts to reintroduce power into institutional theory are at the core of the literature on institutional entrepreneurship, current research falls short in accomplishing this task because it focuses on too narrow a spectrum of cases. We suggest that one might more successfully read, examine, and understand agency by looking at more extreme cases of power and resistance.

Almost two decades after DiMaggio's (1988) call to bring power, agency, and interest back into research on institutions and Powell's slightly later (1991) quest to expand the scope of institutional analysis, significant advances have been made in understanding how institutions are created, transformed, disrupted, and replaced by new ones. However, a comprehensive examination of recent empirical studies on institutional work reveals two dominant patterns: (1) the predominant focus is on cases in the developed world; and (2) the emphasis is on powerful actors. In what follows we briefly elaborate on these two patterns and on how breaking free from them might advance our understanding of institutional work.

Context

Empirical research on institutions has typically taken the field as the unit of analysis (DiMaggio, 1991; Scott, 1994; Fligstein, 2001). Thus a broad variety of fields, with different structural characteristics, have been examined in studies looking at institutional reproduction or change. Stable and relatively mature fields have received much attention. Examples include studies on the professional business services field in Canada (Greenwood, Suddaby & Hinings, 2002), fisheries in Norway (Holm, 1995), the gastronomic field in France (Rao, Monin & Durand, 2005), or the United States radio broadcasting industry (Leblebici *et al.*, 1991). Researchers have also recently focused on processes of institutional change in emerging fields such as the HIV/AIDS advocacy treatment field in Canada (Maguire, Hardy & Lawrence, 2004), or non-profit consumer watchdog organizations in the United States (Rao, 1998). This by no means exhaustive list reveals an important variety of settings.

However, studies on institutional work are also predominately located in the so-called developed world. Very little work has been done in developing countries (for two remarkable exceptions see Lawrence, Hardy & Phillips, 2002; and Khan, Munir & Willmott, 2007). This is surprising – and we believe unfortunate – particularly if we consider the work of authors who, coming from a disparate set of research traditions, have shaped our current understandings of institutions and of institutional work. Authors such us Bourdieu (1977, 1979), Douglas (1986), Lévi-Strauss (1967), and Geertz (1963)[2] offered illuminating examples for the study of institutions and institutional change extracted from their research in the developing world. For example, Bourdieu's concepts of field and habitus can be traced back to his early work in Algeria in the 1960s. And Lévi-Strauss' imagery of the bricoleur, extensively used by institutional scholars, was introduced in his book *The Savage Mind* (1967), which discusses mythical thought in primitive societies.

Accordingly, it seems to us that much can be gained by expanding our focus and looking at processes of institutional reproduction and change in more diverse contexts. As suggested by Fligstein (1997), the skills and strategies used by institutional "workers" are likely to vary in different contexts, and therefore a broader scope of research settings is desirable in order to achieve a comprehensive understanding of institutional work.

Actors

Over the past fifteen years a new emphasis in institutional studies has emerged, which centers on understanding the role of actors in creating, maintaining, and transforming institutions and fields. That said, most of this research has focused on the activities of powerful actors, such as state organizations (Dobbin, 2001), large corporations (Garud, Jain & Kumarswamy, 2002), or professional associations (Greenwood *et al.*, 2002).

As highlighted by Battilana (2006), relatively few studies have looked at individuals as institutional entrepreneurs. Interestingly, these few studies have typically emphasized powerful actors with a strong bias towards featuring prominent and successful individuals.[3] In

---

[2] This is not intended to be an exhaustive list by any means. The objective here is merely to observe that many valuable insights can be gained by turning our attention to processes of institutional change in the developing world.

[3] Fligstein and Mara-Drita's (1996) study of the activities of Jacques Delors as builder of the European Single Market, or Hirsch and Bermiss' (this volume, Chapter 10) account of Vaclav Klaus' ability to – apparently – fool IMF representatives and international analysts for almost a decade, can be considered examples of this tendency.

addition, given that "creating new institutions is expensive" (DiMaggio, 1988: 14), the preference for powerful actors has been accompanied by an emphasis on the importance of having abundant resources.

This schematic picture of the "typical" actors featured in empirical studies of institutional entrepreneurship provokes two reflections. First, if we are to look at powerful actors, we probably need to understand why they are powerful and what confers upon them the power they have. Second, we know much about powerful actors who control abundant resources, but little attention has been paid to how less powerful and poorly resourced actors initiate or contribute to institutional change or maintenance. The objective in this chapter is to examine more carefully the institutional work of those we normally assume are powerless in order to advance our understanding of institutional change.

Power, resistance, and institutional work

Previous studies suggest that entrepreneurial actors create new institutions and transform existing ones by recombining the institutions and resources that they have at hand, such as rules (Fligstein, 1997), organizational models (Clemens, 1993), or cultural logics (Creed, Scully & Austin, 2002). As mentioned, little empirical research in organizational institutional theory has looked at the role of poorly resourced, less powerful, and peripheral actors, who are usually labeled as marginal actors. One notable exception is Lawrence, Hardy, and Phillips' (2002) study showing how the collaborative efforts of a small non-governmental organization (NGO) in Palestine were followed by the creation of proto-institutions.

Despite this and other scattered efforts, the challenge remains to provide a more detailed account of the toolkit, i.e. the strategies and actions, of actors with limited power – and, by extension, with limited resources – to promote institutional change. We need to advance our knowledge of – to use Scott's (1985) expression – the weapons of the weak. When power and resources are concentrated in the hands of a few and there is limited interest in challenging the status quo, the questions that remain are: how is change possible; who initiates change; and what are the mechanisms at play?

Michel Foucault (1980) reminds us that where there is power, there is resistance. Obvious as they might sound, these words open up a whole spectrum of forms of institutional work done by very different actors to those typically examined in existing empirical research. In his remarkable analysis of confrontations between the powerless and the powerful, James Scott (1990) explores how the powerless and oppressed make use of different "arts of resistance." One of the core insights of Scott's analysis is that most of the political activities of subordinate groups sit somewhere between collective defiance of the powerful and "hegemonic compliance." In other words, portraying agency as lying somewhere on a continuum between a great deal of agency (for the powerful) and limited agency (for the powerless) is, at the very least, simplistic. Agency of the powerless is present in more subtle, hidden forms of institutional work. It is an agency that is not so much about new ways of doing things or initiating change but is more one of enlightenment and emancipation.

In the rest of this chapter we wish to reinforce the potential that we believe the study of actors with limited resources and power may have for understanding agency in institutional theory. In particular, we see the purposeful efforts of such actors to alleviate poverty in the developing world as providing a unique opportunity for students of institutions to refine the understanding of institutional work by reassessing institutional actors, processes, and outcomes.

Why poverty alleviation?

Stern and Barley (1996) have urged organizational scholars to consider the impact that organizations have on the broader social systems in which they are embedded. One particular issue that has received limited attention from organizational scholars is the alleviation of poverty in the developing world (Margolis & Walsh, 2003; Pearce, 2005).

In a world where almost 3 billion people live on less than two dollars per day[4] (Easterly, 2006b), global poverty is one of the most important challenges of our time. Its omnipresence, together with the failure of a vast number of poverty-alleviation schemes (Scott, 1998) – and in particular of what William Easterly (2006a) compellingly calls

---

[4] After adjusting for purchasing power.

"Big Push" approaches[5] – provide a moral obligation for scholars across fields to stop overlooking poverty issues. In addition, we argue that the study of poverty alleviation provides an exciting opportunity to advance existing theory. More specifically, we put forward three reasons why studying poverty alleviation has the potential to both enrich and inform existing notions of agency in institutional research.

First, discussions about overcoming the poverty trap that exists in many developing countries have thus far mostly centered on macro-level variables such as geography, trade policy, property rights, economic growth, and cultural values (Pearce, 2005). Similarly, research has typically focused – once again – on the role of powerful actors, such as states (Bates, 1981), international multilateral organizations such as the World Bank or the International Monetary Fund (Easterly, 2006b; Sachs, 2005), domestic business groups (Leff, 1978; Khanna & Palepu, 2000), and, more recently, multinational corporations, in tapping the "fortune" at the base-of-the-pyramid (Prahalad & Hart, 2002). However, as suggested by several authors working in different research traditions, this focus on macro-solutions and on powerful actors might have precluded the attention to and support of micro- (or grassroots) solutions (Banerjee & He, 2004; Scott, 1985, 1998). Not surprisingly, research on organizations has also to a large extent neglected grassroots efforts where less powerful actors with limited resources attempt to transform and deinstitutionalize rules that impede social and economic development.

Second, there is a need to unpack the institutional forces that make poverty so persistent and to understand how to act upon them. The dramatic failure of the majority of aid-led development efforts (Banerjee & He, 2004; Easterly, 2006a) painfully demonstrates not only the limitations but also the perils of ignoring the importance of particular social structures as well as political and social networks. Studying how the wide array of legacy institutions, traditions, myths, and customary practices that underlie poverty are reproduced and maintained, and by whom, is of utmost importance. Yet even more important is the understanding of how these institutional arrangements impede, among other things: access to basic health, education, financial or legal services; market development and market participation; access

---

[5] For Easterly (2006a), two recent examples of these "Big Push" approaches are the call made by Jeffrey Sachs (2005) to end world poverty in our lifetime and the United Nations Global Millennium Goals.

to formal justice or to alternative means of mediation; and, ultimately, understanding how to act upon such institutional arrangements in order to transform or deinstitutionalize them.[6]

Third, poverty-alleviation initiatives have often been based on a rather narrow materialist conceptualization of poverty. Such a view holds that the task of poverty alleviation consists in ensuring that households meet a certain minimum of material or physiological needs. However, emerging discourses within the field of development see poverty as a multidimensional construct, in which the material or physiological aspects are important but not exclusively so. Increasing attention is given to gender issues, as well as to issues of injustice, illiteracy, violence, or security (Narayan-Parker, 2000; World Bank, 2001). The main message is that poverty is multidimensional and multi-faceted and the poor are not a homogeneous group. This is important because it calls for more holistic approaches to poverty alleviation that would span several societal domains and different and often contradictory institutional logics (Friedland & Alford, 1991). As a result, research on poverty and poverty alleviation not only constitutes a moral obligation; it also provides a unique opportunity to study agency in the midst of institutional pluralism (Kraatz & Block, 2008).

Actors and poverty alleviation

For many years social scientists have debated which are the most effective strategies to alleviate poverty. Some advocate shock therapy involving mega-reforms and structural adjustment, both requiring major top–down interventions. Others favor incremental approaches based on small moves and paying attention to local institutions, knowledge, and actors.

In line with the incremental approach although with a different focus, a selected body of work has looked at the strategies deployed by the

---

[6] Using the market case as an example, we might wonder why so many remain excluded from participating in markets. For some economists, such as Hernando de Soto (1989), the issue is chiefly one of setting clear property rights and strong enforcing mechanisms. However, when they conflict with prevailing existing institutions, the problem seems to be of a more complex nature, as experienced by poor women in rural Cameroon living under the norm of *purdah* or by peasants in some areas of rural Bangladesh where kinship norms – reinforced by Muslim inheritance laws – prescribe the obligation to sell land and other goods to kin (Mair & Martí, in press).

poor to cope with their situation. Researchers have studied peasant rebellions, often applying a social movement perspective and, more recently, participatory democracy approaches (Baiocchi, 2005; Cohen & Rogers, 1995). Arguing that these forms of political activity were "rarely afforded" by the most subordinate classes (Scott, 1985), a group of researchers shifted its interest towards studying how the poor do what Hobsbawm (1973) called "working the system … to their minimum disadvantage." This body of research further illustrates that studying agency and the institutional work of the poor, the powerless, and the disenfranchised constitutes a promising avenue to push our thinking – and hopefully our acting – on institutional and social change. In parallel to the rising interest of development organizations in incremental bottom–up approaches, management and organizational scholars are paying increasing attention to a phenomenon that has a long heritage as a practice: that of social entrepreneurship (Mair & Martí, 2006; Peredo & Chrisman, 2006). Still in a stage of theoretical infancy, the concept of social entrepreneurship means different things to different people and researchers (Dees, 1998). In this chapter we narrowly refer to it as the innovative use and combination of a disparate set of resources to alleviate poverty.

Institutional work and poverty alleviation

What can be learned from the efforts of social entrepreneurs to alleviate poverty? One important insight from our previous discussion is that poverty is multidimensional and its causes are rooted in the set of practices, rules, and technologies institutionalized in a determinate context. Hence, efforts to alleviate poverty are likely to encompass a great deal of institutional work. It is our intention in what follows to examine how the study of social entrepreneurs' efforts to alleviate poverty in the developing world can enrich our current understanding of the nature, as well as the content, of institutional work. Building on our empirical work in Egypt, Bangladesh, and India (Mair, Martí & Ganly, 2007; Mair & Martí, in press; Seelos & Mair, 2007), we identify six specific features of social entrepreneurs' activities that invite us to refine and complement the concept of institutional work. We do not argue that these features are unique or exclusive to social entrepreneurs: rather we wish to draw attention to how our findings might enrich the repertoire of institutional work. In particular, these features suggest that the typical portrayal of agency in institutional work fails to capture the whole picture. The typical portrayal is one in which only a special type of actor – either powerful and central, or highly innovative, peripheral, and often aggressive – is able to create and transform institutions. Our research indicates that other types of actors, often powerless, disenfranchised, and under-resourced, who seemingly have no choice other than compliance, are also doing important institutional work. These actors employ a number of strategies including: (1) engaging in experimental projects; (2) probing for weaknesses and exploiting small advantages in non-aggressive ways; (3) working – often behind the scenes – for the enhancement of existing institutions; (4) challenging existing myths, traditions, cultural beliefs, and structures of dominance that not only prevent them from having a more active role in their communities but also generate practices and rituals of denigration and insult; (5) building provisional institutions; and (6) navigating across different institutional logics. We believe that by turning our attention to these neglected features we extend the scope of institutional work and enrich current views of agency.

Features of institutional work

Experimental

The debate over big push versus incremental approaches to poverty alleviation mirrors a long-lasting debate among social scientists. The issue of whether institutional change results from jolts or is a gradual process has been extensively discussed and addressed by institutional scholars (Streeck & Thelen, 2005; Campbell, 2004). We contend, how-ever, that an important aspect of this debate has been overlooked in empirical studies of institutional work: that of experimentation.

The activities of social entrepreneurs in their efforts to address the institutional conditions that lie behind poverty encompass a great deal of experimentation. Given the limited resources at their disposal and their comparative lack of power, social entrepreneurs tend to favor what Scott (1998), in his review of failed top–down plans, referred to as "small steps" and "reversibility." Thus, for instance, engaging women in market-based activities in countries where the norm of *purdah*[7]

---

[7] *Purdah* literally means "curtain." It refers to the obligation – for women only – to stay close to their family groups, visit primarily with female friends, and to forgo public places such as the village market where they might purchase food or clothing.

heavily constrains their participation in public life requires a great deal of caution. Offering micro-loans in areas where credit has been traditionally given by powerful patrons demands alertness towards local power relations and reactions. In such contexts and conditions, institutional work is necessarily occurring in small and tentative steps. Otherwise, strong resistance and countermobilization from elites or, more generally, from those interested in maintaining the status quo, are likely to bring these initiatives to a rapid end. Thus the relationship between the powerful and the powerless, between elites and subordinates, must be seen as an ongoing struggle in which both sides are "continually probing for weaknesses and exploiting small advantages" (Scott, 1990: 184; see also Bourdieu, 1977).[8]

In their influential examination of agency, Emirbayer and Mische (1998) pay special attention to experimentation, in particular when discussing the projective dimension of agency. In fact, much of their project revolves around this concept. However, accounts of institutional work thus far have paid limited attention to experimentation or to trial-and-error processes. As a result, in empirical studies of institutional work, we rarely find stories of failures, of paths not taken, or of paths taken and then abandoned (Schneiberg, 2007). This can be partly understood as a consequence of the focus on why and how actors actually succeed in promoting institutional change. In that respect, we echo and welcome the call for a focus on the activities rather than on the accomplishments of institutional work that Lawrence, Suddaby, and Leca make in the introduction to the present volume.

Arguably, the imagery of the institutional entrepreneur as a bricoleur (Fligstein, 1997; Creed, Scully & Austin, 2002; Rao, Monin & Durand, 2005) somehow captures this experimental nature of institutional work. Yet, while existing accounts of institutional bricolage emphasize the deployment and re-combination of different resources, they say little about how and why these elements are combined, what actors learn from those combinations, or about how that learning affects future combinations and paths. Limited attention has also been paid to why bricoleurs abandon previously utilized resources.

---

[8] As Schumacher reminds us, poverty alleviation cannot be an act of creation, cannot be ordered, bought, and comprehensively planned: it requires a gradual process of change and evolution (1999: 140).

Finally, these reflections point to a fundamental issue that we believe has also been largely neglected in existing studies: the unintended consequences of action (for an exception, see Khan, Munir & Willmott, 2007). Most of our current efforts – and this book is an example of this trend – center on understanding how and under what conditions agency is possible (Emirbayer & Mische, 1998; Sewell, 1992). However, we also know that the consequences of action – both for the agents and those affected by them – cannot be entirely foreseen in advance (Arendt, 1957; Emirbayer & Mische, 1998). Lawrence highlights the lack of attention to the "side effects" of institutions "on the myriad of actors who are neither party to their creation nor are contemplated in their design" (2008: 191). Similarly, we believe that the lack of attention to the unintended effects and consequences of any effort to create, maintain, or transform institutions is striking. By emphasizing the experimental nature of any type of institutional work, we purposively point towards unexpected positive or negative effects. For instance, one of the effects of microcredit programs in rural Bangladesh has been an increasing rate of violence against the female borrowers (Wahed & Bhuiya, 2007). Possible explanations for this phenomenon include the increased tension that is associated with enhanced economic opportunities for women (Mair & Martí, in press).[9]

Accordingly, the approach of social entrepreneurs to work in small steps should be understood not only as a consequence of their limited resources, but also as a purposive attempt to minimize negative unintended consequences – e.g. aggressive overreaction, countermobilization, or wasting limited resources – by favoring small steps and reversibility (Schumacher, 1999; Bourdieu, 1977).

Being marginal, being aggressive?

Interestingly, accounts of the institutional work of marginal or less-powerful actors by institutional scholars have very often paid more attention to allegedly aggressive strategies. Thus, for instance, Suchman (1995) referred to advocacy practices, Lawrence and Suddaby (2006) to lobbying, advertising, and litigation, and Elsbach and Sutton (1992) to coercion and illegitimate activities. The use of such practices is, no

---

[9] It is important to highlight that recent empirical studies suggest that the level of violence diminishes with the length of involvement with the microcredit organization.

doubt, present in revolutionary social movements demanding civil and legal rights in developing countries.[10] Yet the occurrence as well as the willingness of the poor to use aggressive techniques in many developing countries is rare (Hobsbawm, 1973; Moore, 1987). Moreover, in countries where corruption within the legal system, the judiciary, and at different levels of the government is pervasive, lobbying and litigation (strategies which may be quite effective in developed countries) are typically not widely used by actors with limited power and resources. We do not mean to conclude that these practices of advocacy are not important. However, it seems to us that aggressive practices and forms of advocacy may be counterproductive in contexts where important asymmetries exist between the powerful and the powerless (Bourdieu, 1977). As Hobsbawm observes, this does not imply the impossibility of revolution or change at all, rather revolution might be made "*de facto* by peasants who do not deny the legitimacy of the existing power structure, the law, the state, or even the landlords" (1973: 12).

Our research on rural Bangladesh, where we studied the activities of a social entrepreneur – BRAC – in its efforts to strengthen mechanisms for the protection and enforcement of the rights of the poor speaks to this point. In Bangladesh, the poor have limited access to the formal legal system because they can neither afford to pay bribes nor to wait eternally for dispute settlements. As a result, informal means of resolving disputes – called *shalish*, meaning mediation – are preferred in rural areas. However, these traditional forms of dealing with conflicts are dominated by the male elite; a fact that limits women's participation and also enhances the level of corruption. Notwithstanding such limitations, BRAC has consistently made efforts to engage its female members in *shalish* as an important and culturally relevant process of local dispute resolution. Accordingly, instead of directly denying the potential as well as the legitimacy of *shalish* to resolve disputes and protect their rights, BRAC deliberately encourages the women to take part. By taking part, women are contributing, in subtle, non-aggressive – and often very slow – ways, to undermining or transforming some of the existing institutions – e.g. the seclusion of women from public life that ensures lack of access to enforcing mechanisms.

---

[10] For a recent example see Wolford's (2003) study of the "Movimento dos Trabalhadores Rurais Sem Terra" (Movement of Rural Landless Workers) in Brazil.

In other words, the point is not to displace elites or to act aggressively against them. Rather, the objective is to obtain significant benefits for non-elites on a continuing basis. However, even in these cases, social entrepreneurs are likely to find strong and even aggressive resistance. For instance, in the 1980s and 1990s BRAC, along with other NGOs providing primary education in rural areas, was making important efforts to gather as much support as possible for its programs at the community level by attempting to engage local elites and religious leaders. However, back in the 1990s some of their schools were set on fire by radicals who, making use of religious arguments, claimed that mixing boys and girls in class was going against the values and norms of Bangladeshi society.[11] Similarly, poor women – who as a result of their participation in microcredit schemes engaged in income-generating activities – often began by working on activities within their homes. However, many who attempted to work outside of but close to the home were forcefully reminded by other villagers that they were breaking the norms of *purdah*.

Enhancing institutions

An important facet of the work of social entrepreneurs to alleviate poverty has to do with the enhancement of existing institutions. This is interesting since the focus on how actors create and transform institutions seems to preclude attention to the work done by other, arguably smaller, actors to complement, broaden, and enhance those institutions.

Much of the work of poverty alleviation consists in enabling the poor to benefit from various institutions from which they remain excluded – e.g. education, health or financial services, systems of property rights, and channels of political and civic participation.

The efforts of social entrepreneurs to strengthen and ensure the enforcement of property rights for a larger number of people can be used as an illustration. Clearly defined property rights and well-developed enforcement mechanisms, while important, may be meaningless for all but a small portion of a society if most people are excluded from the formal legal system because of the prevalence of informal institutions based on relations of power, systems of belief, and other social norms. In rural Bangladesh as well as in some rural areas of India, for example,

---

[11] Riaz (2005) reports that in the early 1990s, over 110 BRAC schools were allegedly set on fire.

high bribes must be paid to those in power; therefore justice is generally only obtained by those who can afford it. In addition, customary practices that expect women to subjugate their own rights to those of their male family members prevent women from obtaining equal justice. Other social norms in Bangladesh include the obligation to sell assets to kin before offering them to "outsiders." In other words, the poor are forced to sell to their richer kin at less than market prices.

A particular definition of property rights used may favor some and lead to the exclusion of many others. Addressing such diverse sets of factors is a difficult and long-term task; however, different actors are making important efforts to ensure that the excluded can also benefit from existing systems of property rights. The aforementioned initiative by BRAC to engage women in *shalish* processes can be seen to guarantee the protection of property rights as well as the enforcement of contracts. In fact, economic sociologists and political scientists have shown how organized parties try to affect the constitution of property rights in their own interest (Campbell & Lindberg, 1990; Fligstein, 1996). We believe that understanding how actors attempt to ensure that the excluded can also benefit from systems of property rights is of utmost practical importance as well as theoretically relevant to understanding market-building processes and, notably, market inclusion and exclusion.

All in all, the work of enhancing institutions can be seen as complementing and broadening the scope of institutions that are created and maintained by other actors such as the government or financial service providers. This characterization is, we believe, important, since it serves to point out the differences with other forms of institutional work that bear a resemblance to the work of enhancement. For example, this aspect of the institutional work of social entrepreneurs partly resembles the work of what DiMaggio (1988) calls subsidiary actors. For DiMaggio, subsidiary actors contribute by "provid[ing] legitimacy to the new organizational form[s]" (1988: 15) created by institutional entrepreneurs, and thus "gain from the success of the institutionalization project." Yet the work of enhancing institutions, as we see it, has less to do with contributing to their legitimacy than to broadening their scope and breadth so that others – i.e. the excluded – can also benefit from them.

"Enhancing" institutional work triggers associations with the notion of "enabling work" as well, which Lawrence and Suddaby define as "the creation of rules that facilitate, supplement and support institutions" (2006: 230). However, while Lawrence and Suddaby place the emphasis on how powerful actors – e.g. government or professional associations – enable institutions by creating authorizing agents or by diverting resources (2006: 230–231), we want to call attention to how other non-central, less powerful actors enhance institutions. For example, the emergence of different forms of microfinance can be understood as an effort to extend access to basic financial services – i.e. credit – to those excluded from the formal banking system (Mair & Martí, 2006). In this sense, it should not be seen as an attempt to undermine the banking system but to change it in order to make it more inclusive. This is done by relaxing or disrupting some of the practices and norms that impede access to banking services for the poor – specifically the need for collateral to receive a loan.

Finally, an intriguing feature of the work of enhancement is that it does not seem to fit neatly with any of the three broad categories – creating, maintaining, or disrupting institutions – used by Lawrence and Suddaby (2006) to describe institutional work. Rather, it seems to encompass all three. In this respect, it could be seen as contributing to the ongoing creation of institutions (DiMaggio, 1988); to the mainte-nance of existing institutions – hence the resemblance with the enabling work (Lawrence & Suddaby, 2006) as suggested above; as well as to the disruption of those institutionalized rules, technologies, and practices that impede some people from benefiting from existing institutional arrangements (Mair & Martí, in press).

Transforming and disrupting cultural beliefs, myths, and traditions
Institutional analysis has focused on three analytical elements that compose institutions (Scott, 1995), namely regulative systems, normative systems, and cultural-cognitive systems. The latter have been typically theorized as exogenous logics which become taken for granted, which has "inhibited the development of theories about how cultural beliefs can become deinstitutionalized or change once they achieve taken-for-granted status" (Lounsbury, Ventresca & Hirsch, 2003: 76). As a consequence, we do not know much about how actors contribute to the disruption of cultural and belief systems (for a recent exception, see Dacin & Dacin, 2008). However, we have already briefly referred throughout this chapter to a rich body of literature that suggests that actors with limited power and resources may contribute to the disruption of such systems (Bourdieu, 1977; Moore, 1987; Scott, 1985, 1990).

The provision of basic health services is a particularly illuminating example. Recognizing the strong correlation between ill-health and extreme poverty (Hulme & Shepherd, 2003), social entrepreneurial organizations have developed health programs to deliver preventive medicine and basic cures for common diseases to communities in rural Bangladesh. Yet local realities in these rural areas often mean that women relate particular illnesses to evil spirits and, accordingly, believe that the pronunciation of *Allahar kalam* (divine verses) will heal them (Mahbub & Ahmed, 1997). As a consequence, providing the necessary infrastructure to deliver health services is not enough: it is equally important to work on disrupting existing beliefs and myths that might prevent the effectiveness of health services and infrastructure.

We have previously referred to the emergence of the microfinance movement as a challenge to the long-institutionalized practice among formal financial service providers of requiring collateral for any credit operation. An additional challenge faced by microfinance programs targeting women in rural areas of countries such as India, Bangladesh, or Cameroon is the seclusion of women within their houses sanctioned by the norm of *purdah*. Anecdotal evidence from Bangladesh suggests that microfinance institutions have been able to gradually contribute to relaxing the strength of *purdah* by making their programs specifically accessible to women, i.e. by encouraging the women to start micro businesses that could be conducted within the home – raising chickens, milking cows, etc. Indeed, the fact that women manage to form and join microfinance groups in the face of strong opposition from their husbands and fathers reflects a significant departure from existing traditional patriarchal social contracts.

Lawrence and Suddaby (2006) identify three different forms of institutional work that contribute to the disruption of institutions. Two out of the three – disconnecting sanctions and disassociating moral foundations – are effectively restricted to actors who are able to manipulate the status apparatus – i.e. elites. However, the third form – undermining assumptions and beliefs – largely corresponds to some of the strategies that the powerless do make use of, mainly through contrary practice. In particular, these actors are probably not "powerful or culturally sophisticated actors" (Lawrence & Suddaby, 2006: 238). And very much in line with our argument throughout this chapter, Lawrence and Suddaby suggest that these different forms of institutional work "demand different categories of actor, ones that are immune or somehow less affected by the governance mechanisms of their institutional environment" (2006: 238). This implies that the institutional pressures might be less "totalizing" for some actors in some contexts. While Lawrence and Suddaby refer to the state, the judiciary, or professions and elites, their argument can also be extended, we believe, to other categories of actors: for instance, to those women living in extreme poverty who consciously break with the norm of *purdah* not because they consider it to be unjust but because their dire situations do not allow them to respect these social prohibitions, and hence they are forced to act in countercultural ways.

In sum, the study of how social entrepreneurs in developing countries attempt to create new institutions and enhance or change existing ones provides an important opportunity to study processes of transformation and disruption of cultural beliefs, traditions, and customary practices that lie at the basis of poverty and dominance.

Provisional institutions

One of the main tenets of institutional theory is that institutions endure. But does this mean that they are created to last forever? Or, to put it differently, can institutions be created to be provisional? These questions pose two analytically different but related issues. The first has to do with the intentions behind creating institutions and the second with the final outcome of provisional institutional arrangements.

In his seminal paper DiMaggio states that "new institutions arise when organized actors with sufficient resources see in them an opportunity to realize interests that they value highly" (1988: 14). Following the opportunistic tone in this definition of institutional entrepreneurship, it might be plausible that institutional entrepreneurs also opportunistically created provisional institutions that served their interests for a certain – more or less defined – period of time.

An example might be illuminating here. In our work in rural Bangladesh we studied BRAC's efforts to facilitate market access and participation for the poorest of the poor. BRAC launched a new program in 2002 named "Challenging the Frontiers of Poverty Reduction" (CFPR). One of the most innovative elements of this program was the transfer of assets – e.g. poultry, cows, seeds, etc. – to its beneficiaries. However, BRAC soon realized that many of the women in the CFPR program were exposed to a high risk that the assets they had received would be stolen (or simply taken from them), damaged, or sabotaged.

Too poor to be clients, the program participants were not able to ensure the support of elite community members as patrons in either the formal or informal courts to enforce their own rights over their assets. To address this issue, BRAC organized what were called Village Poverty Reduction Committees. The objective was to create a set of practices and rules to provide support and security to the women; to do this BRAC built on traditional responsibilities of village elites with respect to the poor as well as creating a new forum to ensure these responsibilities were enacted. Five years after their introduction, such practices and rules, although varying in the degree of institutionalization (Jepperson, 1991), have contributed to building a more enabling and supportive environment for these women.

An interesting feature of this experiment, however, is that BRAC considers these practices and rules to be just a small step towards guaranteeing and enforcing property rights for the poorest of the poor and providing them with the opportunity to have access to mainstream development activities such as microfinance. Indeed, some accounts suggest that these practices and structures of support in this context might have the perverse effect of strengthening relations of patronage, and hence reinforcing social structures that sustain poverty. Notwithstanding these potential negative effects – which brings us back to the aforementioned issue of the unintended consequences of action – BRAC believes that the institutionalization of these practices and structures contributes at this moment in time to its objective of building a more enabling environment for the ultra poor. In other words, while BRAC is aware that such practices and rules still fall short, they have been purposively created to accomplish a particular function at a particular moment in time.

The second issue identified above, i.e. the final outcome of provisional institutional arrangements, raises a set of methodological questions. What is the empirical evidence that allows us to support the claim that an institution is provisional? Is the label "provisional" just a statement about a stage in the life cycle of institutions (Scott, 1995; Tolbert & Zucker, 1996) or the degree of institutionalization (Jepperson, 1991; Barley & Tolbert, 1997)?

We see the intentions of "institutional workers" as fundamental to answer these and related questions. As the previous example suggests, actors might conceive the institutions they create as provisional because they think that after a certain period of time they themselves will deactivate them – once they have accomplished their role. Alternatively, actors might also create such institutions under the assumption or the expectation that other actors will disrupt them in the future. In either case, the provisional nature of institutions has to do less with the degree of institutionalization than with how their creators and even people involved in their maintenance see them.

The idea of provisional institutions poses additional questions and theoretical issues. If it is, then, possible to think of institutions created to endure for a certain period of time, what are the implications for the study of institutional work? What kind of contexts necessitate actors to engage in work aimed at provisional institutions? Why do they need to create provisional institutions? Is it necessary to do so or is this a second-best alternative? Do actors know that such practices will be provisional and, hence, finite? An intriguing feature of institutions is that, at some point, they take on a life of their own. If this is the case, are their creators, or others, able to deactivate them? If so, how? Furthermore, given that institutionalized practices and rules serve as "important causal sources of stable patterns of behaviour" (Tolbert & Zucker, 1996: 179), what are the consequences of intentionally creating provisional institutions?

Navigating across different institutional logics

One of the aspects of poverty that makes its alleviation a complex task is its multidimensionality. Images of poverty vary. Often it has a female face reinforced by deep-rooted customary practices of seclusion and by religious belief systems. In other cases the image portrays situations of asymmetric relations of dependence and patronage, castes or classes, buttressed by myths and legacy institutions. Poverty is many-faceted and therefore poverty-alleviation efforts should be able to navigate across different institutional fields, each with different institutional logics (Bourdieu, 1993; Friedland & Alford, 1991).

The idea of conflicting and contradictory institutional logics has been fruitfully used to explain how actors legitimate identity accounts and also to provide explanations for the paradox of embedded agency (Creed *et al.*, 2002; Greenwood & Suddaby, 2006). The main insight is that actors are able to apply, enact, and use multiple institutional logics across different fields in order to promote change in one particular field of activity. For instance, in order to sensitize rural communities towards health issues, social entrepreneurs and development organizations proactively borrowed elements from the cultural and religious domains to frame and communicate arguments. BRAC for example promotes sanitation by emphasizing "*amongst the Muslim ... members that cleanliness is part of the Iman (religious faith/piety/fidelity), so they should keep their houses, clothes, and their bodies clean*" (Research and Evaluation Division [RED], 2004: 30).

While poverty alleviation certainly builds on this ability to integrate elements from the cultural and religious domains, it also requires entrepreneurs to go one step further and to work simultaneously in different domains. In other words, it is not simply about making use of and transposing bits and pieces of institutions or institutional logics from one field to another, but an issue of "embodiment and incarnation of multiple and often contradictory institutional logics" (Kraatz & Block, 2008: 244). For instance, engaging women in productive activities by providing microcredit in rural Bangladesh implies juggling financial and business logics. Yet it also requires the entrepreneurial actor to navigate subtly between a range of other logics since the provision of loans for productive purposes challenges existing cultural and religious norms that sanction the seclusion of those women in their houses, the patriarchal system, or the gendered division of labor that restricts the involvement of women to a very limited range of "public" activities. We still know very little about how actors navigate and work with different institutional and often contradictory logics at the same time; what are the main challenges and opportunities for organizations doing so; and what sort of skills do these actors need?

Summary and concluding remarks

The goal of this chapter has been to suggest that the study of poverty-alleviation efforts by social entrepreneurs in the developing world can contribute to a more nuanced understanding and richer portrayal of institutional work. Turning attention towards this setting means exploring new, or refining existing aspects of institutional work in contexts where power asymmetries, religious and legacy institutions, customary practices, and myths are particularly stubborn.

Empirical studies of institutional work have largely neglected processes related to the change and/or maintenance of institutions in the developing world. We have argued that this is somewhat surprising – and unfortunate – given the rich tradition and the influence of studies in such settings. We have also argued that the largest body of empirical work on institutional change and institutional entrepreneurship in organizational theory has focused on the role of powerful actors endowed with abundant resources. The limited work available on less powerful actors, typically characterized as marginal, has often portrayed their strategies and actions as aggressive. Our research, looking at how social entrepreneurs attempt to enhance and broaden the scope of existing institutional arrangements, suggests that additional types of less aggressive strategies and practices are at play.

By focusing on poverty-alleviation initiatives we have attempted to introduce some new perspectives into the scholarly discussion on institutional work. First, we have observed in our research the experimental nature of that work and, to use Schumacher's (1999) happy expression, the "beautifulness of smallness." Given the complexity as well as the delicate nature of poverty issues, efforts to alleviate poverty must be resolute, but also gradual (Scott, 1998). In hailing the importance of smallness and reversibility we also suggested that more thought should be devoted to the possibility and the consequences of provisional institutional arrangements. We then elaborated on the importance of enhancement work in facilitating access to and broadening the scope of existing institutions, in particular when such work enables the excluded to have a more active role in the economy and society at large. Finally, we suggested that the study of developing country contexts, and, specifically, of social entrepreneurship in these contexts, promises to offer new insights into how cultural beliefs, traditions, and customary practices become deinstitutionalized and transformed, as well as better understanding of how actors navigate across and cope with multiple institutional logics.

It has been our intention to suggest potential ways to widen current views of agency in institutional studies by giving voice to neglected actors and ignored contexts. There are two additional issues that we wish to highlight in concluding. First, that the study of agency cannot be detached from the analysis of its consequences – either intended or, particularly, unintended. And second, while we believe the study of poverty and poverty-alleviation schemes is a scholarly obligation, we also draw attention to its rich potential as an opportunity for institutional theorists to both deepen and widen our understanding of institutional processes.

References

Arendt, H. (1957) *The Human Condition*. New York: Free Press.

Baiocchi, G. (2005) *Militants and Citizens: The Politics of Participatory Democracy in Porto Alegre*. Stanford, CA: Stanford University Press.

Banerjee, A. V. & He, R. (2004) Making aid work. MIT mimeo, February 10.

Barley, S. & Tolbert, P. S.. (1997) Institutionalization and structuration: studying the links between action and institutions. *Organization Studies*, 18(1): 93–117.

Bates, R. (1981) *Markets and States in Tropical Africa*. Berkeley: University of California Press.

Battilana, J. (2006) Agency and institutions: the enabling role of individuals' social position. *Organization*, 13(5): 653–676.

Bourdieu, P. (1977) *Outline of a Theory of Practice*. Cambridge: Cambridge University Press.

(1979) *Algeria 1960*. Cambridge: Cambridge University Press for Editions de la Sciences de l'Homme, Paris.

(1993) *Sociology in Question*. London: Sage.

Campbell, J. L. (2004) *Institutional Change and Globalization*. Princeton, NJ: Princeton University Press.

Campbell, J. L. & Lindberg, L. N. (1990) Property rights and the organization of economic activity by the State. *American Sociological Review*, 55(October): 634–647.

Clemens, E. S. (1993) Organizational repertoires and institutional change: women's groups and the transformation of US politics, 1890–1920. *American Journal of Sociology*, 98(4): 755–798.

Cohen, J. & Rogers, J. (1995) *Associations and Democracy*. New York: Verso.

Creed, W. E. D., Scully, M. A. & Austin, J. R. (2002) Clothes make the person? The tailoring of legitimating accounts and the social construction of identity. *Organization Science*, 13(5): 475–496.

Dacin, M. T. & Dacin, P. A. (2008) Traditions as institutionalized practices: implications for deinstitutionalization. In R. Greenwood, C. Oliver, K. Sahlin & R. Suddaby (eds.), *Handbook of Organizational Institutionalism*, pp. 327–351. London: Sage.

De Certeau, M. (1984) *The Practice of Everyday Life*. Berkeley: University of California Press.

De Soto, H. (1989) *The Other Path: The Invisible Revolution in the Third World*. New York: Harper & Row.

Dees, G. (1998) The meaning of social entrepreneurship. www.fuqua.duke.edu/centers/case/documents/dees_SE.pdf. Accessed on February 2, 2009.

DiMaggio, J. (1988) Interest and agency in institutional theory. In L. G. Zucker (ed.), *Institutional Patterns and Organizations: Culture and Environment*, pp. 3–22. Cambridge, MA: Ballinger.

(1991) Constructing an organizational field as a professional project: US art museums, 1920–1940. In W. W. Powell & P. J. DiMaggio (eds.), *The New Institutionalism in Organizational Analysis*, pp. 267–292. Chicago: Chicago University Press.

Dobbin, F. (2001) Why the economy reflects the polity: early rail policy in Britain, France, and the United States. In M. Granovetter & R. Swedberg (eds.), *The Sociology of Economic Life*, 2nd edn., pp. 401–424. Boulder, CO: Westview Press.

Douglas, M. (1986) *How Institutions Think*. Syracuse: Syracuse University Press.

Easterly, W. (2006a) The big push déjà vu: a review of Jeffrey Sachs's *The End of Poverty: Economic Possibilities for Our Time*. *Journal of Economic Literature*, 44(1): 96–105.

(2006b) *The White Man's Burden: Why the West's Efforts to Aid the Rest Have Done So Much Ill and So Little Good*. New York: Penguin.

Elsbach, K. & Sutton, R. I. (1992) Acquiring organizational legitimacy through illegitimate actions: a marriage of institutional and impression management theories. *Academy of Management Journal*, 35(4): 699–738.

Emirbayer, M. & Mische, A. (1998) What is agency? *American Journal of Sociology*, 103: 962–1023.

Fligstein, N. (1996) Markets as politics: a political cultural approach to market institutions. *American Sociological Review*, 61(4): 656–673.

(1997) Social skill and institutional theory. *American Behavioral Scientist*, 40: 397–405.

(2001) Social skill and the theory of the fields. *Sociological Theory*, 19(2): 105–125.

Fligstein, N. & Mara-Drita, I. (1996) How to make a market: reflections on the European Union's single market program. *American Journal of Sociology*, 102: 1–33.

Foucault, M. (1980) *The History of Sexuality: An Introduction*, vol. I. New York: Vintage Books.

Friedland, R. & Alford, R. R. (1991) Bringing society back in: symbols, practices, and institutional contradictions. In W. W. Powell & P. DiMaggio (eds.), *The New Institutionalism in Organizational Analysis*, pp. 232–263. Chicago: University of Chicago Press.

Garud, R., Jain, S. & Kumaraswamy, A. (2002) Institutional entrepreneurship in the sponsorship of common technological standards: the case of Sun Microsystems and Java. *Academy of Management Journal*, 45(1): 196–214.

Gaventa, J. (1982) *Power and Powerlessness: Quiescence and Rebellion in an Appalachian Valley*. Urbana: University of Illinois Press.

Geertz, C. (1963) *Peddlers and Princes: Social Development and Economic Change in Two Indonesian Towns*. Chicago: University of Chicago Press.

Giddens, A. (1984) *The Constitution of Society*. Berkeley: University of California Press.

Greenwood, R. & Suddaby, R. (2006) Institutional entrepreneurship in mature fields: the big five accounting firms. *Academy of Management Journal*, 49(1): 27–48.

Greenwood, R., Suddaby, R. & Hinings, C. R. (2002) Theorizing change: the role of professional associations in the transformation of institutionalized fields. *Academy of Management Journal*, 45(1): 58–80.

Hobsbawm, E. (1973) Peasants and politics. *Journal of Peasant Studies*, 1(1): 3–22.

Holm, P. (1995) The dynamics of institutionalization: transformation processes in Norwegian fisheries. *Administrative Science Quarterly*, 40(3): 398–422.

Hulme, D. & Shepherd, A. (2003) Conceptualizing chronic poverty. *World Development*, 31(3): 403–423.

Jepperson, R. L. (1991) Institutions, institutional effects, and institutionalization. In W. W. Powell & J. DiMaggio (eds.), *The New Institutionalism in Organizational Analysis*, pp. 143–163. Chicago: University of Chicago Press.

Khan, F. R., Munir, K. A. & Willmott, H. (2007) A dark side of institutional entrepreneurship: soccer balls, child labour and postcolonial impoverishment. *Organization Studies*, 28(7): 1055–1077.

Khanna, T. & Palepu, K. (2000) The future of business groups in emerging markets: long-run evidence from Chile. *Academy of Management Journal*, 43(3): 268–285.

Kraatz, M. S. & Block, E. S. (2008) Organizational implications of institutional pluralism. In R. Greenwood, C. Oliver, K. Sahlin & R. Suddaby (eds.), *Handbook of Organizational Institutionalism*, pp. 243–275. London: Sage.

Lawrence, T. B. (2008) Power, institutions and organizations. In R. Greenwood, C. Oliver, K. Sahlin & R. Suddaby (eds.), *Handbook of Organizational Institutionalism*, pp. 170–197. London: Sage.

Lawrence, T. B., Hardy, C. & Phillips, N. (2002) Institutional effects of interorganizational collaboration: the emergence of proto-institutions. *Academy of Managament Journal*, 45(1): 281–290.

Lawrence, T. B. & Suddaby, R. (2006) Institutions and institutional work. In S. Clegg, W. R. Nord & T. B. Lawrence (eds.), *Handbook of Organization Studies*, pp. 215–254. London: Sage.

Leblebici, H., Salancik, G. R., Copay, A. & King, T. (1991) Institutional change and the transformation of interorganizational fields: an organizational history of the US radio broadcasting industry. *Administrative Science Quarterly*, 36(3): 333–363.

Leca, B. & Naccache, P. (2006) A critical realist approach to institutional entrepreneurship. *Organization*, 13(5): 627–651.

Leff, N. (1978) Industrial organization and entrepreneurship in the developing countries: the economic groups. *Economic Development and Cultural Change*, 26: 661–675.

Lévi-Strauss, C. (1967) *The Savage Mind*. Chicago: University of Chicago Press.

Lounsbury, M., Ventresca, M. & Hirsch, P. M. (2003) Social movements, field frames and industry emergence: a cultural-political perspective on US recycling. *Socio-Economic Review*, 1: 71–104.

Maguire, S., Hardy, C. & Lawrence, T. B. (2004) Institutional entrepreneurship in emerging fields: HIV/AIDS treatment advocacy in Canada. *Academy of Management Journal*, 47(5): 657–679.

Mahbub, A. & Ahmed, S. M. (1997) Perspective of women about their own illness. Dhaka: BRAC-ICDDR, B Joint Research Project: Working paper number 16.

Mair, J. & Martí, I. (2006) Social entrepreneurship research: a source of explanation, prediction, and delight. *Journal of World Business*, 41: 36–44.
    (In press) Entrepreneurship in and around institutional voids: a case study from Bangladesh. *Journal of Business Venturing*.

Mair, J., Martí, I. & Ganly, K. (2007) Social entrepreneurship: seeing institutional voids as spaces of opportunity. *European Business Forum*, 31 (Winter): 34–39.

Margolis, J. D. & Walsh, J. P. (2003) Misery loves companies: rethinking social initiatives by business. *Administrative Science Quarterly*, 48(2): 268–305.

Moore, B. (1987) *Injustice: The Social Bases of Obedience and Revolt*. White Plains, NY: M. E. Sharpe.

Narayan-Parker, D. (2000) *Voices of the Poor: Can Anyone Hear Us?* New York: Oxford University Press for the World Bank.

Oliver, C. (1991) Strategic responses to institutional processes. *Academy of Management Review*, 16(1): 145.

Oliver, C. (1992) The antecedents of deinstitutionalization. *Organization Studies*, 13(4): 563.

Pearce, J. L. (2005) Organizational scholarship and the eradication of global poverty. *Academy of Management Journal*, 48(6): 970–972.

Peredo, A. M. & Chrisman, J. J. (2006) Toward a theory of community-based enterprise. *Academy of Management Review*, 31(2): 309–328.

Powell, W. W. (1991) Expanding the scope of institutional analysis. In W. W. Powell & J. DiMaggio (eds.), *The New Institutionalism in Organizational Analysis*, pp. 183–203. Chicago: University of Chicago Press.

Prahalad, C. K. & Hart, S. L. (2002) The fortune at the bottom of the pyramid. *Strategy + Business*, 26: 54–67.

Rao, H. (1998) Caveat emptor: the construction of nonprofit consumer watchdog organizations. *American Journal of Sociology*, 103: 912–961.

Rao, H., Monin, P. & Durand, R. (2005) Border crossing: bricolage and the erosion of categorical boundaries in French gastronomy. *American Sociological Review*, 70: 968–991.

Research and Evaluation Division (RED) (2004) Process documentation on the implementation aspects of the CFPR/TUP program. Available: www.bracresearch.org. Accessed April 10, 2008.

Riaz, A. (2005) Traditional institutions as tools of political Islam in Bangladesh. *Journal of Asian and African Studies*, 40(3): 171–196.

Sachs, J. (2005) *The End of Poverty: Economic Possibilities for Our Time.* New York: Penguin.

Scott, J. C. (1985) *Weapons of the Weak: Everyday Forms of Peasant Resistance*. New Haven: Yale University Press.

(1990) *Domination and the Arts of Resistance: Hidden Transcripts*. New Haven, CT: Yale University Press.

(1998) *Seeing Like a State: How Certain Schemes to Improve the Human Condition Have Failed*. New Haven, CT: Yale University Press.

Scott, W. R. (1994) Conceptualizing institutional fields: linking organizations and societal systems. In H.-U. Derlien, U. Gerhardt & F. W. Scharpf (eds.), *Systemrationalitat und Partialinteresse (Systems Rationality and Partial Interests)*, pp. 203–219. Baden-Baden, Germany: Nomos.

(1995) *Institutions and Organizations*. Thousand Oaks, CA: Sage.

Schneiberg, M. (2007) What's on the path? Path dependence, organizational diversity and the problem of institutional change in the US economy, 1900–1950. *Socio-Economic Review*, 5: 47–80.

Schumacher, E. F. (1999) *Small Is Beautiful: Economics as if People Mattered*, 3rd edn. Vancouver: Hartley & Marks.

Seelos, C. & Mair, J. (2007) How social entrepreneurs enable human, social, and economic development. In V. Rangan, J. Quelch, G. Herrero & B. Barton (eds.), *Business Solutions for the Global Poor: Creating Social and Economic Value*, pp. 271–294. San Francisco: Jossey-Bass.

Seo, M. & Creed, W. E. D. (2002) Institutional contradictions, praxis and institutional change: a dialectical perspective. *Academy of Management Journal*, 3: 222–247.

Sewell, W. H. (1992) A theory of structure: duality, agency, and transformation. *American Journal of Sociology*, 98(1): 1–29.

Stern, R. N. & Barley, S. R. (1996) Organizations and social systems: organization theory's neglected mandate. *Administrative Science Quarterly*, 41(1): 146–162.

Streeck, W. & Thelen, K. (eds.) (2005) *Beyond Continuity: Institutional Change in Advanced Political Economies*. Oxford: Oxford University Press.

Suchman, M. (1995) Managing legitimacy: strategic and institutional approaches. *Academy of Management Review*, 20: 571–611.

Tolbert, P. S. & Zucker, L. G. (1996) Institutionalization of institutional theory. In S. Clegg, C. Hardy & W. Nord (eds.), *Handbook of Organization Studies*, pp. 175–190. Thousand Oaks, CA: Sage.

Wahed, T. & Bhuiya, A. (2007) Battered bodies & shattered minds: violence against women in Bangladesh. *Indian Journal of Medical Research*, 126 (October): 341–354.

Wolford, W. (2003) Families, fields and fighting for land: the spatial dynamics of contention in rural Brazil. *Mobilization: An International Quarterly*, 8(2): 157–172.

World Bank (2001) *Engendering Development: Through Gender Equality in Rights, Resources, and Voice*. New York: Oxford University Press.

5 | Institutional work as the creative embrace of contradiction

TIMOTHY J. HARGRAVE AND
ANDREW H. VAN DE VEN

Introduction

In 2006, Lawrence and Suddaby introduced the concept of institutional work into the study of institutions and institutional change. They define institutional work as "the purposive action of individuals and organizations aimed at creating, maintaining and disrupting institutions" (2006: 215). Their effort represents an important advance within a series of efforts to systematically incorporate agency into neo-institutional theory (DiMaggio, 1988; Fligstein, 1997; Oliver, 1991). Lawrence and Suddaby point out that neo-institutionalists have given relatively little attention to "the relationship between institutional work and the contradictions that are inherent in organization fields" (2006: 248). In this chapter we address this gap. We do so by presenting a dialectical perspective on institutional change and then examining different approaches to managing institutional contradictions. Our main argument is that an important aspect of institutional work is the ability to use the tension between contradictory elements as a source of innovation. We refer to the work of the noted community organizer Saul Alinsky to illustrate this argument.

Our perspective suggests that the effective institutional actor, whether incumbent or challenger, takes actions to both stabilize and change institutions. Incumbents must not only maintain institutions, but also disrupt disrupters and refine existing arrangements. Similarly, challengers must attempt to preserve parts of existing institutions as well as suggest alternative arrangements. Our perspective further suggests that effective institutional actors recognize the interdependence of incumbents' and challengers' strategies; exploit gaps between espoused values and actual behavior; and undertake mutually reinforcing institutional work practices across levels of organization.

We argue that the effective institutional actor embraces both structural and processual contradictions as well as the contradiction between structure and process – between principle and spontaneity, planning

120

and emergence, acceptance and control. Because no two social situations are exactly alike, successful institutional work requires comfort with uncertainty and practical imagination. Thus our arguments contribute to the development of the pragmatic sociology of institutional work that views agency as "intelligent, situated institutional action" (Lawrence & Suddaby, 2006: 219).

We proceed as follows. In the next section we present a dialectical perspective on institutional work, emphasizing that institutional processes are not deterministic but rather contingent upon the relative power and political skill of opposed parties. In the chapter's third section we argue that effective institutional work involves the creative use of contradiction. We illustrate our argument by referring to the strategies and tactics of Saul Alinsky. In the chapter's fourth section we present the implications of our argument for understanding institutional work. In the final section we discuss our conclusions.

Dialectics and institutions

Neo-institutionalists study the relationship between actors and institutions. Institutions are the humanly devised rules that enable and constrain action and make social life predictable and meaningful (Scott, 2001). They are composed of material and ideal elements (Giddens, 1984; Sewell, 1992). Rao, Monin, and Durand define institutions as composed of institutional logics, which are "belief systems that furnish guidelines for practical action," and governance structures, which are "the arrangements by which field-level power and authority are exercised" (2003: 795–796). Institutional actors revise and replicate institutions through practices (Barley & Tolbert, 1997; Giddens, 1984), which are "embodied, materially mediated arrays of human activity centrally organized around shared practical understanding" (Schatzki, Knorr-Cetina & von Savigny, 2001: 2). Institutional processes are the sequence of actions by which institutional arrangements are created, maintained, and disrupted (Hargrave & Van de Ven, 2006; Lawrence & Suddaby, 2006).

As noted throughout this volume, neo-institutional scholars are increasingly giving attention to the role of agency in institutional processes. Oliver (1991) incorporated agency into institutional theory by identifying actors' "strategic responses to institutional processes." She proposed responses ranging from acquiescence to defiance and manipulation. Fligstein (1997) identified specific social skills and behaviors of institutional entrepreneurs. More recently, Lawrence and Suddaby (2006) introduced the concept of institutional work into the study of institutions and institutional change. They define institutional work as "the purposive action of individuals and organizations aimed at creating, maintaining and disrupting institutions" (2006: 215).

In this chapter we seek to further develop understanding of institutional work by taking a dialectical perspective. In dialectical processes, change emerges from interactions between proponents of current institutional arrangements and parties espousing contradictory arrangements. The new arrangements that emerge are then challenged by proponents of alternative arrangements as the dialectical process recycles.

As Poole and Van de Ven (2004) discuss, there are many variations of dialectical process theories. They can be distinguished by their views on how contradictions are resolved and the determinacy of the process (Nielsen, 1996). Hegelian and Marxian dialectical perspectives see conflict as the motor of change. According to this view, change occurs when opposing parties have sufficient power to confront each other and engage in struggle. Interactions between opposing parties take place only when both parties have sufficient power. If opponents of existing arrangements are powerless, then their position will remain latent and existing arrangements will go unchallenged. In contrast, Socratic dialectical perspectives view opposing perspectives as complementary and necessary for appreciating the relevant dimensions of an issue (Nielsen, 1996). Thus, for example, it is not possible to understand the perspective of proponents for an institutional change without examining the views of opponents. Contradictions are central to dialectical processes of change. A contradiction is "the dynamic tension between unified opposites in a system" (Werner & Baxter, 1994: 350). Thus contradictions are more than dualities; they exist only when there is dynamic tension between oppositions that are interdependent, which together compose a unity, and which logically presuppose each other.

Scholars also take different views of the level of determinacy of dialectical processes. In Marxian and Hegelian dialectical processes, incumbents who support and are supported by current institutional arrangements (thesis) are challenged by an opposing group espousing an antithesis, setting the stage for a transformative synthesis which both negates and preserves the thesis and antithesis (Schneider, 1971). This synthesis is seen as a product of historical forces and therefore as not contingent upon the behavior or skills of particular actors. Other models, such as Bakhtinian (1981) dialectics, view this dualism between thesis and antithesis as only a special and limiting case of many more oppositions ever-present in pluralistic organizations and communities. They view change as occurring through more indeterminate, contingent processes in which opposing parties "continue their ongoing struggle of negation" (Werner & Baxter, 1994: 352). According to this view, institutional arrangements are not transformative syntheses but rather temporary truces that reflect the relative power and political skill of opposing parties (Hargrave & Van de Ven, 2006; Seo & Creed, 2002; Van de Ven & Poole, 1995).

Dialectical scholars often focus on structural contradictions, and particularly the tensions between the material and ideal elements of structure (Hegel, 1807; Marx, 1859). Seo and Creed (2002) identify four contradictions within and between material and ideal elements. These are the contradictions between legitimacy demands and functional efficiency, which is the main focus of the neo-institutional stream that begins with Meyer and Rowan's (1977) seminal work; between the imperatives of change and existing identities and routines; between the structures governing different spheres of society (Clemens & Cook, 1999; Friedland & Alford, 1991; Sewell, 1992); and in actors' interests. Drawing on Benson (1977), Seo and Creed note that multiple contradictions exist at a single level of analysis, and also across levels of analysis. They write that "multilevel processes produce a complex array of interrelated but often mutually incompatible institutional arrangements" which together "provide a continuous source of tension and conflicts within and across institutions" (2002: 225).

Seo and Creed argue that acute structural contradictions catalyze social change. Citizens become agents of change and exercise praxis when institutional arrangements do not adequately serve their interests or meet their aspirations (Benson, 1977; Seo & Creed, 2002). Praxis is "the free and creative reconstruction of social patterns on the basis of a reasoned analysis of both the limits and the potentials of present social forms" (Benson, 1977: 5).

Empirical work on structural contradictions has tended to focus on contests of logics among segments of the organizational field. For example, Braithwaite and Drahos (2000) characterize the international business regulatory process as a contest in which proponents of strong regulation make their case by appealing to principles such as transparency and harmonization, while opponents of regulation wield the principles of sovereignty and autonomy. Hoffman conceptualized organizational fields as arenas of debate "in which competing interests negotiate over issue interpretation" (1999: 351). Townley (2002) finds that the introduction of planning and performance measurement into a cultural organization led to clashes in all four types of rationalities (substantive, practical, theoretical, and formal) identified by Weber (1978). Lounsbury and Crumley (2007) document the struggle that started in the 1960s in the mutual fund industry between proponents of active money management and an "old guard" that favored the logic of passive money management.

Contradictions inhere in institutional processes as well as in institutional arrangements. One of these processual contradictions is the stability/change contradiction: institutional processes contain pressures for stability and pressures for change (Hegel, 1807; Marx, 1859; Seo & Creed, 2002; Van de Ven & Poole, 1995). Another is the structure/action contradiction, which neo-institutionalists currently label "the paradox of embedded agency" (Battilana & D'Aunno, this volume; Leca, Battilana & Boxenbaum, 2006; Leca & Naccache, 2006; Garud, Hardy & McGuire, 2007).[1] At issue is the tension that arises because actors are seen as simultaneously agentic (internally motivated) yet also inescapably embedded within institutions and influenced by the actors who carry them. A third important (and related) processual contradiction is the internal/external contradiction: actors must simultaneously develop and manage their organizations' internal capabilities, culture, and systems on the one hand, and attend to the external environment on the other.

Just as structural contradictions occur across levels of analysis, so do processual contradictions. Scott (2001: 83) identifies six levels of institutional analysis (world system, society, organizational field, organizational population, organization, and organizational sub-system). Scott notes that processes of stability and change play out at each level of analysis, and that the conditions of stability and change at one level influence those at other levels.

---

[1] Paradox and contradiction are closely related concepts. Cameron and Quinn write that "the key characteristic in paradox is the simultaneous presence of two contradictory elements" (1988: 2). Ford and Backoff write that terms including paradox, contradiction, dilemma, dialectic, and irony "all reflect the notion of constructed dualities" (1988: 89).

The management of contradictions

As they have become more actor-oriented and less deterministic, neo-institutionalists have begun to identify the institutional work practices that actors use to manage contradictions. To date, however, they have not systematically catalogued these practices. The broader literature on dialectics addresses this gap. Echoing Poole and Van de Ven (1989), Werner and Baxter (1994) identify four basic approaches to managing contradiction. These include: simply ignoring one pole and satisfying the other (with strategies of selection, denial, and negation); satisfying the poles sequentially (segmentation, alternation); satisfying them both at once (moderation); and reframing them as complementary.

Bundling Werner and Baxter's second and third categories, we present three approaches to managing contradiction: the "either/or" approach, moderation, and the "both/and" approach (Ford & Backoff, 1988; Gharajedaghi, 1982; Martin, 2007; Werner & Baxter, 1994). The both/and and moderation approaches address both poles of a contradiction, while the either/or approach addresses only one. The both/and and moderation approaches are distinguished by their orientation toward contradiction: the both/and approach frames contradictory poles as complementary elements of a unity. In contrast, the moderation approach treats them as competing and irreconcilable. We now review these three approaches. Our major conclusion is that institutional actors will be most effective when they take a both/and approach to the management of contradictions.

Either/or approaches

Either/or approaches separate different poles of a contradiction, and tend to deny one pole by proceeding as if that pole does not exist, or seek to satisfy one pole while ignoring, or at the expense of, the other. An incumbent who sought to silence and deter proponents would be practicing an either/or approach. Lawrence and Suddaby's taxonomy of institutional work practices identifies numerous practices that constitute an either/or approach. One such practice is policing, which Lawrence and Suddaby define as "ensuring compliance through enforcement, monitoring, auditing" (2006: 230). This practice is designed to squelch practices that contradict the prevailing institutional logic. Lawrence and Suddaby illustrate policing by citing Jones (2001), who found that Thomas Edison brought thirty-three copyright and patent right lawsuits in federal court between 1897 and 1905 to ensure that his patent rights were enforced.

Deterrence is another either/or practice used by institutional incumbents. Lawrence and Suddaby define deterrence as "establishing coercive barriers to institutional change" (2006: 230). Here Lawrence and Suddaby cite Hargadon and Douglas (2001), who also studied Edison and found that politicians interested in maintaining an electric lighting system based on natural gas used any number of measures to deter Edison's electric lighting scheme, including proposing that Edison pay $1000 per mile of wiring and 3 percent of gross receipts.

Oakes, Townley, and Cooper (1998) provide evidence of an either/or approach in their study of the introduction of business planning into cultural organizations in Alberta. They find that the actors who introduced business planning used the pedagogic practices of naming, categorizing, and regularizing to replace one understanding of cultural organizations, defined by those working in the field, with another understanding that was defined in reference to the external market. Oakes and colleagues write that "the power of pedagogy" – its ability to negate alternatives – "lies in its ability to name things in a way that diminishes the possibility of resisting because the process appears neutral and normal – 'technical'" (272).

Garud, Jain, and Kumaraswamy (2002) document the use of an either/or approach by Sun Microsystems in its sponsorship of the Java technological standard. Garud and colleagues suggest that because managers at Sun were unaware of the dialectical nature of institutional change processes, they were caught off-guard by the unintended consequences of their own actions. They find, for example, that Sun's efforts to mobilize collective action bred resistance from vested interests and inadvertently undermined Sun's legitimacy, because other actors were inclined to view Sun's actions as self-interested but not in the best interests of the field as a whole. This study provides evidence that "either/or" approaches can be ineffective and even counterproductive. They may inadvertently undermine themselves by creating pressure for satisfying the negated pole, thereby unleashing unintended consequences. Marquis and Lounsbury (2007) reach a similar conclusion in their study of the US banking industry. They found that "national banks' efforts to introduce a banking logic emphasizing efficiencies of geographic diversification" bred its own resistance, catalyzing "new forms of professional entrepreneurialism intended to preserve a community logic of banking" (799).

Moderation

Moderation refers to the dividing of resources between contradictory poles. The actor's underlying view is that the poles are opposed, and therefore that tradeoffs must be made between them. There are no opportunities for synergies, and efforts to satisfy one pole reduces the resources available for satisfying the other.

Since its inception, neo-institutional theory has posited that organizations manage the contradiction between technical and legitimacy demands by engaging in ceremonial conformity (Meyer & Rowan, 1977). Such decoupling constitutes a moderation approach because it enables organizations to live with – but not embrace or resolve – the contradiction between material and symbolic activities.

Zilber (2007) provides empirical evidence of moderation in her study of institutional entrepreneurship in Israel's high tech sector after the dot-com crash of 2000. She finds that "actors who represented different groups … were engaged in constructing a shared story of the crisis that reflected and further strengthened the established institutional order. Concurrently, the same actors were also telling a counter-story of indictment, blaming other groups for the crisis and calling for changes in the institutional order" (1035). Zilber concludes that institutional entrepreneurship involves both collaboration and contestation, and that storytelling was critical to the achievement of both.

Both/and approaches

The actor using a both/and approach acknowledges both poles of a contradiction, frames these poles as complementary, and uses the contradiction as a source of innovation. Both/and approaches involve the ability to simultaneously hold contradictory positions in mind (Martin, 2007). This distinguishes it from either/or thinking, in which one tries to satisfy a single criterion. We propose that in pluralistic settings in which multiple legitimate and competing groups seek to exercise their rights and pursue their interests, institutional actors are most likely to be successful in navigating contradictions by taking a both/and approach.

The advantage of the both/and approach is that it provides a source of creativity. The framing of contradictory ideas as interdependent elements of a unity rather than as opposed provides a source of creative tension. Cameron and Quinn argue that without tension between simultaneous opposites, unproductive schismogenesis occurs. They define schismogenesis as "a process of self-reinforcement where one action or attribute perpetuates itself until it becomes extreme and therefore dysfunctional" (1988: 6). Eisenhardt and Wescott write that "tension between opposing forces ... creates the unfreezing that is necessary for innovation and change" (1988: 173). In their study of just-in-time manufacturing, they argue that the simultaneous pursuit of multiple, contradictory goals drives the questioning of assumptions, broad search, greater insight into phenomena and relationships, continuous experimentation, and the creation of small crises. These in turn lead to innovation, which improves performance.

Some of the institutional work practices identified by Lawrence and Suddaby (2006) are both/and approaches, in that they simultaneously address pressures for both stability and change. For example, Lawrence and Suddaby discuss "mimicry" as "associating new practices with existing sets of taken-for-granted practices, technologies and rules in order to ease adoption" (2006: 221). Mimicry embraces the stability/change contradiction by recognizing that institutional entrepreneurs will be more successful in making change if they provide stability by building upon existing arrangements. Similarly, the practice of "valorizing/demonizing" recognizes that institutional stability depends upon both celebration of socially sanctioned behavior and diminution of the challenger's reputation. It therefore embraces the internal/external contradiction.

In their study of the introduction of multidivisional practices (MDPs) into the accounting field, Suddaby and Greenwood (2005) advance the literature on the management of institutional contradictions by providing evidence of a both/and approach. They find that the rhetoric of both proponents and opponents of the MDP form exploited inherent contradictions that historically had been suppressed in the accounting industry's discourse of professionalism. Suddaby and Greenwood write that proponents of MDPs used "economic language [which] defined legitimacy as responding to consumer demands" while opponents, "relying on a call to 'core values,' invoked traditional connotations of an ideal type of professional identity to define legitimacy as promoting the public welfare" (2005: 51). Suddaby and Greenwood conclude that the shaping and sharpening of perceptions of institutional contradictions through careful "language selection, common metaphors, and the use of common referents is ... a key component in challenging the taken-for-granted nature of an existing institutional order" (2005: 59). Suddaby and Greenwood also speak to the dangers of the either/or approach when they note that tensions that have been denied in favor of apparent unity eventually become overt and must be addressed.

Institutional work as the creative use of contradiction

Institutional actors, whether incumbents or challengers, will be most effective when they take a both/and rather than either/or orientation to managing contradictions. The simultaneous embrace of contradictory poles can stimulate creativity and innovation. In contrast, practices that address one pole of a contradiction but not the other might inadvertently work against themselves by releasing pressure to satisfy the contradictory pole.

While neo-institutionalists are currently preoccupied with the structure/agency contradiction, we have pointed out that institutional actors must manage many other contradictions as well. In the remainder of this section we offer propositions that further explore the both/and management of some of these contradictions.

Institutional actors both stabilize and change institutions

As noted, one fundamental processual contradiction that institutional actors must embrace is the stability/change contradiction. Prior work has suggested that institutional entrepreneurs create institutions, incumbents maintain them, and challengers disrupt them (Lawrence & Suddaby, 2006). In contrast, the both/and perspective suggests that both incumbents and challengers will be more effective when they take actions to both stabilize and change institutions.

The danger that incumbents face is a lack of dynamism. Even members who benefit from current arrangements may feel bored, frustrated, and hungry for excitement. As a result, the incumbent must offer the promise of change and convince constituents that they are better served by addressing change. This requires incumbents to explain why they are more effective than the challengers. Thus to stabilize and maintain

Table 5.1. *Alinsky's rules for radicals*

- Power is not only what you have but what the enemy thinks you have
- Never go outside the experience of your people
- Wherever possible go outside of the experience of the enemy
- Make the enemy live up to their own book of rules
- Ridicule is man's most potent weapon
- A good tactic is one that your people enjoy
- A tactic that drags on too long becomes a drag
- Keep the pressure on
- The threat is usually more terrifying than the thing itself
- Maintain a constant pressure upon the opposition
- Push a negative hard enough, it will break through into its counterside
- The price of a successful attack is a constructive alternative
- Pick the target, freeze it, personalize it and polarize it.

Source: Alinsky, 1971.

institutions, incumbents must disrupt disrupters and respond to changing conditions by continually revising existing arrangements.

Challengers, of course, seek to change institutions. To do so they must challenge existing arrangements and suggest alternatives. In addition, they must provide their members with a sense of security. Followers must have a sense that the organization and its leadership are stable and capable before they are willing to enlist in the battle for change. Further, leaders must preserve desirable elements of current institutions during the process of disrupting these institutions. Preserving the attractive elements of existing institutions makes new institutions more recognizable and makes institutional change less abrupt. In addition, it enables the challenger to demonstrate that he or she can be relied upon in the future to be constructive.

Renowned community organizer Saul Alinsky understood the importance of creatively embracing the stability/change contradiction. While we agree with the typical characterization of Alinsky's approach to organizing as unsentimental and confrontational, we argue that this view of Alinsky has obscured his nuanced, creative, and pragmatic ability to understand and exploit contradictions. Alinsky's (1971) "rules for radicals" are presented in Table 5.1.

Alinsky recognized that his efforts to change institutions were more effective when he was able to provide members with a sense of stability. To do so Alinsky relied upon tactics that were familiar, interesting, and enjoyable to members. This is reflected in Alinsky's rules "never go outside the experience of your people," "a good tactic is one that your people enjoy," and "a tactic that drags on too long becomes a drag" (again see Table 5.1).

Many of the institutional work practices that have been identified in the institutional literature implicitly embrace one pole of the stability/ change contradiction but not the other. As such they could undermine themselves by inadvertently releasing contrary pressures. Just as the entrepreneurs at Sun unintentionally bred their own resistance (Garud *et al.*, 2002), so a challenger who stoked ideological fires by "disconnecting moral foundations" and "undermining assumptions and beliefs" (Lawrence & Suddaby, 2006) but failed to frame change in familiar, resonant terms would run the risk of unsettling and losing members.

The either/or practices that have been identified in the literature would be more effective if revised to address the contradictory pole. For example, the practice of "disconnecting sanctions/rewards" (Lawrence & Suddaby, 2006) (e.g. using the courts to nullify the incumbents' source of competitive advantage) could be reshaped to simultaneously favor the challenger. The practice of "constructing normative networks" could be redefined as "divide and conquer," the political practice in which an actor simultaneously strengthens his/her coalition and weakens his/her opponent by attracting members away from the opponent's coalition.

If the institutional actor cannot establish practices due to practical reasons such as political conditions, then s/he should bundle practices that address one pole of a contradiction with practices that address the other. For example, Alinsky suggests that agents of change concerned about causing a sense of confusion and loss among members could bundle their institutional creation activities with institutional maintenance activities such as mimicry, which preserves the attractive elements of old institutions. Similarly, an institutional incumbent concerned about the possibility of organizational torpor could bundle institutional maintenance activities with institutional creation and disruption activities that provide members with a sense of stimulation and excitement.

Incumbents' and challengers' strategies are interdependent

Another important contradiction that institutional actors should embrace is the internal/external contradiction. This contradiction plays out across levels and in different forms. A both/and approach to this contradiction would view internal and external work as mutually supportive rather than as competing. Our earlier example of challengers motivating their members by disrupting incumbents illustrates effective management of the internal/external contradiction as well as the stability/change contradiction.

A both/and approach to the internal/external contradiction also would recognize that incumbents' and challengers' strategies are interdependent. Effective institutional strategy (Lawrence, 1999) is predicated upon a careful reading of other actors' interests, strategies, and expected moves and countermoves. Further, because organizations (like individuals) define their identities and strategies based on their perceptions of others (Deephouse, 1999; Strandgaard Pedersen & Dobbin, 2006), they can benefit from managing opponents' perceptions of them, and by influencing others' perceptions of opponents.

In their study of social movement tactics, Elsbach and Sutton (1992) document the importance of impression management in institutional work. Elsbach and Sutton find that the two social movement organizations they studied, ACT UP and Earth First!, faced a tension between the desire to accomplish their goal of radical change and the need for legitimacy. They addressed this tension by engaging in both illegal activities and socially legitimate activities such as press conferences and workshops, and they used these two types of activities in a mutually reinforcing way. Specifically, activists used controversial activities to generate publicity and more conventional activities to gain legitimacy for themselves and their social goals. By carefully managing public perceptions, ACT UP and Earth First! were able to make progress toward their instrumental goals.

Saul Alinsky's work also speaks to the importance to institutional work of impression management. Alinsky's view that possible courses of action should be evaluated based upon the impressions they create and the responses they provoke is reflected in several of his rules, including "power is not only what you have but what the enemy thinks you have" and "the threat is usually more terrifying than the thing itself" (see Table 5.1). "The real action is in the enemy's reaction," Alinsky wrote; "the enemy properly goaded and guided in his reaction will be your major strength" (1971: 136).

Another way in which Alinsky embraced the internal/external contradiction was by viewing internal organization-building and external work as interdependent and mutually supportive rather than as mutually exclusive activities competing for scarce resources. Alinsky feared that once the organization was established and stable, members would turn their aggressions inward if not given an external target. As a result, he felt that attacking incumbents was essential to maintaining his coalition. In addition, Alinsky recognized that the incumbents he faced were often complacent and bounded by routines. Therefore he emphasized that challengers' actions should be unpredictable:

Each blow, each move [by the opposition] is based upon a conviction that you will respond in a foreseen manner. Don't respond in that manner and your opponent's plans reach an impasse. Don't react in the conventional manner; don't follow a plan of your own. Go into a state of complete confusion and draw your opponent into the vortex of the same confusion. (1946: 150–151)

Institutional work at one level influences work at other levels

Institutional actors must also embrace contradictions between the demands of different levels of organization; effective institutional work involves mutually reinforcing efforts across levels. Organizational stability depends on stable interpersonal relationships, and it also enables efforts to make field-level change. Similarly, changes in personal relationships can necessitate organizational change, as can changes in field-level conditions. The effective institutional actor is aware of these interconnections.

Warren (2001) provides an excellent example of cross-level institutional work in his study of Alinsky disciple Ernesto Cortes, the leader of the Texas chapter of the Industrial Areas Foundation (IAF). Warren observes that the Texas IAF effectively builds both "bonding capital" within communities and "bridging capital" among them (25). Building bridging capital keeps community organizations from becoming inward-looking, leads them to develop broader identities and a commitment to the common good, and facilitates the development of a network that can exert power at the state level. At the same time, state-level efforts to impact public policy depend upon the expertise, initiative, and relationships of community activists. Local and global institutional work recursively facilitate each other.

Institutional work involves exploiting gaps between ideals and behavior

Finally, institutional actors must embrace the contradiction between the material and cultural-ideal elements of social structure. As already noted, this tension historically has been of central concern to social theorists but has received relatively little attention from neo-institutionalists, who have focused more on the structure/agency tension. While we have already noted that challengers seek to call attention to and shape understanding of disparities between expectations and material realities, we also want to point out that material/ideal contradictions inhere not only in institutional arrangements but also inside actors themselves. Institutional actors are motivated not only by material/ideal disparities such as extreme poverty and inequality but also by more personal tensions such as failure to live up to their own aspirations. As demonstrated by Alinsky, institutional actors can strategically exploit these internal material/ideal contradictions as well.

Alinsky cleverly exploited tensions between ideal and material reality, and in particular, differences between actors' stated values and actual behaviors. Alinsky took the view that nearly all people "espouse a morality which they do not practice ... The vast separation between their moral standards and actual ways of living resolves itself into extraordinary inconsistencies and inner conflict" (1946: 93–94). Alinsky exploited this inner conflict by providing individuals with the opportunity to reconcile their morals and behavior. For example, he enlisted business people to his community organizations by emphasizing the promotional benefits of joining, while also recognizing that these people would claim to have joined for nobler reasons.

Concluding discussion

The management of contradictions is an important but undertheorized and underresearched aspect of institutional work. We have suggested that recognizing and managing contradictions is an important element of institutional work. We have further suggested that effective institutional actors frame contradictory poles as complementary, rather than denying one pole or treating the poles as competing. The both/ and approach unlocks creativity and reduces adverse unintended consequences.

We have identified the stability/change, structure/agency, material/ideal, and internal/external contradictions as some of the major contradictions inherent in institutional structures and processes. An important implication here is that institutional actors must be concerned with more contradictions than just the "paradox of embedded agency." While neo-institutionalists are rightly giving attention to this contradiction, they may be doing so to the exclusion of other important tensions that institutional actors face.

Our main argument, that managing contradictions requires a both/and approach, glosses over the point that institutional work requires a working understanding of the actors, networks, tensions, and mechanisms that comprise the organizational field. More fundamentally, one cannot creatively manage contradictions if one does not recognize that processes of change are dialectical and contradictions must be creatively managed. Alinsky wrote that:

It is in these contradictions and their incessant interacting tensions that creativity begins. As we begin to accept the concept of contradictions we see every problem or issue in its whole, interrelated sense. We then recognize that for every positive there is a negative, and that there is nothing positive without its concomitant negative, nor any political paradise without its negative side ... The interplay of seemingly conflicting forces or opposites is the actual harmony of nature. (1971: 15–16)

We distinguished structural contradictions from processual ones, recognizing that structure and process themselves stand in contradiction. One aspect of the structure/process contradiction that institutional actors face is the tension between planned and emergent strategy. Organizations will be more effective if their members are empowered to pursue their interests and establish the organization's goals, while, paradoxically, these same members will be more committed to the organization if its espoused mission and goals are inspiring. Alinsky expressed his comfort with this contradiction when he wrote that "the organization is born out of the issues and the issues are born out of the organization" (1971: 120).

A second and related dimension of the structure/process contradiction is the tension between rule-following and adaptability to context. Institutional actors will be more effective in making change or preserving stability if they embrace this tension rather than rigidly following plans or taking only unplanned activities (the latter are either/or approaches). One both/and strategy that reconciles this contradiction is the pragmatic and spontaneous application of orienting guidelines. Alinsky understood this approach as the embrace of both analysis and instinct. Recognizing that "there can be no prescriptions for particular situations because the same situation rarely recurs" (1971: 138), Alinsky stated that:

Analytical logic is required to appraise where you are, what you can do next, the risks and hopes that you can look forward to ... But I cannot overemphasize that the tactic itself comes out of the free flow of action and reaction, and requires on the part of the organizer an easy acceptance of apparent disorganization. (1971: 165)

Alinsky is sometimes viewed as an ideological diehard radical. This is unfortunate, for it camouflages his profound insights into the political dynamics of institutional work. Alinsky's strategy of applying guidelines in a flexible fashion reflects an important attitude of pragmatism to accomplishing institutional work. This pragmatic attitude is similar to that of John Dewey, who saw "general principles [as] often indispensable as improvable tools to experimentally develop a situation's individualized meanings" (Fesmire, 2003: 58). Institutional actors and scholars would do well to remember the words of the great jazz musician Charles Mingus, who pragmatically noted of his craft that "you can't improvise on nothin' man... You gotta improvise on somethin'" (Fesmire, 2003: 96).

References

Alinsky, S. (1946/1969) *Reveille for Radicals: A Practical Primer for Realistic Radicals*. New York: Random House.
   (1971) *Rules for Radicals: A Practical Primer for Realistic Radicals.* New York: Random House.
Bakhtin, M. M. (1981) *The Dialogic Imagination: Four Essays by M. M. Bakhtin*, trans. C. Emerson & M. Holquist. Austin, TX: University of Texas Press.
Barley, S. R. & Tolbert, P. S. (1997) Institutionalization and structuration: studying the links between action and institution. *Organization Science*, 18(1): 93–117.
Benson, J. K. (1977) Organizations: a dialectical view. *Administrative Science Quarterly*, 22: 1–21.

Braithwaite, J. & Drahos, P. (2000) *Global Business Regulation*. New York: Cambridge University Press.

Cameron, K. S. & Quinn, R. E. (1988) Organizational paradox and transformation. In R. E. Quinn & K. S. Cameron (eds.), *Paradox and Transformation: Toward a Theory of Change in Organization and Management*, pp. 1–18. Cambridge, MA: Ballinger.

Clemens, E. & Cook, J. (1999) Politics and institutionalism: explaining durability and change. *Annual Review of Sociology*, 25: 441–466.

Deephouse, D. L. (1999) To be different, or to be the same? It's a question (and theory) of strategic balance. *Strategic Management Journal*, 20: 147–166.

DiMaggio, P. (1988) Interest and agency in institutional theory. In L. G. Zucker (ed.), *Institutional Patterns and Organizations: Culture and Environment*, pp. 3–22. Cambridge, MA: Ballinger.

Eisenhardt, K. M. & Wescott, B. J. (1988) Paradoxical demands and the creation of excellence: the case of just-in-time manufacturing. In R. E. Quinn & K. S. Cameron (eds.), *Paradox and Transformation: Toward a Theory of Change in Organization and Management*, pp. 169–193. Cambridge, MA: Ballinger.

Elsbach, K. D. & Sutton, R. I. (1992) Acquiring organizational legitimacy through illegitimate actions: a marriage of institutional and impression management theories. *Academy of Management Journal*, 35(4): 699–738.

Fesmire, S. (2003) *John Dewey and Moral Imagination: Pragmatism in Ethics*. Bloomington, IN: Indiana University Press.

Fligstein, N. (1997) Social skills and institutional theory. *American Behavioral Scientist*, 40(4): 397–405.

Ford, J. D. & Backoff, R. W. (1988) Organizational change in and out of dualities and paradox. In R. E. Quinn & K. S. Cameron (eds.), *Paradox and Transformation: Toward a Theory of Change in Organization and Management*, pp. 81–121. Cambridge, MA: Ballinger.

Friedland, R. & Alford, R. R. (1991) Bringing society back in: symbols, practices, and institutional contradictions. In W. W. Powell & P. J. DiMaggio (eds.), *The New Institutionalism in Organizational Analysis*, pp. 232–263. Chicago: University of Chicago Press.

Garud, R., Hardy, C. & Maguire, S. (2007) Institutional entrepreneurship as embedded agency: an introduction to the special issue. *Organization Studies*, 28: 957–969.

Garud, R., Jain, S. & Kumaraswamy, A. (2002) Institutional entrepreneurship in the sponsorship of common technological standards: the case of Sun Microsystems and Java. *Academy of Management Journal*, 45(1): 196–214.

Gharajedaghi, J. (1982) Social dynamics (dichotomy or dialectic). *General Systems*, 27: 251–268.

Giddens, A. (1984) *The Constitution of Society*. Berkeley: University of California Press.

Hargadon, A. & Douglas, Y. (2001) When innovations meet institutions: Edison and the design of the electric light. *Administrative Science Quarterly*, 46: 476–501.

Hargrave, T. J. & Van de Ven, A. H. (2006) A collective action model of institutional change. *Academy of Management Review*, 31(4): 864–888.

Hegel, G. W. F. ([1807] 1977) *Phenomenology of Spirit*. Oxford: Oxford University Press.

Hoffman, A. J. (1999) Institutional evolution and change: environmentalism and the US chemical industry. *Academy of Management Journal*, 42(4): 351–371.

Jones, C. (2001) Co-evolution of entrepreneurial careers, institutional rules and competitive dynamics in American film. *Organization Studies*, 22(6): 91–144.

Lawrence, T. B. (1999) Institutional strategy. *Journal of Management*, 25(2): 161–188.

Lawrence, T. B. & Suddaby, R. (2006) Institutions and institutional work. In S. R. Clegg, C. Hardy & W. R. Nord (eds.), *Handbook of Organization Studies*, 2nd edn., pp. 215–254. London and Thousand Oaks, CA: Sage.

Leca, B., Battilana, J. & Boxenbaum, E. (2006) Taking stock on institutional entrepreneurship: what do we know? Where do we go? Working paper presented at Academy of Management Meeting, 2006.

Leca, B. & Naccache, P. (2006) A critical realist approach to institutional entrepreneurship. *Organization*, 13(5): 627–651.

Lounsbury, M. & Crumley, E. T. (2007) New practice creation: an institutional perspective on innovation. *Organization Studies*, special issue on Institutional Entrepreneurship, 28: 993–1012.

Marquis, C. & Lounsbury, M. (2007) Vive la résistance: competing logics and the consolidation of US community banking. *Academy of Management Journal*, 50(4): 799–820.

Martin, R. (2007) *The Opposable Mind: How Successful Leaders Win Through Integrative Thinking*. Cambridge, MA: Harvard Business School Press.

Marx, K. (1971 [1859]) Preface to a contribution to the critique of political economy. In E. Fischer (ed.), *The Essential Theory of Karl Marx*. New York: Herder & Herder.

Meyer, J. R. & Rowan, B. (1977) Institutionalized organizations: formal structure as myth and ceremony. *American Journal of Sociology*, 83: 340–363.

Nielsen, R. P. (1996) Varieties of dialectic change processes. *Journal of Management Inquiry*, 5(3): 276–292.

Oakes, L. S., Townley, B. & Cooper, D. J. (1998) Business planning as pedagogy: language and control in a changing institutional field. *Administrative Science Quarterly*, 43: 257–292.

Oliver, C. (1991) Strategic responses to institutional processes. *Academy of Management Review*, 16: 145–179.

Poole, M. S. & Van de Ven, A. H. (1989) Using paradox to build management and organization theories. *Academy of Management Review*, 14(4): 562–578.

(2004) Theories of organizational change and innovation processes. In M. S. Poole & A. H. Van de Ven (eds.), *Handbook of Organizational Change and Innovation*, pp. 374–397. Oxford: Oxford University Press.

Rao, H., Monin, P. & Durand, R. (2003) Institutional change in Toque Ville: nouvelle cuisine as an identity movement in French gastronomy. *American Journal of Sociology*, 108(4): 795–843.

Schatzki, T. R., Knorr-Cetina, K. & von Savigny, E. (2001) *The Practice Turn in Contemporary Theory*. London: Routledge.

Schneider, L. (1971) Dialectic in sociology. *American Sociological Review*, 36(4): 667–678.

Scott, W. R. (2001 [1995]) *Institutions and Organizations*, 2nd edn. Thousand Oaks, CA: Sage.

Seo, M. & Creed, W. E. D. (2002) Institutional contradictions, praxis, and institutional change: a dialectical perspective. *Academy of Management Review*, 27(2): 222–247.

Sewell, W. H., Jr. (1992) A theory of structure: duality, agency, and transformation. *American Journal of Sociology*, 98(1): 1–29.

Suddaby, R. & Greenwood, R. (2005) Rhetorical strategies of legitimacy. *Administrative Science Quarterly*, 50: 35–67.

Strandgaard Pedersen, J. & Dobbin, F. (2006) In search of identity and legitimation: bridging organizational culture and neo-institutionalism. *American Behavioral Scientist*, 49(7): 897–907.

Townley, B. (2002) The role of competing rationalities in institutional change. *Academy of Management Journal*, 45(1): 163–179.

Van de Ven, A. H. & Poole, M. S. (1988) Paradoxical requirements for a theory of organizational change. In R. Quinn & K. Cameron (eds.), *Paradox and Transformation: Toward a Theory of Change in Organization and Management*, pp. 19–63. Cambridge, MA: Ballinger.

(1995) Explaining development and change in organizations. *Academy of Management Review*, 20: 510–540.

Warren, M. R. (2001) *Dry Bones Rattling: Community Building to Revitalize American Democracy*. Princeton, NJ: Princeton University Press.

Weber, M. (1978 [1921]) *Economy and Society*, trans. and ed. G. Roth. Berkeley and Los Angeles: University of California Press.

Werner, C. M. & Baxter, L. A. (1994) Temporal qualities of relationships: organismic, transactional, and dialectical views. In M. Knapp & G. Miller (eds.), *Handbook of Interpersonal Communication*, 2nd edn., pp. 323–379. Thousand Oaks, CA: Sage.

Zilber, T. B. (2007) Stories and the discursive dynamics of institutional entrepreneurship: the case of Israeli high-tech after the bubble. *Organization Studies*, 28: 1035–1054.

Studies of institutional work

6 Building the iron cage: institutional creation work in the context of competing proto-institutions

CHARLENE ZIETSMA AND BRENT MCKNIGHT

A unique contribution of institutional theory is the insight that organizations need legitimacy as well as technical efficiency to survive and thrive in their environments (DiMaggio & Powell, 1983; Meyer & Rowan, 1977). The institutionalized norms, practices, and logics which structure organizational fields exert isomorphic pressures, forming an "iron cage" which constrains organizational actions. Organizations are seen as legitimate when they conform to field structures and operate within the iron cage (DiMaggio & Powell, 1983). Much work in institutional theory has focused on the diffusion of institutional structures and the forces which support institutional isomorphism.

Yet not all institutional environments are highly institutionalized, and not all actors are equally constrained by institutional arrangements. A great deal of work in the last two decades has shown that institutional entrepreneurs may arise to question institutional arrangements (DiMaggio, 1988), resisting them strategically (Oliver, 1991; Ang & Cummings, 1997), disrupting and deinstitutionalizing them (Ahmadjian & Robinson, 2001; Oliver, 1992), and reconstructing them to suit the desires of different actors (Anand & Peterson, 2000; Hargadon & Douglas, 2001; Zilber, 2002).

Much of the prior work on institutional entrepreneurship has tended to focus retrospectively on the path of a single institutional innovation as it gained support in an emerging or existing field, often displacing an existing set of institutional arrangements (e.g. Greenwood, Suddaby & Hinings, 2002; Maguire, Hardy & Lawrence, 2004; Munir, 2005).

* This chapter has benefited significantly from feedback received at the 2007 Vancouver Conference on Institutional Work, and especially from the editorial direction and comments of Roy Suddaby, Bernard Leca, and Tom Lawrence. We gratefully acknowledge the support of the Social Science and Humanities Research Council in funding this research.

Throughout this work, competing or independently evolving innovations which may also have been candidates for institutionalization are generally not discussed. Yet institutional change does not always occur as a solution, pre-formed, to a problem that may not previously have been acknowledged. Instead, disruptive activities by activists or insurgents may erode the legitimacy of one set of institutional arrangements without providing widely accepted arrangements to replace them.

When fields have been sufficiently disrupted by deinstitutionalization work, there exist no legitimate institutionalized templates for field members to mimetically adopt to gain legitimacy. The iron cage of institutional structures has been breached, and the means for attaining legitimacy is uncertain. In such uncertain circumstances, Beckert (1999) has argued that institutional entrepreneurs will arise to promote institutional arrangements that favor their interests. They will seek to rebuild the iron cage with new institutional arrangements (patterns, forms, practices, logics) that can be considered legitimate by those both inside and outside the organizational field, therefore protecting the field from further disruption. An actor within an organizational field could then adopt those arrangements to reduce the likelihood that its legitimacy could be challenged by those either within or outside the field.

Yet there is no guarantee that only a *single* institutional entrepreneur will arise. Frequently, there is significant disagreement among field constituents as to which arrangements should be adopted, or how new arrangements should be designed. Several groups may engage in parallel institutional work, and find they are competing against, and impacted by, other actors sponsoring different arrangements. Yet we know little about the processes by which new institutional innovations emerge, compete, and resolve into shared logics and practices over time.

In this research, we investigate the processes by which competing candidates for institutionalization, or proto-institutions (Lawrence, Hardy & Phillips, 2002), coalesce into shared practices and logics. We study these processes in the context of the coastal forest industry of British Columbia (BC), Canada, from 1992 to 2006; an industry which had faced significant social and environmental criticism, and whose institutional arrangements had been delegitimated by insurgents. We identify the institutional work undertaken by leaders competing to promote their preferred institutional arrangements within an uncertain institutional environment.

We find a process of co-creation of institutions involving multiple members of the organizational field, who compete and collaborate through multiple iterations of institutional development until a common template becomes diffused. This co-creation process moves beyond heroic conceptions of institutional entrepreneurs that effect institutional change by sheer will alone. Instead, we find ongoing negotiations, experimentation, competition, and learning, which resolve over time into shared conceptions of problems and solutions in organizational fields. This co-creation institutional work occurs simultaneously with continued disruption work, and involves concurrent development of maintenance mechanisms designed to hold institutions in place as they diffuse.

We thus offer several contributions. First, we show that institutional creation work can be a process of collaborative co-creation and/or competitive convergence, involving experimentation undertaken by multiple actors. This process leads to a solution that embeds the interests of multiple parties. In a collaborative process, shared templates emerge from consensus, negotiation, and active co-creation. In a competitive process, templates emerge from competitive convergence, in which actors translate some elements of others' templates into their own in response to feedback from potential adopters. Second, in these collaborative co-creation and competitive convergence processes, we find that institutional disruption, creation, and maintenance may occur simultaneously as actors try to discredit prior institutional templates, create and promote their own, and develop the means to diffuse and maintain their preferred templates at the same time. Furthermore, we identify the effects of institutional detritus – the bits of logics, practices, and identities remaining from the previously stable context and the process by which it was disrupted (Schneiberg, 2007). We find that institutional entrepreneurs remain constrained by some deeply held identities and logics, which they are only able to get beyond using collaborative co-creation processes.

The chapter proceeds as follows. First, we discuss the character of institutions and the growing literature on agentic institutional change. We briefly review literature on institutional work, including institutional creation, disruption, and maintenance, then focus attention on prior work which pertains to institutional creation work in disrupted environments and competition over institutional arrangements. We then present our empirical study, discussing the methodology, and reviewing our findings. Finally, we discuss our findings in the context of the literature on institutional work.

Literature review

The purpose of institutions

Institutions have been defined as "humanly devised constraints that structure political, economic and social interaction" (North, 1990: 97). They result in "socially constructed, routine-reproduced, program or rule systems" (Jepperson, 1991: 149) that "provide stability and meaning to social life" (Scott, 2001: 48). Institutions reduce environmental uncertainty by establishing the standards and behaviors required for legitimacy within an environment. Because "organizational decision makers have a strong preference for certainty, stability, and predictability in organizational life" (Oliver, 1991: 170, citing DiMaggio, 1988; DiMaggio & Powell, 1983; Pfeffer & Salancik, 1978; Zucker, 1977), strong institutional frameworks provide significant benefits for organizations. In highly institutionalized organizational fields, institutional arrangements are supported by cognitive, normative, and regulative pillars, meaning they are taken for granted as natural, normatively valued beyond their technical usefulness, and reinforced by coercive mechanisms which sanction deviants (Scott, 2001). Institutions include rule systems, laws, accepted practices, and common knowledge.

Institutions are at the same time highly constraining. They affect patterns of social relationships and domination which determine who holds power and access to valuable resources (DiMaggio & Powell, 1983; Fligstein, 2001). These institutional arrangements are also self-reinforcing in that they reproduce power positions and motivate dominant elites to maintain institutional arrangements in order to preserve their positions of privilege (Greenwood & Hinings, 1996). The same institutional arrangements put other actors at a disadvantage and reduce their ability to effect change (Fligstein, 1991). Highly institutionalized environments have thus been described as "iron cages" which constrain actors and drive isomorphism within organizational fields (DiMaggio & Powell, 1983).

Enduring institutions are well noted in the literature; however, much of the recent literature adopting the institutional perspective has focused on institutional change. Earlier work identified exogenous forces for institutional change, including political, legal, or administrative shifts (Fox-Wolfgramm, Boal & Hunt, 1998; Hoffman, 1999; Oliver, 1991), technological changes (Barley, 1986), or changes in markets or stakeholders' demands (Greenwood & Hinings, 1996; Oliver, 1992). Other work has focused on institutional entrepreneurship as a mechanism for institutional change (Beckert, 1999; Greenwood, Suddaby & Hinings, 2002; Maguire, Hardy & Lawrence, 2004; and many others). Much of this work has described nearly heroic institutional entrepreneurs, or "modern princes" (Levy & Scully, 2007), challenging an organizational field and molding it to suit their interests (Greenwood *et al.*, 2002; Hargadon & Douglas, 2001; Hensmans, 2003). However, the ability of a new institution to become sufficiently diffused and taken for granted depends to a large degree on the willingness of incumbent actors to adopt the change. This presents institutional theory with a paradox of embeddedness, since it is not obvious how embedded actors are able to effect change to the very institutions they take for granted (Holm, 1995; Seo & Creed, 2002).

Recent work sheds light on the mechanisms of endogenous institutional change. In studying Big Five accounting firms, Greenwood and Suddaby (2006) found that when elite firms identified substantial contradictions, either through exposure to neighboring fields or as a result of clear misalignment within their own field, the firms became less embedded. This lower level of embeddedness provided these firms with increased awareness of and motivation for change.

Complementing this work, other research has proposed a competitive, dialectic struggle between opposing viewpoints that, once resolved, forms the basis for new variation in a diffusion model of institutional change (Hargrave & Van de Ven, 2006). Building on the social movement literature (McAdam & Scott, 2005), actors are seen to engage in framing contests, construct cooperative and competitive networks, manipulate institutional arrangements or incentive structures, and collectively mobilize in order to effect change (Wijen & Ansari, 2007; Hargrave & Van de Ven, 2006). These battles between insurgents and countermovements of incumbents (Hensmans, 2003) disrupt existing arrangements, yet ready-made solutions may not be available, leaving much institutional work to be done.

Once an environment has been disrupted and its conventions deinstitutionalized, legitimate and appropriate templates for behavior in a field may be unknown. This may be especially true when new actors or newly powerful actors differ significantly from former elites in their conceptions of what is appropriate. The result is an uncomfortable state of uncertainty for organizational decision makers (Oliver, 1991; DiMaggio, 1988; DiMaggio & Powell, 1983). Contributing to this uncertainty are competing logics and the detritus of institutional materials left over from previous institutional work, including political networks, alternative systems, and community associations (Schneiberg, 2007).

Institutional creation work in disrupted environments

In this chapter we are particularly interested in the work done by actors to create institutions within these disrupted environments. As Lawrence and Suddaby (2006) described, institutional creation work involves defining rule systems and vesting them with the ability to confer property rights, constructing normative networks of actors possessing defined identities in relation to the new rule systems, and developing support for those rule systems through advocacy, theorizing, and educating. Actors develop proto-institutions: "new practices, rules, and technologies" which "may become new institutions if they diffuse sufficiently" (Lawrence *et al.*, 2002: 281). When actors are promoting a particular set of institutional arrangements as a solution to some problem in the field, we refer to that set of arrangements as a proto-institution. Proto-institutions are candidates for institutionalization, if only enough members of the field will adopt them. Where multiple proto-institutions have been proposed for the same purpose, it is not clear which proto-institution, if any, will become dominant. It is important to note that, since institutional arrangements confer property rights and status, the competition over proto-institutions implies a competition over power and dominance within an organizational field. The opposite is also true. Having more power in an organizational field implies that an actor can impose or influence the adoption of a set of institutional arrangements that will privilege its interests.

Competition to define legitimate practices has received limited attention in the literature. Galvin (2002) described how medical professional associations competed with regulators and advocacy organizations for influence in the medical field, implying increased ability to influence institutional arrangements. Galvin's study stopped short of examining the fine-grained dynamics of competition among those advocacy and professional organizations. Washington (2004) examined the competition between the National Collegiate Athletic Association (NCAA) and National Association of Intercollegiate Athletics (NAIA) in college athletics, finding that the NCAA extended its membership criteria to the very groups that the NAIA was better serving in order to fend off the

NAIA's competitive threat. In Reay and Hinings' (2005) study of the Alberta government's move to exclude physicians from health-care decisions by forming regional health networks, physicians publicly attacked the normative legitimacy of the health networks, and used the support mobilized to negotiate an influential role for themselves within the new system. Perhaps the most thorough empirical description of institutional competition is found in Garud, Jain, and Kumaraswamy's (2002) study of Sun's efforts to promote its Java open programming standards to a broad group of users. Competitors Microsoft and Hewlett Packard responded by introducing and/or supporting rival standards, countermobilizing users, and discrediting Sun.

While each of these studies sheds some light on how actors compete for the right to set field-structuring rules and standards, they do not delve into the processes by which standards emerge and are changed through the competition. In this chapter we seek to address how institutional actors create new institutional arrangements, and adapt them as they compete for dominance in disrupted environments. How do actors compete and collaborate in constructing their collective iron cage when the basis for choosing among proto-institutions is unknown? We address this research question via a longitudinal study of sustainable forest management standard development in the forest industry. In this context, actors (including forest companies, environmental groups, governments, and others) promoted a variety of proto-institutions, including certification and labeling schemes, regulations, and land use processes. We describe our methods, and then present our findings.

Methods

To investigate proto-institutional competition we conducted a longitudinal study leveraging a detailed, multisource data set situated within the British Columbia (BC), Canada, forestry context. Since the BC setting is also influenced by transnational conflict over standard setting (McNichol, 2006), we also attend to global influences. While our study focused on the 1992 to 2006 time period relevant to the study of the proto-institutions, our analysis was informed by a deep knowledge of the context from prior work dating back to 1985. The intensity and duration of the institutional disruption provided an ideal context for the study of the creation and competition of proto-institutions in disrupted contexts.

Data

The data for this research are based on an extensive qualitative database of interviews, organizational documents, news articles, press releases, and third-party reports. The semi-structured interviews averaged 90 minutes and include interviews with 52 forest company participants, 10 environmentalists, 3 government officials, 4 forest-dependent community members, and 3 certification body officials. The interviews were conducted between 1996 and 2007 with the majority completed in 1999–2000, in close proximity to the events under study (Miles & Huberman, 1984).

In addition, 147 press releases from companies and environmental non-governmental organizations (ENGOs), over 50 news articles pertaining specifically to the proto-institutions under study, and extensive news summaries detailing the BC forest industry from 1992 to 2006 were gathered. Secondary reports were also consulted, including annual federal government reports on Canadian forests, firm annual reports, NGO reports, and other academic studies conducted in the context.

Analysis

The first step in the data analysis was to create a narrative describing competing proto-institutions and their development over time (Langley, 1999). The narrative, which was constructed from the raw data and secondary sources, was supplemented by extensive comparison tables and a timeline describing the milestones in the development of the proto-institutions. This narrative provided a strong foundation and served as an important reference and analytical tool throughout the duration of the project.

As a second step, we sought evidence of proto-institution construction and adaptation and the factors that influenced it. We noted that proto-institution sponsors (the group that initially created the proto-institution) developed and adapted features for their proto-institutions, and promoted them to target groups. We noted additional patterns of interaction between competing proto-institution sponsors and among proto-institution sponsors and the broader set of actors in the organization field. We sought evidence of how the core features and target supporters of each proto-institution changed over time, and we looked for causal influences of those changes.

For the third step, we traversed the entire data set, coding passages to illuminate the behavior of the actors in the context as they promoted or supported specific proto-institutions. Guided by Lawrence and Suddaby's (2006) discussion of institutional creation, maintenance, and disruption work, but maintaining sensitivity to emerging themes in the data, we iterated between theory and data to identify behavioral themes and their interrelationships, and processes of proto-institutional competition. Since we noted that the proto-institutions were constantly evolving, we chose to focus mainly on institutional creation work, though we noted that maintenance and disruption work occurred concurrently. When possible, multiple data sources were leveraged in order to triangulate and validate our interpretation of the data (Jick, 1979). This process was repeated, moving from the behavior of individual actors to the behavior of classes of actors, identifying similarities and differences. This method resulted in an analysis of how proto-institutions became co-created through the institutional work of multiple actors in the BC forestry context.

Findings

To present our findings, we first provide an overview of the BC coastal forest industry and the emergence of the competing proto-institutions. We then describe the institutional work undertaken by a variety of actors to construct and promote their favored proto-institutions in the context of others' competitive and collaborative actions.

The BC coastal forest industry: a disrupted context

Forests cover about 500,000 square kilometres of BC, and, until recently, forestry was the primary industry, accounting for about half of BC exports, and nearly 300,000 jobs. Most (95–97 percent) forests were harvested using clear cutting, a broadly accepted method which removed all trees from a logging site. In BC during the 1980s and 1990s, a proliferation of environmental groups began demonstrating against both the BC government and forest companies, building on international concerns about the negative environmental impacts of deforestation in the Amazon basin.[1] Environmental groups claimed that

---

[1] Environmentalists later labeled BC the "Brazil of the North."

clearcutting was rapacious, that the government and forest companies were in bed together and could not be trusted to safeguard the environment, and that the public had a right to be involved in forestry decision-making, since forests were a public, even planetary, resource. Forestry firms and the BC government initially considered the environmentalists to be an ill-informed fringe group and either ignored them or had them arrested. However, the conflict escalated and was internationalized over many years of protest campaigns culminating in the summer of 1993 with the arrest of over 700 protesters.[2]

By the mid 1990s, leading ENGOs adopted a new strategy by targeting international customers of forest products to persuade and coerce them into changing their purchasing behavior. These customers, "fed up [with] buying B.C. lumber that seems to come with a protester attached to every two-by-four...,"[3] in turn put pressure on BC forest companies to practice sustainable forest management. Both forest companies and their customers were highly motivated to find a workable solution to this dilemma.

While the dominant harvesting practices were considered illegitimate by many outside the industry, and actors were motivated to change, a broadly acceptable system of sustainable forest management (SFM) did not exist. Worldwide, retailers and ENGOs were "clamoring for a transparent, credible and uniform system" of demonstrating legitimate forest management to fill the void (McNichol, 2006: 369). International certification schemes began to emerge in the 1990s, targeted at providing credible information to purchasers and guidance to forest companies. Yet there was little consensus on appropriate harvesting practices, and the certification schemes themselves became a focus for the conflict.

For an SFM system to be broadly accepted in the BC context, it had to meet the varied objectives of a number of stakeholders. For environmentalists it had to (1) delineate a set of SFM practices (*SFM practices*), (2) ensure the protection of the most ecologically sensitive forests (*protected areas*), and (3) provide a permanent role for stakeholders in decision-making processes associated with forest management (*open process*). Collectively these can be referred to as satisfying *social legitimacy criteria*. To satisfy the forest industry and gain firm acceptance, a system of SFM had to (4) increase access to national and international markets through universal recognition and acceptance (*market access*),

---

[2] *Vancouver Sun*, May 22, 1999, A13.   [3] *Vancouver Sun*, May 5, 2000, A1.

(5) impose the least costs in terms of compliance (*ease of implementation*), and (6) reduce uncertainty by maximizing industry's control over forest practice and harvest area decisions (*industry control*). Collectively, these can be referred to as *firm acceptance criteria*. There are clear conflicts in these objectives, such as the industry's desire for control vs. the ENGOs' desire for an open process. Further, more stringent forest practices and greater protection of ecologically sensitive areas generally reduce the ease of implementation for forest companies. Despite these opposing objectives, all actors shared the higher-order objective of finding a system of sustainable forest management that reduced the conflict around forest practices for all stakeholders (forest companies, ENGOs, governments, and customers) and could be considered legitimate by all.

Emerging proto-institutions

The field was left with fragments of institutional detritus: a dominant logic of clear cutting among forest companies which was contested by others, incomplete and controversial systems of SFM, a shared history of conflict and distrust between environmentalists and forest companies, and the ENGOs' widely accepted rhetorical claims that the public had to protect forests from untrustworthy forest companies and governments. Into this disrupted environment, several different proto-institutions were introduced as candidates for systems of SFM. These were introduced in a relatively short period of time by four different types or groups of actors: activists, industry associations, the BC government, and elite organizational field members.

The *Forest Stewardship Council (FSC)*, a largely environmentalist-driven organization which emerged from the Earth Summit in Rio de Janeiro in 1992, was the first to announce a certification standard, though the regional standards for BC were not finalized until 2002.[4] Forest industry associations around the world responded to the threat of FSC certification by initiating industry- and government-based forest certifications, including the American Forest and Paper Association's *Sustainable Forestry Initiative (SFI)* certification and the Forest

---

[4] FSC standards involved ten international principles plus a number of regional criteria that were to be negotiated through a multi-stakeholder process involving four chambers of environmental, social, economic, and indigenous actors respectively.

Table 6.1. *Overview of proto-institutions*

	FSC	Industry certification (SFI and CSA)	FPC	EBM
Full name	Forest Stewardship Council	Sustainable Forest Initiative and Canadian Standards Association	Forest Practices Code	Eco-System Based Management
Year of founding	1993; 1996 in BC; BC standards ratified in 2002.	1994, 1996	1996	2003
Features	Chain of custody; labeling; practices and processes (minimum threshold, outcome- and process-based).	Chain of custody; labeling; practices and processes (minimum threshold, outcome-based).	Regulations of harvesting; land-use decision-making; stakeholder engagement.	Practices/processes: harvesting; land-use decision-making; stakeholder engagement.
Sponsors	ENGOs and NGOs; forest company customers; traders.	Industry-prompted.	BC government.	Elite forest companies and ENGOs.
Key supporters/adopters	Leading ENGOs; social groups; indigenous peoples; customers of forest companies; peripheral forest companies.	Most forest companies and forest industry associations; peripheral NGOs.	All BC forest companies (compliance regulated).	Leading forest companies and ENGOs; ratified by a multi-stakeholder process and the BC government.
Perceived disadvantages	Seen to be associated with ENGOs; hard to implement.	Industry driven.	Considered largely irrelevant to conflict.	Not internationally recognized; hard to implement.

Products Association of Canada-initiated *CSA SFM* standard (controlled by the Canadian Standards Association), introduced in 1994 and 1996 respectively. The BC government introduced the *Forest Practices Code (FPC)* in 1996 to ensure sustainable forest management and therefore respond to the ongoing conflict in the BC forest industry. Finally, elite actors in the field also proposed programs to ensure sustainable forest management. MacMillan Bloedel, the leading forest company, initially proposed a variable retention program and promoted it to other forest companies. Later this program was adapted into an *Eco-System Based Management (EBM)* program, and it was promoted by elite forest companies and elite ENGOs in the organizational field. Table 6.1 provides an overview and captures the important features, sponsors, key adopters and supporters, and perceived disadvantages of each proto-institution.

Institutional co-creation in competitive contexts

We initially summarize our findings here and then present them in detail. In our analysis of the institutional creation work undertaken by actors in the BC coastal forestry context, we found a process of co-creation (shown in Figure 6.1), in which the sponsors of each proto-institution developed an experimental set of features designed to achieve specific objectives. They consulted and promoted the proto-institution with an elite set of potential supporters. These supporters usually suggested or negotiated features in the proto-institution in exchange for their support, in what we are calling a *collaborative co-creation process*. When sufficient support had been obtained, the sponsors and supporters of the proto-institution positioned and promoted their proto-institution to the entire institutional context, and simultaneously disrupted competing proto-institutions. To promote the proto-institutions, they employed logics that were shared by at least some members of the disrupted environment, and that fell into one of three categories: (1) they had been institutionalized within the industry prior to disruption by ENGOs, (2) they had become a shared part of the new institutional context through the disruption process, or (3) they were linked to discourses which had become institutionalized in the broader societal field. By using these logics, developing supportive networks, and setting up coercive mechanisms, proto-institution sponsors were establishing the cognitive, normative, and regulative foundations to maintain their

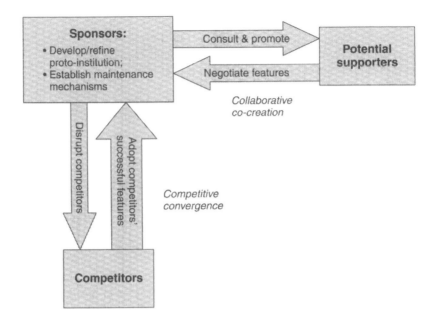

Figure 6.1 Model of institutional co-creation work in a competitive context

proto-institutions. As other proto-institutions were also introduced, each of the competitors observed how members of the organizational field responded to them, tried to influence these responses by disrupting their competitors, and then adopted the features that were valued by the market in a process of *competitive convergence*.

The process of institutional creation work we present in Figure 6.1 was not linear, but iterative: the initial development of a proto-institution usually included some elements of collaborative co-creation and competitive convergence, and these processes continued regularly throughout the years of competition. Sponsors of proto-institutions regularly engaged in disruption of competitors, and promotion of their own proto-institutions. During initial development, they also established the maintenance mechanisms that would, over time, hold their proto-institutions in place. They enhanced the proto-institutions over time with feedback from the institutional environment.

Despite its iterative nature, we describe the model in a linear fashion for clarity. We first describe the initial development, promotion, and disruption activities, then the collaborative co-creation and competitive convergence activities, and finally the maintenance mechanisms.

Initial development

To come up with an initial set of features for its proto-institution, each sponsor identified its own objectives and the objectives of other actors in the context that would be likely to support or oppose the proto-institution. For industry-sponsored programs (CSA and SFI), the dominant objectives were of course to maximize the firm acceptance criteria of industry control, market access, and ease of implementation. However, these programs also had to perform well enough on the forest practices, protected areas, and open-process dimensions to achieve the social legitimacy necessary to maintain market access. For ENGOs and the FSC program, on the other hand, the social legitimacy aspects were dominant, while the firm acceptance aspects were secondary. For the BC government's FPC, all stakeholders had to be satisfied in order to have a successful proto-institution. Because of the forest industry's importance to the BC economy, the industry acceptance criteria were slightly favored by the government. For the elite actors sponsoring the EBM proto-institution, social legitimacy and firm acceptance criteria had to be jointly maximized since both leading firms and leading ENGOs were involved.

The sponsors of each proto-institution initially consulted with their targeted stakeholders in order to understand what features would be acceptable. FSC had the most intensive consultation process, involving representatives from social, environmental, economic, and indigenous peoples' groups from the outset. Similarly the BC government held consultations with forest companies and environmental interests before introducing the FPC. MacMillan Bloedel consulted with ENGOs, the public, the government, academics, consultants, and other industry representatives before it launched variable retention, and later used that research to help convince others to join the group of organizations sponsoring EBM. This group of elite ENGOs and forest companies further conducted joint research on social, ecological, and economic factors, negotiated rules, and then proposed them to a multi-stakeholder group charged with approving any agreements. SFI's and CSA's consultation process focused inwardly on their own forest industry members and on government. Each also had to react to the competing FSC standard, however, necessitating the inclusion of the same components, albeit with greater process- rather than outcome-based standards.

Figure 6.2 illustrates the competitive position of each of the proto-institutions based on its performance on the six objectives, and further

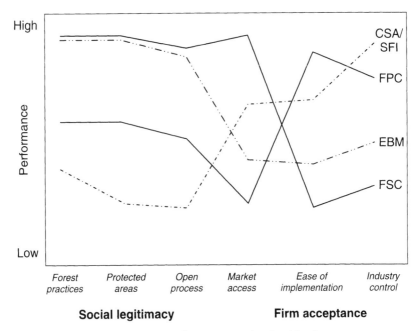

Figure 6.2 Proto-institutions' performance on the six objectives

details are available in the appendix to this chapter. EBM and FSC maximized the social legitimacy criteria, while SFI/CSA maximized the industry acceptance criteria and performed much lower on the social legitimacy criteria. EBM performed slightly better than FSC on ease of implementation and industry control, but potentially poorer on market access due to its local scope; international customers' purchasing criteria were more likely to specify FSC than EBM. Implementation of FSC was challenging for industry members, due to extensive stakeholder involvement including lengthy approval processes and ongoing changes. The BC government's FPC, trying to be all things to all people, was accepted by none. It provided limited social legitimacy performance by protecting new parks, specifying some more sustainable forest practices, and initiating ongoing stakeholder consultation processes, but provided very limited market access benefits and yet still offered industry little control.

Promotion

Proto-institution sponsors and supporters expended considerable effort promoting their proto-institution. We conceptualize these promotional activities as constructing and reinforcing the cognitive, normative, and regulative institutional pillars that form the structure of institutions (Scott, 2001). In doing so, these actors not only added new institutional material but drew on the institutional "detritus" remaining from the disruption of the institutions in the forestry field (Schneiberg, 2007).

Cognitive

According to Scott (2001), the cognitive pillar is associated with comprehensibility, taken-for-grantedness, and a logic of orthodoxy. Actions associated with the cognitive pillar are taken simply because they are considered right and natural. Since the BC forestry field had been so thoroughly disrupted through years of conflict, there was only limited orthodoxy with which to work. However, some of the sponsors linked their proto-institutions to orthodox logics from other fields. For example, the FSC justified the involvement of multiple stakeholders in the development of SFM standards by drawing upon a widely accepted logic that the public should be involved in decisions regarding publicly owned land. While dominant in other areas of public discourse, this notion represented a radical departure from the way forestry had previously been accomplished. Furthermore, FSC borrowed the logic associated with indigenous peoples' land claims, which were surfacing as a significant political issue in the mid-1990s, to justify extensive involvement of environment-friendly indigenous peoples in land-use decisions. Finally, FSC used a market logic to encourage or coerce forest company customers to support FSC (or face consumer boycotts), and to encourage or coerce forest companies to adopt FSC (or face diminished market access). Similarly, the BC government used the orthodoxy of government regulation in the service of protecting public goods when supporting the FPC. The Canadian Standards Association was selected as the organizing body for CSA certification because it was trusted to administer multiple standards across many other categories, suggesting its right to produce the CSA SFM standard would be taken for granted.

Normative

The normative pillar refers to social obligations and moral standards that actors are obliged to follow (Scott, 2001). ENGO supporters set the normative context for FSC, attracting public support through advertising campaigns demonizing the destruction of BC forests. This logic was left over from the disruption of the forestry field. ENGOs promoted the FSC standard as the only certification system able to meet acceptable

moral standards. In one advertisement in *Time* magazine, Pierce
Brosnan, who played British secret agent James Bond, urged consumers
to be "an action hero" and purchase only FSC-certified wood.[5] The FSC
used the resultant public support to appeal to the social and environmental responsibilities and obligations of a cross-section of firms including large retailers, publishers, construction firms, furniture makers, and
homebuilders to gain support for its certification. A spokeswoman for a
large retailer stated: "we have a responsibility as the market leader"
(with respect to sustainably harvested wood), and "we take that very
seriously."[6] Another spokesperson for a different retailer admitted that
while he did not know where the Great Bear Rainforest (a disputed
area) was on a map, "it's certainly a name that means a lot to a lot of
people."[7] The BC government and forest companies also used normative framing: they claimed that adopting the FPC and EBM was "doing
the right thing" to protect the environment. EBM attached itself to the
BC government's multi-stakeholder consultation process, so that the
initial announcement of EBM came from multiple stakeholders in
agreement, suggesting moral appropriateness.

All sponsors constructed supportive networks for their proto-institution
to build a normative community. For example, one ENGO assisted two
leading forest companies in applying for and obtaining FSC certification
for their forest operations.[8,9] MacMillan Bloedel arranged meetings
with other leading forest companies to discuss the conflict with
ENGOs, gave away its research into variable retention harvesting practices, and supported competing firms in improving their ability to
employ variable retention. When that did not work, the firm was
instrumental in establishing the group that sponsored EBM, inviting
other elite firms and ENGOs to participate. The ENGOs in this group
also met other ENGOs to encourage them to accept the EBM process.
Similarly, the forest industry association sponsors of CSA and SFI urged
industry solidarity on forest certification using normative logics.

---

[5] *Vancouver Sun*, January 15, 1999, pp. D1, D12.
[6] *Seattle Times*, November 22, 1999.
[7] Michael McCullough, "Building supplies giant won't buy wood from 'Great Bear
   Rainforest'," *Vancouver Sun*, August 9, 2000, p. A1.
[8] April 25, 2002 press release from WWF. www.wwf.ca/NewsAndFacts/
   NewsRoom/Default.asp, accessed July 19, 2006.
[9] November 14, 2003 press release from WWF. www.wwf.ca/NewsAndFacts/
   NewsRoom/Default.asp, accessed July 19, 2006.

Regulative

Finally, the regulative pillar pertains to laws, rules, and the resulting sanctions that actors are subject to should they deviate. The logic is one of instrumentality (Scott, 2001). Each of the proto-institution sponsors reinforced the regulative pillar by using coercive forces to gain support. For example, the government-backed FPC and EBM carried the weight of law while the American Forest & Paper Association and the Forest Products Association of Canada coerced its members into obtaining certification by establishing it as a membership criterion.

More generally, once firms join any voluntary certification program or standard, they submit to the coercive pressures inherent in the standard and its monitoring (Prakash & Potoski, 2006). Even in cases where firms are not initially coerced into adopting a particular proto-institution, once they became members, proto-institution sponsors are able to apply sanctions including publicly communicating members' violations and revoking membership. The FSC provided an example of this when it removed from membership a firm that was not performing to the standards the FSC and its supporters deemed appropriate.[10]

FSC and its ENGO supporters quite aggressively used coercive forces, co-opting customers of forest products in order to apply market pressure to coerce forest companies into adopting standards. For example, the FSC campaigned to get printing firms to adopt FSC certification, resulting in over twenty-five printers receiving FSC chain of custody certification between 2003 and 2005.[11] This put implicit pressure on providers of pulp and paper products to provide FSC-certified supplies so that printers could provide FSC-certified products. ENGOs demonstrated at large retailers such as Home Depot and Lowe's in order to influence retailers' purchasing policies in favor of FSC-certified wood.[12]

Disrupting alternatives

In addition to promoting their preferred proto-institutions, creators and supporters engaged in activities to discredit alternative proto-institutions.

[10] "Forest giant's operations get ISO approval: Interfor receives certification after passing an independent audit by KPMG Quality Registrar," *Vancouver Sun*, January 22, 2000, p. D3.
[11] "Canadian printers lead the way in FSC," August 4, 2005, FSC press release.
[12] *Vancouver Sun*, August 17, 1999, p. D4.

The most active actors in this endeavor were the ENGOs who actively targeted the "environmentally destructive forest practices endorsed by industry-backed"[13] and "bogus" certifications including the CSA and SFI. They claimed the FPC was "soft" regulation and that the government was "in bed with the forest companies." Both the FPC and the CSA were said to be examples of "putting the fox in charge of the henhouse," and SFI was similarly criticized.

Actors also used legal means to challenge alternatives. For example, in October 2004, the Sierra Legal Defence Fund, on behalf of the Sierra Club of Canada and the National Aboriginal Forestry Association, initiated eleven appeals of forest certifications issued by the CSA, claiming the certified companies did not meet the CSA's own standards.[14] While public critique came mostly from activist organizations rather than firms or governments, privately, forest companies expressed serious concerns about the requirements of the FSC, FPC, and EBM, referring to the "unfinishable agenda" of ENGOs.

Disruptions of alternative standards by the sponsors and supporters occurred throughout the process of creating proto-institutions. The supporters also engaged in promoting proto-institutions and disrupting alternative standards as they contributed to the collaborative co-creation of a particular proto-institution. The next section describes the co-creation process.

Co-creation – competition and collaboration

Over time, the leading proto-institutions became more like each other, while the FPC failed as a standard of sustainable forest management.[15] Sponsors of proto-institutions revised and refined the proto-institutions for two reasons: first, to respond to competitive moves, and second, at the behest of existing or potential supporters, who offered their conditional support. The more dominant players in industry, environmental

[13] "Environmentalists release report warning 'Buyers beware' of bogus forest certification schemes," Greenpeace PR, March 26, 2003.
[14] www.sierraclub.ca/national/programs/biodiversity/forests/campaign.shtml? x=750, accessed May 1, 2007.
[15] Note: the FPC succeeded as an institution, since it was a set of regulations that forest companies in BC had to follow to ensure access to public forests, and 95 percent of the forests in BC are public. However, the FPC had no legitimacy as a signifier of sustainable forest management.

groups, and government took strong leadership roles in the shaping of proto-institutions, leveraging their ability to influence others to gain concessions in the institutional arrangements.

Competitive convergence

As actors promoted their proto-institutions, they adapted their strategy and product offering to match the emerging competitive environment. This involved blending elements of the accepted strategies of other proto-institutions, while balancing the stringency of requirements against their ease of implementation. For example, a CSA representative originally expressed the opinion that labeling programs result in a "hodgepodge of competing claims."[16] However, as the FSC labeling system began to gain acceptance, the CSA shifted gears and in 2001 adopted its own forest products labeling program.[17] SFI and CSA each enhanced their stakeholder consultation processes and implemented some performance-based measures as a result of FSC's strengths in that area (Von Mirbach, 2004: 21).

The SFI responded to criticisms that it only served industry interests by constructing an independent board to manage the program.[18] FSC was similarly criticized for being too close to ENGOs; it countered with public relations messages distancing itself from them. Both SFI and CSA responded to FSC's transnational approach (featuring global principles for international recognition and local customization for stakeholder support) by gaining the support of the Program for the Endorsement of Forest Certifications, a European certifier of certifiers.

This competitive convergence is not unique to the BC context. As McNichol (2006: 372) described, "Competing alternative programs that originally appeared to thwart the FSC's efforts have slowly morphed, seemingly paradoxically, to embrace and embody (at least on paper) many of the same rules and norms within their operations."

Collaborative co-creation

Proto-institution sponsors also responded to the demands of supporters both in the initial design of proto-institutions, and in subsequent

---

[16] 1996, State of Canada's Forest Industry.
[17] CSA Press Release, July 20, 2001. www.csagroup.org/news/releases/default.asp, accessed July 19, 2006.
[18] www.sfiprogram.org/aboutsfi.cfm, accessed May 5, 2007.

adaptations. As the proto-institution was implemented, supporters were able to judge its effectiveness with respect to their criteria and put pressure on sponsors to make changes. For example, when the BC government's stance shifted to become more industry-friendly, the government adapted the FPC to the needs of industry by simplifying its implementation, changing it from a process and results-focused standard, to a results-only standard to be self-monitored by the industry.[19] The development of the EBM and FSC standards represented similar collaborative efforts among multiple stakeholder groups. When FSC was faced with customer complaints that FSC-certified products were not available in sufficient quantities to achieve the targets ENGOs demanded of customers, FSC responded with a number of changes. First, they allowed small woodlot owners to band together to save time and resources in achieving FSC certification. Next, they also relaxed the percentage of FSC-certified wood required for labeling in a manufactured product. Finally, FSC partnered with two forest companies (Tembec and Domtar) to encourage additional supply. In short, many actors had to negotiate features with supporters both in the early phases of proto-institution development, and later on to adapt the proto-institution. Supporters thus helped to co-create the proto-institutions by negotiating features in exchange for their support.

Establishing maintenance mechanisms

The final form of institutional co-creation work we found focused on constructing institutional maintenance mechanisms to facilitate the persistence of proto-institutions. Starting at initial creation, each of the proto-institutions studied included planned or actual mechanisms for their own maintenance both to ensure the proto-institution "stuck" among early adopters and to stabilize the proto-institution once it became more widely adopted. The mechanisms worked by reinforcing the regulative, cognitive, and normative pillars of the proto-institution.

Sponsors and supporters created these maintenance mechanisms in a variety of ways. First, they changed or established incentive structures and coercive mechanisms that reinforced desired behaviors. They constructed normative networks and reinforced solidarity among existing ones to establish a community of shared meanings which would

---

[19] BC Government Forest Practices Home Page – www.for.gov.bc.ca/tasb/legsregs/fpc/, accessed May 5, 2007.

reproduce the institution. Finally, sponsors and supporters continued to link proto-institutions to existing logics in the field through ongoing promotion and maintenance efforts.

Specifically, the industry associations modified their membership rules to require members to obtain their preferred certifications.[20] This coercive pressure had the added effect of creating a normative network that built and enhanced solidarity among industry members, particularly with respect to SFI. The solidarity not only acted as a normative foundation for compliance, but was probably responsible for the FSC's inability to generate sufficient timber supply in North America, which led to a relaxation of FSC standards (Gale, 2004). Auditing and monitoring functions also served as common regulative maintenance mechanisms. The BC government's Ministry of Forests actively monitored companies' compliance with the FPC. Each of the standards mandated that its requirements be embedded in a forest company's standard operating procedures, and certification bodies required ongoing re-certifications. The FPC, EBM, and FSC also relied on deterrence to maintain proto-institutional compliance by emphasizing that ongoing conflict could only be avoided if companies followed the rules.

Discussion

We have described the institutional creation work associated with "building the iron cage" in disrupted and competitive contexts by examining the efforts of actors who developed and supported competing proto-institutions. We have described five categories of activities including initial development, promotion, disrupting alternatives, co-creation, and establishing maintenance mechanisms. These activities are found to operate in no fixed order and in a highly iterative manner. Institutional work does not proceed in a linear fashion from disruption to creation to maintenance, but instead involves all three of these activities at the same time and during substantially overlapping time periods.

We find that institutional creation work involves two co-creation mechanisms which each operate to ensure proto-institutions embed

[20] Members of the American Forest Products Association were required to obtain SFI certification. Members of the Forest Products Association of Canada were required to obtain at least one of CSA, SFI, or FSC certification.

the interests of multiple actors in the institutional context. The first mechanism is *collaborative co-creation* where adjustments are made to proto-institutions in response to the demands of potential supporters. The second mechanism is *competitive convergence*, where proto-institutions are adjusted in response to feedback from potential adopters of the proto-institution on creators' own proto-institutions as well as on competing proto-institutions. Actors create experimental proposals for adoption and discuss and promote them with potential supporters. They adapt them to accommodate supporters' needs, promote them more broadly, and simultaneously work to disrupt competing institutions. The proto-institutions are refined by competitive convergence, where successful features of other proto-institutions are imitated, and by collaborative co-creation, where through extensive discussion and collective decision-making among multiple supporters of a proto-institution, a common meaning system emerges, facilitating proto-institution adoption. Finally, proto-institution sponsors create mechanisms to maintain their proto-institutions, both while they are in the development stage and going forward. We have thus addressed our research question concerning how institutional actors create new institutional arrangements, forming a new iron cage, and how they adapt these arrangements as they compete for dominance in disrupted environments. We have shown that the iron cage is the work of many craftspeople that knowingly and unknowingly, competitively and collaboratively, work together towards the development of a dominant logic and taken-for-granted practices.

Institutional creation work in the context of competition

Prior studies frequently describe institution creation work in the absence of competition, highlighting institutional entrepreneurs with singular visions and relatively unconstrained agency pursuing specific projects. While it has been understood that these institutional entrepreneurs must build support for their institutional change projects, prior work has not emphasized the tradeoffs inherent in such promotion work.[21] Support comes with a price, and usually involves an adaptation of the proto-institution to embed something that will privilege or

---

[21] Though such tradeoffs seem similar in nature to Selznick's (1949) notion of co-optation.

protect the interests of supporters. Even non-supporters' interests constrain an institutional entrepreneur's actions if those interests have attracted sufficient attention.

Interests among groups often conflict; proto-institution creators are thus unable to satisfy the demands of all people. Since actors have several competing proto-institutions which they can adopt, they are able to leverage their influence to demand revisions and thereby co-create institutions with proto-institution sponsors. The set of features in any proto-institution that is sufficiently diffused is likely to reflect the relative power positions of each actor in the institutional context. In our study, ENGOs were able to generate sufficient support to require inclusion of features like stakeholder consultation and forest practices in every proposed proto-institution. The ENGOs' influence significantly changed the nature of mainstream decision-making in forestry. Yet they had not, as of the time of writing, been able to completely dictate the nature of new proto-institutions because forest companies continued to maintain a strong power position in the BC coastal forestry context.

More generally, regardless of which proto-institution wins the contest for dominance (if any do), institutional creation is not likely to be a winner-take-all game. The mechanisms of collaborative co-creation and competitive convergence ensure that the interests of various actors will be embedded in the winning proto-institution to the extent that those actors are able to command support and resources for their institutional projects.

Thus, instead of the institutional design work featured in the institutional entrepreneurship literature, we see a much greater emphasis on collective action (Hargrave & Van de Ven, 2006: 882), involving "political action among distributed, partisan, and embedded actors" which we see as playing out through collaborative co-creation and competitive convergence mechanisms. Each actor (with influence), striving for their own interests, will add their own design features to the iron cage. Through the mechanisms of co-creation and convergence, the final institutional arrangements are likely to embed the interests of all the key players, at a particular point in time, into a tightly woven structure. The complexity of the iron cage structure (due to the multiple embedded interests) makes the cage durable and constraining in the face of efforts to change it; each component of the cage supports the interests of some relatively influential members of the organizational field. While the empirical story presented here and other research demonstrate that institutional change is possible and the iron cage is not impervious to attack and destruction, this process of co-creation illustrates some of the reasons behind the constraining force of the iron cage.

While we believe that collaborative co-creation and competitive convergence are both likely to occur and operate together in disrupted environments, based on the analysis of our empirical context, we speculate that they may lead to different outcomes. In processes of collaborative co-creation, actors with different agendas and meaning systems work together to construct the institutional arrangements, and in doing so, they develop the *common* meaning systems that characterize stable organizational fields (Scott, 2001). Collaboratively created proto-institutions are much more likely to diffuse to the actors that have developed the shared meaning systems to support them. Co-creators can then adjust the way they frame the solutions to align with the meaning systems that dominate within their own networks, to diffuse the innovations further, assisted by the social capital they have within their own networks. The iron cage becomes stronger, and the institution diffuses among a larger group of actors.

On the contrary, we believe that where competitive creation dominates over co-creation, it is much more likely that the field will segment into niches, each supporting a particular set of arrangements. Through competitive convergence, the same features may exist across different proto-institutions, but they may have different interpretations within niches, and niche participants may disagree violently with the interpretations of other niches. Furthermore, the logics of competition and conflict themselves will limit the willingness of actors to adopt other proto-institutions across niches, even when they have similar features. For example, while FSC and EBM similarly protect forest practices and ecologically sensitive areas and are equally onerous to implement, the inclusive development process of EBM made it much more acceptable to the forest companies than FSC, and not less acceptable to the ENGOs. Forest companies have been constrained by their previously institutionalized beliefs about environmentalists (and vice versa), and thus had trouble understanding ENGO demands even while they understood they needed to respond to them. Forest companies believed that ENGOs had an "unfinishable agenda" that would permanently create uncertainty for them, and so any solution developed predominantly by ENGOs was distrusted. Accepting FSC would be "giving in" to environmentalists' demands. Similarly, the ENGOs' belief that you couldn't leave the "fox in charge of the henhouse" prevented them from accepting CSA or SFI, even as these systems became more convergent with more stringent proto-institutions.

These competitive logics are examples of detritus left over from the prior periods of institutional stability and disruptive conflict (Schneiberg, 2007). While Schneiberg (2007) spoke of the leftover institutional material from paths not taken, this paper also identified the leftover institutional material from paths taken, then disrupted.

These bits of detritus, like the institutions once associated with them, can be both enabling and constraining. As a number of authors have suggested, the institutional material can be enabling because it can be overlain onto new innovations, facilitating their acceptance (e.g. Aldrich & Fiol, 1994; Hargadon & Douglas, 2001; Rao, Monin & Durand, 2003). Further, the detritus can be used by institutional entrepreneurs as a starting point around which they can build support (Schneiberg, 2007; Marquis & Lounsbury, 2007). Conversely, the detritus can be constraining because even in disrupted contexts, certain institutional materials will still have significant influence among some groups, and institutional entrepreneurs must find a way to navigate through the leftover logics, practices, and relationships that continue to exist in the institutional context, since these contradictory logics are resources which can be used to contest the legitimacy of innovations (Suddaby & Greenwood, 2005).

Implications for theories of institutional change

Our findings have implications for theories of institutional change. We address the criticism of the many stories that exist in the literature of heroic institutional entrepreneurs, who, either as individuals (e.g. Hargadon & Douglas, 2001; Maguire *et al.*, 2004), or as organizations (e.g. Garud *et al.*, 2002; Greenwood *et al.*, 2002; Hensmans, 2003), bring about institutional change through sheer force of will and who are somehow undersocialized and unconstrained by institutional arrangements. Instead, we share with other authors an image of interest-driven actions by actors in an institutional context who are not undersocialized, but who may be both constrained by some logics and enabled by others because of the existence of competing logics and a diversity of institutional materials (Schneiberg, 2007; Greenwood & Suddaby, 2006).

Yet we also identify that there are multiple actors that are navigating the diverse institutional debris, and several of them may be acting independently and concurrently as institutional entrepreneurs. These actors craft strategies to effect institutional change; however, they pursue their projects while other actors are simultaneously pursuing different projects. Through the mechanisms of collaborative co-creation and competitive convergence, the proto-institutions they develop are significantly modified by each other's presence, and as a result, much more reflective of the interests of multiple actors in the field. Proposed changes are experimented with and the demand for various features is assessed in a market for acceptance of the institutional arrangement. In short, institutional change is emergent, resulting from the interests of multiple actors embedded in the new institutional arrangements, reinforcing the arrangement's durability in the face of future changes.

This study also deals with the divergence between some examples of institutional change that suggest that institutional entrepreneurs must overlay new institutional arrangements with existing features (e.g. Aldrich & Fiol, 1994; Hargadon & Douglas, 2001) and others that describe actors who reject and vilify existing institutional logics (e.g. Hensmans, 2003). Extending the work of Schneiberg (2007), we show that in disrupted organizational fields both examples are valid. The detritus from past institutions *and* the institutional material from the conflict itself exist in the context, along with societal logics to which field members are exposed. Actors draw widely from the institutional material littering the path, either applying it or vilifying it, recognizing that elements will resonate with some groups more than with others. Through co-creation processes, actors may find a way to integrate competing and diverse logics. Through competitive convergence processes, actors may find a way to build enough elements into a proto-institution that appeal to those with competing logics that the proto-institution becomes accepted. Yet diffusion may be prevented if actors are unable to shed their past identities as enemies. We thus find that even in very disrupted institutional environments, the detritus of past arrangements and battles constrains the acceptance of institutional change projects, but also enables them due to a richer set of material available to institutional entrepreneurs.

Conclusions

We have focused attention on the competition among proto-institutions in disrupted and competitive field contexts, identifying the institutional work undertaken by actors to create, promote, and refine their proto-institutions and respond to competitive moves. This research fills a gap in the study of institutional emergence by focusing on the study of institutions in the making, arising within heavily disrupted organizational fields. Proto-institutions in competitive contexts are adapted and refined until they begin to converge on acceptable institutional arrangements. This process of collaborative refinement and competitive convergence explains how the interests of influential actors both inside and outside the organizational field become embedded in institutional arrangements. The process of competition or collaboration surfaces their demands, and the support those demands are able to attract determines whether or not they become embedded in convergent solutions. We also observed that institutional creation, disruption, and maintenance occur simultaneously during institutional competitions, and that some new institutional creation is driven by a desire to preserve the power positions of incumbents in organizational fields.

We expect that this co-creation process by multiple actors of different types is much more common than the current literature suggests. Furthermore, it may be rising in importance over time, as more actors, and more non-traditional actors, involve themselves in new arenas, especially through the rise of social and environmental sustainability issues. We submit that the co-creation of institutional arrangements represents a promising area for future study.

References

Ahmadjian, C. L. & Robinson, P. (2001) Safety in numbers: downsizing and the deinstitutionalization of permanent employment in Japan. *Administrative Science Quarterly*, 46(4): 622–654.

Aldrich, H. E. & Fiol, C. M. (1994) Fools rush in? The institutional context of industry creation. *Academy of Management Review*, 19(4): 645–670.

Anand, N. & Peterson, R. A. (2000) When market information constitutes fields: sensemaking of markets in the commercial music industry. *Organization Science*, 11(3): 270–284.

Ang, S. & Cummings, L. L. (1997) Strategic response to institutional influences on information systems outsourcing. *Organization Science*, 8(3): 235–256.

Barley, S. R. (1986) Technology as an occasion for structuring: evidence from observations of CT scanners and the social order of radiology departments. *Administrative Science Quarterly*, 31(1): 78–108.

Beckert, J. (1999) Agency, entrepreneurs, and institutional change: the role of strategic choice and institutionalized practices in organizations. *Organization Studies*, 20(5): 777–799.

DiMaggio, P. J. (1988) Interest and agency in institutional theory. In L. Zucker (ed.), *Institutional Patterns and Organizations: Culture and Environment*, pp. 3–21. Cambridge, MA: Ballinger.

DiMaggio, P. J. & Powell, W. W. (1983) The iron cage revisited: institutional isomorphism and collective rationality in organizational fields. *American Sociological Review*, 48(2): 147–160.

Fligstein, N. (1991) The structural transformation of American industry: an institutional account of the causes of diversification in the largest firms, 1919–1979. In W. W. Powell & P. J. DiMaggio (eds.), *The New Institutionalism in Organizational Analysis*, pp. 311–336. Chicago: University of Chicago Press.

　(2001) *The Architecture of Markets: An Economic Sociology of Twenty-First-Century Capitalist Societies*. Princeton, NJ: Princeton University Press.

Fox-Wolfgramm, S. J., Boal, K. B. & Hunt, J. G. (1998) Organizational adaptation to institutional change: a comparative study of first-order change in prospector and defender banks. *Administrative Science Quarterly*, 43 (1): 87–126.

Gale, F. (2004) The consultation dilemma in private regulatory regimes: negotiating FSC regional standards in the United States and Canada. *Journal of Environmental Policy & Planning*, 6(1): 57–84.

Galvin, T. L. (2002) Examining institutional change: evidence from the founding dynamics of US health care interest associations. *Academy of Management Journal*, 45(4): 673–699.

Garud, R., Jain, S. & Kumaraswamy, A. (2002) Institutional entrepreneurship in the sponsorship of common technological standards: the case of Sun Microsystems and Java. *Academy of Management Journal*, 45(1): 196–214.

Greenwood, R. & Hinings, C. (1996) Understanding radical organizational change: bringing together the old and the new institutionalism. *Academy of Management Review*, 21(4): 1022–1054.

Greenwood, R. & Suddaby, R. (2006) Institutional entrepreneurship in mature fields: the big five accounting firms. *Academy of Management Journal*, 49(1): 27–48.

Greenwood, R., Suddaby, R. & Hinings, C. R. (2002) Theorizing change: the role of professional associations in the transformation of institutionalized fields. *Academy of Management Journal*, 45(1): 58–80.

Hargadon, A. B. & Douglas, Y. (2001) When innovations meet institutions: Edison and the design of the electric light. *Administrative Science Quarterly*, 46(3): 476–501.

Hargrave, T. J. & Van de Ven, A. H. (2006) A collective action model of institutional innovation. *Academy of Management Review*, 31(4): 864–888.

Hensmans, M. (2003) Social movement organizations: a metaphor for strategic actors in institutional fields. *Organization Studies*, 24(3): 355–381.

Hoffman, A. J. (1999) Institutional evolution and change: environmentalism and the US chemical industry. *Academy of Management Journal*, 42(4): 351–371.

Holm, P. (1995) The dynamics of institutionalization: transformation processes in Norwegian fisheries. *Administrative Science Quarterly*, 40(3): 398–422.

Jepperson, R. L. (1991) Institutions, institutional effects, and institutionalism. In W. W. Powell & P. J. DiMaggio (eds.), *The New Institutionalism in Organizational Analysis*, pp. 143–163. Chicago: University of Chicago Press.

Jick, T. D. (1979) Mixing qualitative and quantitative methods: triangulation in action. *Administrative Science Quarterly*, 24(4): 602–611.

Langley, A. (1999) Strategies for theorizing from process data. *Academy of Management Review*, 24(4): 691–710.

Lawrence, T. B., Hardy, C. & Phillips, N. (2002) Institutional effects of interorganizational collaboration: the emergence of proto-institutions. *Academy of Management Journal*, 45(1): 281–290.

Lawrence, T. B. & Suddaby, R. (2006) Institutions and institutional work. In S. R. Clegg, C. Hardy, T. B. Lawrence & W. R. Nord (eds.), *Handbook of Organization Studies*, 2nd edn., pp. 214–254. London: Sage.

Levy, D. & Scully, M. (2007) The institutional entrepreneur as modern prince: the strategic face of power in contested fields. *Organization Studies*, 28(7): 971–991.

Maguire, S., Hardy, C. & Lawrence, T. B. (2004) Institutional entrepreneurship in emerging fields: HIV/AIDS treatment advocacy in Canada. *Academy of Management Journal*, 47(5): 657–679.

Marquis, C. & Lounsbury, M. (2007) Vive la résistance: competing logics and the consolidation of US community banking. *Academy of Management Journal*, 50(4): 799–820.

McAdam, D. & Scott, W. R. (2005) Organizations and social movements. In G. Davis, D. McAdam, W. Scott & M. Zald (eds.), *Social Movements and Organization Theory*, pp. 4–40. Cambridge: Cambridge University Press.

McNichol, J. (2006) Transnational NGO certification programs as new regulatory forms: lessons from the forestry sector. In M. L. Djelic & K. Sahlin-Andersson (eds.), *Transnational Governance: Institutional*

Dynamics of Regulation, pp. 349–375. Cambridge: Cambridge University Press.

Meyer, J.W. & Rowan, B. (1977) Institutionalized organizations: formal structure as myth and ceremony. *American Journal of Sociology*, 83(2): 340–363.

Miles, M.B. & Huberman, A.M. (1984) *Analysing Qualitative Data: A Source Book for New Methods*. Beverly Hills, CA: Sage.

Munir, K.A. (2005) The social construction of events: a study of institutional change in the photographic field. *Organization Studies*, 26(1): 93–112.

North, D.C. (1990) *Institutions, Institutional Change and Economic Performance*. Cambridge: Cambridge University Press.

Oliver, C. (1991) Strategic responses to institutional processes. *Academy of Management Review*, 16(1): 145–179.

(1992) The antecedents of deinstitutionalization. *Organization Studies*, 13 (4): 563–588.

Pfeffer, J. & Salancik, G.R. (1978) *The External Control of Organizations*. New York: Harper & Row.

Prakash, A. & Potoski, M. (2006) *The Voluntary Environmentalists: Green Clubs, ISO 14001, and Voluntary Environmental Regulations*. Cambridge: Cambridge University Press.

Rao, H., Monin, P. & Durand, R. (2003) Institutional change in Toque Ville: nouvelle cuisine as an identity movement in French gastronomy. *American Journal of Sociology*, 108(4): 795–843.

Reay, T. & Hinings, C. (2005) The recomposition of an organizational field: health care in Alberta. *Organization Studies*, 26(3): 351–384.

Schneiberg, M. (2007) What's on the path? Path dependence, organizational diversity and the problem of institutional change in the US economy, 1900–1950. *Socio-Economic Review*, 5(1): 47–80.

Scott, W.R. (2001) *Institutions and Organizations*, 2nd edn. Thousand Oaks, CA: Sage.

Selznick, P. (1949) *TVA and the Grass Roots*. Berkeley: University of California Press.

Seo, M.G. & Creed, W.E.D. (2002) Institutional contradictions, praxis, and institutional change: a dialectical perspective. *Academy of Management review*, 27(2): 222–247.

Suddaby, R. & Greenwood, R. (2005) Rhetorical strategies of legitimacy. *Administrative Science Quarterly*, 50(1): 35–67.

Von Mirbach, M. (2004) *Footprints in the Forest: Current Practice and Future Challenges in Forest Certification*. Ottawa: Sierra Club.

Washington, M. (2004) Field approaches to institutional change: the evolution of the National Collegiate Athletic Association 1906–1995. *Organization Studies*, 25(3): 393.

Wijen, F. & Ansari, S. (2007) Overcoming inaction through collective institutional entrepreneurship: insights from regime theory. *Organization Studies*, 28 (7): 1079.

Zilber, T. B. (2002) Institutionalization as an interplay between actions, meanings, and actors: the case of a rape crisis center in Israel. *Academy of Management Journal*, 45(1): 234–254.

Zucker, L. G. (1977) The role of institutionalization in cultural persistence. *American Sociological Review*, 42(5): 726–743.

Appendix. *Detailed assessment of each proto-institution*

	FSC	FPC	SFI	CSA	EBM
Principal target supporters	ENGOs; customers of forest companies; consumers.	Forest companies; ENGOs; the public.	Forest companies; customers of forest companies.	Forest companies; customers of forest companies.	Forest companies; ENGOs; government; customers of forest companies; other stakeholders.
Geographic focus	Transnational	BC	US	Canada	Coastal BC
Value of proposition	*Consensus-based to protect environmental, social, and economic values; locally customized; specialized markets for wood; stops pressure.*	*Strengthened government regulations to protect the environment and answer critics.*	*US forest company rallying point to define certification on industry terms, to answer some critics, and present an alternative to FSC.*	*Industry-friendly certification to answer some critics and present an alternative to FSC.*	*Forest Cos: stops pressure; ENGOs: protects eco-systems; provides an open decision process; Gov't: stops pressure, resolves stakeholder conflict; Other stakeholders: protects interests.*
Social legitimacy (forest practices, protected areas, and process)	**High:** Universally recognized by ENGOs as strong acceptable standard.	**Low:** Considered baseline by ENGOs.	**Low:** Viewed as insufficient by ENGOs.	**Low:** Viewed as insufficient by ENGOs.	**High:** Strong broad local support suggests effective at reducing disruptions.

Market access benefits	High: Internationally recognized – satisfies most stringent purchasing policies.	Low: Not part of customer purchasing policies.	Moderate: Approved by Program for Endorsement of Forest Certifications.	Moderate: Approved by Program for Endorsement of Forest Certifications.	Low to moderate: A British Columbia-specific arrangement.
Ease of implementation	Difficult: Significantly different forest practices required and subject to ongoing stakeholder input.	Moderately difficult at first, easier with structures in place.	Relatively simple	Relatively simple	Difficult: Significantly different forest practices required and subject to ongoing stakeholder input.
Industry control	Low: The stakeholder consultation process is ongoing and firms are subject to revisions. Industry interests are weakly represented.	High: Reproduces prior industry/government control of process.	High: The industry initially set these standards and continued to wield significant influence.	Moderate to high: This standard has more.	Moderate: Ongoing stakeholder input.

7 | Scandinavian institutionalism – a case of institutional work

EVA BOXENBAUM AND
JESPER STRANDGAARD PEDERSEN

INSTITUTIONAL theory has witnessed a fairly successful stream of research and has witnessed a renaissance within the social sciences over the last couple of decades. This has created a diffusion of institutional theory into a number of disciplines within the social sciences and resulted in the creation of a distinction between different types of institutionalisms like economical, sociological, and historical institutionalism (Scott, 1995, 2008). A widely used distinction within institutional theory has also been a division between "old institutionalism" and "new institutionalism" (see, for example, DiMaggio & Powell, 1991; Czarniawska & Sevón, 1996; Hirsch & Lounsbury, 1997). Lately it has also become customary to talk about a particular Scandinavian approach to organization studies (e.g. Engwall, 2003; Kreiner, 2007; Olsen, 2007) and about a "Scandinavian institutionalism" as a distinctive and identifiable variant of institutionalism (e.g. Czarniawska & Sevón, 1996, 2003; Lægreid, 2007; Røvik, 2007; Greenwood, Sahlin, Oliver & Suddaby, 2008; Sahlin & Wedlin, 2008). This chapter aims at identifying and presenting the origin of what could be termed Scandinavian institutionalism and at characterizing its main features and its emerging boundaries.

In a way it seems like a paradox to claim the existence of a Scandinavian brand of institutional theory. Institutional theory emphasizes processes of isomorphism, homology, and standardization in an

* The authors would like to thank colleagues in the Department of Organization at Copenhagen Business School, notably Søren Christensen, Susse Georg, Peter Kjær, Kristian Kreiner, Chris Mathieu, Majken Schultz, and Ann Westenholz for providing thoughtful input to this chapter. We would also like to thank the editors and other participants in the conference on institutional work held at Vancouver in June 2007, as well as an anonymous reviewer, for drawing attention to this topic, and the editors for assigning us this interesting task.

ever more globalized world, hence it may seem paradoxical to claim that Scandinavia has been shielded from the isomorphic pressures of prevailing institutional theory. Yet, as we will argue, Scandinavian institutionalism highlights organizational variation and distinctiveness rather than isomorphism and standardization. However, variation and distinctiveness are precisely the preconditions that make it interesting and relevant to study processes of convergence. What initially appears as significant variation across organizations may, upon scrunity, turn out to be only slightly different versions of a similar organizational form, and vice versa (Brunsson & Olsen, 1998). This line of inquiry has emerged within Scandinavia in response to a range of contextual factors that we explain in this chapter. We thus agree with other researchers that research traditions are historical products (e.g. Czarniawska & Sevón, 2003; Olsen, 2007; Kreiner, 2007). This feature makes it relevant to talk about a regional variant of institutional theory.

Our narrative is about the birth and characteristics of Scandinavian institutionalism. It is simultaneously an account of institutional work, not least the unintentional effects of institutional work. Institutional work refers to the relatively invisible micro-processes of intentional actions that individuals engage in to further their own interests (Lawrence & Suddaby, 2006). Actions become institutional work when they simultaneously contribute, often in unanticipated ways, to advance institutional projects (see the introduction to this book). In other words, institutional work captures the deliberate actions that produce an institutional effect, regardless of whether this effect is antici-pated and desired at the outset. Our narrative illustrates one case in which the interplay of agency, intentionality, effort, accomplishment, and unintentional consequences, which together make up institutional work, led to the unanticipated creation of Scandinavian institutionalism as a new and distinct field of study.

More specifically, this chapter illustrates how deliberate actions to formalize transatlantic collaborations produced the unintentional institutional effect of giving birth to Scandinavian institutionalism. As we will argue, it was the deliberate efforts of a small group of actors that brought about Scandinavian institutionalism. It started, as we will show, with a few Scandinavian and American researchers who shared a research interest in how public reforms affect organi-zational practice. They first set out to create an informal academic network and then made efforts to formalize this academic network when they launched the Scandinavian Consortium for Organizational Research (SCANCOR) in 1988 at the heart of the Stanford University campus. It was only years later that these deliberate actions to formalize stimulating academic encounters inadvertently gave rise to Scandinavian institutionalism. We describe this unintentional effect and demonstrate that Scandinavian institutionalism has indeed taken on a life of its own in recent years.

We begin the chapter with a chronological account of the intentional efforts of actors. We introduce the actors and explain how they proceeded, quite deliberately, to formalize a research network on organization studies. Having outlined their intentions, actions, and accomplishments, we then turn our attention to the unintentional consequences of their deliberate efforts. We present the distinctive features and boundaries of Scandinavian institutionalism as we perceive them from our situated point of view as Scandinavians. It is thus an inside-out approach to identifying Scandinavian institutionalism. Certainly, close distance and embeddedness in local institutions may lead us to characterize Scandinavian institutionalism in a different way than would others who perceive it from a greater distance or from a different vantage point. Thus this is not an authoritative account but rather a situated narrative of the creation of a new institution. Nevertheless, we conclude the chapter with a discussion of what our narrative tells us about institutional work and what we think Scandinavian institutionalism can bring to the institutionalist literature.

Deliberate actions

From informal network to formal organization (1970–1988)

It is always difficult to determine the origins of something and when it began. This also goes for the history and development of what has been coined as, and captured by, the notion of Scandinavian institutionalism. One might claim that the roots of Scandinavian institutionalism goes back to the 1970s and 1980s. During the 1970s an informal network of scholars gradually formed around Professor James G. March from Stanford University. March had on several occasions been visiting Scandinavia and the research institutions in Denmark, Finland, Norway, and Sweden where he engaged in different kinds of collaboration with researchers from business schools and universities. The book

Ambiguity and Choice in Organizations, edited by March and Olsen (1976, 1979), contains contributions from a number of Scandinavian researchers and is one example and early evidence of this collaboration. The book is about decision-making with a particular focus on loose coupling. It challenges the notions of organizations as densely linked systems, marked by clear means–end goals and aligned with intentional plans, a research theme in which March and the Scandinavian researchers had a common interest.[1] An informal research network gradually emerged around March with a core group of Scandinavian scholars consisting of Nils Brunsson from the Stockholm School of Economics (Sweden), Søren Christensen from Copenhagen Business School (Denmark), Johan P. Olsen from LOS Centeret (Norway), and Guje Sevón from the Swedish School of Economics in Helsinki (Finland).

For more than a decade, from the mid 1970s to the late 1980s, this informal network around March was gradually developed and expanded. Over the years, researchers from Scandinavian business schools and universities visited March at Stanford University on longer- or shorter-term bases. During these stays at Stanford University, the Scandinavian researchers (visiting professors, PhD students, etc.) attended meetings, seminars, and courses, through which they came into contact with Stanford faculty and PhD students. Prominent institutional scholars such as W. Richard Scott and John W. Meyer and their respective PhD students were among the first acquaintances of the Scandinavian scholars visiting Stanford University. This is how many Scandinavian researchers were exposed to new ideas and new organizational theories, including institutional theory.[2]

Creating an institution (1988–1995)

At the end of the 1980s the Stanford–Scandinavian network had grown to proportions that were increasingly difficult to handle on an informal basis. At this time, something occurred that could be identified as institutional work in the sense of institutional creation: the informal network became formalized and institutionalized through the establishment

---

[1] See also Hallett and Ventresca (2006) for a depiction of the American research community of organizational sociologists, political scientists, and social psychologists studying educational bureaucracies as exemplars of loosely coupled organizations.

[2] The significance of this contact between Scandinavian and American researchers is also noted in Lægreid (2007).

of the Scandinavian Consortium for Organizational Research (SCANCOR). On September 15, 1988, a formal organization was created at Stanford University with a board, a director, and a secretary. The board was composed of Scandinavian researchers, one representative per country, and James G. March was elected director. The mission of SCANCOR became "to advance research and development in the social sciences, particularly in the area of organizational studies; to operate facilities at Stanford University to support Scandinavian visiting scholars at Stanford; to facilitate and support collaboration among its member institutions; and, to facilitate and encourage collaboration among scholars at Stanford, in Scandinavia, and in other research centers in Europe."[3]

The funding for SCANCOR came from seven educational institutions (universities and business schools) in the Scandinavian countries.[4] Each member paid a fee that secured sufficient financial resources to rent office space at Stanford University. Hence, on March 10, 1989, SCANCOR established its physical premises within the Department of Education on the Stanford University campus. The visits from Scandinavia, which had previously been organized informally, became subject to a formal application procedure, wherein the board (Nils Brunsson from Sweden, Søren Christensen from Denmark, Johan P. Olsen from Norway, and Guje Sevón from Finland) made decisions in collaboration with James G. March on the formal applications to visit SCANCOR.

Another example of institutional work and institutional agency is the creation in 1990 of a junior network of scholars among Scandinavian PhD students and assistant professors. The network was founded on the initiative of, and with financial support from, the SCANCOR board. Over the next four to five years, the Scandinavian Young Scholars Network developed into a network that held annual workshops and conferences in the various Scandinavian countries. SCANCOR also made arrangements with senior researchers, notably James G. March,

---

[3] Source: SCANCOR homepage.
[4] The seven Scandinavian universities and business schools behind the creation of SCANCOR were Copenhagen Business School (Denmark), Stockholm School of Economics (Sweden), Norwegian School of Economics, University of Bergen and Norwegian Research Centre in Organization and Management (Norway), Swedish School of Economics in Helsinki, Helsinki School of Economics, and Åbo Akademi (Finland). Later on Iceland joined the other countries with the University of Iceland as a member.

W. Richard Scott, and John W. Meyer, to give talks, lectures, and research seminars at the annual meetings in the Scandinavian Young Scholars Network. These activities were important for the creation and maintenance of the network, and for the diffusion of ideas and theories among the community of young Scandinavian scholars. The network of young scholars was not created with the intent of diffusing institutional theory throughout Scandinavia but this effect nevertheless occurred in the early 1990s when institutional theory came to be one of the new and exciting theories of social science in Scandinavia (as well as in Europe and the United States).

Scandinavian organizational research had a strong emphasis on organizational culture and symbolism in the 1980s. In the early 1990s, the Scandinavian research interest in organizational culture gradually shifted in the direction of new institutional theory. This shift was initially driven by research in public organizations and public reforms that were taking place in Norway and Sweden at the time.[5] The books *Rediscovering Institutions – The Organizational Basis of Politics*, by March and Olsen (1989), and *The Reforming Organization*, edited by Brunsson and Olsen (1993), are good examples of this budding interest in new institutionalism and public organizations. During the early 1990s, many activities took place that can be characterized as acts of institutional work, including seminars, workshops, and mini-conferences attended by researchers from both Scandinavia and Stanford University. In 1992, for example, a group of eight scholars from Copenhagen Business School visited researchers from both New York University (Charles Fombrun, Steven Mezias, Theresa Lant, and Raghu Garud) and Stanford University (James G. March, John W. Meyer, W. Richard Scott, Mark C. Suchman, Patricia Thornton, and Marc Ventresca). These visits resulted the following year in a mini-conference held on the island of Moen in Denmark. This mini-conference led to the publication in 1995 of the book *The Institutional Construction of Organizations – International and Longitudinal Studies*, edited by Scott and Christensen.[6] Another outcome of this conference was that the "traffic" of researchers between Scandinavia and US over the next

---

[5] The shift was also significantly stimulated by the publication of *The New Institutionalism in Organizational Analysis*, edited by Powell and DiMaggio (1991).

[6] This publication was one of the first joint publications within institutional theory including researchers from Scandinavia as well as the USA.

couple of years became multidirectional: some North American scholars spent a semester or an entire year at Scandinavian research institutions.[7]

Institutional maintenance and consolidation (1995–)

One might argue that in the early years, the work of Scandinavian institutionalist researchers was difficult to distinguish from the institutionalist research being conducted elsewhere. At the very least, their work was not as articulated and distinct as we argue that it has become in recent years. After many years of network building and academic exchange of scholars and ideas, institutionalist research in Scandinavia seems to have found a voice of its own. This voice is apparent in the articulation of specific research agendas within institutional theory, which are reflected in recent publications and in conferences and seminars that Scandinavian institutionalists have organized since the mid 1990s. One example is the symposium on "Action in Institutions," held in conjunction with the 1995 Academy of Management Meeting in Vancouver. The Scandinavian voice is evident in the announced call, which states that "the purpose of the symposium is to address the troubling gap in new institutional analyses of organizations – the seeming lack of a theory of action." On the initiative of Scandinavian researchers, the symposium explicitly explored the role of actors and action in institutional analysis. Scholars from both Scandinavia and North America attended the symposium, which gave rise in 1997 to the special issue on "Action and Institutions" in *American Behavioral Scientist* (edited by Christensen, Karnøe, Strandgaard Pedersen, and Dobbin).[8]

---

[7] For instance, Frank Dobbin, who is now professor at Harvard University, was visiting scholar at Copenhagen Business School (CBS) in 1994–1995. Frank Dobbin is a former PhD student of John W. Meyer from Stanford University and was at that time working at Princeton University. In collaboration with researchers from CBS, he launched a PhD course in "New Institutional Theory," which has now run for more than ten years at CBS.

[8] Eight years later, in 2005 a new group of institutional scholars from Scandinavia, Europe, and the United States gathered in Denmark for a conference on "New Public and Private Models of Management: Sense-making and Institutions," which resulted in a special issue of *American Behavioral Scientist* in 2006, edited by Westenholz, Strandgaard Pedersen, and Dobbin.

During the late 1990s, SCANCOR also hosted several seminars and conferences, including a seminar on standardization in 1997, followed by the publication of the book *A World of Standards*, edited by Brunsson and Jacobsson in 2000.[9]

Perhaps the most significant landmark of this period was the volume *Translating Organizational Change*, edited by Czarniawska and Sevón (1996). This book, which brought together Scandinavian and non-Scandinavian researchers, articulated several important research agendas within institutional theory. This volume introduced the concept of Scandinavian institutionalism and also imported the notion of translation from actor network theory into institutional theory. The concept of translation refers to the notion that ideas change when they travel from one context to another, an idea borrowed from French scholars like Bruno Latour and Michel Callon (Callon & Latour, 1981; Latour, 1986, 1987; Callon, 1986). The institutional approach to translation challenged the notions of isomorphic diffusion that had so far dominated institutional research and became a core feature of Scandinavian institutionalism.

A third initiative occurred in the late 1990s when Lars Engwall from the University of Uppsala in Sweden launched a research program on "Creating European Management Practice" (CEMP). This research program studied processes of production, circulation, and consumption of management ideas from an institutional perspective. Through a series of workshops and seminar activities, the research program brought together a number of Scandinavian (as well as other European) scholars working with institutional theory. For several years, Lars Engwall organized sub-themes on this topic during the annual meeting of the European Group of Organization Studies (EGOS), whereby he further consolidated process-oriented approaches to institutional theory within Scandinavia and Europe. In relation to this research program, SCANCOR also organized a conference on "Carriers of Management Knowledge" at Stanford University in 1999.[10]

The year 1999 marked an important change at SCANCOR. The founding fathers and the first generation of board members at SCANCOR (March, Brunsson, Christensen, Olsen, and Sevón) decided

[9] Røvik (1998) is another significant publication and example of Scandinavian institutionalism from the 1990s.

[10] The CEMP research program has resulted in various publications, e.g. Sahlin-Andersson and Engwall (2002), Amdam, Kvålshaugen, and Larsen (2003), and Alvarez, Mazza, and Strandgaard Pedersen (2005).

to step down to leave room for the next generation. Professor Walter W. Powell replaced James G. March as director of SCANCOR and Stanford representative, and Kristian Kreiner (Denmark), Kari Lilja (Finland), Per Lægreid (Norway), and Kerstin Sahlin-Andersson (Sweden) became the new board of Scandinavian representatives.[11]

Since the turn of the century, the annual meeting of EGOS (European Group of Organization Studies) has played a particularly instrumental role in the institutional maintenance and further consolidation of Scandinavian institutionalism and, more generally, of institutional theory in Europe. Apart from the above-mentioned subtheme headed by Lars Engwall (Uppsala), Finn Borum (CBS) and Walter W. Powell (Stanford/SCANCOR) also organized a couple of subthemes at EGOS on institutional theory, notably on institutional change and on field formation and transformation. Since 2004, in what could be seen as another act of institutional work, SCANCOR has been organizing a PhD course that brings PhD students from the Scandinavian member organizations into contact with one another as well as with PhD students and faculty from the United States.[12] The most recent example of institutional work is probably the formal establishment of alumni networks in each of the Scandinavian countries, which was initiated in fall 2007. Since their foundation, the alumni networks have reached approximately 225 Scandinavian scholars that have visited SCANCOR over the years. On November 21, 2008, SCANCOR celebrated its twentieth anniversary in the company of its alumni network and friends of SCANCOR. Their shared experiences give rise to an emerging sense of collective identity that may extend far into the future.

This narrative of the birth of Scandinavian institutionalism sum-marizes what we consider to be the intentional actions and manifesta-tions of agency. The formation of SCANCOR, joint book projects, exchange of visiting scholars, joint seminars and conferences, young scholars' network, joint PhD courses, and alumni networks are examples of the institutional work that led to the unintentional creation of Scandinavian institutionalism. The unintentional consequence of these

---

[11] From 2001 a principle of rotation was introduced involving an automatic shift of one board member per year. New board members are nominated by their respective countries.

[12] Taking place in California, 2004; Copenhagen, 2005; Finland, 2006; and Copenhagen, 2007.

actions was to formalize a research network between organizational researchers in Scandinavia and at Stanford University, accomplished through the creation of SCANCOR. Yet these actions also had the unintended consequence of creating the field of Scandinavian institutionalism. Let us now turn to the characteristics of Scandinavian institutionalism as it has come to be known and explore its emergent boundaries.

Unintentional effects

Identifying Scandinavian institutionalism

The institutionalist literature that has emerged and developed within Scandinavia is perhaps best captured as a literature concerned with how organizations respond to institutional pressure. Scandinavian institutionalists display a keen interest in understanding how organizations perceive and interpret institutional pressure and how these perceptions and interpretations affect everyday organizational practice. They are more interested in studying intra-organizational dynamics than in the structuration of organizational fields, which is a prominent topic in the prevailing institutionalist literature. Whether a cause or an effect, this interest has predisposed Scandinavian institutionalists to engage more readily with practice-oriented literatures. We see a general preference in Scandinavian organization studies for research objects that are situated, dynamic, unique, ambiguous, fragmented, and emergent (Kreiner, 2007) and for research that combines institutional theory with practice-oriented literature (e.g. Czarniawska & Sevón, 1996).

Our conception of Scandinavian institutionalism is that it revolves around the concepts of loose coupling, sense-making, and translation.[13] These concepts, drawn from the respective works of James G. March, Karl E. Weick, Bruno Latour, and Michel Callon, have all strongly influenced and shaped the development of Scandinavian institutionalism into a distinct research tradition (see e.g. Olsen, 2007 and Kreiner, 2007 for a review of the influence of James G. March on organizational research in

---

[13] This claim is generally supported by Lægreid (2007: 79) who in depicting "the Scandinavian way" notes that "the cognitive, neo-institutional and cultural approaches have had a strong foothold in the Scandinavian way of studying organizations."

Scandinavia). Upon closer examination of the Scandinavian institution-alist literature, we would argue that at least two separate lines of inquiry can be identified: (1) loose coupling and (2) sense-making and transla-tion. Loose coupling refers to a weak link that an organization makes among various components of organizational life, such as decisions, strategies, practices, structures, and events (Weick, 1979, 1995, 2001). Sense-making and translation occur when actors seek to grasp a new organizational element and try to implement it in their organizational context. This division is not sharp, but there is nevertheless a tendency for political scientists to work on loose coupling (e.g. Brunsson & Olsen, 1993, 1998) and for culturalists to engage more readily with translation and sense-making (e.g. Czarniawska & Sevón, 1996; Sahlin-Andersson, 1996, 2001; Røvik, 1998, 2007). The distinction is not arbitrary but seems to partially result from historical contingencies related to the previously described efforts to formalize a network of researchers.

The line of inquiry on loose coupling seems to be most strongly represented among the first generation of Scandinavians who took part in the initial efforts to formalize the network. Many of the initiators of the network were trained in political science and shared with their American colleagues in the 1970s an emerging research interest in loose couplings:

> The idea of "coupling," and loose coupling in particular, came to prominence in the ideas and writings of a group of dissenting organizational sociologists and social psychologists working on problems of change and reform in public schools in the mid 1970s. [This topic was debated at a 1974 conference at the Stanford School of Education, which was attended by oganization theorists, sociologists, and historians of education.] (Hallett & Ventresca, 2006: 910)

As this quote shows, loose coupling was in the 1970s associated with the Stanford School of Education, which formally hosts SCANCOR within Stanford University. The Scandinavians who pursue research on loose coupling within Scandinavian institutionalism tend to be first-generation members of the SCANCOR community or their academic descendants. The early members (i.e. Brunsson, Christensen, Olsen, and Sevón) brought the concept of loose coupling back to the Scandinavian political science community, where it developed into a distinct line of inquiry.

The line of inquiry on sense-making and translation is predominantly associated with the second generation of Scandinavians who joined the network around SCANCOR in the 1980s. Many of these researchers have a background in cultural studies and became interested in the interpretative and symbolic aspects of organizational life in the 1980s. They took an interest in studying how organizational actors make sense of public reforms and how their interpretations affect daily organizational practice. Some of them introduced agency and politics into their analysis while others claimed that sense-making and translation are inherently subconscious processes. Let us turn to a more detailed picture of these two lines of inquiry within Scandinavian institutionalism.

The Scandinavian loose coupling literature

Beyond any doubt, the work of Karl E. Weick and James G. March on loose coupling has exerted an important influence on the Scandinavian literature on loosely coupled systems (Engwall, 2003; Kreiner, 2007; Olsen, 2007). Loose coupling refers to the ability of actors to couple and decouple organizational elements and activities, whether unintentionally or as they see fit in a particular situation (Weick, 2001). Empirical examination is directed at identifying how various organizational elements relate to one another in everyday organizational practice. Decoupling is explored as one among many types of loose couplings among organizational elements, ranging from formal structure and organizational policy to operational procedures, managerial decisions, and external communication.

One example of this tradition is a study of radical reform at Swedish Rail that Nils Brunsson and Johan P. Olsen conducted (Brunsson & Olsen, 1993). They showed in this study that the radical reform was formally implemented at the structural level without significantly impacting daily operations. While management thought that the reform would result in near chaos, they discovered to their surprise that rail traffic and operational supervisors were virtually undisrupted by the reform. Their findings suggest that deliberate loose coupling produced this outcome. Management could obtain collaboration from operational departments on the decision to reform only as long as the reform did not in any significant way affect the daily routines of the operational departments. Brunsson and Olsen also identified other loose couplings in the organization that made the radical reform have only a marginal effect on organizational practice.

Another example of the Scandinavian loose coupling literature is a historical analysis of Copenhagen Business School. In this study, Borum and Westenholz (1995) show that Copenhagen Business School, since its foundation in 1917, gradually absorbed elements of different myths from its institutional environment. This ongoing process resulted in an organization that, in the early 1990s, embodied five different models that were loosely coupled to one another. They conclude that what appeared on occasion to be a case of decoupling was in fact an organization that continuously integrated new institutional elements into its organizational practice without fully discarding old ones. By engaging in loose coupling, the business school maintained its operational efficiency while also assuring legitimacy over time and with different constituents. This study testifies to the organizational complexities that underpin how organizations respond to institutional pressure.

Sense-making, translation, and the question of agency

This line of research, which focuses on interpretive processes, takes inspiration from Karl E. Weick's work on sense-making (e.g. Weick, 1979, 1995, 2001). Its source of inspiration stems from empirical observations that ideas or practices may diffuse under the same label but acquire different meaning when they are implemented in different organizational contexts. Sense-making refers to the act of making sense of ongoing events and actions, often in a retrospective light. Implied in this concept is a recognition that actors' understanding and interests make them interpret the same occurrences differently. A characteristic of the sense-making literature is therefore that it positions actors as interpreters of institutional pressure and hence as mediators of the institutional pressures on organizations. As they try to comprehend the institutional pressures, interpreting actors inescapably shape the effects of the institutional pressure on the organization. This interpretive process is often implicit and institutionally embedded, but it can certainly also be partially deliberate on occasion. Sense-making becomes a source of strategizing when actors gain awareness of several possible interpretations and use these interpretations strategically to further their own interests. These two approaches to sense-making, embeddedness versus strategizing, are subject to some debate within the community of Scandinavian institutionalists much like "institutional entrepreneurship" is within the international community (see e.g. Dacin, Goodstein & Scott, 2002). Both approaches are reflected in the Scandinavian translation literature.

Translation refers in the Scandinavian institutionalist literature to the modification that a practice or an idea undergoes when it is implemented in a new organizational context. As mentioned previously, the notion of translation takes inspiration from actor network theory, and, in particular, from the work of French scholars like Bruno Latour and Michel Callon (Callon & Latour, 1981; Latour, 1986, 1987; Callon, 1986). They posit that a phenomenon undergoes change every time it is applied in a new organizational context because meaning derives exclusively from connection to other elements in the organizational context. Meaning changes when some contextual elements are removed and other contextual elements added, a process that occurs every time an idea, technology, or practice "travels" to a new organizational context. In the institutionalist version of translation, attention is focused on how apparently isomorphic organizational forms become heterogeneous when implemented in practice in different organizational contexts. When implemented in practice, an organizational form gains connection to some new contextual elements and loses connection to others, producing different translations of the organizational form (Sahlin-Andersson, 1996; Czarniawska & Joerges, 1996; Røvik, 1998, 2007). This line of inquiry is evident in empirical research conducted by Scandinavian institutionalists (Strandgaard Pedersen & Dobbin, 1997; Røvik, 1998, 2007; Lippi, 2000; Mazza, Sahlin-Andersson & Strandgaard Pedersen, 2005; Boxenbaum, 2006, 2008).

The first stream of Scandinavian research on sense-making and translation emphasized the implicit aspects of the interpretation process. This stream, initiated in the mid 1990s, is primarily associated with Czarniawska and Joerges (1996), Sahlin-Andersson (1996, 2001), and Røvik (1998, 2007). Czarniawska and Joerges (1996) proposed that ideas are translated when individuals engage in organizational practice. The translation process is not a consciously mediated act of strategizing, they argue, but an implicit search for pragmatic solutions. Translation occurs when an idea that seems promising for alleviating an organizational problem is selected and then objectified and materialized. This approach is also apparent in Sahlin-Andersson's model of translation in which she outlines how practices are packaged for export (Sahlin-Andersson, 2001). She proposed that local practices are edited by means of three editing rules that make the practices relevant and attractive to potential adopters. The editing rules pertain to context, logic, and formulation, she argued, and they constitute implicit principles of action rather than deliberate tools of strategizing.

Within the same line of inquiry, Røvik (1998, 2007) traces the various trends that have defined management ideas and practices around the turn of the century. He gives attention to what distinguishes a successful management concept from an unsuccessful one in the diffusion process and also to what characterizes the adopting "modern" organization. According to Røvik (1998), a successful concept is characterized by the following seven features: (1) social authorization, (2) theorizing, (3) productivization, (4) time marking, (5) harmonization, (6) dramatization, and (7) individualization (Røvik, 1998: 108–111). He further characterizes the adopting "modern" organization as a "multistandard organization" that is marked by (a) a high intake capacity, (b) a high decoupling capacity, (c) a high translation capacity, (d) a high take-out capacity, and (e) a high storage capacity (Røvik, 1998: 279–319).

The second stream of research on sense-making and translation in Scandinavia took form fairly recently. It highlights the strategic opportunities associated with different interpretations and recognizes that there is more than one way in which an actor can interpret and translate an idea or a practice within a given organizational context. To the extent that actors gain awareness of alternative frames of interpretations, they may deliberately try to translate an idea or a practice in a manner that aligns with their own interests. Research conducted within this strategic branch of translation seeks to illuminate how and why actors choose one interpretation over other available interpretations. The argument is that their choice of interpretative frame holds the key to a better understanding of how organizations respond to institutional pressure. An example of this tradition is Borum's (2004) study of how key actors in Danish hospitals strategically reinterpreted the same institutionalized belief to fit their own political preferences. The actors were aware of the strategic dimension of interpretation and negotiated the interpretation that should guide organizational practice. Similar strategic implications are also apparent in the study that Strandgaard Pedersen and colleagues conducted on film-making in different countries (Alvarez, Mazza, Strandgaard Pedersen & Srejenova, 2005). They found that maverick film directors relied on their own strategic interpretations when they decided to differentiate themselves from other film directors in the field. They shielded themselves from institutional pressure, as a market strategy, through three different types of shielding in order to create and protect their creative space. A final example of this line of inquiry is Boxenbaum's study of how diversity management was translated to a

Danish context (Boxenbaum & Battilana, 2005; Boxenbaum, 2006). The translating actors generated different interpretations of diversity management on the basis of their own individual preferences. They then selected the frame that they believed would have most strategic appeal to top management and that would also appeal pragmatically to the organizational members who were to implement diversity management in practice. All three studies reflect an agentic line of inquiry within the translation literature in Scandinavian institutionalism,[14] a characteristic that aligns them with the international literature on institutional work and institutional entrepreneurship.[15]

Emerging boundaries of Scandinavian institutionalism

The reader may wonder if we have indeed captured the emerging field of Scandinavian institutionalism in the above description and, if so, how we determine the boundaries of Scandinavian institutionalism. This task is rendered difficult by the tendency to publish much of the Scandinavian institutionalist literature in books, not in journals, and in the Scandinavian languages rather than in English. However, it makes little sense to talk of Scandinavian institutionalism as an emerging field unless it is accessible to non-Scandinavians. Hence, we have tried to capture manifestations of the emerging field of Scandinavian institutionalism in English-language journal articles, monographs, and book chapters.

We first conducted a keyword search (all text) in the EBSCO database. This search generated three articles: Boons and Strannegård (2000); Becker-Ritterspach (2006); and Lervik *et al.* (2005). We then searched the index of several authoritative books and edited volumes within institutional theory for the term "Scandinavian institutionalism": Scott (1995, 2001, 2008); Powell and DiMaggio (1991); and Greenwood *et al.* (2008). Only the latter edited volume, *The Sage Handbook of Organizational Institutionalism*, contained references to

---

[14] For other empirically based studies, see, for example, Amdam *et al.* (2003); for a theorization on social transformation processes, see, for example, Holm (1995), Strandgaard Pedersen and Dobbin (2006), and Strandgaard Pedersen, Svejenova, and Jones (2006).

[15] For a review of the institutional entrepreneurship literature, see Leca, Battilana, and Boxenbaum (2006).

Scandinavian institutionalism. According to the index, this keyword appeared in the introduction (Greenwood *et al.*, 2008) and in four chapters: Boxenbaum and Jonsson (2008); Sahlin and Wedlin (2008); Meyer (2008); and Czarniawska (2008). We based our analysis of the boundaries of Scandinavian institutionalism on these three journal articles and five book chapters.

From these eight data sources, we selected all paragraphs that specifically mentioned the term "Scandinavian institutionalism" and copied them into a separate file along with any associated footnotes. We then noted all references and key names that appeared in the selected paragraphs mentioning Scandinavian institutionalism. We extracted all self-references, i.e. authors referring to their own work, and all publication references that had no Scandinavian author (e.g. Powell & DiMaggio, 1991). This procedure left us with a list of publications that had at least one Scandinavian author and a list of key names that were associated with Scandinavian institutionalism. The publications constitute what we propose to be the canon of Scandinavian institutionalism, while the key names may be thought of as its inspirational figures. Finally, to assign weight to the different references and inspirational figures, we counted in how many of the eight texts a given reference or name appeared in conjunction with Scandinavian institutionalism. The findings are reproduced in Tables 7.1 and 7.2.

Table 7.1 shows that Scandinavian institutionalism is most strongly associated with Czarniawska and Sevón's edited volume from 1996 but that a number of other books and journal publications also define this emerging field. This finding supports Czarniawska's claim that "Guje Sevón and I coined the term 'Scandinavian institutionalism' (Czarniawska & Sevón, 1996) to denote works from Denmark, Norway, and Sweden, written under the influence of Richard W. Scott, James G. March, and John W. Meyer" (2008: 770). This citation also aligns with our findings on the most inspirational figures: Table 7.2 shows James G. March, John W. Meyer, W. Richard Scott, Bruno Latour, and Michel Callon as the most prominent non-Scandinavian figures that are associated with Scandinavian institutionalism. The latter two are actor network theorists and primarily associated with the translation literature.

Some authors do not appear in these tables, a plausible reason being that they publish more readily in the Scandinavian languages. Another reason may be that the number of journal articles, monographs, and

Table 7.1. *The canon of Scandinavian institutionalism*

References related to Scandinavian institutionalism	Number of texts in which the reference is mentioned
Czarniawska & Sevón, 1996	5
Czarniawska & Sevón, 2005	1
Brunsson, 1989	1
Brunsson & Olsen, 1993	1
Brunsson & Olsen, 1998	1
March & Olsen, 1976	1
March & Olsen, 1989	1
Sahlin-Andersson & Engwall, 2002	1
Scott & Christensen, 1995	1
Borum, 2004	1
Alvarez, Mazza, Strandgaard Pedersen & Svejenova, 2005	1
Johansson, 2002	1

Table 7.2. *Inspirational figures for Scandinavian institutionalism*

Key names associated with Scandinavian institutionalism	Number of texts in which the reference is mentioned
James G. March	4
John W. Meyer	3
W. Richard Scott	2
Bruno Latour	2
Michel Callon	2
Peter Berger and Thomas Luckmann	1
Karin Knorr-Cetina	1
Karl E. Weick	1

edited volumes on Scandinavian institutionalism is still relatively small, which makes it difficult to draw a realistic picture. Although Scandinavian institutionalism is an emerging field whose contents and boundaries are constantly being revised and expanded, we find the list of books and key figures to give a reasonably plausible picture of the emerging field of Scandinavian institutionalism.

Apart from the above-mentioned identifiers of Scandinavian institutionalism, certain methodological orientations also seem to distinguish

Scandinavian institutionalism from the prevailing North American version of institutionalism. Let us briefly conclude with a description of some defining methodological features of Scandinavian institutionalism.

Methodological orientations of Scandinavian institutionalism

Scandinavian institutionalism displays a preference for intensive, rich, process-oriented, and qualitative approaches to the study of organizational practice (Sahlin-Andersson & Söderholm, 2002; Czarniawska & Sevón, 2003; Røvik, 1998, 2007). By far the most common methodology is to use qualitative methods, preferably ethnography. Although efforts are made to generate theoretical insight from the detailed observations of practice, the complex nature of the observed phenomena renders the task of theory development rather difficult. Only a fraction of the findings are consequently published in international journals (Engwall, 1995), if they are published at all. However, it is common to engage in dialogue with practitioners about the implications for practice (Kreiner, 2007).

The careful attention to interpretation also applies to the act of research. The researcher interprets the empirical observations and thereby mediates between the empirical world and the academic knowledge that is produced. In that capacity, the researcher produces "situated knowledge." Situated knowledge means that what we find in empirical research is partially a reflection of where we stand when we observe it (Haraway, 1991) and of how we interpret these situated observations (Alvesson, 2003). For instance, Scandinavian institutionalism looks different when observed from within Scandinavia than it does from the outside. The further distanced the observer is, in terms of abstracting or simplifying the object under study, the more isomorphism there will seem to be (Forssell & Jansson, 2000). Similarly, if we study organizational life a century ago, then we are more likely to observe isomorphism than if we collect data on contemporary organizations. The clearest evidence of isomorphism is found within the world systems literature, where the unit of analysis is highly aggregated. If, in contrast, we step inside an organization to study how institutional pressure is interpreted in everyday practice, isomorphism may look like an illusory effect of particular research strategies. In fact, we see a remarkable variation in organizational response to institutional pressures in the findings from case-based research (e.g. Djelic & Quack, 2003; Sahlin-Andersson & Engwall, 2002), which supports our claim that research findings represent a form of situated knowledge.

The key point here is that researchers co-construct their research results from a situated position. This means that the position that researchers occupy relative to the object of study influences what kind of data they will collect and what meaning they will attribute to this data. For instance, Alvesson (2003) describes several different interpretations that can be attributed to the research interview, depending on the researcher's assumptions about the knowledge that can be derived from this data source. In contrast to most North American research, the Scandinavian tradition also approaches the *analysis* of research findings as a contextual act rather than as a normative act (Lægreid, 2007). Accordingly, researchers should show awareness of their position relative to the object of study when reporting findings from empirical research. This is a premise that requires researchers to constantly question the epistemological assumptions upon which they base their research findings and to signal awareness of the situated nature of their own knowledge production. Many Scandinavians are impressively skilled in the exercise of this epistemological stance.

Conclusion

The narrative that we presented in this chapter told the story of how Scandinavian institutionalism was born and how it has developed into a distinct field of institutionalist inquiry in recent years. This emerging field of study is concerned with how organizations respond heterogeneously to institutional pressures. Our narrative also testifies to the power of institutional work. We hope to have demonstrated to the reader that although the first generation of Scandinavian institutionalists engaged in deliberate actions, and did so successfully, the effects of their actions surpassed their own imagination and deliberate intentions. The creation of SCANCOR, joint book projects, exchange of visiting scholars, joint seminars and conferences, young scholars network, joint PhD courses, and alumni networks were all activities deliberately undertaken to formalize a research community among Scandinavian researchers and researchers from Stanford University. Yet these activities also became part of the institutional work that inadvertently, as an unintentional consequence, led to the creation of Scandinavian institutionalism as an emerging field of institutional inquiry. In other words, our narrative did not stop when the first generation of Scandinavian institutionalists reached their deliberate goal by launching SCANCOR in 1988. It continued with the second generation of Scandinavian institutionalists who coined the term, formulated new realms of institutional inquiry, and engaged North American and European researchers in their hybrid ideas. Their actions had unintentional consequences in as much as Scandinavian institutionalism emerged as a distinct line of inquiry within institutionalism, sustained by a large community of researchers within, and even beyond, Scandinavia.

We find it interesting that new fields can arise as unintentional consequences of deliberate actions that were neither anticipated nor explicitly desired at the outset. Although the institutional effects flowed from the deliberate actions of strategic individuals, the most important effects were not intended. This finding raises interesting questions about the role of agency in institutional work. For instance, do intentions evolve over time, or do actions produce effects regardless of the intentions behind the actions? These questions merit further attention in future empirical research on institutional work. It could be interesting to explore, for instance, whether it is actions or intentions that produce the most significant institutional effects.

If we compare the Scandinavian lines of inquiry with the international literature on institutionalism, we recognize some of the same theoretical debates. For instance, a key question in both traditions is whether individuals are able to shape, block, or initiate institutions by engaging in institutional work, or whether their range of choice, and the choice itself, is so strongly conditioned by institutional forces that it makes little sense to study individuals (Holm, 1995). The Scandinavian institutionalist literature may contribute to resolving this tenacious issue.

A related and intriguing question that arises from our narrative is how Scandinavian institutionalism contributes to the development of institutional theory. The Scandinavian institutionalist literature has produced insightful accounts of the complex processes that unfold inside organizations that are subjected to institutional pressures. These complex processes revolve around the notions of loose coupling, sense-making, and translation, which we identified to be the key theoretical characteristics of Scandinavian institutionalism. These insights may be of some interest to the research community that is forming around the notion of institutional work. It is paradoxical that the primarily North American institutionalists who launched some of these lines of inquiry in the 1970s subsequently neglected them in favor of studying field-level dynamics and are now reintroduced to them decades later by Scandinavians. Indeed, Scandinavian institutionalists did pursue this line of inquiry in relative isolation from the prevailing institutional literature and their line of inquiry is only now converging with the international research agenda (Boxenbaum & Jonsson, 2008).

We think that the Scandinavian line of inquiry may help illuminate some important feedback mechanisms in institutional change, notably how organizational responses produce institutional change. For instance, do loose couplings precipitate a process of deinstitutionalization, or do they, in contrast, help maintain institutions precisely because organizational practices are not disrupted in the process? Such feedback mechanisms have largely escaped inquiry, yet they represent an intriguing avenue for future research. We propose to leverage decades of Scandinavian institutionalist research on organizational responses to institutional pressures to study complex, intra-organizational processes of institutional work. The practice-oriented approach of Scandinavian institutionalism may compel other institutionalists to complement the isomorphic macro-studies that predominate in North America with the process-oriented micro-studies that are more common in Scandinavia. Perhaps, ideas from Scandinavian institutionalism will travel to research settings outside Scandinavia where they will be translated into ever new forms of situated knowledge of institutional work.

References

Alvarez, J. L., Mazza, C. & Strandgaard Pedersen, J. (2005) Editorial: the role of mass media in the consumption of management knowledge. *Scandinavian Journal of Management*, 21(2): 127–132.

Alvarez, J. L., Mazza, C., Strandgaard Pedersen, J. & Svejenova, S. (2005) Shielding idiosyncrasy from isomorphic pressures: towards optimal distinctiveness in European filmmaking. *Organization*, 12: 863–888.

Alvesson, M. (2003) Beyond neo-positivists, romantics, and localists: a reflexive approach to interviews in organizational research. *Academy of Management Review*, 28(1): 13–33.

Amdam, R. P., Kvålshaugen, R. & Larsen, E. (eds.) (2003) *Inside the Business Schools: The Content of European Business Education*. Oslo: Abstrakt–Liber–Copenhagen Business School Press.

Becker-Ritterspach, F. A. A. (2006) The social constitution of knowledge integration in MNEs: a theoretical framework. *Journal of International Management*, 12(3): 358–377.

Boons, F. & Strannegård, L. (2000) Organizations coping with their natural environment. *International Studies of Management & Organization*, 30(3): 7–17.

Borum, F. (2004) Means–end frames and the politics and myths of organizational fields. *Organization Studies*, 25: 897–922.

Borum, F. & Westenholz, A. (1995) The incorporation of multiple institutional models: organizational field multiplicity and the role of actors. In R. W. Scott & S. Christensen (eds.), *The Institutional Construction of Organizations – International and Longitudinal Studies*, pp. 113–131. Thousand Oaks, CA: Sage.

Boxenbaum, E. (2006) Lost in translation? The making of Danish diversity management. *American Behavioral Scientist*, 49(7): 939–948.

(2008) The process of legitimation. In S. Scheuer & J. Damm Scheuer (eds.), *The Anatomy of Change*, pp. 239–264. Copenhagen: Copenhagen Business School Press.

Boxenbaum, E. & Battilana, J. (2005) Importation as innovation: transposing managerial practices across fields. *Strategic Organization*, 3(4): 355–383.

Boxenbaum, E. & Jonsson, S. (2008) Isomorphism, diffusion and decoupling. In R. Greenwood, C. Oliver, K. Sahlin & R. Suddaby (eds.), *Handbook of Organizational Institutionalism*, pp. 78–98. Thousand Oaks, CA: Sage.

Brunsson, N. (1989) *The Organization of Hypocrisy: Talk, Decision, and Actions in Organizations*. Chichester: Wiley.

Brunsson, N. & Jacobsson, B. (2000) *A World of Standards*. Oxford: Oxford University Press.

Brunsson, N. & Olsen, J. P. (eds.) (1993) *The Reforming Organization*. London: Routledge.

(eds.) (1998) *Organizing Organizations*. Bergen-Sandviken: Fagbokvorlag.

Callon, M. (1986) Some elements of a sociology of translation: domestication of the scallops and the fishermen of St. Brieuc Bay. In J. Law (ed.), *Power, Action and Belief*, pp. 196–233. London: Routledge & Kegan Paul.

Callon, M. & Latour, B. (1981) Unscrewing the Big Leviathan: how actors macro-structure reality and how sociologists help them to do so. In K. Knorr-Cetina & A. V. Cicourel (eds.), *Advances in Social Theory and Methodology*, pp. 277–303. London: Routledge & Kegan Paul.

Christensen, S., Karnøe, P., Strandgaard Pedersen, J. & Dobbin, F. (eds.) (1997) Actors and institutions: editors' introduction. *American Behavioral Scientist*, 40(4): 392–396.

Czarniawska, B. (2008) How to misuse institutions and get away with it: some reflections on institutional theory(ies). In R. Greenwood, C. Oliver, K. Sahlin & R. Suddaby (eds.), *Handbook of Organizational Institutionalism*, pp. 769–782. Thousand Oaks, CA: Sage.

Czarniawska, B. & Joerges, B. (1996) Travels of ideas. In B. Czarniawska & G. Sevón (eds.), *Translating Organizational Change*, pp. 13–47. Berlin: Walter de Gruyter.

Czarniawska, B. & Sevón, G. (eds.) (1996) *Translating Organizational Change*. Berlin: Walter de Gruyter.

(eds.) (2003) *The Northern Lights: Organization Theory in Scandinavia*. Copenhagen: Copenhagen Business School Press.

(2005) *Global Ideas: How Ideas, Objects and Practices Travel in the Global Economy*. Malmö: Liber; Copenhagen: Copenhagen Business School Press.

Dacin, T., Goodstein, J. & Scott, W. R. (2002) Institutional theory and institutional change: introduction to the special research forum. *Academy of Management Journal*, 45(1): 45–56.

DiMaggio, P. J. & Powell, W. W. (1991) Introduction. In W. W. Powell & P. J. DiMaggio (eds.), *The New Institutionalism in Organizational Analysis*, pp. 1–38. Chicago: University of Chicago Press.

Djelic, M.-L. & Quack, S. (2003) *Globalization and Institutions: Redefining the Rules of the Economic Game*. Cheltenham: Edward Elgar.

Engwall, L. (1995) The Vikings vs. the world: an examination of Nordic business research. *Proceedings of the 13th Nordic Conference on Business Studies*, 1: 303–312.

(2003) On the origin of the Northern Lights. In B. Czarniawska & G. Sevón (eds.), *The Northern Lights: Organization Theory in Scandinavia*, pp. 395–411. Copenhagen: Copenhagen Business School Press.

Forssell, A. & Jansson, D. (2000) *Idéer som Fängslar. Recept för en Offentlig Reformation [Ideas that Imprison: A Recipe for Reform of Public Management]*. Malmö: Liber.

Greenwood, R., Oliver, C., Sahlin, K. & Suddaby, R. (2008) Introduction. In R. Greenwood, C. Oliver, K. Sahlin & R. Suddaby (eds.), *Handbook of Organizational Institutionalism*, pp. 1–46. Thousand Oaks, CA: Sage.

Hallett, T. & Ventresca, M. (2006) How institutions form: loose coupling as mechanism in Gouldner's *Patterns of Industrial Bureaucracy*. *American Behavioral Scientist*, 49(7): 908–924.

Haraway, D. (1991) Situated knowledges: the science question in feminism and the privilege of partial perspective. In *Simians, Cyborgs and Women: The Reinvention of Nature*, pp. 183–202. New York: Routledge.

Hirsch, P. & Lounsbury, M. (1997) Ending the family quarrel: toward a reconciliation of "old" and "new" institutionalisms. *American Behavioral Scientist*, 40(4): 406–418.

Holm, P. (1995) The dynamics of institutionalization: transformation processes in Norwegian fisheries. *Administrative Science Quarterly*, 40: 398–422.

Johansson, R. (2002) *Nyinstitutionalismen inom Organisationsanalysen [New Institutionalism within Organizational Analysis]*. Lund: Studentlitteratur.

Kreiner, K. (2007) A Scandinavian way in organization theory: what is the evidence, and does evidence matter? *Nordiske Organisasjionsstudier* 9(1): 83–92.

Lægreid, P. (2007) Organization theory – the Scandinavian way. *Nordiske Organisasjionsstudier*, 9(1): 77–82.

Latour, B. (1986) The power of association. In J. Law (ed.), *Power, Action and Belief*, pp. 164–280. London: Routledge & Kegan Paul.

   (1987) *Science in Action: How to Follow Scientists and Engineers Through Society*. Cambridge, MA: Harvard University Press.

Lawrence, T. B. & Suddaby, R. (2006) Institutions and institutional work. In S. R. Clegg, C. Hardy, T. B. Lawrence & W. R. Nord (eds.), *Handbook of Organization Studies*, 2nd edn., pp. 215–254. Thousand Oaks, CA: Sage.

Leca, B., Battilana, J. & Boxenbaum, E. (2006) Taking stock on institutional entrepreneurship: what do we know? Where do we go? Online working paper at Copenhagen Business School. Available at http://ir.lib.cbs.dk/paper/ISBN/x65651767x.

Lervik, J. E., Hennestad, B. W., Amdam, R. P., Lunnan, R. & Nilsen, S. M. (2005) Implementing human resource development best practices: replication or re-creation? *Human Resource Development International*, 8(3): 345–360.

Lippi, A. (2000) One theory, many practices: institutional allomorphism in the managerialist reorganization of Italian governments. *Scandinavian Journal of Management*, 16: 455–477.

March, J. G. & Olsen, J. P. (1976; 1979) *Ambiguity and Choice in Organizations*. Bergen: Universitetsforlag.

   (1989) *Rediscovering Institutions – The Organizational Basis of Politics*. New York: Free Press.

Mazza, C., Sahlin-Andersson, K. & Strandgaard Pedersen, J. (2005) European constructions of an American model. *Journal of Management Learning*, 36(4): 471–491.

Meyer, R. (2008) New sociology of knowledge: historical legacy and contributions to current debates in institutional research. In R. Greenwood, C. Oliver, K. Sahlin & R. Suddaby (eds.), *Handbook of Organizational Institutionalism*, pp. 519–538. Thousand Oaks, CA: Sage.

Olsen, J. P. (2007) Organization theory, public administration, democratic governance. *Nordiske Organisasjionsstudier*, 9(1): 93–110.

Powell, W. W. & DiMaggio, P. J. (eds.) (1991) *The New Institutionalism in Organizational Analysis*. Chicago: University of Chicago Press.

Røvik, K. A. (1996) Deinstitutionalization and the logic of fashion. In B. Czarniawska & G. Sevón (eds.), *Translating Organizational Change*, pp. 139–172. Berlin: De Gruyter.

   (1998) *Moderne Organisasjoner: Trender i Organisasjonstenkningen ved Tusenårsskiftet* [Modern organizations: trends in organizational research by millennium]. Bergen-Sandviken: Fakboklaget.

   (2007) *Trender og Translasjoner – Ideer som former det 21. århundrets organisasjon* [Trends and translations – ideas that shape the organization of the 21st century]. Oslo: Universitetsforlaget.

Sahlin, K. & Wedlin, L. (2008) Circulating ideas: imitation, translation and editing. In R. Greenwood, C. Oliver, K. Sahlin & R. Suddaby (eds.), *Handbook of Organizational Institutionalism*, pp. 218–242. Thousand Oaks, CA: Sage.

Sahlin-Andersson, K. (1996) Imitating by editing success: the construction of organizational fields and identities. In B. Czarniawska & G. Sevón (eds.), *Translating Organizational Change*, pp. 69–92. Berlin: Walter de Gruyter.

   (2001) National, international and transnational constructions of new public management. In T. Christensen & P. Lægreid (eds.), *New Public Management: The Transformation of Ideas and Practice*, pp. 43–72. Aldershot: Ashgate.

Sahlin-Andersson, K. & Engwall, L. (2002) *The Expansion of Management Knowledge – Carriers, Flows and Sources*. Stanford, CA: Stanford University Press.

Sahlin-Andersson, K. & Söderholm, A. (2002) The Scandinavian school of studies. In K. Sahlin-Andersson & A. Söderholm (eds.), *Beyond Project Management: New Perspectives on the Temporary–Permanent Dilemma*. Malmö: Liber.

Scott, W. R. (1995/2001/2008) *Institutions and Organizations*, 1st, 2nd, 3rd edns. London: Sage.

Scott, W. R. & Christensen, S. (1995) *The Institutional Construction of Organizations – International and Longitudinal Studies*. Thousand Oaks, CA: Sage.

Strandgaard Pedersen, J. & Dobbin, F. (1997) The social invention of collective actors: on the rise of the organization. *American Behavioral Scientist*, 40: 431–443.

   (2006) In search of identity and legitimation – bridging organizational culture and neo-institutionalism. *American Behavioral Scientist*, 49: 897–907.

Strandgaard Pedersen, J., Svejenova, S. & Jones, C. (2006) Editorial, special issue: Transforming creative industries: strategies of and structures around creative entrepreneurs. *Creativity and Innovation Management*, 15(3): 221–223.

Weick, K. E. (1979) *The Social Psychology of Organizing*. Reading, MA: Addison Wesley.

(1995) *Sensemaking in Organizations*. London: Sage.

(2001) *Making Sense of the Organization*. Malden, MA: Blackwell.

Westenholz, A., Strandgaard Pedersen, J. & Dobbin, F. (2006) Introduction. Institutions in the making: identity, power, and the emergence of new organizational forums. *American Behavioral Scientist*, 49: 889–896.

8 | Institutional maintenance as narrative acts

TAMMAR B. ZILBER

I N this chapter, I address the forms of institutional work involved in symbolic institutional maintenance. Taking a narrative approach, I define symbolic institutional maintenance as the travel of institutional stories across social levels, and I explore the forms of institutional work used to translate societal meta-narratives into organizations and the lives of individuals. Based on the study of a rape crisis center in Israel, I examine the maintenance of the feminist and therapeutic institutions within which the organization was embedded. I follow the feminist and therapeutic meta-narratives prevalent in Israeli society, as they traveled into, and were modified by, the rape crisis center. Further, I follow the use of these societal-level narratives, and the organizational versions thereof, by organizational members, as they strove to make sense of their own lives and identities. I conceptualize this series of narrative acts as institutional maintenance, worked out in the interfaces of various social levels; embedded in power relations; and involving the delicate balance of duplication and change. At the societal level, institutions are embodied within diverse meta-narratives that encode the "taken-for-granted" in shared poetic tropes, like protagonists and villains, dramatic settings and plots. Organizational members carry these institutional meta-narratives into the organization. Still, societal

* I thank the people at "Orot" rape crisis center for accepting me into their community. Research was supported by the Israeli Foundation Trustees (1997) and by various funds at the Hebrew University of Jerusalem: Eshkol Institute, Schein Center (1996–1997), and the Morris Ginsberg Foundation (1999–2000) of the Social Science Faculty; by the Lafer Center for Women's Studies (1995–1996); and by the Leon Recanati Fund of the Jerusalem School of Business Administration. An early version of this chapter was presented at the International Workshop on Institutional Work at the Segal Graduate School of Business, Simon Fraser University, Vancouver, Canada. Thanks to all participants for the inspiring discussion of the paper; to the editors, Bernard Leca, Tom Lawrence, and Roy Suddaby for their encouragement and insightful comments and suggestions; and special thanks to Yehuda Goodman for the ongoing dialogue on the ideas presented in this chapter.

meta-narratives that are taken up within organizations do not simply duplicate the institutional order. Rather, through reinterpretation organizational elites translate them into local – more specific and selective – versions, which are then used in organizational sense-making processes. Organizational socialization processes make these stories available to newcomers and veteran members. Further, individual organizational members use these organizational stories and the institutional meta-narratives to construct their own personal life stories. Once again, however, the individuals' stories do not simply duplicate the organizational versions of institutional meta-narratives or the institutional meta-narratives, but are rather translations thereof, on the basis of members' reinterpretations. The travel of stories across social levels is a process of institutional maintenance, as the use of societal-level meta-narratives on the organizational and individual levels both reflects and further strengthens the institutional order.

Studying institutional maintenance through a narrative perspective highlights three aspects thereof. First, it underlies the delicate balancing between duplication and transformation involved in institutional maintenance. Second, it shows the various kinds of agency involved in institutional maintenance, as interests and power relations affect the translation process. Finally, it focuses attention on the complex interfaces of actors at various social levels (society, organizations, and individuals) in the work of institutions.

A narrative take on symbolic institutional maintenance

Like all social constructions, institutions require collective efforts at reconfiguration through interactions among their constituents in a continuous, cyclic process (Berger & Luckmann, 1967; Giddens, 1984; Barley & Tolbert, 1997). Since the institutional order is "unfinished" (DiMaggio, 1988: 12), institutions require ongoing work. Maintaining the institutional order by supporting, correcting, or recreating the mechanisms that guarantee social compliance with it (Lawrence & Suddaby, 2006: 230) is crucial for institutional stability (Scott, 2008).

Two aspects of institutions need maintenance – rules and symbols (Lawrence & Suddaby, 2006; Scott, 2008). Rules relate to the regulative and normative pillars of institutions, and their maintenance requires disciplinary acts to keep their system of rewards and punishments. Symbols, on which I focus here, relate to the cultural-cognitive pillar of institutions, and their maintenance involves the efforts at making sense of the institutional order and reproducing its values and meanings. These latter work may include, for instance, positive, negative, or nostalgic constructions of the past, present, and potential future ("valorizing," "demonizing," and "mythologizing"; Lawrence & Suddaby, 2006) that embody and strengthen the meaningful underpinning of an institution.

So far, institutional maintenance has attracted only modest empirical interest (Lawerence & Suddaby, 2006), and the few relevant studies (Angus, 1993; Kilduff, 1993; Miller, 1994; Zilber, 2002) touch only briefly on its symbolic aspects. Thus, I set out to explore how symbolic institutional work is carried out.

My study of symbolic institutional maintenance is based on a discursive approach to institutions, which holds that institutions are built upon, and are supported by, shared systems of meanings (Phillips, Lawrence & Hardy, 2004). These shared understandings, termed discourses, are comprised of spoken, written, performative, and spatial texts, grounded in specific contexts and power relations (Clegg, 1993; Fairclough, 1992; Hardy & Phillips, 2004). Discourses constitute institutions by defining the taken-for-granted structures, practices, and beliefs in a specific field. Thus, institutionalization involves the production, dissemination, and consumption of texts (Phillips *et al.*, 2004). The emergence of new institutions (Lawrence & Phillips, 2004; Maguire & Hardy, 2006), as well as institutional change (Greenwood, Suddaby & Hinings, 2002; Munir & Phillips, 2005; Rao, Monin & Durand, 2003), entails a change in the underlying discourses, and is initiated by interested actors who engage in the writing and rewriting of various documents. Institutionalization, then, is a "textual affair" (Munir & Phillips, 2005: 1669).

While the discursive approach to institutionalization is by now well established (for a review see Zilber, 2008) – testifying to the important role of texts and discourses in supporting institutions, their creation and change – we know much less about the role of discourse in the process of institutional maintenance. Thus, in this chapter I try to further develop our understanding of the discursive dynamics of symbolic institutional maintenance. To do so, I focus on a specific discursive device – stories.

Narratives[1] hold much epistemological, methodological, and empirical potential for the study of the discursive dynamics of institutional

---

[1] Notwithstanding some differential definitions and uses in literary theory and elsewhere, I use "story" and "narrative" interchangeably throughout this chapter.

maintenance: to begin with, stories as discrete and patterned units of meanings take part in the ever going process of social construction by combining in complex ways reality, experience, belief, behavior, interpretation, and interest. Narration involves the selection, combination, editing, and molding of events into a story form – in particular, organizing them with the help of plots, protagonists, scenes, and morality – by which they are given meaning (Garro & Mattingly, 2000: 22; Ochs & Capps, 1996). At the same time, these narrativized interpretations of the past influence people's understandings, behaviors, and invested interests in the present and future (Czarniawska, 1998; Gabriel, 2000). Hence, the stories we tell reflect and express – and also *shape* and *create* – realities and experiences thereof. As institutions are social constructions, and their maintenance involves the reconstruction of the institutional order, the narration of stories as social action offers a unique window into the micro-dynamics of the process.

Further, stories are collective creations. They are co-authored by multiple actors (Boje, 2001; Gabriel, 2000), in a process that involves interests, power relations, and political maneuvering (Mumby, 1993). The study of institutional maintenance from a narrative perspective may help us explore its political dynamics.

Finally, stories take part in the social construction of individual, organizational, and societal realities. On the individual level, life stories – stories people tell to themselves and to others about their lives – are reconstructions of the past, as influenced by the present, and in light of imagined futures. These reconstructions are "born out of experience and give shape to experience. In this sense, narrative and self are inseparable" (Ochs & Capps, 1996: 20), so that personal life stories constitute "identity," or the "self" (Bruner, 1986, 1990; Gergen & Gergen, 1987; McAdams, 1988, 1993). Thus, in constructing personal identity as the "unfolding reflective awareness of 'being-in-the-world'" (Ochs & Capps, 1996: 21), storytelling holds a central role. Organizations as well are "storytelling" systems (Boje, 1991). Organizational identity – the shared understanding of "who we are" (Albert & Whetten, 1985) – is constituted by the "stories about organizations that actors author in their efforts to understand, or make sense of, the collective entities with which they identify" (Brown, 2006: 734). These may include multiple stories of various types, like stories told in conversations, corporate websites, and annual reports. Likewise, shared understandings and meaning systems in the broad sociocultural environment may take the form of "meta-narratives." Also called "grand narratives," "master narratives," or "dominant narratives" (see Lyotard, 1984), these views and beliefs about human nature and behavior as well as the physical world are organized as templates or scripts that individuals use when making sense through the construction of stories. The "cultural stock of stories" available to narrators within a specific cultural domain (Bruner, 1990; Polkinghorne, 1988: 107; Ricoeur, 1991: 33; Rosenwald & Ochberg, 1992: 5–7) underlies and gives sense to any particular story (Polkinghorne, 1988: 153; Wertsch & O'Connor, 1994). As stories operate on multiple social levels, a narrative perspective allows us to understand and explore institutional maintenance at the interfaces of multiple social levels.

To sum, I examine the discursive dynamics of institutional maintenance as carried out through the specific medium of stories. My case study is an Israeli rape crisis center, operating under the influence of two institutions: a feminist ideology and a psychotherapeutic world view. I aim at offering an *interpretative account* of the center and the discursive dynamics of institutional maintenance within it. Specifically, I follow the travel of stories across multiple social levels and their interpretations and translations along the way. I focus on the forms of institutional work that are used to carry – embed and translate – societal meta-narratives into organizations and the lives of their members.

Methods

The case study: Orot rape crisis center

My study is based on fieldwork in "Orot" (pseudonym) rape crisis center in Israel (to which I will refer as "the center," as its members do). Originally, I was drawn to explore the relations between ideology and practice in a feminist organization, but later on I came to understand the center through the perspective of neo-institutionalism, and in particular as an organization that operated under the effect of two diverse institutions, the feminist ideology and the psychotherapeutic world view (Zilber, 2002). The rape crisis center was established by feminist women as a non-governmental and non-profit organization. Its objectives, methods of operation, definitions of rape, and actual exercise of assistance to rape victims were rooted in a feminist ideology. With the years, many non-feminist, therapeutically oriented women and men joined the center, carrying with them a new, therapeutic institution. This institution pushed forward a process of professionalization that changed the power relations within the organization. It also affected the language through which members of the organization made sense of rape, victims, and relations among themselves. In particular, it turned the support work into the central script for all types of relations within the center. The two institutions complemented each other in some respects, and competed in others, affecting intra- and interorganizational structures, practices, and meanings (for a detailed description and analysis, see Zilber, 2002). At the time I gathered the empirical data, the organization operated crisis hotlines to victims of rape, mostly by volunteers. Aside from telephone and face-to-face support, its activities included prevention of rape, especially by lobbying for changes in the attitudes toward rapists and rape victims as manifested in Israel's law and in the practices and understandings of various state agencies (police, juridical systems, health-care organizations, and the educational system). Most funding came from donations, and only a small part derived from quite irregular governmental support. The center held a small number of salaried employees (administrators) who aimed at working as a non-hierarchical collective body, and was run by a committee elected annually from among the volunteers.

There were altogether some 160 registered volunteers at the center (80 percent women), but only a third were active on a regular basis. Some joined on the basis of their feminist convictions, others in relation to the psychotherapeutic activity carried out in the center (especially students of clinical psychology and social work), and still others came in because of a desire "to contribute to society." Upon joining the center all volunteers participated in a training course. The annual turnover at the center was high, usually about 50 percent. Volunteers who had been active at the center for over two years were known as "seniors" (a few volunteers had been there for five to ten years, and one was active at the center for eighteen years).

Data and analysis

Data were collected in two different research projects. First, in the years 1995–1996, I conducted eighteen months' fieldwork at the center. This research included participant observation, interviews, and the collection of archival data. Like all newcomers to the organization, I participated in the eighteen-week-long training course. Later, I volunteered on the hotline throughout the research period. I spent two days per week in the center, observing a variety of meetings, social gatherings, and other activities. I also conducted interviews with thirty-six volunteers (all recorded and later transcribed), dealing with their perceptions of the center's identity. As part of my fieldwork, I collected many organizational-level stories – stories about the organization and its identity as well as stories about events, members, and support relations, told in decision-making processes, meetings, and social gatherings. I also noted the way these stories echoed societal-level meta-narratives (Zilber, 1998). In 2002, a student of mine, Etty Levy, herself a volunteer at the center, conducted under my guidance another study in the organization, this time focusing on the experience of the volunteers. As part of this study, she interviewed twelve volunteers (again, all interviews were recorded and later transcribed). Each interview started with a general request that the interviewee tell her "life story." To assist them, Levy first asked them to divide their lives into chapters, as if they were about to write a book about their lives (see Lieblich, Tuval-Mashiach & Zilber, 1998). Based on these chapters, the researcher guided the interviewee through the story of her life, asking for details about each period. The second half of each interview touched upon the experience of volunteering in the center – especially interviewees' motivation and the role and effect of the center in their lives.

Levy (2004) found that there was much similarity between life stories told by different interviewees. While the content of the stories was quite different and unique to each, they resembled each other structurally. Narrators seemed to follow a similar plot of trauma and recovery. These findings resonated with my previous study, and led me to explore more deeply the interplay of stories across social levels, which I then conceptualized as institutional maintenance (Lawrence & Suddaby, 2006). My narrative analysis (Boje, 2001; Gabriel, 2000) proceeded in the following stages.

In the first stage, I reread cultural studies of Israel, looking for the analysis of feminist and therapeutic discourses. I reread the available data from my own study (interviews, field notes, transcripts of meetings and social gatherings, including the training course), looking for stories – heroes, villains, complications and their resolutions. Finally, I reread Levy's (2004) analysis of volunteers' life stories.

In the second stage, I analyzed the stories according to their poetical tropes, like characters, plot lines, and causal attributions. Once I

Table 8.1. *Narrating stories at three social levels*

Level of analysis	Societal level of institutional meta-narratives		Organizational narration of the institutional	Individuals' narration of the institutional and the organizational
Narrative dimension	Feminist	Therapeutic	Feminist/therapeutic	Feminist/therapeutic
Protagonist	Female	The individual	Weak victim	The narrator
Villain	Male	"Significant others" and their inner representations	Powerful offender	Specific people in her life
Supporting roles	Sisterhood	Therapist, the "healthy self"	Rape crisis center volunteers	Inner strength
Plot	From powerlessness to empowerment	From misery to well-being	From sexual trauma to recovery, through support	From trauma to empowerment
Causal factors	Broad social order	Inner psychological processes	Both broad social and inner forces	Both broad social and inner forces
Attribution of responsibility	Society	Protagonist	Offender, society	Offender, protagonist
Content	Gender inequality	Individual and collective behaviors and choices	Sexual assault	Variety of personal crises

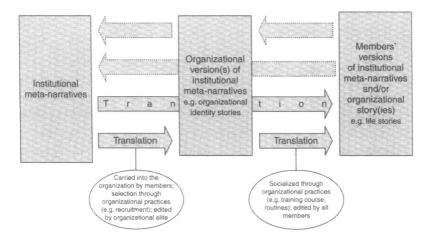

Figure 8.1 Institutional maintenance as narrative acts

identified the content and form of the stories, I was able to characterize the "ideal" story at each social level. I use the term "ideal" story after Weber (Shils & Finch, 1949), to denote story types that do not exist, but rather represent the typical attributes of groups of stories. The results of this stage of the analysis are summarized in Table 8.1.

In the third stage, after reinterpreting the materials through narrative analysis, I came to understand the micro-dynamics of institutional maintenance within the center as a drama of stories. Here I integrated my knowledge of the dynamics at various levels of analysis: combining the analysis of societal-level meta-narratives, organizational-level stories and dynamics (the center's recruitment practices, socialization processes through the training course, and power relations and inner politics) based on my previous research (Zilber, 1998, 2002), and individual-level stories (based on Levy, 2004). The wealth of data allowed me to offer an interpretative account of institutional maintenance as the travel of stories across social levels. The results of this stage of the analysis are summarized in Figure 8.1, which offers a graphic representation of the process of institutional maintenance through narrative acts.

Maintaining the symbolic institutional order: Orot rape crisis center

I will first present my reading of the institutional stories told at the societal, organizational, and individual levels, and highlight the strong parallels between them, as well as their interpretation and translation at each level. I will then move to suggest the organizational practices through which the institutional meta-narratives were translated into the center and the lives of its members.

From powerlessness/misery to empowerment/well-being: feminist and therapeutic societal-level institutional meta-narratives

The feminist and therapeutic institutions are both salient in Israeli society. Feminism – a diverse and contested ideology, theory, and social action – holds that women are discriminated against on the basis of their gender. While the causes of this discrimination, as well as its consequences and potential strategies for its elimination, are contested among various feminist streams, they all agree that gender equality is to be sought (Whelehan, 1995). Striving to be part of the democratic and liberal western world, and still working within the impact of other traditions and tendencies, Israel may be characterized by conflicting tendencies regarding the status of women and feminism. On the one hand, Israeli law is progressive, protecting women's equality and offering various mechanisms to encourage their involvement in public life (Radai, 1983). On the other hand, various forces and sociopolitical arrangements reinforce traditional roles and the marginalization of women, among them religious beliefs and norms backed by state structures and practices (Radai, 1991), the centrality of the family and motherhood (Berkovitch, 1997), and the centrality of the military as a patriarchal organization in the society at large (Izraeli, 1997; Levy-Schreiber & Ben-Ari, 2000). The feminist movement in Israel was established in the early 1970s, but it is still fighting for social and political status and impact. Israeli society, for the most part, is still cautious and suspicious of feminist activism (Rapoport & El-Or, 1997; Rozin, 2005; Safran, 2006).

The therapeutic institution in Israel, like feminist ideology, is derived from, and is localized on the basis of, the therapeutic institution in the West. Therapy has become a cultural phenomenon (Bellah, Madsen, Sullivan, Swidler & Tipton, 1985) and therapeutic notions have become a folk model, guiding the process of understanding and sense-making among professionals and lay persons alike (Rose, 1998). The therapeutic institution focuses on the individual, and emphasizes emotional and cognitive inner processes. It highlights the power of talk in curing processes. Given the professionalization of therapy, it enjoys high status in Israeli society.

The feminist and therapeutic institutions were prevalent then at the societal level in which Orot rape crisis center has been operating. In narrative terms, each of these institutions was embodied in a meta-narrative, a story template that includes characters and roles (e.g. heroes, villains, victims), a plot line (a problem, a solution state, and the potential activities that may move the protagonist from the problematic state to its resolution), attributions (e.g. of causal connection and responsibility), and common contents (e.g. various kinds of crisis).

The feminist institution was based upon a feminist meta-narrative (see Table 8.1) common in the modern West, and which can be put to use to explain a variety of phenomena, from wage differences between the genders, to differential representation in political systems, to gender stereotypes in advertisements (to name just a few). The crisis, conflict, or deficiency state that stands at the heart of the feminist plot is discrimination against women. It casts the central characters and roles in the story – victims/heroines (usually women, as a social category, not individuals), and villains/oppressors (usually men, again as a social category). Other women may play supporting roles, helping the protagonist to find her inner powers through sisterhood. The explanations feminists offer for women's subordination in its numerous manifestations attribute the differences to social, political, and cultural constructions of gender and gender relations. Hence, the story is located within a broad social, cultural, political, and historical context. The themes of gender inequality and oppression serve as the logic that links the various actions and stages in the story (offering a generic causal sequence). The desired goal according to the feminist meta-narrative is to eliminate harmful gender power relations, a goal that can be achieved through a political struggle of women acting consciously together. The story is about empowerment.

The therapeutic institution was based upon a therapeutic meta-narrative (see Table 8.1), as this cultural construct is used – in psych-professional circles and popularized in the modern West – to explain a variety of phenomena. These include individual behaviors and life choices (e.g. divorce, educational or occupational success or failure), as well as collective and even national-level behaviors. According to this meta-narrative, the world is viewed through an individual-focused lens.

Notwithstanding the variety of psychological, psychiatric, and therapeutic discourses, the therapeutic meta-narrative revolves around an
intra-psychic, individual distress. Following the dominance of the post-
trauma and object-relations paradigms in the last few decades, it is most
commonly phrased in terms of traumatic events, or problematic relations with "significant others," and their inner representations. These
inner conflicts, ambivalences, and traumas may have various manifesta-
tions, usually maladaptive behaviors, as well as cognitive and emotional
dynamics at the individual or collective level. The solution lies in resolving the problem by bringing it to consciousness and through talk-cure
and other individual-centered technologies of self-management. The
main character in this therapeutic meta-narrative is a sufferer – a victim
of life circumstances, misdoings by others, or her own behavior. To her
side we may find another character in a supporting role. A psychody-
namic or post-traumatic logic ties the various actions in the story. It is
also a story of transformation, but the driving force is not political as
much as professional, with therapeutically trained characters helping
individuals in distress to re-establish their well-being.

Sexual trauma and recovery: the organizational-level story

The feminist and therapeutic institutional meta-narratives were actively
translated as they traveled into the rape crisis center. One organizational
version of these institutional meta-narratives was built on selective
motifs from the two, relating more concretely to the organization's
main activity, that is helping victims of sexual assault (see Table 8.1).
It included three main parts: a story of trauma, like rape or sexual abuse;
a post-traumatic reaction; and recovery. The trauma was usually
depicted as sudden, unpredicted, capturing the victim unguarded and
unable to prevent it. The post-traumatic reaction included feelings of
helplessness, shame, and inability to ask for help. The recovery was
marked by finding inner strength or outside support, coming to terms
with what had happened and feeling re-empowered. Further, the organizational version was constructed by using a limited set of characters.
The victim was the main character, a protagonist that was usually
depicted at the beginning of the story as weak. The offender(s) were
stronger than the victim – men versus women, grown-ups versus a child,
a group versus an individual. They were able to take command over the
protagonist's life and make her do as they wished. Most stories included

another character, a rape crisis volunteer, in a supporting role of helping the victim find her inner strength. The story was transformative. By its end the victim emerged out of the trauma empowered. Finally, the organizational version contained various "poetic tropes" (Gabriel, 2000), centered on issues of power and domination (attribution of motives, and of blame and credit) as well as self-reflection and retrospect (attribution of emotion, and of agency).

This organizational version of the institutional meta-narratives was apparent in a variety of organizational texts, like the "blue notebook" that explicated guidelines for support, volunteers' entries in the hotline log, and stories of the center's history as told to me in interviews (Zilber, 1998).

Individual stories of trauma-and-empowerment

The power of the institutional meta-narratives and their organizational version is further evident when we explore their use on the individual level. Levy (2004), who studied the experience of volunteering in the center, asked her interviewees to tell her the story of their lives, hoping to find how the center and their involvement with it were woven into their stories. It turned out that the impact of the center on their stories was profound. The interviewees seemed to construct their life stories – their identities according to narrative psychology (Bruner, 1986, 1990) – using the organizational version of the institutional meta-narratives. Yet, they did so while further translating and adapting it to their needs (see Table 8.1). One interviewee, for example, spoke of her troubled relations with her sister. She described her sister as constantly hurting her, invading her privacy by reading her letters and diary; insulting her to the point that she lost her self-confidence; and enforcing her preferences over those of other members of the family (like changing the channel on TV and always making everyone watch whatever she wanted). The interviewee described her parents as too weak to put any boundaries on her sister, thus leaving her to cope with her by herself. Another interviewee told a story about her conflicted relations with her mother after the death of her father. Stricken by grief, the mother demanded that the interviewee, who was a child at the time, took some of the father's roles and responsibilities upon herself. Among them, she asked the child to put her to sleep at night and physically comfort her in bed. The interviewee described her feeling of disgust and repulsion from the touch of her mother's body against hers. While she did not talk about sexual abuse, she constructed the story using many themes of stories of incest. Another interviewee told a story about her problematic romantic relations. The man she loved and lived with at the time used to weigh her every morning, in an effort to "help" her to lose weight and look "perfect." In retrospect, the interviewee saw these relations as problematic, and interpreted her partner's behavior as dominating, controlling, and humiliating.

But the stories did not end with the experience of vulnerability and pain. Rather, all these interviewees told stories that ended up with an optimistic note, as they told how they managed to recover from the early offenses inflicted upon them. Some of them highlighted a psychological process of getting to know themselves, learning to hear and respect their inner voices, to acknowledge their true wishes and aspirations, and pursue them with the help of their newly found self-awareness. Others told a story about a struggle in which they found the strength to stand up against those hurting them, and fight for their rights.

I will present here one detailed story to exemplify the individual translations and use of the organizational version of institutional meta-narratives in the life stories of volunteers in the center. Alice (pseudonym), in her late twenties, had been volunteering in the center for about a year prior to the interview. She was single, and lived in a rented flat with other tenants. She had an academic education in the social sciences and was just beginning her professional career. Her life story included a few episodes of trauma and recovery, and I will describe one here. When in first grade, living in a small town, a group of second graders extorted her for marbles. "Because I was a fragile child," she said,

[A]nd there was another girl from another small town [in the school], and they were frightening. She had two friends from second grade, and at the time it was very frightening and intimidating ... they made her bring them marbles every day, marbles to play, and she, my friend from that small town, she told me to bring marbles, like a gift to them. And then, and I remember that as a very difficult experience, because, what happened is, that almost every day I stole marbles from my parents, so I can bring her one marble every day, so she can give it to them. Because, I think they knew it was me who brings the marbles, and if I hadn't brought them, I think it would have ended badly, they threatened to do this and that. (Levy, 2004: 83; translated from Hebrew)

Alice constructed her story in a way that echoed stories of gang-rape. In gang-rape, a girl or a woman is attacked by a group of boys or men, who depict her as weak and vulnerable, helpless against the power of the group. The group acts out of confidence that the victim will not share with others what is happening to her, and members of the group seem to believe that they are entitled to exploit her weakness and the benefits she can provide them with (see, for example, Sanday, 2007). Similarly, Alice tells a gendered story of herself as a weak girl, bullied by two intimidating boys through the mediation of a shared friend. Their threats prevented her from asking for help, and they managed to rub her for a long time.

But eventually Alice managed to stop them from hurting her anymore:

And then, I remember that as a turning point, that ... one time, that girlfriend from the small town, the one to which I had to bring the marbles, she made me very angry, I don't remember, she called me names or something, and I became very irritated, and I started to beat her up, and people were in quite a shock, I have never beaten anyone before, and I was quite weak, and this was a turning point for me, no one will abuse me anymore. (Levy, 2004: 84; translated from Hebrew)

Alice fought back, not only against the abusing girlfriend and the two boys, but also against her own depiction of herself as weak and vulnerable. She changed her own ways, acting against her usual pattern. According to her story, this transformation brought about a major change in her life ever since, as she was never again victimized.

Note how a seemingly "simple," trivial story of childhood rivalry and conflict, similar to experiences which many of us remember from our own childhood, is constructed here as a significant, painful, yet eventually empowering experience. It is through the use of the organizational trauma-and-empowerment story that this transformation had occurred, or represented to the listener (and to the teller). Indeed, analyzing this and other stories suggests that most of the interviewees used the trauma-and-empowerment story (trauma, struggle to cope, a renewed strength) to construct their lives. However, personal narratives are translations of organizational narratives: while the content of the organizational version was focused on sexual trauma and abuse, members' life stories were much more varied in terms of content (Levy, 2004).

Institutional work: linking societal meta-narratives to organizational and individual stories

So far I have shown how the stories at three social levels echo each other. I will now turn to exemplify the forms of institutional work involved in linking the institutional meta-narratives to the organizational and individual stories. To begin with, organizational recruitment practices explain how the two institutional meta-narratives traveled into the center. As well, the organizational version of the institutional meta-narratives was actively conveyed to newcomers through the training course. Finally, organizational routines – like the keeping of a hotline log – further strengthen the linkage between stories on various social levels.

My study of the organization (Zilber, 1998, 2002) suggests that both institutional meta-narratives were carried into the center by feminist and therapeutically oriented professionals. As the organization suffered from high turnover, recruiting new volunteers was always a pressing concern. But recruitment practices were limited in scope, as members believed it takes a certain character and background to join the center. Specifically, the organization relied on reaching out to both a close network of feminist circles and students of social work and psychology (Zilber, 2002). By limiting the entry of new volunteers to these two populations, the center ensured that only the feminist and therapeutic institutions will be carried into it, and that both institutions will be represented. Thus, recruitment practices account for the co-presence of these two institutions within the center.

The mandatory training course, which all members had to pass before officially joining the center as volunteers, is another form of institutional work that helped to link societal-level institutional meta-narratives to the organizational and individual stories. All new members went through a fifteen- to eighteen-week training course, which encompassed some sixty hours of lectures, workshops, group dynamics, and role-playing. Each training course was guided by two experienced volunteers, who usually had professional training in group dynamics. The group – some fifteen participants – was gender homogeneous, all women or all men. In my training course we were fourteen women, ages ranging from 20+ to 50+, with a variety of backgrounds, employment status, and professional affiliations.

The training course involves learning of much information about various kinds of sexual assault, victims' reactions and behaviors, support relations, processing of rape by state apparatuses, as well as about the center itself. It also included dynamic work on management of emotions and cognitions, and in particular raising the self-awareness of future volunteers aimed at enhancing their capacities in supporting and being sensitive to victims and their needs. My interviews and informal talks with a few course instructors, as well as the analysis of course outlines that they shared with me, suggest that the course structure and format emerged out of much trial-and-error as well as deliberate efforts by staff, board members, and instructors to define the core elements and beliefs according to which the center is organized and operates, and deliver them to newcomers. Those involved with the design and delivery of the training courses were aware of their importance and potential as socialization tools (Saks & Ashforth, 1997), and they were striving to make best use of that.

Most important for my argument are the ways by which this learning and training were taking place. The training course was led as a dynamic group. There were hardly any frontal lectures. Instead, most meetings were run as an open exchange, enhanced by exercises and role playing. The course's instructors as well as all the guest lecturers shared with the participants their personal experiences, and encouraged participants to do the same. As I reread my field notes and transcriptions from the course, I noted the many *stories* told throughout: stories of victims of sexual assault, stories of volunteers about support relations, and stories of participants about their own sexual and other traumas. The wealth of data shared during the course – about various kinds of sexual assault, the common reactions to rape, and the processing of victims by the state – were delivered through many anecdotes and exemplary stories.

I argue, therefore, that the socialization into the center was enhanced by the learning and mastering of specific storytelling, the organizational version of the societal-level institutional meta-narratives. Participants learned this organizational-level story in both direct and indirect ways. They became familiar with it through listening to the stories and anecdotes told by the instructors and guest lecturers. They learned it through the information delivered to them, as it too was offered in the form of stories. They learned their role as supporters within this story, through role-playing. Finally, they learned to think and construct their own experiences through this meta-narrative, for instance when they were asked to tell their own experience of sexual assaults. As it turned out, many (including myself) were discovering anew, and learning to tell, their identity and their life story as related to, and richly reframed within, this organizational story.

Let me exemplify this last point by describing what is considered to be the highlight of the course, the session of three meetings, lasting twelve hours altogether, entitled "personal stories." Scheduled in the middle of the four-month course, these "personal stories" meetings were usually held in participants' homes (rather than in the center, like all the other activities). The importance of these meetings was stressed from the very beginning, as participants were asked to note the dates on their calendars and make all efforts not to miss them. In these meetings, all participants were asked to tell a personal story of sexual assault. The goals of these sessions, as noted in organizational texts, were threefold – to allow future volunteers to process their personal experience of sexual assault, in the hope that it would not interfere with their ability to support others; to serve as an opportunity for future volunteers to experience giving support to others; and to allow them to experience support from the side of those being helped. The inclusion of these meetings as part of the course reflected the assumption that all women have gone through some experience of sexual assault. Indeed, all women in my course had a story to tell. When we were first told about these meetings, at the beginning of the course, I had no recollection of a sexual assault. Two months later, I had already recalled three such stories, and was wondering which one I should share with the group. The course itself, with the many stories told in it, acted as a consciousness-raising group that guided participants to redefine past experiences in the terminology, and narrative form, offered through the course. Moreover, the instructors, as well as fellow participants, all actively listened to the stories told by their colleagues, expressing empathy and asking questions, and thus taking part in the constructions of the stories (Boje, 2001) in line with the organizational version of the institutional meta-narratives.

A third form of institutional work that helped to link the organizational story to the lives of individuals is the organizational routine of keeping a hotline log. All calls to the hotline were to be recorded by the volunteers in the "log" – a heavy, thick notebook that was always to be kept near the phone. And all entries were to be read by the volunteers first thing as they came in for a new "shift." This routine, which was strictly kept, was meant to ensure the continuity of care and support relations across various volunteers (as many clients called the center on a regular basis, each time answered by another volunteer). It also allowed the gathering of statistical data on the number of calls and their nature, often used in grant applications and lobbying activity. This meant that volunteers routinely wrote, and read, short entries – stories – of victims and their experiences of sexual assault. The entries in the log were varied – some short and others longer, some seemingly objective and cold and others more emotionally loaded, some structured by the progress of the talk and others offering an analytical account of the issues discussed. And yet most entries echo, at their deep structure, the organizational version of the institutional story. That is, most volunteers used this story as a template, when trying to summarize and communicate their talks with victims over the phone. By routinely writing, and reading, these entries, then, volunteers were exposed to, and used, the organizational version of the institutional meta-narratives. In this way, this organizational routine further linked the organizational story with individuals' lives.

Organizational recruitment practices, socialization processes, and routines all served, then, as forms of institutional work that linked societal meta-narratives to the organizational and individual stories.

Discussion: symbolic institutional maintenance from a narrative perspective

My analysis of Orot rape crisis center exemplifies how institutions are maintained through narrative work (see Figure 8.1). I showed that organizational processes made a specific version of institutional meta-narratives available for organizational members, and that this version was used by members even in their personal efforts at making sense of their own lives. In so doing, they reproduce the institutional order, as their stories make sense of the institutional order and reproduce its values and meanings.

The institutional environment contains meta-narratives that denote the webs of meanings and understandings that legitimate institutional structures, practices, and beliefs, and guide actors in making sense of the organizational field (otherwise conceptualized, in the lingo of institutional theory, as "rational myths" [Meyer & Rowan, 1977] or "discourses"

[Phillips *et al.*, 2004]). Institutional meta-narratives are story templates that chart a space of possibilities in terms of characters, roles, plot lines, and other poetical tropes.

As institutional environments contain multiple meaning systems (Friedland & Alford, 1991), they contain multiple meta-narratives as well. Narrators use meta-narratives as cultural "tools" (Swidler, 1986) to choose from and work out their specific lines of action, meaning-making, and interpretation. Given the multiplicity of meta-narratives and of narratives, the relation between them is quite complex and multidirectional: each meta-narrative can support various particular stories, and each particular story may build on various meta-narratives. Meta-narratives restrict and direct, to some extent, the narration of particular stories within their domain. At the same time, these institutional meta-narratives are generic and flexible, in the sense that they can be quite easily adopted and adapted to narrate (make sense of) different circumstances, on different levels (e.g. from the individual to the national).

Institutional maintenance is the process through which institutional meta-narratives common at the societal level are used to make sense of the world by organizations and by individuals within them. Hence both organizations and individuals within them carry (Scott, 2003), or reproduce, the institutional order. In a cyclic process of storytelling, the institutional order is maintained, as stories at each level reflect higher-level stories, and further strengthen them.

Organizational members carry institutional meta-narratives into the organization. While the institutional environment contains multiple meta-narratives, not all institutional meta-narratives are carried into organizations. It is a selective process that involves various organizational practices, like recruitment and socialization processes. Further, those stories which do travel across organizational boundaries are translated, that is modified, adapted, and aligned to the organization. They are made available to organizational members through socialization processes and through their distribution in organizational texts. Organizational members may use these stories to make sense of their own lives, while further interpreting and translating them.

Institutional maintenance through narrative acts is more complicated than the linear depiction outlined above. Members of the center used institutional meta-narratives in their life stories, not only in relation to the organizational-specific version they were socialized into and trained to use. Rather, they used this version as it echoed societal institutional meta-narratives they were familiar with (long arrows at the back, in Figure 8.1). Thus, institutional meta-narratives were legitimated on the societal level; they were given specific meaning in the organizational level; and thus were known enough and productive enough for members to use in their efforts to make sense of their own lives. As well, in my study I focused only on one side of the process, following the travel of stories from the societal, through the organizational, to the individual level. But the process is bilateral. With time, individual and organizational translations of institutional meta-narratives may reflect back on the societal level, and change the institutional meta-narratives themselves (dotted arrows in Figure 8.1).[2]

My study of symbolic institutional maintenance from a narrative perspective offers three main contributions to our understanding of institutional maintenance. First, it highlights maintenance as operating between duplication and change, and specifically worked out through interpretation and translation. Second, it highlights the political aspects of symbolic institutional maintenance. Finally, it highlights maintenance as institutional work carried out at the interface of various social levels. More generally, it testifies to the merits of a narrative perspective on institutional work, and offers some interesting avenues for future research.

Institutional maintenance between duplication and change: the dynamics of interpretation and translation

Institutional maintenance carried out through storytelling is not a simple process of replication. When organizations construct their own versions of institutional meta-narratives, they do so through acts of interpretation that in fact creatively modify or translate (Czarniawska & Joerges, 1996; Sahlin-Andersson, 1996; Zilber, 2006) societal-level meanings to serve their interests and goals, and to fit their specific conditions. Likewise, organizational members' use of

---

[2] For example, the rape crisis center, as part of the Israeli feminist movement, did manage to affect the discourse of sexual assault and rape in Israel (e.g. Safran, 2006).

organizational versions of institutional meta-narratives involves further interpretation and translation.

The feminist and therapeutic institutions, as developed in the West (Whelehan, 1995; Rose, 1998), and translated into Israeli society (Rozin, 2005), were further translated to fit the issues, concerns, and everyday experiences within the center. The organizational version reflects, and further recreates, the web of meaning characteristics of the feminist and therapeutic institutions that govern the center. It reflects the political, feminist understanding of rape as a crime of domination, best understood within the wide, gendered social order (rather than within the narrow and individualized interaction between a specific man and a woman; Brownmiller, 1975; Stock, 1991). Thus the stories depict unequal power relations, a weak victim and a strong offender, and they celebrate the ability to change this situation (for victims to emerge empowered). At the same time, the stories also reflect the therapeutic institution by highlighting the psychological response to sexual trauma and the importance of self-awareness and talk-cure in the process of coping with it (Nudelman, 1997). The combined organizational version of these institutional meta-narratives played down the political and critical zeal of the feminist meta-narrative, while also softening the strict professional gaze on inner-psychological dimensions as suggested by the therapeutic meta-narrative. Individuals' stories as well, while reflecting the organizational version, further modified it. The most striking adaptation relates to the content of the personal identity stories. Whereas the organizational narrative of trauma and empowerment was usually carrying specific contents of sexual abuse, rape or incest, many of the interviewees used this plot-line while charging it with non-sexual contents.

Thus, symbolic institutional maintenance is a balancing act, as organizations and individuals rely on institutional meta-narratives while modifying them. Too many modifications may result, with time, in institutional change. Not enough modifications may deem institutional meta-narratives useless (i.e. not being relevant enough) in organizational and individual sense-making, and thus may result, with time, in deinstitutionalization (Oliver, 1992). Institutional maintenance is not an automatic duplication of the institutional order, nor is it an unconstrained adaptation thereof. Future work may shed more light on the delicate balance between duplication and change involved in symbolic institutional maintenance.

The political aspects of symbolic institutional maintenance

Storytelling and translation are political acts (Sahlin-Andersson, 1996; Mumby, 1993). To tell a story, actors need to be in a subject position that allows them to voice their versions, or constructions, of reality (Maguire, Hardy & Lawrence, 2004). Translation involves editing: it is the work of actors who actively rewrite institutional texts (Sahlin-Andersson, 1996). In the translation of societal-level meta-narratives into organizational stories, the organizational elite (managers, powerful individuals) turn their constructions into "reality." At the rape crisis center, the training-course instructors and guest lecturers were the elite – committed, veteran, feminist, experienced, and professionally trained. They had access to a crucial organizational resource, a powerful socialization tool, and they used it to voice their version and turn it into the "formal," "organizational" version. The translation of the feminist and therapeutic meta-narratives into one organizational version served the interests of the organizational elite in two principal ways. First, maintaining the institutional order also sustained their privileged position within the organization (and the institutional order). Second, it served the survival of the organization on which they thrived. In particular, it allowed both institutions, the feminist and the therapeutic, to govern the organization, without an overt conflict between them. It also allowed the organization to be flexible in the way it presented itself outwardly, highlighting feminist or therapeutic characteristics in keeping with audience preferences, and thus made it easier for the organization to gain legitimacy (Zilber, 1998, 2002). The elite members were thus trying to make sure members kept the right balance between a feminist ideology (like the interpretation of rape in sociopolitical terms) and therapeutic skills (like improving the art of listening), which in fact reflected also the delicate power relations within the organization. More generally, then, it seems that actors are motivated to maintain the institutional order within which their interests are vested (Zilber, 2007).

But this is only half the story. For the institutional order to be maintained, it is not enough to make some institutional meta-narratives available for consumption by organizational members. It is not even enough to implement the organizational version in various organizational texts. Rather, for the institutional order to be retained, its symbolic realm needs to be actively consumed by members, that is, used by members in their daily personal sense-making efforts. This personal processing of the institutional order by actors is a more mundane type of agency. In the translation of societal-level meta-narratives into organizational stories, the organizational elite turn their constructions into "reality." In the translation of organizational versions of institutional meta-narratives into individual life stories, however, all members take part. Thus, institutional maintenance involves "institutional entrepreneurship" (DiMaggio, 1988) by powerful actors within the institutional order based on personal merits (DiMaggio, 1991; Fligstein, 1997) and unique positions within the field (Greenwood & Suddaby, 2006), but it also involves more mundane and distributed acts of agency-as-interpretation (Zilber, 2002; and see Zietsma & McKnight, this volume).

The narrative perspective taken in this chapter allowed us to move beyond the tendency of the discursive approach to focus on formal texts. The emphasis on organizational written texts, edited and official, highlights well-calculated intentions and actions, while overlooking and under-theorizing the ways in which meanings are processed in organizations through other kinds of texts. Looking at narrative acts, and trying to provide an interpretive account thereof, may allow scholars to better appreciate the complexity of institutionalization as combining not only meanings and actions as given and as a calculated outcome of the "rational actor," but the ways in which people experience, digest, interpret, and manipulate in action (consciously, but also in less conscious or less acknowledged ways) their lives in light of the institutionalized meanings and practices. In particular, when looking at organization members' narrations of the institutionalized meanings and practices within their own lives, through their life stories, it seems that what they are doing is not just working out clear-cut meanings and well-calculated lines of actions, but rather struggling for an insight, and busy at integrating their experiences, beliefs, actions, and meanings through the use and reinterpretation of available meta-narratives. Thus, the narrative perspective followed here allows us to move from the depiction of institutional agency as acts of heroic entrepreneurial individuals alone, to a more varied and inclusive understanding of agency (Emirbayer & Mische, 1998). Future work may follow suit in examining diverse types of agentive acts (including the mundane) carried out by various actors (including the less powerful) for multiple aims (including the less calculative).

Maintenance at the interface between social levels

Previous studies that touched upon institutional maintenance (as reviewed by Lawrence & Suddaby, 2006) focused on the organizational level, exploring how organizational dynamics (such as recruitment and sense-making) maintain the institutions within which organizations operate (e.g. Angus, 1993; Kilduff, 1993; Miller, 1994; Zilber, 2002). In the same vein, most discursive studies of institutions explore the production and dissemination of texts, assuming but not exploring processes of consumption (e.g. Maguire & Hardy, 2006; Suddaby & Greenwood, 2005; Zilber, 2006; for an exception see Trank & Washington, this volume). Thus, we know little about the ways institutional texts are consumed and used by organizations and individuals. More generally, most institutional studies focus on inter-organizational levels, assuming but not exploring the intra-organizational dynamics of institutions, and the roles and experiences of individuals in institutionalization (Battilana & D'Aunno, this volume).

Institutions, however, operate on multiple levels (Scott, 2008), including society, organizational field, organizations, and individuals. Thus it makes sense to assume that institutional maintenance as well works on multiple levels.[3] For symbols to have the effect of explaining and legitimating institutions they need to be embedded within the larger institutional order, and thus echo societal-level institutions. At the same time, they need to be consumed by members of organizations within the institutional domain, and thus be interpreted and reproduced by social actors. The narrative perspective used in this study, and in particular looking at the various social levels in which narratives are produced and processed, helped in exploring these multilevel dynamics. Institutional maintenance, thus, is a series of narrative acts, each building on higher-level narrative resources (meta-narratives), while adapting them to local contexts (recreating then-specific narratives). The process is creative, delicate, and

---

[3] Logically, one assumes that the organizational-field level should have been part of the process in the rape crisis as well. However, in this particular case, and for historical and political reasons, members at Orot rape crisis center did not experience themselves, and the organization, as operating within a field of organizations. Feeling that the organization is unique and not like any other, they saw themselves as operating within the broad societal level. My interpretation reflects this perception.

political, resulting in a web of stories that echo and further reconstruct the institutional order.

Our understanding of institutional work more generally, and specifically the interplay of social levels involved, may benefit from a
narrative perspective. Stories may take part not only in institutional
maintenance, but also in institutional creation and disruption. Still,
the specific narrative work involved, and its dynamics, will be somewhat different in each type of institutional work. Institutional maintenance requires the use of stories from a higher level in subordinate
ones, and vice versa. While this is a cyclic process, we may analytically
say that our starting point is well-institutionalized narratives, on the
societal level, thus called meta-narratives.[4] These meta-narratives are
re-enacted at other, subordinate levels. In institutional maintenance,
we see no substantive change in the societal meta-narratives.
Institutional creation, by contrast, entails the establishment of *new*
meta-narratives or determining anew the balance and hierarchy
between existing meta-narratives. Rather than building on the institutional meta-narrative, particular stories may build on a different meta-
narrative, borrowed, for instance, from another institutional domain
(or imported from another society). Analytically, in institutional creation the focus is on the "new" stories that add up in the creation of a
new meta-narrative. Institutional change does not involve the creation
of new meta-narratives, nor the reproduction of existing ones, but
demands the *radical transformation* of an established meta-narrative.[5]
Institutional work from a narrative perspective may be conceptualized
thus as involving the narration and travel of stories across institutional
levels, but the relations between meta-narratives and stories, and the
dynamics of the process, will be different in different types of institutional work. Further research could shed more light on these
distinctions.

---

[4] The narrative/meta-narrative distinction is relative and analytic. One could of
course start the analysis from a more global perspective, and view local societies as
embedded within, or in relation with, other societies.

[5] In practice, however, we are looking at times at a continuum, so that institutional
maintenance as the acts of narration, interpretation, and translation of existing
individual or organizational-level stories may add up, with time, in new or at least
changed meta-narratives.

References

Albert, S. & Whetten, D. A. (1985) Organizational identity. *Research in Organizational Behavior*, 7: 263–295.

Angus, L. B. (1993) Masculinity and women teachers at Christian Brothers College. *Organization Studies*, 14(2): 235–260.

Barley, S. R. & Tolbert, P. S. (1997) Institutionalization and structuration: studying the links between action and institution. *Organization Studies*, 18(1): 93–117.

Bellah, R. N., Madsen, R., Sullivan, W. M., Swidler, A. & Tipton, S. M. (1985) *Habits of the Heart: Individualism and Commitment in American Life*. Berkeley: University of California Press.

Berger, P. L. & Luckmann, T. (1967) *The Social Construction of Reality: A Treatise in the Sociology of Knowledge*. New York: Anchor Books.

Berkovitch, N. (1997) Motherhood as a national mission: the construction of womanhood in the legal discourse in Israel. *Women's Studies International Forum*, 20(5–6): 605–619.

Boje, D. M. (1991) The storytelling organization: a study of story performance in an office-supply firm. *Administrative Science Quarterly*, 36(1): 106–126.

(2001) *Narrative Methods for Organizational and Communication Research*. London: Sage.

Brown, A. D. (2006) A narrative approach to collective identities. *Journal of Management Studies*, 43(4): 731–753.

Brownmiller, S. (1975) *Against Our Will: Men, Women and Rape*. New York: Simon & Schuster.

Bruner, J. (1986) *Actual Minds, Possible Worlds*. Cambridge, MA: Harvard University Press.

(1990) *Acts of Meaning*. Cambridge, MA: Harvard University Press.

Clegg, S. R. (1993) Narrative, power and social theory. In D. K. Mumby (ed.), *Narrative and Social Control: Critical Perspectives*, pp. 15–45. Newbury Park, CA: Sage.

Czarniawska, B. (1998) *A Narrative Approach to Organization Studies*. Thousand Oaks, CA: Sage.

Czarniawska-Joerges, B. & Joerges, B. (1996) Travels of ideas. In B. Czarniawska-Joerges & G. Sevón (eds.), *Translating Organizational Change*, pp. 13–48. Berlin: Walter de Gruyter.

DiMaggio, P. J. (1988) Interest and agency in institutional theory. In L. G. Zucker (ed.), *Institutional Patterns and Organizations: Culture and Environment*, pp. 3–21. Cambridge, MA: Ballinger.

(1991) Constructing an organizational field as a professional project: US art museums, 1920–1940. In W. W. Powell & P. J. DiMggio (eds.), *The*

New Institutionalism in Organizational Analysis, pp. 267–292. Chicago: University of Chicago Press.

Emirbayer, M. & Mische, A. (1998) What is agency? *American Journal of Sociology*, 103(4): 962–1023.

Fairclough, N. (1992) *Discourse and Social Change*. London: Polity.

Fligstein, N. (1997) Social skill and institutional theory. *American Behavioral Scientist*, 40(4): 397–405.

Friedland, R. & Alford, R. R. (1991) Bringing society back in: symbols, practice, and institutional contradictions. In W. W. Powell & P. J. DiMaggio (eds.), *The New Institutionalism in Organizational Analysis*, pp. 232–263. Chicago: University of Chicago Press.

Gabriel, Y. (2000) *Storytelling in Organizations: Facts, Fictions, and Fantasies*. Oxford: Oxford University Press.

Garro, L. C. & Mattingly, C. (2000) Narrative as construct and construction. In C. Mattingly & L. C. Garro (eds.), *Narrative and the Cultural Construction of Illness and Healing*, pp. 1–49. Berkeley: University of California Press.

Gergen, K. J. & Gergen, M. (1987) Narratives as relationships. In R. Burnett, P. McGee & D. C. Clarke (eds.), *Accounting for Relationships*, pp. 269–315. London: Methuen.

Giddens, A. (1984) *The Constitution of Society: Outline of the Theory of Structuration*. Berkeley: University of California Press.

Greenwood, R., Suddaby, R. & Hinings, C. R. (2002) Theorizing change: the role of professional associations in the transformation of institutionalized fields. *Academy of Management Journal*, 45(1): 58–80.

Greenwood, R. & Suddaby, R. (2006) Institutional entrepreneurship in mature fields: the big five accounting firms. *Academy of Management Journal*, 49(1): 27–48.

Hardy, C. & Phillips, N. (2004) Discourse and power. In D. Grant, C. Hardy, C. Oswick & L. Putnam (eds.), *Handbook of Organizational Discourse*, pp. 299–316. London: Sage.

Izraeli, D. (1997) Gendering military service in the Israeli defense forces. *Israel Social Science Research*, 12(1): 129–166.

Kilduff, M. (1993) The reproduction of inertia in multinational corporations. In S. Ghoshal & D. E. Westney (eds.), *Organization Theory and the Multinational Corporation*, pp. 259–274. New York: St. Martin's.

Lawrence, T. B. & Phillips, N. (2004) From Moby Dick to Free Willy: macro-cultural discourse and institutional entrepreneurship in emerging institutional fields. *Organization*, 11(5): 689–711.

Lawrence, T. B. & Suddaby, R. (2006) Institutions and institutional work. In S. R. Clegg, C. Hardy, W. R. Nord & T. Lawrence (eds.), *Handbook of Organization Studies*. Thousand Oaks, CA: Sage.

Levy, E. (2004) The experience of women volunteers at a rape crisis center. Unpublished MA thesis, Jerusalem, Israel (in Hebrew).

Levy-Schreiber, E. & Ben Ari, E. (2000) Body-building, character-building and nation-building: Gender and military service in Israel. *Studies in Contemporary Jewry*, 16: 171–190.

Lieblich, A., Tuval-Mashiach, R. & Zilber, T. (1998) *Narrative Research: Reading, Analysis and Interpretation*. Newbury Park, CA: Sage.

Lyotard, J.-F. (1984) *The Postmodern Condition: A Report on Knowledge*. Minneapolis: University of Minnesota Press

Maguire, S., Hardy, C. & Lawrence, T. B. (2004) Institutional entrepreneurship in emerging fields: HIV/AIDS treatment advocacy in Canada. *Academy of Management Journal*, 47(5): 657–679.

Maguire, S. & Hardy, C. (2006) The emergence of new global institutions: a discursive perspective. *Organization Studies*, 27(1): 7–29.

McAdams, D. P. (1988) *Power, Intimacy and the Life Story: Personological Inquiries into Identity*. New York: Guilford Press.

(1993) *The Stories We Live by: Personal Myths and the Making of the Self*. New York: William Morrow.

Meyer, J. W. & Rowan, B. (1977) Institutionalized organizations: formal structure as myth and ceremony. *American Journal of Sociology*, 83: 340–363.

Miller, J. (1994) *The Social Control of Religious Zeal: A Study of Organizational Contradictions*. New Brunswick, NJ: Rutgers University Press.

Mumby, D. K. (1993) *Narrative and Social Control: Critical Perspectives*. Newbury Park, CA: Sage.

Munir, K. A. & Phillips, N. (2005) The birth of the "Kodak moment": institutional entrepreneurship and the adoption of new technologies. *Organization Studies*, 26(11): 1665–1687.

Nudelman, F. (1997) Beyond the talking cure: listening to female testimony on the Oprah Winfrey Show. In J. Pfister & N. Schnog (eds.), *Inventing the Psychological: Toward a Cultural History of Emotional Life in America*, pp. 297–315. New Haven, CT: Yale University Press.

Ochs, E. & Capps, L. (1996) Narrating the self. *Annual Review of Anthropology*, 25: 19–43.

Oliver, C. (1992) The antecedents of deinstitutionalization. *Organization Studies*, 13(4): 563–588.

Phillips, N., Lawrence, T. B. & Hardy, C. (2004) Discourse and institutions. *Academy of Management Review*, 29(4): 635–652.

Polkinghorne, D. E. (1988) *Narrative Knowing and the Human Sciences*. New York: State University of New York Press.

Radai, F. (1983) Equality of women under Israeli law. *Jerusalem Quarterly*, 27: 81–108.

(1991) The concept of gender equality in a Jewish state. In B. S. Swirski & M. P. Safir (eds.), *Calling the Equality Bluff: Women in Israel*, pp. 18–28. New York: Pergamon Press.

Rao, H., Monin, P. & Durand, R. (2003) Institutional change in Toque Ville: nouvelle cuisine as an identity movement in French gastronomy. *American Journal of Sociology*, 108(4): 795–843.

Rapoport, T. & El-Or, T. (1997) Cultures of womanhood in Israel: social agencies and gender production. *Women's Studies International Forum*, 20(5/6): 573–580.

Ricoeur, P. (1991) Narrative identity. *Philosophy Today*, 35(1): 73–81.

Rose, N. (1998) *Inventing Ourselves: Psychology, Power and Personhood*. Cambridge: Cambridge University Press.

Rosenwald, G. C. & Ochberg, R. L. (eds.) (1992) *Storied Lives: The Cultural Politics of Self-understanding*. New Haven, CT: Yale University Press.

Rozin, T. (2005) *What is Feminism?* Tel Aviv: Zemora-Bitan (in Hebrew).

Safran, H. (2006) *Don't Want to Be Nice*. Tel Aviv: Pardes (in Hebrew).

Sahlin-Andersson, K. (1996) Imitating by editing success: the construction of organization fields. In B. Czarniawska-Joerges & G. Sevón (eds.), *Translating Organizational Change*, pp. 69–92. Berlin: Walter de Gruyter.

Saks, A. M. & Ashforth, B. E. (1997) Organizational socialization: making sense of the past and present as a prologue for the future. *Journal of Vocational Behavior*, 51(2): 234–279.

Sanday, P. R. (2007) *Fraternity Gang Rape: Sex, Brotherhood, and Privilege on Campus*. New York: New York University Press.

Scott, W. R. (2003) Institutional carriers: reviewing modes of transporting ideas over time and space and considering their consequences. *Industrial and Corporate Change*, 12(4): 879–894.

(2008) *Institutions and Organizations*, 3rd edn. Thousand Oaks, CA: Sage.

Shils, E. & Finch, H. A. (eds.) (1949) *Max Weber on the Methodology of the Social Sciences*. New York: Free Press.

Stock, W. E. (1991) Feminist explanations: male power, hostility, and sexual coercion. In E. K. Grauerholz & M. A. Koralewski (eds.), *Sexual Coercion: A Sourcebook on its Nature, Causes, and Prevention*, pp. 61–73. Lexington, MA: Lexington Books.

Suddaby, R. & Greenwood, R. (2005) Rhetorical strategies of legitimacy. *Administrative Science Quarterly*, 50: 35–67.

Swidler, A. (1986) Culture in action: symbols and strategies. *American Sociological Review*, 51: 273–286.

Wertsch, J. V. & O'Connor, K. (1994) Multivoicedness in historical representation: American college students' accounts of the origins of the United States. *Journal of Narrative and Life History*, 4(4): 295–309.

Whelehan, I. (1995) *Modern Feminist Thought*. New York: New York University Press.

Zilber, T. B. (1998) Ideology, practice and ambiguity in organizations: a rape crisis center as a feminist organization. Unpublished PhD dissertation, Hebrew University of Jerusalem (In Hebrew).

(2002) Institutionalization as an interplay between actions, meanings and actors: the case of a rape crisis center in Israel. *Academy of Management Journal*, 45(1): 234–254.

(2006) The work of the symbolic in institutional processes: translation of rational myths in Israeli high-tech. *Academy of Management Journal*, 49: 279–301.

(2007) Stories and the discursive dynamics of institutional entrepreneurship: the case of Israeli high-tech after the burst of the bubble. *Organization Studies*, 28(7): 1035–1054.

(2008) The work of meanings in institutional processes and thinking. In R. Greenwood, C. Oliver, R. Suddaby & K. Sahlin-Andersson (eds.), *Handbook of Organizational Institutionalism*. London: Sage.

9 Maintaining an institution in a contested organizational field: the work of the AACSB and its constituents

CHRISTINE QUINN TRANK AND
MARVIN WASHINGTON

T HE concept of institutional work (Lawrence & Suddaby, 2006) offers an important new way to frame institutional analysis, connecting disparate (at least in the empirical literature) institutional processes such as creating, maintaining, and disrupting institutions. With its focus on practical action within organizational fields, institutional work is concerned with the status of the institution itself, rather than simply the impact of institutions on other actors in an organizational field (Lawrence & Suddaby, 2006). We contribute to the study of institutional work by theoretically and empirically examining the question of how an institution maintains its impact on an organizational field in the face of change and the emergence of alternative mechanisms for structuring a field. As such, we are working with a case of institutional work that Battilana and D'Aunno (this volume) describe as practical-evaluative agency aimed at maintaining institutions. Specifically, we examine this in the context of legitimating organizations – organizations such as accrediting bodies, regulatory organizations, and governance associations – established to maintain particular institutional arrangements.

Individuals and organizations play an important role in organizational fields and the ongoing reproduction of institutions (Berger & Luckmann, 1966). Legitimating organizations maintain particular institutional arrangements by conferring legitimacy on other social actors and establishing mechanisms of compliance and membership (e.g. Lawrence, 2004). Although institutions represent a mechanism through which new processes, actors, and organizational forms can be integrated into a field (Greenwood, Suddaby & Hinings, 2002), legitimating organizations are often the public vehicle and symbolic touchstone for these institutional processes. In many ways, these organizations are often the focal and public face of complex institutional arrangements.

Because legitimating organizations, established to confer legitimacy to other actors and organizations, play a central role in organizational fields, they have become an increasingly important focus of attention in organization theory. Consumer watchdog agencies (Rao, 1998), professional associations (Greenwood *et al.*, 2002), collegiate sports associations (Washington, 2004), ISO 9000 quality certification (Guler, Guillen & MacPherson, 2002), and the internationalization of business school accreditation (Durand & McGuire, 2005) are examples of studies of legitimating organizations that have appeared in the organizational literature.

This chapter extends the literature on legitimating organizations and institutional work by examining the institutional work performed by legitimating organizations to maintain *their own* legitimacy and the legitimacy of the institutional arrangements for which they are guardians when alternative structuring mechanisms gain power within a field. At the same time, however, we look at the processes of enactment and reification of this institutional work by constituent organizations in the field. Because legitimating organizations are embedded in larger social and political systems (Holm, 1995), their ability to structure any field is conditioned on the availability of other sources of capital to constituent organizations and the continued reliance of those constituent organizations on the legitimating organization's sanction. By studying not just the work of the legitimating organizations to maintain institutional arrangements, but the extent to which constituent targets enact the institution-reifying work, rather than appropriating other sources of capital, we may assess the validity of a legitimating organization's claims to power in a field. This approach recognizes legitimacy and its value as an intersubjective understanding that requires ongoing reproduction in activities and interactions. It also recognizes the possibility and effects of other, competing bases of power in an organizational field (Bourdieu, 1986).

We use university-based business education as a context. Through this analysis we seek to uncover and describe the institutional work of maintaining the institution of accreditation and the role of the Association to Advance Collegiate Schools of Business – International (AACSB) as a legitimating organization purposively attempting to preserve accreditation as the mechanism of social control in the field of business education in the face of alternative sources of social and cultural capital available for many schools. A significant alternative source of capital in the field of business education is reputation measures such as media rankings. In addition, some schools hold positions of social status that provide field-level capital and privilege. Still other schools hold positions of regional centrality and prominence, and others disciplinary standing that offer an alternative source of legitimacy within a field. These alternative sources of social and cultural capital can affect a legitimating organization's power in a field. Further, by looking at which schools publicly enact the institutional work of the AACSB, as well as at the ways legitimating themes are enacted and used (as opposed to reputation, market, or status themes), we gain a better understanding of the structuring of the field itself.

In the sections that follow, we expand upon our conception of legitimating organizations and discuss their institutional work. We then examine the institutional work of the AACSB in the field of business education, and the penetration of AACSB-generated themes in the public presentation of member schools. After presenting the data, we provide a discussion of how the AACSB attempts to maintain the legitimacy of AACSB accreditation within the field. We conclude with a description of how our work contributes to the growing literature on institutional work.

Institutional work of maintaining institutions

Although there are a number of studies that have examined the institutional work associated with creating and disrupting institutions (see Lawrence & Suddaby, 2006, for a summary), much less is known about the processes of maintaining institutions (Scott, 2001). This appears to be somewhat ironic, given that institutions are assumed to be relatively enduring. Perhaps because the focus of attention on the creation and disruption of institutions is more obviously the purposive action of social actors, institutional work in those contexts is more obvious. In any case, with a few exceptions, the institutional work of maintaining institutions has been something of a black box in institutional research.

Lawrence and Suddaby (2006: 36) assert that the institutional work of maintaining institutions "involves supporting, repairing or recreating the social mechanisms that ensure compliance." It is important to note that institutional work in this definition may include repetition and support of existing practices as well as changes in the social mechanisms of compliance that may be needed to maintain institutions. For example, democracy as an institution persists not only because there are deliberate activities designed to reproduce it (Jepperson, 1991), but also because membership boundaries and rules of participation are changed (as in the case of women's suffrage and the Voting Rights Act in the United States) in response to challenges that problematize practices associated with the institution.

Maintenance work is the active, strategic process of institutions to maintain their status and power in the field. Lawrence and Suddaby (2006: 37) identified two major categories of maintenance work. The first category involves the use of forms of regulatory and legitimate authority: the creation of rules and standards; establishing policing and enforcement processes; and the use of deterrence strategies designed to thwart threats to the institution. The second category of institutional work relies less on forms of legitimate authority, and more upon processes of internalization by reinforcing the normative and cognitive bases for the institution (Selznick, 1957; Washington, Boal & Davis, 2008). These include valorizing or demonizing people who represent positive or negative aspects of normative foundations; the artful repetition of stories from the past to represent the normative bases of the institution; and processes that actively infuse normative meaning into the routines and practices of everyday institutional life.

A legitimating organization must resolve two problems in the process of maintaining institutional arrangements. First, whatever the form of certification conferred by the legitimating organization, it must offer constituents meaningful consequences, either through sanctioning participation in the field or by facilitating constituent organizations' capacity to acquire resources (Oliver, 1997). Legitimating organizations thus facilitate membership and control. Likewise, to the extent that potential constituents can survive and accrue resources without the endorsement of the legitimating organization, the power of the legitimating agency to structure the field (and preserve the institution it serves) is attenuated.

Second, in some fields there are challenges to a legitimating organization's position. For example, in his study of the emergence of consumer watchdog agencies, Rao (1998) describes the competition between for-profit and not-for-profit consumer protection organizations and between alternative not-for-profit models of consumer protection. The competition for legitimacy, however, need not be so direct. There are different types of legitimacy (Suchman, 1995), and more than one type may be operating in a single organizational field (Hoffman, 1999). These legitimacies also may affect organizations in the same field differently (Ruef & Scott, 1998). In their study of hospitals, for example, Ruef and Scott (1998) showed that the relative importance of various types of legitimacy changes over time, and that the antecedents to legitimacy also vary over time. Suddaby and Greenwood (2005) describe the different imperatives affecting the field of accounting, including that of the (then) Big Five accounting firms, which often called up market-based legitimacy, and other professional service firms, which employed normative or moral legitimacy, in the debate over multidisciplinary partnerships. These studies emphasize the notion that "legitimacy" is rarely a monolithic phenomenon and rarely static in an organizational field. Rather, multiple sources of legitimacy often coexist in the same field and become more or less powerful as a resource over time (Dacin, 1997).

For legitimating organizations supporting institutions, this means that some level of institutional work is likely to be necessary in order to survive significant shifts in the organizational fields in which they operate. Legitimating organizations may need to engage in deliberate, conscious action to maintain their field-level power and their gate-keeping role if confronted with a contender legitimating organization (Durand & McGuire, 2005) or just the weakening of the institutional arrangements they preserve in the field. This leads to our first research question: what are the practices that legitimating organizations use to maintain the institutional arrangements they represent and preserve their power to affect the institutional arrangements in an organizational field? Our second question involves the responses from the constituent organizations: how is the institutional work of legitimating organizations to preserve and promote the institutions they represent reflected in the practices and processes of organizations in the organizational field? To shed light on these questions, we examine the field of business education.

The AACSB's coercive system adaptation as institutional work

For many years, the AACSB accredited only those organizations that might be considered to be the most elite business schools in the United States. Originally established in the early 1900s as a means for schools of business to assure the equivalence and transfer of course credit between schools, the body grew to include schools that followed relatively stable sets of curricular and administrative standards. In the early 1990s, significantly in response to the establishment of competing accrediting bodies in the United States and a desire to extend its reach abroad (Durand & McGuire, 2005; McKenna, Cotton & Van Auken, 1997; Miles, Hazeldin & Munilla, 2004), the AACSB expanded membership.

Expansion, however, posed problems for the organization as an accrediting body. Conceptually, accreditation represents a mechanism through which common standards and practices are determined and enforced (Schray, 2006). Now seeking to accredit schools with fewer resources and located in countries with different systems of education than in the United States, the relatively rigid standards for curricular content and faculty qualification were no longer useful (Durand & McGuire, 2005). The AACSB's solution was a mission-based system, in which schools are accredited based on their work toward accomplishing their particular missions. For example, a school's mission may set as its priority any rank ordering of intellectual contribution, teaching, or service. Likewise, scholarship may focus on any ordering of basic, applied, or instructional research. The relative importance of these and other processes is to be determined in consultation with various organizational stakeholders, but it is a school-based priority-setting. The extent to which the school has marshaled its resources in order to achieve the purposes stated in the mission, as assessed by a team of peers, became the basis for accreditation.

By making this change, the number of schools that could potentially qualify for accreditation increased considerably. Under the new processes, accreditation could be conferred on schools emphasizing any combination or ordering of activities, as long as they showed evidence of effectively marshalling resources to achieve their chosen mission. This enabled schools that did not meet earlier standards to become accredited by the AACSB, and offered an index of processes that schools aspiring to accreditation could use to achieve it. Because curriculum and content matters were no longer specified as rigidly, schools with more limited offerings, resources, and different outcome expectations than the legacy schools could be considered for accreditation (Miles *et al.*, 2004).

However, the expansion that resulted from the changes in standards created a situation in which the value of accreditation itself may be compromised from the schools' perspective, and, particularly, to those already accredited (Durand & McGuire, 2005). Critics also asserted that the changes may actually diminish not just the status, but the substance of business education (Trank & Rynes, 2003). Thus, with the AACSB's change in the rules of accreditation – virtually no distinction in accreditation status between a school with a predominantly research mission and a basic research focus, and schools with a primary commitment to teaching and a focus on mostly instructional scholarship – the meaning of membership and the capital available to both legacy and new players shifted (Schmotter, 2000). With the mission-based process, the status configuration changed markedly. The AACSB appears to be aware of potential concern about differentiation when in its preamble to its accreditation guidelines it states:

Acknowledging the diversity within AACSB, all accredited members share a common purpose – the preparation of students to enter useful professional, societal, and personal lives ... Substantial opportunity remains for accredited members to differentiate themselves through a variety of activities. (AACSB, 2006a)

The change has implications for the AACSB as a legitimating organization sustaining accreditation. In many ways, the status of the legacy members is a resource for the AACSB, imbuing cultural value to AACSB accreditation over and above the assurance of meeting particular standards. With expansion, the AACSB's membership becomes less homogeneous, more diverse with regard to status, and, as a consequence, institutional work to maintain its role in structuring the field is necessary. For example, a new focus on measuring "process" and "continuous improvement," rather than common content, was emphasized in the AACSB's public presentations, connecting its rationalization process to broader-quality themes in the business environment (Durand & McGuire, 2005).

Perhaps more critically, at roughly the same time the AACSB was making these changes (and likely as an antecedent to them), the idea of accreditation as the institutional mechanism of regulation in higher education was being challenged by a number of interests. Accreditation, at its heart, is a means of self-regulation by universities away from direct governmental or market oversight. This decentralized system gave colleges and universities considerable autonomy (Schray, 2006: 2). Critics of self-regulation complain that accreditation has become "a crazy-quilt of activities, processes and structures that is fragmented, arcane, more historical than logical" (Dickeson, 2006). Self-regulation, it is argued, is neither rigorous nor transparent, so that the public purposes of accreditation are not met, while benefits to the member universities (and their autonomy) are preserved.

It is in this environment within higher education that the AACSB moved to a mission-based accreditation model, but, significantly, also changed its mechanisms of compliance to adapt to these pressures. Many specialized accrediting organizations, such as those that accredit law and medicine, have symbiotic relationships with professionals in practice and with state certification organizations. Their accreditation, as a result, is tied to professional standards, institutionalized by the state and professional organizations, rather than to specific local interests (Abbott, 1988). Business schools (outside accounting, which has a separate accreditation) have no such institutional link, but, probably more than other areas in higher education, are affected directly and locally by demands for accountability from students, businesses, and alumni (Rynes & Trank, 1999; Trank & Rynes, 2003). The new accreditation processes the AACSB implemented recognize these stakeholder interests directly as part of the rules of accreditation, and constituent organizations must offer evidence that these interests have been addressed.

The changes in the mechanisms of sanctioning membership and compliance were designed to preserve the institution of accreditation in business education and the AACSB's role as a legitimating organization in the face of field-level pressures. The changes, however, may have led to the unintended consequence of violating some of the normative foundations of accreditation that the AACSB represents (Durand & McGuire, 2005).

Reinforcing normative foundations

Institutional work designed to reproduce norms and beliefs may be particularly relevant in the case of the AACSB. Because AACSB accreditation is voluntary, its coercive power is sustained only insofar as the availability of critical resources for constituents accrues from it. Although the organization has responded to pressure from competing accreditation bodies and to calls for accountability to key stakeholders in the field, other problems remain.

One of the key functions of accreditation in education is to provide some measure of validity to the credential acquired by students. Its value lies in the extent to which

employers, students, and other third parties perceive accreditation as adding value to the educational credentials the institution awards. To earn a degree is one thing; to earn it from an accredited institution is something more. (Miller & Boswell, 1979)

It has been argued by a number of observers that accreditation has lost its institutional value in the face of alternative means of validation. One of the AACSB's greatest concerns is the power of media outlets such as *Business Week*, *The Financial Times*, and *US News and World Report* to structure the field as an alternative to accreditation as an arbiter of quality. Perhaps more than accreditation, many schools chase the criteria associated with rankings, some investing considerable resources into being ranked and moving up in the rankings (Policano, 2001; Gioia & Thomas, 1996).

Empirical studies also have shown that AACSB accreditation may not be an indicator of validity in employer decision-making. For example, in an employer survey conducted in the Houston metropolitan area (Shipley & Johnson, 1991), only 40 percent of employers recruiting at universities in Texas were familiar with AACSB accreditation; only 36 percent considered it important. Approximately 88 percent of the firms in the survey indicated that AACSB accreditation made no difference in starting salary or position. Although there are no studies we could find that directly compare the impact of accreditation versus media rankings for employer preference, the level of attention paid to rankings by deans in their strategic decisions would appear to indicate that rankings play a large part in their decisions.

In the last few years, the AACSB has embarked on an active campaign that appears to be designed to reinforce its normative foundations in the face of field-level change and its own adaptive, coercive institutional work, particularly with reference to rankings. Part of this strategy has been to reaffirm its role as "the premier accrediting body" for business schools. The following sections will examine the strategies that the AACSB is using to reassert the value of accreditation and its own position – and its legitimacy – in the field after changing membership boundaries, standards, and its review processes. The material we examine includes press releases, publications targeted to constituents and the public, brochures and other materials targeted to specific audiences (including employers and students), and publications and public pronouncements intended to elevate the status of the AACSB, along with the values and norms associated with accreditation. We also examine the penetration of these arguments to constituent organizations by examining the use of accreditation information and other references to external legitimating sources in brochures and websites.

The institutional work of the AACSB: promoting accreditation

The "promoting accreditation" materials are part of a larger "value of accreditation" campaign designed specifically to preserve the institution of accreditation, not just in the face of the AACSB's adaptations, but to changes in the organizational field of management education, particularly the growing power of media organizations to define quality. In these promotional materials it also reinforces its role as the legitimating organization for accreditation. In the report of its taskforce on business school rankings, the AACSB was urged to take direct action to assert the AACSB's position to define the field (AACSB, 2005: 9):

In the past, AACSB International has not taken an active position regarding the media rankings of business schools. However, recent changes in the business school environment and mission of AACSB have converged to force and enable action. Intensifying competition for students has caused accredited schools and schools seeking accreditation to insist that the association take steps to increase the external recognition of its accreditation brand. Historically, the value of AACSB accreditation has been mostly internal – relying on schools' innate desire to excel and improve. As market power in education has shifted from providers to consumers, however, the external focus of rankings has increased in importance over accreditation. Without intervention, ranked schools may begin to question the need for AACSB accreditation.

The promotional materials are organized on a single website with links to the suggested materials, introduced by the following (AACSB, 2006b):

The links on this page can help you spread the good news to the stakeholders in your community. One is a generic, "fill-in-the-blank" press release, designed as a model with correct figures and accreditation terminology. It is only a suggested format – a guide for you to use in preparing your own school-specific

release. Fill in the appropriate information and include quotes from your
school dignitaries. Be sure to send to both institutional and student publications, as well as your local media.

The campaign to promote the value of accreditation thus represents a
clear instance of institutional work. Using NVivo 7, a software program
designed to aid in the content analysis of text and graphic material, we
identified a number of thematic categories associated with the maintenance of the institution of AACSB accreditation from the promotional
documents. These appear in Table 9.1. It is important to note that in
none of the materials were competing institutions, media rankings, or
accountability pressures explicitly referenced. The specter of each, however, seems implicit in several of the themes. In this preliminary stage,
we focused on creating categories that were descriptive of the content.

Perhaps the most visible theme in the material is the notion of
excellence. In fact, one of the new accreditation logos includes the
puzzling sobriquet "Earned Excellence" along with the tag line, "Best
Business Schools in the World." The emphasis on the, perhaps, hyp-
erbolic words "excellence" and "best" and the global reach of "the
highest standards in the world" appear to attempt to position the
AACSB as an international organization, but also as one that distinguishes its members qualitatively from all others. Although it may be
difficult to imagine what "unearned excellence" might be, the term
"earned excellence" makes sense when interpreted more specifically
with reference to the notion that the certification process for accreditation goes beyond reputation, status halo or data-manipulation,
argued to be associated with ranking systems (Policano, 2001) –
accreditation is valid – earned.

The collection of standards mentioned in the promotion documents is
mostly notable for their benevolent ambiguity. "Quality" and "continuous
improvement" have no content markers. Knowledge is "current" and
"relevant." Measurement of learning goals is specified as a standard, but
the content of the goals is not. The ambiguity, of course, is a function of
the mission-linked accreditation process, and the assessment of quality
based on "marshalling resources" to achieve mission objectives. The
only document which gave an indication of the meaning of "mission-
linked" was the flash presentation, which includes a slide that says,
"Every business school has its own mission. Choose the one that best
serves your career goals." This is the only indication in any of the

Table 9.1. *Major themes in AACSB promotional materials*

Theme	Typical indicators from promotional texts
Excellence	The best faculty, the best students, the best employers, and the best business recruiters in the world recognize and seek out schools whose programs have earned AACSB International accreditation.
	One business school accreditation represents the highest standards in the world, and has since 1916: AACSB International.
	Best of the best graduates.
	Most widely sought after and widely recognized endorsement.
Standards	Institutions that earn accreditation confirm their commitment to quality and continuous improvement through a rigorous and comprehensive peer review process.
	AACSB International accreditation continuously challenges business schools to perform at the highest level. AACSB International accreditation informs the world that a business school manages resources to achieve a vibrant and relevant mission.
	It speaks of faculty scholarship, high-caliber teaching of quality and current curricula, and meaningful interaction between students and faculty.
	Advance business and management knowledge through faculty scholarship.
	Provide high-caliber teaching of quality and current curricula.
	Cultivate meaningful interaction between students and a qualified faculty.
	Produce graduates who have achieved specified learning goals.
Exclusivity	Less than 1/3 of US business schools and 15% of programs worldwide meet the rigorous standards.
	Seventeen of the most prominent business schools in the United States, including Columbia University, Cornell University, Dartmouth College, and Harvard University, founded AACSB. As longstanding members of AACSB, these prestigious institutions speak to a timeless tradition of exclusivity and excellence.
	Enrolling in an AACSB institution makes you a member of an elite group of emerging, competitive business leaders.
	You've attended an elite institution where learning matters.
Process	AACSB institutions have passed rigorous peer review.
	Peer review of content and quality are meticulously evaluated by a team including deans from some of the most prestigious schools.

Table 9.1. (*cont.*)

Theme	Typical indicators from promotional texts
	Curricula are evaluated in terms of outcome, e.g. employers are often polled as to a graduate's performance.
	AACSB accreditation is based on the highest standards developed by deans, faculty, and thought leaders.
	Guided by best practices and continuous improvement.
Continuous change	Economic organizations must perform to high standards and rising expectations, so should AACSB.
	Facing challenges such as global economic forces, conflicting values, changing technology in products and processes.
Value added	For students and employers seeking the best.
	Graduates of AACSB have an advantage.
	Rigorous peer review – so you get the competitive edge.
	Assures stakeholders of earned excellence.

documents that the content of schools' curricula may be diverse. Most interesting, there is no comparable statement in the brochure for the business community that may indicate that employers should target schools based on diverse missions. As a consequence, the material side-steps issues concerning comparability across schools, promoting the notion that there are content differences and "choice" for students, but downplaying potential differences to employers, where the implicit choice implied in the materials is between accredited versus non-accredited schools.

Exclusivity is asserted in two ways. The first approach is statistical, indicating that a relatively small percentage of schools that could be accredited are. The business community materials reveal an interesting semantic choice by indicating that "15% of programs worldwide meet the rigorous standards." This wording is important because it implies that the reason why some are not accredited is because they failed to meet the rigorous standards. In fact, a number of schools outside the United States choose not to be accredited by the AACSB as a matter of principle (Durand & McGuire, 2005). A second approach used in the material is the use of the term "elite" in each of the brochures and in the flash presentation. As a referent for elite status, materials referred to several of the high-status founding schools, such as Columbia, Cornell,

Dartmouth, and Harvard. Although it is difficult to assess how to interpret the choice of Ivy League schools in the list of founders, it is worth noting that a number of other schools were involved in the founding (Wisconsin, Northwestern, Illinois, to name just a few). It may be that narrowing the list to Ivy League schools offered a way to communicate exclusivity that including, for example, Big Ten schools might not.

The process theme emphasizes how a school comes to be accredited and the sources for accreditation standards. Again, some level of ambiguity remains in the description of processes associated with accreditation. Rigorous evaluation and peer review is highlighted, but not what is being evaluated. Many references are made to the difficulty of the accreditation process. Prestige is explicitly appropriated in the description of process by including an indication that evaluation teams include deans from high-status schools, and that standards are developed by faculty, deans, and "thought leaders" in management education.

The business-centered theme links the changes in the business environment to the need for responsiveness in management education. Businesses face rising expectations of performance, and so, by extension, should business schools. Businesses are facing particular environmental challenges so business schools, as a result, need to be prepared to recognize those complexities. This theme anchors the school to the business community. There is an implicit commitment to serve the business community (rather than markets, society, or broad value systems such as professions).

Finally, the promotional material contained a number of ideas that specify AACSB accreditation as adding meaningful value to employers and students. With a degree from an AACSB-accredited school, a student has a "competitive edge" or "advantage" that they would not have from an alternative school. Employers who want the best graduates, the materials argue, tap AACSB schools.

Clearly, there is overlap between the categories, and, occasionally, contradiction. But these constitute a pool of arguments from which schools wishing to represent accreditation to various stakeholders may choose. In the following section, we examine the extent to which AACSB accreditation is incorporated into schools' routines and processes; the extent to which and how schools in our pilot sample use the AACSB themes; and the extent to which alternative legitimizing sources are used.

Enactment of accreditation constituent schools

The process of maintaining institutions is tightly linked to institutionalized action of those in the field. For example, carrying out the requirements of ISO 9000, or even preparing for an audit for renewal of ISO 9000 certification, is institutionalized action by a participating organization, but the use of audit and renewal by ISO 9000 is a mechanism of policing the institution and is maintenance work (Guler *et al.*, 2002; Lawrence & Suddaby, 2006). The effectiveness of the latter is realized in the actions of the former. Although the AACSB's promotional materials assert its power in the field, the validity of the assertions can only be assessed by looking at the extent to which constituent organizations use the AACSB as a resource in their image and identity work.

To highlight the success of the AACSB in their institutional work, we chose to examine the webpages of three AACSB-accredited schools: Northwestern University, representing a founding legacy school; Boston College, representing a legacy school accredited before the 1991 change; and Abilene Christian University, representing a school accredited after 1991. The sampling strategy was designed to capture differences in the meaning of accreditation to schools in these categories. Founding legacy schools established accreditation as a means of assuring the transferability of credit among that small group of elite schools. Legacy schools accredited before 1991 but not founding members achieved accreditation under relatively rigorous content requirements and requirements for faculty credentialing. Schools accredited after 1991 came in on the mission-based approach.

For each school, we began with an examination of the content on the home page of the college of business, coding for AACSB artifacts (logo, pop-up, flash presentation), and mention of AACSB accreditation. We then looked for any dedicated link on the home page to accreditation information. Next, we conducted a site search with "AACSB" as the keyword, and copied the content of the first ten "hits." We examined search results for relevant items (eliminating redundant or dated information, such as mention of accreditation in multiple years' editions of the catalog). We then examined the home page and any dedicated links for references to other legitimating institutions, and did a keyword search on the term "ranking" on the site. Finally, we examined admissions and transfer of credit policies, and other parts of the student-focused and employer-focused links, for evidence of AACSB connections to organizational routines. In reviewing the material, we remained sensitive to any other contextual information that may be relevant to our study.

Northwestern University (legacy founder school)

There were no AACSB artifacts anywhere on the Northwestern website, nor did accreditation appear in any of the promotional sections for students or employers. There were, however, a number of indirect AACSB references. Several articles from the national press are available in Northwestern's online archive – reproductions of articles in the press posted for more extensive media attention. Two of them are AACSB-sourced articles concerning major issues in management education. In the case of a 2001 *Wall Street Journal* article on women in business schools, Northwestern was named by recruiters as being the school best for recruiting women. A *Business Week* article on the shortage of PhDs in business mentioned the AACSB's paradoxical "endorsement of using untrained execs for schools hit by faculty shortages, even as it pointed to the need for a fuller PhD pipeline" (Merritt, 2004). Northwestern's associate dean commented in the article that the approach was "not the way to go." Although the *Business Week* story was critical of the AACSB, Northwestern appears to be using the articles to show the expertise of Northwestern faculty and staff being represented in the news. Faculty members were noted for particular attention if they were used as sources for expert information in the popular and elite business press. It would appear that the efforts to create a normative role for accreditation was less successful at Northwestern than the school's emphasis on its own resources – its faculty as expert commentators in the media.

The AACSB appears to have a role in terms of reproduction of routines. For example, whether Northwestern was accredited was a "frequently asked question" for prospective students. This may be a particularly relevant item for schools hoping to recruit international students, given that accreditation is often a consideration in distribution of financial aid. In addition, in discussing transfer of credit from other schools, only credit from AACSB-accredited schools is considered. The transfer, however, is not automatic – the content must be similar to the content of courses at Northwestern. Thus, Northwestern must add another layer of decision-making to the issue of transfer of credit. Given that assuring the quality of courses and transferability of academic credit was a primary impetus for creating the AACSB, it is notable that the traditional bye given to AACSB courses appears, but is conditioned on a specific review of content.

Although ranking information did not appear on the school's home page, there were more than 100 articles that surfaced in the keyword search, including press releases announcing rankings, and references in student and alumni communications about rankings. Rankings were not a primary presence on the website, where information and image management appears to be more anchored in the nature of, and quality of the content of, courses and opportunities offered at Northwestern. Although it is regularly ranked among the very best schools across media rankings, its ranking is much less a part of its image than would be expected by its rank.

Boston College (legacy school)

Boston College does not use any of the artifacts offered by the AACSB on their web materials or in the print brochures produced for prospective students. It does, like Northwestern, incorporate AACSB accreditation information in informational and procedural parts of its material for prospective students. It considers transfer credit from AACSB-accredited schools, but also accepts credit from equivalent international programs that may not be AACSB accredited. It is also willing to accept transfer credit from non-accredited schools for a limited, specific group of courses at the undergraduate level. Boston College's website also does not promote rankings on its home page, but does list various rankings at several points on its website. Like Northwestern, Boston College focuses on faculty as expert resources in the press, with a major focus on the extent to which faculty have used expertise to comment on major current issues. The faculty are a resource, but, more important, they act as thought leaders.

Abilene Christian University (post-1991 accreditation)

The AACSB logo (without the tag line text) appears on the home page of the business school at Abilene Christian University (ACU). The accreditation link is the first one under the "About Us" link. The accreditation page emphasizes a number of exclusivity statistics, going beyond the AACSB's US and international percentages to assert exclusivity within a range of more specific comparison targets. The accreditation information emphasizes that it is one of the two Church of Christ-affiliated schools to have AACSB accreditation, and one of only two schools of more than 100 members of the Council for Christian Colleges and Universities. It also indicates that of the more than forty private schools in Texas, it is one of the six that is accredited. This would seem to indicate effort on the part of ACU to leverage AACSB exclusivity claims into image- and identity-crafting strategies (Hogg & Terry, 2000). In addition to the exclusivity claims, ACU adopts the AACSB-supplied language concerning excellence, the nature of standards, and the rigors of the process on its accreditation page.

ACU also provides a link to the 2004 press release announcing its accreditation. Again, ACU adopts AACSB exclusivity and excellence language and extends it. The dean commented that, "Moving from our national ACBSP business accreditation to AACSB global accreditation is comparable to an intercollegiate athletics program moving from NCAA Division III to NCAA Division I." The press release repeats the reference group comparisons, but also includes information related to the process accreditation and the effort it took to complete it, reproducing, but customizing process themes in AACSB promotional material. Further, the press release references the everyday routines and practices embedded in the procedures at other schools when it notes that accreditation will give ACU graduates access to graduate programs and highlights ACU's accreditation in position announcements for faculty positions, referencing value-added themes suggested in AACSB materials.

Prior to accreditation and in the school's vision, the goal of achieving accreditation is a key part of the school's fundraising as described in its "Vision of Excellence" capital campaign materials:

Accreditation from AACSB International will associate Abilene Christian's business program with such schools as Harvard, Yale, Purdue, Stanford and the University of Texas. In the United States, there are only 430 AACSB International accredited programs, including seven private universities in Texas: Baylor, Lamar, Rice, St. Mary's, SMU, Trinity and TCU. We hope to join Pepperdine University as the only Church of Christ-affiliated universities with this accreditation.

The benefits of AACSB International accreditation are vast. Some employers only hire business graduates from AACSB International accredited schools. Also, many foreign governments will only send and sponsor students to study at AACSB International accredited schools of business in the United States. Students may experience greater success gaining entrance into top-tier graduate programs in business if their undergraduate business education is accredited by AACSB International.

Accreditation also creates a variety of internship and placement opportunities for students with companies who specifically require an AACSB International affiliation. The framework for "continuous improvement" and "mission-driven excellence" that AACSB International utilizes is, in fact, the best in its class.

To achieve its distinctive vision of excellence, the College of Business Administration needs an additional $35 million in new endowment, strategically focused on five areas of strength and development ...

ACU thus customizes AACSB themes to craft its identity, but also adopts those themes to acquire specific resources. It also uses the AACSB as a way to couple itself with elite universities. In general, the AACSB appeared much more central to the image work of ACU.

Discussion

The research questions of this project are, what is the institutional work of the AACSB with regards to maintaining the legitimacy of accreditation and its own role as a legitimating organization in a field in which competing sources of power have emerged, and how is the institutional work reflected in the practices and processes of colleges? With regard to the first question, we showed the ways in which the AACSB used deterrence strategies to pre-empt the emergence of alternative legitimating organizations by redefining its membership criteria. We also described the ways that the AACSB allows multiple standards to enable the scale of distributed mission-setting, yet centralizes policing of processes. At the same time, the institutional work of adapting compliance mechanisms to maintain the institution of accreditation and the AACSB's role as a legitimating body, as it turned out, required that the AACSB engage in considerable institutional work to maintain the normative and cognitive aspects of accreditation. To explore this work, we examined the discourse of AACSB materials designed to be used by accredited schools to promote AACSB accreditation. These themes were those that the AACSB believed represented the distinct resources offered to schools and their stakeholders.

From this examination seven themes emerged. Each theme is crafted to reinforce the normative foundations of accreditation – the validity of the credential, and the signification of privilege associated with accreditation. Distinct from the rankings that offer reputation endorsements (and based, it is argued, on the halo effects of status or inconsistent and un-validated information provided by colleges and universities; Policano, 2001), accreditation from the AACSB represents excellence and elite status acquired through "rigorous peer review." Rather than global quality assessments, accreditation is asserted to be relevant to particular local stakeholders, making it "relevant" and "current."

Given the reliance upon cognitive and normative content offered to schools to convey the legitimacy of accreditation, it does not come as a surprise that not all of the schools reflected the AACSB's institutional work in their self-presentation processes. The pattern that we identify shows that schools with access to alternative, more socially prominent sources such as ranking-based reputation and status (Northwestern and Boston College) make little or no reference to the AACSB in self-presentations. The role of the AACSB appears mostly in routines and processes or routine decision-making (willingness to take transfer credit from other AACSB schools, answers to a frequently asked question stating that they are accredited). However, for schools without access to high-level rankings or status, AACSB accreditation was displayed more prominently. These schools may have their accreditation as a primary source of legitimacy in the organizational field of business education, distinguishing them from schools that are not accredited.

This effect might appear to be an instance of a middle-status conformity process (Phillips & Zuckerman, 2001), but the situation may be more nuanced. Whereas the middle-status conformity process examines the impact of institutional pressure on organizations (those in the middle of the status hierarchy are most likely to succumb to the pressure), our data suggest that the process might be the result of the loss of status of the institution (in this case, accreditation) itself. Schools with ranking and status advantages don't display AACSB accreditation because it does not add to their status. Accreditation, after all, does not distinguish between top schools but rankings and status do. What is most curious is the fact that Northwestern does little in the way of putting rankings front and center in their self-presentations, despite the fact that it regularly appears in the top ten of virtually every ranking system (and is often first or in the top three). There may be an extent to which high-status organizations might eschew external, "quantified" measures of quality such as rankings. The fact that both Boston College and Northwestern emphasized the extent to which their faculty was called upon as experts in the business media seemed to be a distinct, and unanticipated, positioning strategy.

We started this project by arguing that more institutional research needs to examine the work of creating, maintaining, and disrupting institutions. The research that has been done in this tradition mainly focuses on creating or disrupting institutions. Thus, to contribute to this body of research, we focused our efforts on the processes by which actors maintain the legitimacy and status of their institution. We argue that this institutional work is different from the literature on institutional entrepreneurship as it involves an existing institution (not institution creation) and is also different from institutional change as the mechanism of change is endogenous (not exogenous in terms of a disruption of a jolt) and focused on preserving institutional arrangements. Following Lawrence and Suddaby (2006), we theorize that institutions will rely upon the mechanisms of compliance (deterrence, enabling, and policing of standards) and normative and cognitive reinforcement (a valuable and appropriate way of life) to maintain their legitimacy in the field.

To examine institutional work, we empirically examined the case of the AACSB. The AACSB is an example of a legitimating organization whose role is weakening in a field as a result of challenges to the institution it sustains. To combat this, the AACSB engages in discourse to reinforce its legitimacy, but has done something quite unusual. It has created materials for schools to present to their stakeholders – students, the community, recruiters, and the media – to promote accreditation. The AACSB suggests its discursive themes become the themes of the accredited schools. Thus, while the AACSB engaged in compliance and regulatory maintenance work, it also appears to recognize that its power with its constituents lies in creating a system of normative dependencies throughout the field – not just among constituent organizations, but employers, students, and the media as well. However, the response to the institutional work was mixed. Schools with access to other forms of social and cultural capital were less likely to employ the discourse supplied by the AACSB on their websites than organizations without such access.

The results provide several insights into institutional work. For one thing, AACSB accreditation appears to be a meaningful resource only to schools without access to status, rank, or other types of public exposure (e.g. faculty as thought leaders within the mainstream media). This stands in contrast to the National Collegiate Athletic Association's (NCAA) successful establishment as the dominant legitimating organization in intercollegiate athletics. Even high-status schools identify themselves as associated with the NCAA. For example, today – years after the establishment of the NCAA – Harvard's athletics website displays the NCAA logo prominently on its home page. The AACSB, however, is nowhere to be found on Harvard's business school website. There is an important difference between the AACSB as it expanded its membership and the NCAA at the time it expanded its domain. From its start, the NCAA has sorted schools into categories, preserving status hierarchies in the field of intercollegiate athletics that existed at the time of its establishment and that persist (Washington, 2004). The AACSB makes no such official distinction between schools, yet recognizes the importance of status hierarchies in its promotional materials by referencing Ivy League school founders to the exclusion of other founders.

This research suggests some questions for future research. For example, are markers of legitimacy (accreditation) or reputation (rankings) thought to erode the social status an organization has? For example, would Harvard or Wharton play up "we're number one" or would they play up their history and rich tradition, or their status as a "gold standard" in business education? This study seems to point us toward exploring organizational fields in a more nuanced way. Focusing only on rankings, for example, or only on the regulatory activities of a single legitimating organization, may not give us a complete enough picture of a field. Washington and Zajac (2005) have shown that looking only at one source of capital is inadequate to explain field-level phenomena. The study extends their examination of status and reputation to include regulatory and normative legitimacy as well. Future research should examine these multiple sources of capital in a field at the same time.

The study also puts the difficult problem of defining clear boundaries between institution creation, change, maintenance, and deinstitutionalization in sharp relief. The AACSB changed its rules of membership and compliance mechanisms significantly in response to field-level pressures, but the changes required work to maintain normative foundations of accreditation. The relationship between legitimating organizations and the adaptations they make and the normative arrangements in the institutions they represent merits more study. In many ways, the discursive institutional work of the AACSB, whether or not by design, attempts to preserve the normative understandings of accreditation as a process of standard-setting and certification of quality, while the rule changes appear to undercut assumptions that there are consistent standards. Processes of maintaining institutions by legitimating organizations, then, may be a key source of internal contradictions in institutions. The juxtaposition of compliance mechanisms that enact adaptive change and mechanisms that reference pre-adaptive normative regimes may be worthy of further exploration.

References

AACSB (2005) The business school ranking dilemma: a report from a task force of AACSB International's Committee on Issues in Management Education. www.aacsb.edu/publications/rankings/mediarankingstf.asp. Accessed August 22, 2007.

(2006a) Eligibility procedures and accreditation standards for business accredition. www.aacsb.edu/accreditation/process/documents/AACSB_STANDARDS_Revised_Jan07.pdf. Accessed August 22, 2007.

(2006b) Promoting accreditation. www.aacsb.edu/accreditation/promotion/default.asp. Accessed August 22, 2007.

Abbott, A. (1988) *The System of Professions: An Essay on the Division of Expert Labor*. Chicago: University of Chicago Press.

Berger, P. & Luckmann, T. (1966) *The Social Construction of Reality: A Treatise in the Sociology of Knowledge*. London: Penguin Books.

Bourdieu, P. (1986) The forms of capital. In J. G. Richardson (ed.), *Handbook of Theory and Research for the Sociology of Education*, pp. 241–258. New York: Greenwood Press.

Bourdieu, P. & Wacquant, L. J. D. (1992) *An Invitation to Reflexive Sociology*. Chicago: University of Chicago Press.

Dacin, M. T. (1997) Isomorphism in context: the power and prescription of institutional norms. *Academy of Management Journal*, 40(1): 46–81.

Dickeson, R. C. (2006) The need for accreditation reform. United States Secretary of Education's Commission on the Future of Higher Education. www.ed.gov/about/bdscomm/list/hiedfuture/reports/dickeson.pdf. Accessed July 17, 2007.

DiMaggio, P. J. & Powell, W. W. (1983) The iron cage revisited: institutional isomorphism and collective rationality in organizational fields. *American Sociological Review*, 47: 147–160.

Durand, R. & McGuire, J. (2005) Legitimating agencies in the face of selection: the case of AACSB. *Organization Studies*, 26: 165–196.

Gioia, D. A. & Thomas, J. B. (1996) Identity, image, and issue interpretation: sensemaking during strategic change in academia. *Administrative Science Quarterly*, 41: 370–404.

Greenwood, R. G., Suddaby, R. & Hinings, C. R. (2002) Theorizing change: the role of professional associations in the transformation of institutional fields. *Academy of Management Journal*, 45: 55–81.

Guler, I., Guillen, M. F. & MacPherson, J. M. (2002) Global competition, institutions and the diffusion of organizational practices: the international spread of ISO 9000 quality certificates. *Administrative Science Quarterly*, 47: 207–233.

Hoffman, A. (1999) Institutional evolution and change: environmentalism and the US chemical industry. *Academy of Management Journal*, 42: 351–371.

Hogg, M. A. & Terry, D. J. (2000) Social identity and self-categorization processes in organizational contexts. *Academy of Management Review*, 25: 121–140.

Holm, P. (1995) The dynamics of institutionalization: transformation processes in Norwegian fisheries. *Administrative Science Quarterly*, 40: 398–422.

Jepperson, R. L. (1991) Institutions, institutional effects, and institutionalism. In W. W. Powell & P. J. DiMaggio (eds.), *The New Institutionalism in Organizational Analysis*, pp. 143–163. Chicago: University of Chicago Press.

Lawrence, T. B. (2004) Rituals and resistance: membership dynamics in professional fields. *Human Relations*, 57(2): 115–143.

Lawrence, T. B. & Suddaby, R. (2006) Institutions and institutional work. In S. Clegg, C. Hardy, W. Nord & T. B. Lawrence (eds.), *Handbook of Organization Studies*, pp. 215–254. London: Sage.

McKenna, J. F., Cotton, C. C. & Van Auken, S. (1997) The new AACSB accreditation standards: a prospect of tiering? *Journal of Organizational Change*, 10: 491–502.

Merritt, J. (2004) Is there a doctor in the house? *Business Week*, March 1. BW Online, www.businessweek.com/magazine/content/04_09/b3872103_mz056.htm. Accessed August 20, 2007.

Miles, M. P., Hazeldine, M. F. & Munilla, L. S. (2004) The 2004 AACSB accreditation standards and implications for business faculty: a short note. *Journal of Education for Business*, 80: 29–34.

Miller, J. W. & Boswell, L. E. (1979) Accreditation, assessment, and the credentialing of educational accomplishment. *Journal of Higher Education*, 50: 219–225.

Oliver, C. (1997) Sustainable competitive advantage: combining institutional and resource based views. *Strategic Management Journal*, 18: 697–713.

Phillips, D. & Zuckerman, E. (2001) Middle status conformity: theoretical restatement and empirical demonstration in two markets. *American Journal of Sociology*, 107(2): 379–429.

Policano, A. J. (2001) Ten easy steps to a top-25 MBA program. *Selections*, 1(2): 39–40.

Rao, H. (1998) Caveat emptor: the construction of nonprofit consumer watchdog organizations. *American Journal of Sociology*, 103: 912–961.

Ruef, M. & Scott, W. R. (1998) A multidimensional model of organizational legitimacy: hospital survival in changing institutional environments. *Administrative Science Quarterly*, 43: 877–904.

Rynes, S. L. & Trank, C. Q. (1999) Behavioral science in the business school curriculum: teaching in a changing institutional environment. *Academy of Management Review*, 24: 808–824.

Schmotter, J. (2000) An assignment for the new century. *Selections*, 16(Spring/Summer), 36–39.

Schray, V. (2006) Assuring quality in higher education: key issues and questions for changing accreditation in the United States. United States Secretary of Education's Commission on the Future of Higher Education. www.ed.gov/about/bdscomm/list/hiedfuture/reports/shray.pdf. Accessed July 17, 2007.

Scott, W. R. (2001) *Institutions and Organizations*, 2nd edn. Thousand Oaks, CA: Sage.

Selznick, P. (1957) *Leadership in Administration: A Sociological Interpretation*. Berkeley, CA: University of California Press.

Shipley, M. F. & Johnson, M. (1991) Employment and academic opportunities for graduates of AACSB-accredited schools. *Journal of Education for Business*, 66: 235–239.

Suchman, M. C. (1995) Managing legitimacy: strategic and institutional approaches. *Academy of Management Review*, 20: 571–610.

Suddaby, R. & Greenwood, R. (2005) Rhetorical strategies of legitimacy. *Administrative Science Quarterly*, 50: 35–67.

Trank, C. Q. & Rynes, S. L. (2003) Who moved our cheese? Reclaiming professionalism in business education. *Academy of Management Learning and Education*, 2: 189–213.

Washington, M. (2004) Field approaches to institutional change: the evolution of the National Collegiate Athletic Association 1906–95. *Organization Studies*, 25: 395–417.

Washington, M., Boal, K. & Davis, J. N. (2008) Institutional leadership: past, present, and future. In R. Greenwood, C. Oliver, R. Suddaby & K. Sahlin-Andersson (eds.), *Handbook of Organizational Institutionalism*, pp. 719–734. Thousand Oaks, CA: Sage.

Washington, M. & Zajac, E. (2005) By invitation only: the institutional evolution of status and privilege. *Academy of Management Journal*, 48: 281–296.

10 Institutional "dirty" work: preserving institutions through strategic decoupling

PAUL M. HIRSCH AND Y. SEKOU BERMISS

[The field has paid] insufficient attention to those actors who are able somehow to compromise, avoid or defy systems of institutional control or episodes of interested agency.

(Lawrence, 2008: 189)

Draw attention to behind the scenes, to the actors, writers, and stage-hands that produce them.

(Lawrence & Suddaby, 2006: 249)

Introduction

Two key aspects of institutional work are the entrepreneurship which accompanies the rise of new institutions and the decline which occurs as they move toward deinstitutionalization. As Lawrence and Suddaby (2006) note, studies of each are often separated from each other, as well as from studies of institutions that are in place and being maintained. Their important insight, in calling for a greater integration of work on the creation, maintenance, and decline of institutions is significant, for empirically the creation of new institutions often intersects with existing institutions which are still powerful, as well as those already on their way out. Integrating them in our studies expands the organizational fields to examine, opening up more networks of organizations and purposive actors working to preserve, alter, or replace an institution. These dynamics and the mechanisms they entail focus more attention on the processes and actions involved as institutions undergo changes throughout their life cycles.

In this chapter, we highlight two important areas of institutional study. First, we build upon Lawrence and Suddaby's framework, highlighting the work of *institutional preservation*, a distinct component of institutional work that is most pertinent in the stage between the disruption of incumbent institutions and the creation of nascent institutions. As we define it, institutional preservation instantiates the retention function within the variation–selection–retention evolutionary form (Aldrich, 1999). As applied to institutional work, preservation entails the actions undertaken by actors searching for ways to carry over norms from the previous regime into the construction of the new institutional order. Second, we argue that the process of decoupling, as specifically detailed by Meyer and Rowan (1977), is particularly applicable for the preservation of institutions. We detail the work of preserving institutions through analysis of a rich and dramatic case of macro-institutional change: the Czech Republic's transformation from a communist to a capitalist polity. We highlight how the work of purposive actors resonated with its cultural context, and engaged in various forms of institutional work to preserve specific rules and norms during a tumultuous period.

Following this introduction, we outline a theoretical basis for institutional preservation and its reliance on decoupling. We then analyze and address how the deinstitutionalization of a socialist economic regime and its replacement by a new capitalist regime illustrates key points in Suddaby and Lawrence's program and links strategic decoupling to institutional preservation. We end with a discussion about the importance of drawing on cultural context in the study of institutional work.

Legitimacy and decoupling in institutional theory

As specific practices and structures become infused with normative associations within society they become characteristics that organizations adopt in order to gain or maintain legitimacy (Suchman, 1995). Institutionalized rules, however, are rarely uniform or followed consistently; they are often rife with contradiction. This inconsistency often emerges from the differing interests of separate constituent groups which organizations find themselves dependent upon. For survival purposes, organizations must negotiate between the conflicting institutionalized rules and logics that exist within their social context (Friedland & Alford, 1991).

A solution to this issue, offered by Meyer and Rowan (1977), is a two-pronged approach combining the decoupling of formal structure from technical activities and the use of elaborate displays of confidence to maintain the assumption of good faith. The proposition of decoupling suggests that an organization's formal structure, the rational blueprint of activities within an organization, is only loosely linked to its actual activities (Weick, 1976). As a result, "rules are often violated, decisions are often unimplemented, or if implemented have uncertain consequences, technologies are of problematic efficiency, and evaluation and inspection systems are subverted or rendered so vague as to provide little coordination" (Meyer & Rowan, 1977: 343).

Loosely coupled systems, however, would be untenable without ceremonial displays of confidence. Institutionalized organizations are able to maintain the appearance of legitimacy through practices of good faith whereby everyone is assumed to be acting with competence. One common good faith practice is professional discretion, in which a group of individuals is given discretion to carry out a critical organizational task and are thus protected from obtrusive evaluation and inspection. Research supports the benefits of decoupling with logics of confidence within the fields of education (Meyer & Rowan, 1978), marketing (Beverland & Luxton, 2005), and strategy (Elsbach & Sutton, 1992; Westphal & Zajac, 1994).

In this chapter we adopt an alternative decoupling perspective. The study of decoupling has remained primarily at the firm level (Fiss & Zajac, 2006; Zajac & Westphal, 2004). Much of the research on isomorphism and the subsequent pressure placed on institutional actors to adopt legitimating structures or policies are studied in the context of organizations or individuals within a pre-existing institutional arrangement (Dacin, 1997; Han, 1994; Kraatz & Zajac, 1996). Isomorphic pressures, we argue, also impact on the creation of new institutional arrangements. New institutions are impinged upon by the norms of pre-existing institutional arrangements. Our goal here is to fit institutional theory with an even more macro lens than is normally the custom, just as community ecologists, recognizing that population ecology fails to explain how populations originate, have attempted to expand the explanatory power of the organizational evolution perspective by focusing on the rise of populations as a unit of analysis (Astley, 1985; Barnett, 1990; Korn & Baum, 1994). Individuals who manage and regulate national political and economic systems also face the conflict between generalized, abstract external legitimacy demands, versus the more concrete and context-dependent expectations from their closer-to-home constituencies. We depict the development of loosely coupled systems as an effective mechanism enabling institutional entrepreneurs to maintain stability and consistency within internal political and economic spheres, while appearing to develop new institutional frameworks that adhere to changing external contingencies. Furthermore, while decoupling is useful for the maintenance of institutional arrangements, it can also be utilized in *designing* institutional systems. Especially during times of radical change and deinstitutionalization, such *strategic decoupling* enables institutional entrepreneurs to more "creatively navigate" within their organizational fields (Lawrence & Suddaby, 2006; Oliver, 1991). We highlight and examine this process by reporting on creative techniques of strategic decoupling utilized by political leaders engaged in and surrounded by large-scale institutional change in the Czech Republic.

Privatization in the Czech Republic

After the collapse of the Soviet empire in 1989, there emerged opportunities for the nations of Central and Eastern Europe to establish market economies and join the western-led economic communities from which they had been severed. With this radical environmental shift, questions of redefining and establishing ownership, control, funding, and resource allocation quickly arose. Several templates of "how" to transform the old regimes' top–down, centrally planned forms of economic organization and market control were readily available. The new Russian regime, for example, adopted much of the "shock therapy" program advanced by economists David Lipton and Jeffrey Sachs (1990), the basis of which was to institute a massive, rapid program of economic reform. Speed, it was argued, was required so that economic change could begin before the ineffective political structures could corrupt the efforts. Support for shock therapy reform was readily available from the International Monetary Fund (IMF) and the World Bank, as well as directly from the G-7 industrialized nations. Their programs were all contingent on the recipient nations' agreements to follow the reform programs to be underwritten by this external financial aid.

The Czech government implemented these shock therapy reforms because they were necessary for institutional legitimacy and continued financial assistance. The transmission mechanisms to move a centrally planned economy to a market economy, however, were not automatic, and the diffusion process was far more complicated than a simple command and control system (Stark, 1996). Instead of countries in Central and Eastern Europe smoothly converging toward the economic template propounded by the IMF and World Bank, there were lurches and jolts along the way. Political and economic reversals occurred even after nations had apparently acquired free capital markets (McDermott, 2007). Because institutional and organizational change is rife with conflicts, contests, and controversies (i.e. social control does not just "happen"), isomorphism does not necessarily come free of deviations, social illegitimacies, or temporally bounded compliance. In particular, the "inexorable push toward homogenization" (DiMaggio & Powell, 1991: 64) is complicated by the possible decoupling of promise and delivery, as nation states engage and employ myth and ceremony that presents western governments and financial institutions with the "correct" formal structure, even while the state pursues contrary domestic policies.

A pertinent example of this disconnect occurred in the mass privatization program of state-owned enterprises (SOE) within the Czech Republic. From the end of Word War II until December of 1989, Czechoslovakia was controlled by the Soviet-backed Czechoslovak Communist Party. In November 1989, an organized and officially sanctioned demonstration in memory of students executed by the Nazis during the war attracted a peaceful crowd of 50,000 students, artists, and writers. Eventually, the crowd grew to over 750,000 at various stages, touching off what became known as the Velvet Revolution, which culminated in the regime's departure and the election of Vaclav Havel as president in December 1989.

Soon thereafter the international community became intimately involved in Czech economic reforms. The World Bank and IMF immediately selected Prague as site of their annual meetings in 1990, followed the next year by the World Economic Forum, an elite organization developed for chief executives and political leaders, whose agenda included advising these newer entrants into the global marketplace. These three prominent organizations, as well other smaller foundations and agencies, all met with the newly minted Czech government officials and offered their prescriptions for bringing its state-owned economy in line with western markets and global competition.

In attendance at these meetings was Vaclav Klaus, then the deputy prime minister and minister of finance of the new government, and other members of the newly empowered Civic Democratic Party (CDP). Klaus later became both prime minister and (in 2005) president of the Czech Republic. He is widely regarded as the architect of the Czech economic reforms. As a trained economist, Klaus was well versed in the western ideology of market transformation. His doctoral dissertation was on the economic reforms carried out in England by Margaret Thatcher. Shortly after the Velvet Revolution, Klaus traveled to the best-known capital of free-market capitalism, the University of Chicago's economics department and business school. He subsequently attributed much of his economic program and policy choices to the Chicago school's advocacy of free-market economics, specifically noting his admiration for the writings of Friedman, Becker, Coase, and Stigler (Longworth, 1995). The Czech government, with Klaus' team at the helm, quickly developed an aggressive economic transition strategy calling for the dismantling of state paternalism, a conservative monetary policy to check for inflation, and attending to the devalued exchange rate (Benacek, 1995). The most heralded of these policies was Klaus' innovative mass privatization plan.

Symbol: the mass privatization strategy

As the Czech government proclaimed its commitment to rapidly transform the nation's economic system into a market economy, it put forth a series of mass privatization programs (MPPs), in which a substantial number of state-owned enterprises were put up for sale (Lieberman, 1995).[1] Citizens were encouraged to purchase a booklet of vouchers for 1,000 crowns (US $35.00), which could be later converted into shares of the newly privatized corporations through a centralized auction process.[2] During the first privatization wave in 1993, 63 percent of the shares were purchased via voucher. Vouchers were also a central component of the second wave in 1994, accounting for 43 percent of the shares of privatized companies (Dlouhy & Mladek, 1994: 157).

The speed and magnitude of this innovative mass privatization were praised and applauded by major American and European governmental bodies and foundations as an exemplary model. A 1995 report by the World Bank (Lieberman, 1995) found:

there is no question that the mass privatization program has been a great success. In the Czech Republic alone it has led to the privatization of 70 to

---

[1] Initially piloted in Poland and the Czech and Slovak republics, MPPs were later adopted in Kazakhstan, Lithuania, Romania, Russia, and Ukraine.

[2] Large privatization occurred in five ways: pubic auction, public tender, direct sales to a predetermined buyer, privatization of joint-stock companies (primarily through vouchers), and free transfers to municipalities.

80 percent of state-owned enterprises in a variety of sectors ... It has decentralized the problem of restructuring the Czech industry and has placed it in the hands of new private owners, rather than the hands of the government.

Throughout these mass privatizations, the Czech government's rhetoric emphasized its desire to develop and support free markets. Prime Minister Klaus effectively communicated support for the immediate and early involvement of the public as investors, evoking the metaphor that the government was "throwing things in the air to see, based on the market system, where they come down" (Stevenson & Greenberg, 2000). When President Havel sought to slow down the privatization process, Klaus protested, stating that "a delay of even a month" in the program could cost the country millions of crowns.[3] Klaus opposed industry regulation, calling it an impediment to market competition, and argued that corporate restructuring should be the responsibility of the new private ownership, rather than government agencies.

The international investment community was very pleased with Klaus' strong rhetoric regarding the Czech reform programs (Greenhouse, 1991). He was a featured speaker at many international gatherings, explaining how his economic programs were yielding greater efficiency, promoting market discipline, and invoking higher productivity. A volume of Klaus' pro-free market speeches (Weber, 2003) was published by the conservative Cato Institute in the United States (his inscription on an autographed back cover reads: "The Czech Republic has already crossed the Rubicon"). But, while his advocacy of free-market economic philosophy produced substantial praise and legitimacy from external evaluators, this narrative obscured much of the activity taking place inside the nation's borders. Backstage, Klaus' team's management of the former regime's deinstitutionalization departed significantly from the rhetoric of what appeared as significant economic reform to outsiders.

Substance: preservation of partially planned economy

In 1997, Klaus and the CDP fell out of political favor. Klaus resigned amidst charges of government favoritism and was out of political office for several years. During this period, foreign investors started expressing

---

[3] Foreign desk, "Prague postpones big privatization auction," *New York Times*, 1991, p. A.14.

reservations about the Czechs' economic progress and the effectiveness of Klaus' ambitious programs and promises (McDermott, 2007). What was soon uncovered was an informal system which functioned to preserve the Czechs' state-planned economy.

Changing normative associations between pre-existing practices and their moral foundation is important for the proper creation of new institutions (Lawrence & Suddaby, 2006: 224). The Czech mass privatization plan was explicitly targeted to break the normative association between the powers of the state and commercial firms that operated within the economy. The initiation of the mass privatization plans served as a symbol that the government no longer operated as owner of all commercial enterprises nor did it centrally plan market activity. Subsequent analysis, however, reveals how Klaus and his colleagues approved a system that decoupled the symbols of free markets from the actual market activity. This decoupling was primarily accomplished by two mechanisms: the repurchase of ownership by state-backed investment funds and the absence of strict bankruptcy law.

The most prominent issue surrounding the Czech mass privatization plan was the purchase of the state-owned enterprises by investment privatization funds (IPFs). IPFs undermined the spirit of a market economy in two critical ways. First, IPFs undermined the principle of dispersed stock ownership through the purchase of large amounts of vouchers from Czech citizens when they became available for sale.[4] Shortly after coupon books were distributed, IPFs offered to purchase them at a slightly higher price. After accumulating the majority of vouchers, IPFs dominated the auctioning of enterprises and gained ownership of a very large percentage of privatized firms. In the first wave of privatization, 72 percent of all vouchers were accumulated by IPFs, and 40 percent were accumulated within ten investment funds (Lieberman, 1995).

This concentration of ownership was compounded by the fact that many of the IPFs were subsidiaries of state-owned banks. Thus, another branch of the same government which managed the sale of its assets in the privatization process now owned a large majority of its new "market" economy.

The role of IPFs in the Czech Republic's mass privatization plan is an example of institutional work working on both sides of the same coin.

---

[4] Foreign desk, "Czechs by millions invest $35 in big state sale," *New York Times*, 1992, p. A.7.

While ample effort was put forth by the Czech government officials to formally change the normative associations between commercial firms and the government, there was also substantial work done to preserve these associations within a different set of relationships. In contrast to the mass privatization program's loudly stated goal of "retailing," i.e. creating widespread and dispersed public ownership of shares in these companies, most of these shares wound up in the vaults of fifteen equity funds which were largely backed by the Czech government.

Further conflicts of interest arose because newly privatized firms were also dependent on the Czech banks for financial capital. The consensus among foreign financial advisors was that bankruptcy legislation was necessary so that "market discipline" could punish inefficient, poorly performing firms. Due to ineffective bankruptcy laws (which the government resisted toughening), banks were not forced to foreclose on clients that defaulted on their loans. Eventually, pressure from the international economic community led Czech officials to privatize the banking sector; even this privatization effort, however, was undercut by bank-sponsored IFPs which were permitted to purchase shares of their parent banks' stock (Rao & Hirsch, 2003). The lack of proper bankruptcy procedures allowed the Czech government to proceed with reforms while avoiding the negative externalities, such as sharp rises in unemployment, which are associated with free market creation.

The unraveling of the confidence around the Czechs' new free market led to more critical evaluation of the reforms implemented by Klaus and the CDP and a number of "disconnects" came to light between what had been promised and what had actually unfolded. In 1997, President Havel's state of the union speech to the Czech Parliament attacked many of the "Klausian" policies. Havel noted the gaps between substance and symbolism within the Czech economic transformation, stating:

Under the cloak of an unqualified liberalism, which regarded any kind of economic controls or regulations as left-wing aberrations, the Marxist doctrine of the structure and the superstructure lived on, though paradoxically it was hidden from view. (Carr-Saunders & Wilson, 1933)

Other Czech officials began to describe the "backstage" experience of the mass privatization programs. While spending a year in the US in 1998, Jiri Dienstbier, former foreign minister and deputy prime minister, remarked that the much ballyhooed privatization of big industry in the Czech Republic was a sham (Lewis, 1998).

The preservation of a centrally planned economic system within the burgeoning Czech free-market system was the outcome of several forms of institutional work associated with institution creation (Lawrence & Suddaby, 2006), each with a slight variation to the commonly understood definition. A majority of this work was performed by Vaclav Klaus and other members of the CDP. The most applicable form of institutional work we can observe performed by the CDP is mimicry, which entails associating new practices with older taken-for-granted practices to assist with adoption. The nuanced difference we observe with the mimicry that occurred in the Czech case is that the association with the previous institution, communism, is downplayed or outright rebuked. In the Czech Republic, as with other post-communist transformations, government officials espoused western capitalistic verbiage and adopted western labels and titles, while important components of the political and economic activity remained centrally planned and state-controlled. Often we find that elite communist party members use their political capital to gain wealth in the new market-based system (Szelenyi & Szelenyi, 1995), but former party members also vie for political and cultural capital. Within the Czech economic transformation, CDP members employed the art of mimicry despite the overwhelming rhetoric to the contrary. Mass privatization created new markets but government banks remained in control of much of the economy.

The work of vesting, in which the government creates new rules for property rights, is another component of institutional preservation. Here, the nuanced difference resides in the fact that western concepts of property rights can get lost in translation resulting in unintended consequences. A superb example of this issue is detailed in Kathrine Verdery's anthropological research of the privatization of the agricultural sector in post-socialist Romania (Verdery, 2003). Verdery details how the fundamental driver of capitalism, property rights, had an adverse effect on the economy in Romania. After the fall of the Iron Curtain, state-owned farms in Romania were broken up and distributed as private property to the citizenry in hopes that small profitable family farms would emerge. Instead, however, many of the smaller family farms stopped production entirely due to lack of capital to purchase farming equipment. Farmers found themselves less than adept in navigating the new facets of their occupation, tackling new issues such as product marketing and variable interest rates. As a result, many farmers withdrew from the economic apparatus, looking for more stable ways to run their businesses. Former party officials returned to the fold, this time as supertenants, who monopolized the agrarian sector by financing farm equipment and renting it to smaller farmers. The outcome was a system very similar to the socialist economy with former state officials controlling the nation's agricultural production.

Lastly, institutional preservation requires the construction of normative networks, which Lawrence and Suddaby (2006) describe as the inter-organizational connections through which practices become normatively sanctioned, monitored, and evaluated. Symbolically, the Czech reforms severed connections between the government and business owners to allow market forces to dictate new relationships between a newly privatized firm and its shareholders. This arrangement, however, assumed that the majority of shareholders would be private citizens as a result of the mass privatization plan. Similar to transformation in Romania, individual shareholders were more preoccupied with short-term financial gain, and sold their shares to IPFs for a small but guaranteed profit. The IPFs, who took over the role as majority shareholders in the private sector, remained heavily dependent on the state through state-owned banks (Rao & Hirsch, 2003). Thus we can observe in the Czech case that while new normative links can be highly publicized and visible, important segments of the network also remain opaque. Powerful actors from previous institutional arrangements leverage cultural and political capital to remain centrally positioned in the newly formed normative network. Under these circumstances, actors in these hidden networks can operate in a self-serving fashion which counters the goals of the newly formed institution.

Strategic decoupling

Organizational theory depicts formal organizations as focused both outward, in terms of legitimacy and survival, and inward, in terms of task accomplishment and productivity. This requires elite administrators to manage external uncertainties while also maintaining efficient and predictable internal operations (Thompson, 1967). Meyer and Rowan (1977) outlined three probable outcomes when managers attempt this balancing act in highly elaborated institutional environments: (1) the decoupling of structure from activity, (2) the establishment of the logic of confidence and good faith, and (3) the avoidance of inspection and evaluation. These three components are the cornerstones of a loosely coupled organizational system which in current research is frequently framed as either a management failure or the gradual equilibrium to an organizational system when confronted with overlapping and contradictory institutional logics (Orton & Weick, 1990). We highlight the agency in decoupling and offer an alternative explanation: that loosely coupled systems can also result from the careful strategic design of institutional actors.

Decoupling of structure from activity

The concept of purposeful decoupling is not novel. Oliver (1991) suggests two mechanisms – concealment, the disguising of nonconformity behind a façade of acquiescence, and buffering, the reduction in the extent to which an organization is externally inspected, scrutinized, or evaluated – as a strategic response to institutional processes. Our analysis of the Czech economic reforms, however, explicates these concepts, demonstrating how the specific components of a loosely coupled system work in complementarity.

There is substantial empirical research supporting the notion of strategic decoupling. In consumer product markets, luxury wineries deliberately decouple projected images of authenticity and craftsmanship from their own internal operations that are marketing-based and commercially driven (Beverland & Luxton, 2005). Examples also abound within the research of higher education where colleges and universities use loosely coupled structures to feign change or the lack thereof. An example of the latter is the trend of liberal arts colleges adopting professional programs without reflecting this change in their mission statements (Delucchi, 2000). Conversely, university administrators will also paradoxically promote change in efforts to maintain the status quo. Lutz (1982) describes a university president who organized a committee to research reforms for the university, despite knowing the faculty opposed any major changes. In the end, while there was little change in the university's policies or procedures, the president was able to maintain his reputation as an independent authority trying to "shake things up" at the university.

Logics of confidence

A decoupled organization is not without rules; it is governed by formal structures and logics of confidence and faith. Top executives rhetorically reinforce symbolic structures and ritualized myths while mid- and lower-level employees operate by norms of professionalism and the trust that other individuals are performing their assigned tasks with due diligence. The case of the Czech economic reforms demonstrates that logics of confidence can also work to alternative ends, particularly in the public sector where the behavior of dependent actors (i.e. constituents, beneficiaries) differs from private shareholders. Dependent actors' interests in a focal organization's productivity and efficiency are often secondary to their interests in the organization's persistence and continuity (Meyer & Zucker, 1989). Dependents, in turn, are less concerned about administrators performing their formally "assigned" tasks, and more concerned that administrators are continuing to perform tasks to the direct benefit of their dependents. During the period of mass privatization, Klaus and his political party remained in good favor with the electorate despite the uncertainty of their advocated policies. This was due in part to Klaus' ability to speak of massive change to capitalism while keeping many facets of socialism in place (centralized planning and financing, low unemployment, etc.).

Avoidance of inspection and evaluation

Klaus and the CDP also carefully navigated the practice of integration and separation. While the initial government of Vaclav Havel favored integration with Western Europe, Klaus' party, which came into power in 1992, took a Euroskeptic stance toward economic integration (Hanley, 2002). Klaus argued that rapid economic integration with existing Western European institutions would be a threat to their national sovereignty. He even went so far as to compare the European Union to the coercive regimes of the socialist Soviet bloc. This strategy worked for the CDP in two ways. First, it garnered support for the CDP from Czech citizens who were experiencing a renewed sense of nationalism. Second, it slowed the processes of economic integration with western nations and thus delayed the close inspection and evaluation of the technical core of the Czech economy. It wouldn't be until the late 1990s that, after closer examination, the confidence in the transformation of the Czech economy came under fire.

The art of preserving institutions

> Replacing one institution with another means that income, power and status will be redistributed ... Although institutional change often will be triggered by external events, such change impulses will often be redirected in internal processes and end up in quite unexpected places. (Holm, 1995: 401–402)

> This combination of contradictory indicators yields easy interpretations for both organizational success (market creation and innovations) and failure (markets not working, innovations poorly carried out). (Hirsch & Rao, 2003: 139)

Following the collapse of its communist regime, the challenges of leading the Czech Republic's transformation from a centrally planned to a market economy required substantial institutional work. To implement these massive political and economic changes, new ownership rules at the regulatory level had to be created, along with the privatization of enterprises which employed thousands of workers and managers. To accomplish these goals required institutional entrepreneurship to: (a) create new structures, while simultaneously (b) deinstitutionalizing managerial and administrative frameworks already in place, and (c) deciding which elements from the existing institutional structures to preserve.

Lawrence and Suddaby (2006) call for a more integrated approach to studies of institutional entrepreneurship *or* deinstitutionalization, recognizing the interrelation of issues found in and comprising each of these critical components of institutional work. The reorganizations and mass privatization programs just reviewed provide a rich case in which we see the interrelations of these domains all unfolding *simultaneously*. It may even be argued that had they not so co-occurred, neither the substance nor appearance of these changes would have gone forward. While multiple explanations for the process and outcomes of the privatization program in the Czech Republic are possible (cf. Hirsch & Rao, 2003), we elaborate on the interpretation that Klaus' team succeeded in retaining legitimacy and control over their nation's primary assets, thereby reducing its loss of sovereignty to the advances of global capital. These results recall Suddaby and Lawrence's focus on the interests and agendas of skilled actors, and the dynamics of their establishing new rules, rewards, and potential sanctions.

Klaus' team's strategic decoupling of free-market symbols and structures from the substance of market activity provides valuable illustrations of resistance to institutional processes by use of rhetoric based on cultural capital. The mechanisms utilized were a combination of resistance, persuasion, semiotics, and cultural capital.

The actions noted above provide instances in which three of Oliver's (1991) strategic responses to retain institutional control – compromise, avoidance, and manipulation – were successfully implemented. Though strong reforms were rhetorically promised, they slowed down the loss of control to the isomorphic conformity that had been anticipated and expected by western agencies. In this example, the Klaus team may be seen to have given the appearance of creating new rules and disrupting earlier practices, while purposively acting to maintain some of the earlier institutional arrangements. This enabled the preservation of some of the older arrangements by pretending to dismantle them.

An impressive component of Klaus' success with the western financial community was the cultural capital inherent in his strong knowledge and facility with the neoclassical frameworks and ideologies of free-market capitalism. While this cultural capital contributed to the logic of confidence conveyed to these authorities, Klaus was also very familiar with his nation's experience with other "overseers." Before the advent of western demands for a return to capitalism and free markets, the Czechs had, up until 1918, been subordinate to the royalty of the Austrian Habsburg Empire, followed by the Germans during their take-over in World War II, and most recently by a communist regime supported by the USSR. Figure 10.1 illustrates the breadth and depth of the cultural and material actors in the large organizational field of which Klaus had knowledge and experience. For different audiences, this provided a multitude of potential references and images from which he could draw. More than most leaders from the region, the cultural capital embodied in this institutional entrepreneur – across historical epochs and current geography – also helps account for the multicultural resonance and positive reception of his programs, both at home and abroad.

Inside the Czech Republic, Klaus' public speeches were often as tough and critical of economic inefficiencies as when he spoke before foreign audiences. Interestingly, despite the threat these words posed to voters' prospects for continued employment and state benefits, he and his party continued to be re-elected. To better understand this, we turn to the nation's history and its tacit understanding that outsiders were not to be liked or trusted.

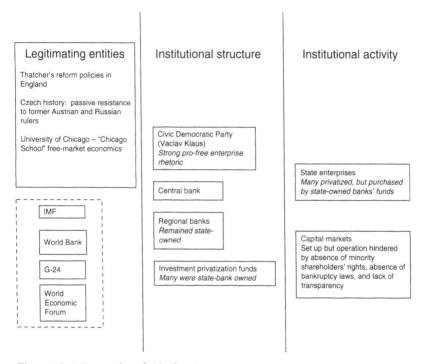

Figure 10.1 Decoupling field of action

This cultural fact is embodied in the nation's fictional hero, the Good Soldier Schweik. Much like most American children know and admire Tom Sawyer and the mischief he caused, nearly all of Central Europe knows Schweik. He is the everyman given orders by superiors, which he then carries out so literally the result is always counterproductive. The superiors are always foreign, and the chapters continue on for four volumes. In recent Czech history, the nation has always been subordinate, taking orders from (respectively) Austria, Germany, Russia, and now the West. In Czech, "to svejk" celebrates the idea of passive resistance; a favorite saying about why the Austrians lost World War I is that they had relied on too many Czech clerks.

Hirsch and Rao (2003) have suggested one reason why the Czechs showed little concern over the implications of Klaus' economic policies is that they saw the speeches as telling outsiders what they liked to hear (following the Good Soldier Schweik). The tacit understanding being that the more socialist culture (pre-Marx) of the Czechs would remain and the impact of the coming changes would be minimized. As stated by

Fox-Wolfgramm, Boal, and Hunt (1998: 120), "organizations whose identity and image are inconsistent with institutional pressures for change will resist change attempts."

We suggest Klaus was so able to satisfy his multiple constituencies by intimately understanding the visions underlying each of their rhetorics, and thereby "leveraging [his] position through the construction of persuasive arguments ... to connect the innovation to broad templates or scenarios of change" (Lawrence & Suddaby, 2006: 240). Interestingly, in the case of the Czech voters, the message to minimize concern (and re-elect him) was more tacit than explicit. We see a connection here to the field's need to take historical narrative and semiotics more seriously. In the example of how the Czechs "pulled it off," we find an interesting suggestion of how the logic of confidence can be turned on its head. Here, it would be the confidence of internal (local, national) participants that the elaborate ceremonies and rituals being introduced were *not* being carried out that kept the loosely coupled system operational.

The type of "backstage" understanding this denotes is captured well by James Scott's distinction between public and private transcripts. In his study, *Domination and the Arts of Resistance* (1990), Scott provides examples of "public" explanations offered by subordinates that conform to models preferred by their superiors, but which backstage, or as "private transcripts" take on widely different formats and interpretations. In Scott's examples, these are protocols that go forward consciously in a fashion that benefits both parties to the ritual performance. On a state level, a similarity we have heard suggested in informal conversations would be if the World Bank fails to verify reports from its grantees before passing along their statements of accomplishment at face value.

While it is hard to pin down the extent to which western governments and elites were aware that the public transcripts proffered by the new Czech regime were decoupled and different from what occurred backstage, it seems apparent that much of the previous regime's institutional arrangements had been preserved and that the West's governments and investors were "officially" the last to know. For entrepreneurs to so successfully preserve aspects of the institutions ostensibly being replaced requires a rich combination of cultural capital, persuasive rhetoric, and political skills.

To so strategically decouple the deinstitutionalization of previous modes of governance while effectively and informally preserving earlier ownership arrangements illustrates well the strategies of compromise and resistance depicted by Oliver (1991), and the effective utilization of rhetoric by actors in organizations elaborated by Eccles and Nohria (1992). Stark found some of the strategic decoupling practices noted above employed more generally throughout what he called East European capitalism. He denoted "recombinant property" as "a form of organizational hedging in ... an attempt to hold resources that can be *justified by more than one legitimating principle*" (1996: 993, emphasis added). We also note that, in contrast to the post-communist "shock therapy" engaged in by the Russian government, China has succeeded (at the time of writing) in preserving its earlier institutions by similarly hedging and decoupling – retaining a dual legitimacy by establishing a stock market and capitalist structure, on the one hand, while under the auspices (and legitimation) of its communist regime, on the other. Here, the distance between public and private transcripts seems closer than in the Soviet bloc.

In their study of early regulatory actions by the United States Securities and Exchange Commission, Bealing, Dirsmith, and Fogarty (1996) show how the consumer relations bureau of a public utility used a combination of Oliver's "Acquiescence" and "Compromise" strategies to protect a state of inaction favored by the utilities, while also adhering to regulatory sanctions demanded by Congress. Analogously, the new Czech government strategically decoupled the policies favored by the International Monetary Fund while also protecting the state of inaction (e.g. preventing bankruptcies, stalling foreign investment) favored by its citizenry. The artful use of rhetoric and cultural capital to preserve institutions while also ostensibly replacing them is also found in Elsbach's (1994) study of how the cattle industry in California managed to overcome attacks on its legitimacy. More recently, we also note that after attacking "big government" and running on campaigns to cut it back, several US administrations (e.g. G. W. Bush, Reagan, and Nixon) have preserved the institution they attacked by leaving office with more government employees and larger deficits than when they arrived.

Conclusion

Suddaby and Lawrence's program to expand on the meaning of institutional work provides exciting opportunities to expand into topical (and analytical) arenas neglected in our literature, and to reclaim some areas warranting reintroduction to the field (Barley, 2007; Hinings & Greenwood, 2002; Stern & Barley, 1996). This chapter took up their essay's invitation to work towards reintegrating our looks at the life cycle of institutions. Taking this edict a step further, we propose a fourth stage within this life cycle in which institutional entrepreneurs work to preserve components of previous institutions within the creation of the new. In the case of the Czech Republic's recent transformation, we found that, in times of large-scale disruption, institutionally disruptive and creative processes do not occur autonomously, but rather are interconnected with each other. New rules cannot be established independent of the deinstitutionalization of what preceded them; nor can we assume that the displaced "older" frameworks just disappear without leaving behind some proponents and legacies. We saw how these all transpired simultaneously, and found a striking example of the institutional entrepreneurship that helped to organize and coordinate them.

We also adopted a perspective on decoupling as a tool purposively used by institutional entrepreneurs to maintain stability and consistency inside the organization's core, while appearing to develop new institutional frameworks that adhere to changing external contingencies. Strategic decoupling by purposive institutional entrepreneurs may be the norm, not its exception – for to better understand both what precedes and what follows isomorphism we must seek out more action and assume less passivity.

References

Aldrich, H. (1999) The evolutionary approach. In *Organizations Evolving*, pp. 20–41. London: Sage.

Astley, W. G. (1985) The two ecologies: population and community perspectives on organizational evolution. *Administrative Science Quarterly*, 30(2): 224–241.

Barley, S. R. (2007) Corporations, democracy, and the public good. *Journal of Management Inquiry*, 16(3): 201–215.

Barnett, W. P. (1990) The organizational ecology of a technological system. *Administrative Science Quarterly*, special issue on Technology, Organizations, and Innovation, 35(1): 31–60.

Bealing, W. E., Dirsmith, M. W. & Fogarty, T. (1996) Early regulatory actions by the SEC: an institutional theory perspective on the dramaturgy of political exchanges. *Accounting Organizations and Society*, 21(4): 317–338.

Benacek, V. (1995) Small businesses and private entrepreneurship during transition – the case of the Czech Republic. *Eastern European Economics*, 33(2): 38–75.

Beverland, M. & Luxton, S. (2005) Managing integrated marketing communication (IMC) through strategic decoupling – how luxury wine firms retain brand leadership while appearing to be wedded to the past. *Journal of Advertising*, 34(4): 103–116.

Carr-Saunders, A. M. & Wilson, P. A. (1933) *The Professions*. Oxford: Clarendon Press.

Dacin, M. T. (1997) Isomorphism in context: the power and prescription of institutional norms. *Academy of Management Journal*, 40(1): 46–81.

Delucchi, M. (2000) Staking a claim: the decoupling of liberal arts mission statements from baccalaureate degrees awarded in higher education. *Sociological Inquiry*, 70(2): 157–171.

DiMaggio, P. & Powell, W. W. (eds.) (1991) *The New Institutionalism in Organizational Analysis*. Chicago: University of Chicago Press.

Dlouhy, V. & Mladek, J. (1994) Privatization and corporate control in the Czech Republic. *Economic Policy*, 9(19): 155–170. (Supplement: Lessons for Reform.)

Eccles, R. G. & Nohria, N. (1992) *Beyond the Hype: Rediscovering the Essence of Management*. Boston, MA: Harvard Business School Press.

Elsbach, K. D. (1994) Managing organizational legitimacy in the California cattle industry – the construction and effectiveness of verbal accounts. *Administrative Science Quarterly*, 39(1): 57–88.

Elsbach, K. D. & Sutton, R. I. (1992) Acquiring organizational legitimacy through illegitimate actions: a marriage of institutional and impression management theories. *Academy of Management Journal*, 35(4): 699–738.

Fiss, P. C. & Zajac, E. J. (2006) The symbolic management of strategic change: sensegiving via framing and decoupling. *Academy of Management Journal*, 49(6): 1173–1193.

Fox-Wolfgramm, S. J., Boal, K. B. & Hunt, J. G. (1998) Organizational adaptation to institutional change: a comparative study of first-order change in prospector and defender banks. *Administrative Science Quarterly*, 43(1): 40.

Friedland, R. & Alford, R. (1991) Bringing society back in: symbols, practices, and institutional contradictions. In W. W. Powell & P. DiMaggio (eds.), *The New Institutionalism in Organizational Analysis*, pp. 223–262. Chicago: University of Chicago Press.

Greenhouse, S. (1991) Czechs begin shift to a free market. *New York Times*, p. 1.3.

Han, S. K. (1994) Mimetic isomorphism and its effect on the audit services market. *Social Forces*, 73(2): 637–663.

Hanley, S. (2002) Party institutionalization and centre-right Euroscepticism in East Central Europe: the case of the Civic Democratic Party in the Czech Republic. Paper presented at the 29th ECPR Joint Sessions of Workshops, Turin.

Hinings, C.R. & Greenwood, R. (2002) ASQ Forum: disconnects and consequences in organizational theory? *Administrative Science Quarterly*, 47(3): 411.

Hirsch, P.M. & Rao, H. (2003) The Schweik syndrome: the narrative power of resistance by agreement. In B. Czarniawska-Joerges & P. Gagliardi (eds.), *Narratives We Organise By*, vol. 2, pp. 137–148. Amsterdam and Philadelphia, PA: John Benjamins.

Holm, P. (1995) The dynamics of institutionalization: transformation processes in Norwegian fisheries. *Administrative Science Quarterly*, 40(3): 25.

Korn, H.J. & Baum, J.A.C. (1994) Community ecology and employment dynamics: a study of large Canadian organizations, 1985–1992. *Social Forces*, 73(1): 1–31.

Kraatz, M.S. & Zajac, E.J. (1996) Exploring the limits of the new institutionalism: the causes and consequences of illegitimate organizational change. *American Sociological Review*, 61: 812–836.

Lawrence, T.B. (2008) Power, institutions and organizations. In R. Greenwood, C. Oliver, R. Suddaby & K. Sahlin-Andersson (eds.), *Handbook of Organizational Institutionalism*, pp. 170–197. Thousand Oaks, CA: Sage.

Lawrence, T.B. & Suddaby, R. (2006) Institutions and institutional work. In S. Clegg, C. Hardy & T. Lawrence (eds.), *Handbook of Organization Studies*, 2nd edn., pp. 215–254. London: Sage.

Lewis, D. (1998) Notes from here and there. *San Francisco Chronicle*, p. A.12.

Lieberman, I.W. (1995) *Mass Privatization in Central and Eastern Europe and the Former Soviet Union: A Comparative Analysis*. Washington, DC: World Bank.

Lipton, D. & Sachs, J. (1990) Creating a market economy in Eastern Europe: the case of Poland. *Brookings Papers on Economic Activity*. Washington DC: The Brookings Institution.

Longworth, R.C. (1995) Czech leader gives U. of C. credit. *Chicago Tribune*, p. 31.

Lutz, F.W. (1982) Tightening up loose coupling in organizations of higher education. *Administrative Science Quarterly*, 27(4): 653.

McDermott, G.A. (2007) Politics, power, and institution building: bank crises and supervision in East Central Europe. *Review of International Political Economy: RIPE*, 14(2): 220.

Meyer, J.W. & Rowan, B. (1977) Institutionalized organizations: formal structure as myth and ceremony. *American Journal of Sociology*, 83(2): 340–363.

(1978) The structure of educational organizations. In M.W. Meyer (ed.), *Environments and Organizations*, pp. 78–109. San Francisco: Jossey-Bass.

Meyer, M.W. & Zucker, L.G. (1989) *Permanently Failing Organizations*. Newbury Park, CA: Sage.

Oliver, C. (1991) Strategic responses to institutional processes. *Academy of Management Review*, 6(1): 145.

Orton, J. D. & Weick, K. E. (1990) Loosely coupled systems: a reconceptualization. *Academy of Management Review*, 15(2): 203.

Rao, H. & Hirsch, P. (2003) "Czechmate": the old banking elite and the construction of investment privatization funds in the Czech Republic. *Socio-Economic Review*, 1: 247–269.

Scott, J. C. (1990) *Domination and the Arts of Resistance: Hidden Transcripts*. New Haven, CT: Yale University Press.

Stark, D. (1996) Recombinant property in East European capitalism. *American Journal of Sociology*, 101(4): 35.

Stern, R. N. & Barley, S. R. (1996) Organizations and social systems: organization theory's neglected mandate. *Administrative Science Quarterly*, 41 (1): 17.

Stevenson, W. B. & Greenberg, D. (2000) Agency and social networks: strategies of action in a social structure of position, opposition, and opportunity. *Administrative Science Quarterly*, 45(4): 651.

Suchman, M. C. (1995) Managing legitimacy: strategic and institutional approaches. *Academy of Management Review*, 20(3): 571–610.

Szelenyi, I. & Szelenyi, S. (1995) Circulation or reproduction of elites during the postcommunist transformation of Eastern Europe – introduction. *Theory and Society*, 24(5): 615–638.

Thompson, J. D. (1967) *Organizations in Action: Social Science Bases of Administrative Theory*. New York: McGraw-Hill.

Verdery, K. (2003) *The Vanishing Hectare: Property and Value in Postsocialist Transylvania*. Ithaca, NY: Cornell University Press.

Weber, K. (2003) Does globalization lead to convergence? Unpublished PhD dissertation, Northwestern University.

Weick, K. E. (1976) Educational organizations as loosely coupled systems. *Administrative Science Quarterly*, 21(1): 1–19.

Westphal, J. D. & Zajac, E. J. (1994) Substance and symbolism in CEOs' long-term incentive plans. *Administrative Science Quarterly*, 39(3): 367.

Zajac, E. J. & Westphal, J. D. (2004) The social construction of market value: institutionalization and learning perspectives on stock market reactions. *American Sociological Review*, 69(3): 433–457.

11 | Doing which work? A practice approach to institutional pluralism

PAULA JARZABKOWSKI, JANE MATTHIESEN,
AND ANDREW H. VAN DE VEN

THIS chapter takes a social theory of practice approach to examining institutional work; that is, how institutions are created, maintained, and disrupted through the actions, interactions, and negotiations of multiple actors. We examine alternative approaches that organizations use to deal with institutional pluralism based on a longitudinal real-time case study of a utility company grappling with opposing market and regulatory logics over time. These two logics required the firm to both mitigate its significant market power and also maintain its commercially competitive focus and responsiveness to shareholders.

Institutional theorists have long acknowledged that institutions have a central logic (Friedland & Alford, 1991) or rationality (DiMaggio & Powell, 1983; Scott, 1995/2001; Townley, 2002), comprising a set of material and symbolic practices and organizing principles that provide logics of action for organizations and individuals, who then reproduce the institutions through their actions (Glynn & Lounsbury, 2005; Suddaby & Greenwood, 2005). Despite a monolithic feel to much institutional theory, in which a dominant institutional logic appears to prevail, institutional theorists also acknowledge the plurality of institutions (e.g. Friedland & Alford, 1991; Kraatz & Block, 2008; Lounsbury, 2007; Meyer & Rowan, 1977; Whittington, 1992). While these pluralistic institutions may be interdependent, they are not considered to coexist in harmony; "There is no question but that many competing and inconsistent logics exist in modern society" (Scott, 1995: 130). Pluralistic institutions are thus a source of contradictory logics (e.g. Friedland & Alford, 1991; Meyer & Rowan, 1977; Seo & Creed, 2002; Townley, 2002), which are expected to generate conflict, contradiction, or

* The authors thank participants at Utilco for their generous access and the Advanced Institute of Management and the Economic and Social Research Council for financial support (award no: RES-331-25-3013).

confusion for organizations and individuals as they seek to realize these logics in action. Kraatz and Block (2008) define this condition as institutional pluralism; organizations operate in multiple institutional spheres, each of which provides different logics that play out in the organization as persistent and deep-rooted tensions.

Pluralism arises from the presence of divergent interest groups, each of which has sufficient power to ensure that their interests remain legitimate (Lindblom, 1965). In pluralistic contexts, divergent interests are neither reconcilable nor able to be suppressed; they must co-exist (Denis, Langley & Rouleau, 2007; Hardy, 1991; Kraatz & Block, 2008; Jarzabkowski & Fenton, 2006). Institutional pluralism thus represents a significant set of organizational challenges. Pluralistic situations entail the coexistence of alternative, legitimate, and potentially competing strategies within a single organization. These situations are contrary to management principles of consensus, unity of command, and structural alignment to a singular vision. Moreover, pluralistic groups are interdependent. They must interact and accommodate each other's interests in creating negotiated orders through partisan mutual adjustment (Lindblom, 1965; Van de Ven, 1992). However, the practice of coping with pluralistic institutions within an organization has received very little empirical study to date (Denis *et al.*, 2007; Kraatz & Block, 2008). Consistent with the underresearched and dynamic nature of the phenomenon, we undertook this study to examine how organizations and the actors within them cope with institutional pluralism over time.

Conceptual background

Institutional pluralism has been examined in institutional theory primarily at the field level. For example, it has been used to explain variation in diffusion of institutionalized practices. Different logics provide viable alternatives that account for practice variation in firms within the same industry (e.g. Hung & Whittington, 1997; Lounsbury, 2007). Other studies examine institutional pluralism as a source of institutional change, either through substitution, in which an existing institutional logic is replaced by a new, competing logic, or by sedimentation, in which new logics layer over and add new meaning to existing logics (e.g. Cooper, Hinings, Greenwood & Brown, 1996; Zilber, 2006), sometimes resulting in one suppressed and one dominant logic (e.g. Reay & Hinings, 2005; Townley, 2002). Competing logics might also engage in a dialectic of opposition which can be reconciled through synthesis of the two. Synthesis is typically achieved through conflict between logics, which provides opportunity for political action as disaffected actors draw upon pluralistic tensions to motivate change (e.g. Greenwood & Hinings, 1996; Hargrave & Van de Ven, 2006; Seo & Creed, 2002; Suddaby & Greenwood, 2005; Van de Ven & Hargrave, 2004). While these field-level studies acknowledge institutional pluralism, they tend to avoid the issue of ongoing coexistence between logics, assuming instead institutional change arising from pluralism. They thus fail to illuminate how different logics coexist inside the organization, which is a key issue for understanding how organizations and their actors cope with institutional pluralism (Denis *et al.*, 2007; Jarzabkowski & Fenton, 2006; Kraatz & Block, 2008). We thus look to alternative explanations in order to understand how organizations and actors cope with ongoing tensions occasioned by managing coexisting, pluralistic interests.

Kraatz and Block (2008) propose that institutional pluralism should be studied at the level of the organization and its actors. Institutional pluralism thus lends itself to an institutional work perspective. Building on concepts of agency within institutional theory (e.g. Barley & Tolbert, 1997; Hargrave & Van de Ven, 2006; Jepperson, 1991; Oliver, 1991), Lawrence and Suddaby (2006) propose that the taken-for-granted presence of institutions is overemphasized, such that their emergence, instantiation, and change within the everyday practices of organizations and their actors is inadequately explained. They develop a research agenda on institutional work, studying how organizations and individuals create, maintain, and disrupt institutions (Lawrence & Suddaby, 2006). This research agenda, which aligns with the level of analysis of our research question, is explained in the introductory chapter of this book. Rather than restating the premises of each category of institutional work, we now consider their implications for coping with institutional pluralism.

Institutional creation examines how new institutions emerge and become established. Lawrence and Suddaby (2006) suggest three main types of work associated with creating institutions, political work, reconfiguring belief systems, and altering meaning system boundaries, each of which might involve different types of practices. The premises of institutional creation furnish some insight into institutional pluralism, in terms of explaining how a new institution is created and inserted into an existing set of institutions. In particular, political practices might be important in ensuring that a new institution can survive within the contested and competing environment of institutional pluralism. We thus suspect that this type of institutional work will be relevant to a study of institutional pluralism. However, it is not clear how the created institution coexists with other institutions that may threaten it. The implicit assumption is that these created institutions will replace or reframe existing institutions by reconfiguring belief systems and altering meaning boundaries. Further empirical research is necessary to examine whether and how these types of work and practices associated with creating new institutions play out in the context of institutional pluralism.

Maintenance, the second category of institutional work identified by Lawrence and Suddaby (2006), examines how institutions are actively produced and reproduced through everyday practice. As the authors note, institutional maintenance is a taken-for-granted premise of institutional theory – institutions persist – yet how such institutions continue to persist is a neglected topic (Scott, 2001). Two main types of institutional work associated with institutional maintenance are: adhering to rule systems and reproducing norms and belief systems. The concept of institutional maintenance is particularly pertinent to a study of institutional pluralism. When multiple, potentially contradictory logics coexist, it seems that any particular institution must continuously be maintained, in order to avoid being dominated by other competing logics. Indeed, Lawrence and Suddaby (2006) suggest that institutional maintenance will be more evident during times of upheaval or threat, when actors must actively preserve the existing institution. We therefore propose that the context of institutional pluralism provides an ideal research setting in which to examine and elaborate the concept of institutional maintenance, as multiple, potentially competing institutions must be maintained in coexistence.

The final category of institutional work that Lawrence and Suddaby (2006) explore is institutional disruption. Institutional disruption occurs where existing institutions do not meet the interests of actors who are able to mobilize sufficient support to attack or undermine these interests. Institutional disruption may thus be seen as a precursor or stage in the process of institutional change (e.g. Greenwood *et al.*, 2002). Lawrence and Suddaby identify three institutional work practices focused upon undermining the prevalence of an existing institution: disconnecting rewards and sanctions from existing rule systems, procedures, and technologies; disconnecting the moral foundations of particular norms; and undermining taken-for-granted assumptions. Institutional disruption is also pertinent to understanding institutional pluralism. For example, competing institutions may seek to disrupt each other. However, as each institution is legitimate and has the necessary resources to persist (Denis *et al.*, 2007; Kraatz & Block, 2008; Lindblom, 1965), disruption will not be possible. As with institutional creation, there is an underlying assumption that disruption involves disrupting an existing institution in order to replace it with a new institution; pluralism is not incorporated sufficiently into the concept. We propose that institutional pluralism provides a context in which to elaborate the concept of institutional work associated with disruption.

Drawing upon the concepts of institutional work, we further developed our research question: "How do organizations and the actors within them engage in different types of institutional work as they endeavor to cope with institutional pluralism over time?" While it is premature to empirically "test" the multiple categories put forward by Lawrence and Suddaby (2006), their concepts can usefully inform an exploratory study such as ours, with a view to elaborating some of these concepts and the associations between them. In particular, our focus upon institutional pluralism provides a critical context (Pettigrew, 1990) in which to observe actors within organizations actively engaged in institutional work.

A practice approach

Lawrence and Suddaby (2006) ground their interest in institutional work within a practice approach to institutions. The practice turn in social theory (Ortner, 1984; Reckwitz, 2002; Schatzki, Knorr Cetina & von Savigny, 2001) has been adopted in a number of management and organization fields, such as technology (e.g. Barley, 1986; Orlikowski, 1992, 2000), accounting (Hopwood & Miller, 1994), and strategy (Jarzabkowski, 2004, 2005; Whittington, 2006). A practice approach examines how actors interact with, construct, and draw upon the social and physical features of context in the everyday activities that constitute practice. Practice theorists address the duality of institutions and action; how institutions are constructed by and, in turn, construct action (e.g. Bourdieu, 1990; Giddens, 1984; Sztompka, 1991; Turner, 1994). While this is also a concern of institutional theory, particularly neo-institutionalists with their interest in instating agency in explanations of institutional change (e.g. Jepperson, 1991; Oliver, 1991; Seo & Creed, 2002), practice scholars take the actions, interactions, and negotiations between multiple actors as their core level of analysis (Jarzabkowski, Balogun & Seidl, 2007). In these actions and interactions actors instantiate, reproduce, and modify institutionalized practices through habit, tacit knowledge, culture, routines, motivations, and emotions (Reckwitz, 2002).

A practice approach is apposite to the study of institutional work because it focuses upon the actions and interactions of actors in creating, maintaining, and disrupting institutions. Furthermore, it hones the level of analysis onto the everyday work of actors and how this work is shaped by institutions, even as it reproduces or modifies those institutions. It has particular value in studying the institutional work involved in institutional pluralism, as it shows how actors go about producing pluralistic institutions within their work, and coping with the tensions between these institutions through their actions and interactions. A practice approach acknowledges that the tensions of institutional pluralism may be part of the ordinary, everyday nature of work, rather than exceptional phenomena. It thus provides deep insights into the institutional work involved in coping with institutional pluralism.

As its name implies, practice theory is concerned with studying praxis (Jarzabkowski *et al.*, 2007; Whittington, 2006). In praxis, actors are knowledgeable agents who construct and reconstruct institutionalized social structures with recognition of the limits and potentials of the current social order (Benson, 1977; Bourdieu, 1990; Giddens, 1984; Seo & Creed, 2002; Sztompka, 1991; Whittington, 2006). While various theoretical bases of praxis might be considered, this chapter will draw upon Sztompka's (1991) theory of social becoming, on the basis that it goes beyond criticisms about the synchronic representations of agent and institutional structure present in structuration theory (Archer, 1995; Barley & Tolbert, 1997), the predisposition toward structural reproduction in habitus (Bohman, 1999; Turner, 1994), or the temporal separation of action and structure present in Archer's (1995) portrayal of realist theory (Clark, 2000).

Sztompka proposes that praxis is a unified "socio-individual field in the process of becoming" (1991: 95). In the theory of social becoming, institutional structures are continuously being operationalized and actors are being mobilized within an ongoing stream of interactions.

This stream of interactions is praxis; the nexus of "what is going on in a society and what people are doing" (Sztompka, 1991: 96; see also Child, 1997; Jarzabkowski, 2004; Whittington, 2006). From this perspective, concepts such as stability and change and structure and action are false representations of a social world that is continuously unfolding. Rather, social order is an ongoing process of "reweaving of actors' webs of beliefs and habits of action to accommodate new experiences obtained through interactions" (Tsoukas & Chia, 2002: 567). Praxis is thus a helpful concept in examining how organizations and their actors construct and reconstruct institutional logics within their work practices over time. We focus upon praxis as the level of analysis in this chapter, examining how actors instantiate the pluralistic institutional logics in which their organization is embedded through their ongoing interactions over time.

Research design

In keeping with the exploratory nature of our topic, we adopted a longitudinal, real-time, case-based approach (Pettigrew, 1990; Yin, 1994). Many utilities in essential industries, such as energy, telecommunications, and water, are subject to economic regulation. These firms are typically former state-owned incumbents which, following privatization, have come to competitive markets with a historic legacy of assets and scale of resources that constitute barriers to entry for other industry players. Most notably, former incumbents are afforded significant market power because of their ownership of the distribution network upon which the industry is dependent.

Our research context is a listed utility company coping with the institutional pluralism that arises when market logic is confronted by regulatory logic.[1] The regulatory logic is to ensure a competitive market, in which one player, despite holding a key part of the value chain, is not able to maximize value from that asset through a monopoly (Kay, 2000). This logic is contrary to a free-market logic, in which a publicly listed company has an obligation to make profit (Friedman, 1970). Under free-market logic a firm would typically maximize a dominant

---

[1] This problem is different from the extant work on institutional pluralism conducted in public sector, professional, and cultural organizations in which a professional, value-based logic is confronted by a market logic (e.g. Glynn & Lounsbury, 2005; Oakes, Townley & Cooper, 1998; Townley, 2002).

market position arising from an integrated value chain (Porter, 1980, 1985). Regulated firms are thus beset by institutional pluralism (Sharratt, Brigham & Brigham, 2007), facing both a market logic of maximizing competitive position and, as listed companies, a strong commercial incentive to maintain this logic, as well as a regulatory logic that requires them to mitigate the advantages afforded by significant market power. We explore our research question in Utilco,[2] a regulated firm coping with these features of institutional pluralism.

As part of an increasing political drive to correct market imbalances in the sector, an agreement was reached between Utilco and the Regulator that Utilco would implement a new Regulatory Framework based on equivalence. Equivalence required Utilco to place its distribution networks within a separate transparent business division. While this new Distribution Division (DD) would remain under the corporate Utilco structure, it would operate independently and provide equal access to the distribution networks to all industry players without favoring downstream Utilco businesses. A critical aspect of equivalence was that DD should not share any commercial information with downstream Utilco businesses or allow its decision-making to be affected by Utilco commercial objectives. Utilco would also have to separate all products it currently offered to the industry through its integrated value chain, so that these could be traded on a transparent market basis between DD and Utilco's Retail Division (RD).

Although this new Framework could not be considered a new institutional logic, it did represent a strengthening of the regulatory logic, containing strong coercive elements of legal redress if Utilco failed to meet the various legally imposed deadlines (LID), which had been set to ensure timely compliance. In order to demonstrate that it fully embraced the strengthening regulatory logic, Utilco also volunteered some self-imposed deadlines (SID) for product separation, which were in advance of the LID and associated with substantial financial penalties if not met. At the LID, Utilco's RD would be the only industry player required to use the equivalent product, although industry would take it up over the next two to three years.

---

[2] In order to preserve the anonymity of the case, all data that might reveal Utilco's identity such as specific dates, names, products, and other contextual features have been disguised. However, the nature and temporal sequence of events are faithfully reproduced.

At the same time, Utilco was a competitive, publicly listed company with a dominant position in the domestic-consumer marketplace and ambitions to further penetrate the highly competitive corporate-consumer marketplace. As such, Utilco had built its value proposition and competitiveness on the basis of superior customer service. A strengthened regulatory logic based on equivalence was thus seen as contradictory to the market logic: "... *people aren't in business to be fair; they're in business to secure an advantage* ..." (RD manager).

Longitudinal qualitative data were collected for an eighteen-month period, tracing the implementation of one of Utilco's major products, Product X, in real-time. Observations took place at the Corporate Center (CC) and across each division of Utilco, including the regulated Distribution Division (DD) and the Retail Division (RD), comprising the two retail divisions, focused on either domestic and small-business customers (RD1) or corporate customers (RD2). The data collected included sixty-nine fully transcribed open-ended interviews with key operational, middle, and senior managers; notes and transcriptions based on non-participant observation of 184 audio-taped meetings across the divisions and at the corporate center; complemented by additional informal observation and interaction, as well as documentary analysis. Together, these data amount to over 1,200 single-spaced A4 pages of data imported into NVivo for coding.

In order to make sense of the mass data, the authors wrote a rich chronological case story of the implementation of Product X from the perspective of the key groups – DD, RD, and CC (Langley, 1999). This story and its associated data formed the basis of our analysis, comprising the unfolding interactions between actors over time as they attempted to cope with the pluralism occasioned by market and regulatory logics. Based on this story, we then identified the different logics being experienced in Utilco. As it is difficult to identify institutional logics empirically, we followed others in searching the raw data for indicators of the market and regulatory logics, such as evidence of norms, beliefs, values, and work practices associated with each logic (e.g. Cooper *et al.*, 1996; Scott, Ruef, Mendel & Caronna, 2000; Reay & Hinings, 2005). Analysis identified and supported the existence of market and regulatory logics. Drawing upon the method used by Reay and Hinings (2005), Table 11.1 presents representative extracts of the raw data and our analysis of these data according to the belief systems, identified as those goals or values and actions to be pursued, that comprise each

Table 11.1. *Representative examples of market and regulatory logics of action*

Logic	Representative data	Logic of action
Regulatory logic	• "We don't compete with our customers anymore and all customers are equally good. ... And there's no benefit to DD in spending lots and lots of sales effort on one customer to the detriment of another. So our customers can sort that out for themselves, they can compete in the end user market" (DD middle manager).	• An equivalent or level playing field for all players is desirable in the marketplace.
	• "Utilco RDs are our biggest customer still, without a doubt, so you have to watch the balance at an industry meeting; the sheer weight of their voice, we need to make sure we have equivalent ..." (DD director).	• DD's purpose is to supply the whole industry in an equivalent way.
	• "What we don't want is for people to have to balance their Utilco versus DD hats; not a good thing. ... Whatever you do, don't not do what's right for DD. If you start doing things that are right for Utilco Group, phew you know" (DD regulation director).	• DD is totally independent from Utilco downstream businesses in its decision-making.
	• "Utilco could meet a lot of the Framework just by ticking the boxes but that wouldn't be in the spirit of it. So we need to meet the spirit of the Framework" (DD regulation director).	• DD voluntarily complies with regulation and does not need to be coerced.
	• "With the Regulator we have to be pretty careful. That's where I think some of the spirit thing comes in because ... if we didn't, there is the potential that the regulator I think will come down pretty hard on you" (DD Product X manager).	• Do not accord advantage to Utilco downstream businesses, regardless of its commercial value to DD.
	• "As long as we're not charging anyone except RD, then we're not getting a complaint from anyone except RD, which is less of a problem [than industry complaints]" (DD manager in meeting).	• Utilco and RD's concerns are of lower priority than regulatory or industry concerns.

Table 11.1. (*cont.*)

Logic	Representative data	Logic of action
Market logic	• "The profit in RDs which are expected to have a good growth profile is key. That will support our share price more than the profit in DD. Share price is obviously … well the major thing we have to take into consideration so if by doing this model we actually alter … if we move profit out of RDs and back up the value chain to the up-stream, so to DD, our share price could be affected" (Utilco finance director).	• Shareholder value and share price are our key concerns as a listed company.
	• "I presume shareholders would expect Utilco's wholly owned selling entity, RD, and its wholly owned producer, DD, to act within the spirit of the law but also to the benefit of its shareholders" (RD2 commercial manager).	• Regulation should not get in the way of profitability. • RD actions should benefit Utilco share price.
	• "So our biggest challenge … at the moment is the setting of customers' expectations … The RD business model incurs losses for every second of customer time added" (RD manager).	• Customer service is central to the Utilco value proposition and profitability.
	• "RD is a big customer of DD; we would expect from any supplier that are part of purchase would give us some advantage because that's the way the world works. That's the law of the world you know, that's how it works. And I expect that to be the same when I deal with DD. So a little start-up company who gives, you know, DD £10,000 a year should not have a better service than me who spend £10 million a year" (RD2 change manager).	• As one of the largest players in the industry, Utilco RDs should be able to gain normal scale advantages in the market.
	• "It goes against everything we've been indoctrinated with over all our years with Utilco … It takes away our cutting edge over customer service" (RD2 operational manager).	• RD should protect customer service at any cost.
	• "What do we owe them to shield them from that kind of pressure? They're dragging down the work we're trying to do to grow our business" (RD regulation manager).	• DD decisions should not be allowed to damage the RD business model.

logic. A more complete report of this methodology can be found in Jarzabkowski, Matthiesen, and Van de Ven (2008).

In particular we were looking for interaction between logics, any mutation of logics that might indicate a shift in their belief systems, or any synthesis or merging of logics. However, the logics remained intact and discrete throughout. Nonetheless, this analysis enabled us to decompose the case story into five distinct phases (Langley, 1999; Van de Ven, 1992), based on the process of Product X implementation and the practices that different groups in Utilco employed as they interacted with each other over Product X. These five phases will be presented in the results. Finally, we used Lawrence and Suddaby's (2006) categories of institutional work to inform our analysis of the phases. We looked specifically for evidence of work practices associated with institutional creation, maintenance, and disruption, drawing upon Lawrence and Suddaby's (2006) concepts and subcategories to inform our coding judgments. These categories are now used in presenting the results of our analysis over five phases of implementing Product X.

Findings[3]

Phase 1 (months 1–4): the regulatory logic is asserted and market logic disrupted

At the outset, Utilco CC was keen to prove itself fully committed to the new Framework. As part of the Framework agreement, the Distribution Division was physically separated from the Retail Division, being placed in a separate building, with new name, logo, and access codes. This physical separation inhibited spontaneous interaction between parts of the business and emphasized the new ideals of equivalence in dealing with downstream Utilco divisions. Physical separation thus enhanced the regulatory logic and, in doing so, disrupted the market logic by disconnecting existing practices of interaction between upstream and downstream businesses. DD was given a separate, independent status within Utilco that began the process of reconfiguring potential value chain advantages to RD.

---

[3] A comprehensive report on the data and results, including a more detailed description of the analysis process, can be found in Jarzabkowski *et al.* (2008).

For the first couple of months, DD and RD worked on the separation of Product X in isolation from each other. RD activity was focused on attempting to develop systems to connect to the DD product, without being sure about the specification of the new DD product. DD activity was focused on the creation of their new boundaries, avoiding any interaction with RD because, under the norms of the regulatory logic, this would be improper conduct. DD insisted that RD should place any requirements for Product X through industry fora, which DD would incorporate only if they met the needs of the whole industry. RD was very worried by this behavior, as it was unable to gain any information on the Product it would be selling to its customers in twelve months' time. In response, RD approached Utilco for support. However, RD had trouble gaining traction, as the dominant regulatory logic gave DD power to resist efforts to interact. DD's refusal to consider RD's needs for Product X further disrupted the market logic by undermining assumptions and beliefs about the importance of RD as a key DD customer.

Eventually in the third month, the two sides realized that they needed to discuss their parallel plans for Product X and meetings between the businesses were arranged. RD expressed its fears about the deterioration of customer service if product testing could not begin at least four months before the SID. A rift quickly became apparent, as RD's market-based values and beliefs were dismissed by DD: "*RD's expectation that the customer experience must NOT be compromised when disintegrating a vertically integrated company is living in cloud cuckoo land*" (DD manager). Such assertions additionally disrupted the market logic by undermining the moral foundations of the Utilco value proposition, which was customer service. DD further advanced the regulatory logic by defining the interaction boundaries. DD emphasized that, under the new Framework, it must not be "*unduly influenced*" by RD in decision-making.

For RD, it was incomprehensible that the customer experience was being invalidated by DD. RD responded by actively maintaining the market logic, drawing on authority structures in an attempt to police and control DD behavior, whilst reaffirming its own belief in customer service as a central tenet of Utilco. The RD aim was to develop interlocked plans with DD that acknowledged the dependencies in developing a workable Product X. Otherwise the SID may not be met.

However, DD rejected this argument, refuting suggestions of interdependence and insisting that collaboration would counteract the regulatory logic: "*They are not interlocked, interdependent plans. DD cannot be dependent on ... one industry player*" (DD manager). DD actively maintained the regulatory logic by adhering to its rule systems and insisting on independent work practices.

CC was keen to project a normative commitment to the new Framework and thus also maintained the regulatory logic by supporting DD's right to work independently. While the CC was already aware of problems with Product X, it was reluctant to shift the balance in favor of the market logic. It thus contributed to embedding the regulatory logic into everyday work practices and disrupting the market logic by suggesting that RD would need to find new work practices. Indeed, the Utilco CEO held a meeting with 350 key managers in the fourth month, emphasizing that achieving the deadlines in the Framework were a priority for everyone.

Phase 2 (months 5–6): incompatibility between logics emerges

Training about the types of information that could be shared under the Framework began to filter through, alleviating concerns about information-sharing between DD and downstream divisions. In addition, CC established an end-to-end management program for Product X. These actions prioritized the regulatory logic but also attempted to alleviate frictions over the development of Product X.

While DD wanted to avoid undue influence, it agreed that there were interdependencies between the two units in meeting the SID. DD felt that it could cooperate with RD without compromising its regulatory values by changing its work practices in order to publish any Product X decisions and solutions to industry, as well as RD. DD thus actively maintained the regulatory logic, adhering to its rules about equivalence and embedding them within work practices that might also enable consideration of RD's position. RD used this as an opportunity to assert the market logic. It pointed out that a testing period of two months, at the barest minimum, was necessary in order to ensure that the Product would work for its customers.

Despite the resolve on both sides to try to work together, incompatibilities emerged, as DD's decision to publish everything to industry began to have consequences for Product X: "*Apparently DD is now considering different products because industry would like that but this is news to us*" (RD manager). The regulatory logic embedded within

DD work practices was incompatible with the market logic embedded in RD work practices; RD could not countenance building a Product X that jeopardized customer service. RD reinforced its own beliefs, stating that the new product spec had unacceptable service times and consequently asking DD to modify it. However, because of the regulatory logic embedded within its work practices, DD needed to check this modification with industry, delaying the response to RD. Misunderstandings accelerated and RD challenged DD's capacity as responsive supplier.

Feeling threatened, RD actively maintained the market logic by calling upon CC to impose deterrents upon DD and demanding that DD be held responsible for risk to market share occasioned by delays in customer service. As such, RD insisted that market-based values should be incorporated in the Product X design. RD also appealed to a higher power, the Utilco CEO, to increase visibility of service issues. Utilco CC was increasingly aware that there were problems with Product X, as rumors abounded that it may not meet the SID. CC responded by emphasizing deterrents to both sides if the SID was not met, in an attempt to balance the two logics. While this prioritized the SID as a normative regulatory objective, hence maintaining the regulatory logic, it did not pay attention to the complementary work practices necessary to achieve this objective.

Phase 3 (months 7–8): polarization of conflict between logics

Conflict between the logics escalated as DD published its Product X spec, which RD had been awaiting, but it was neither what RD thought was agreed nor something capable of fulfilling its customer service needs. RD demonized DD, claiming that DD was using equivalence to bring the level of service down, rather than raising the service components of the product to industry as a whole. The CC end-to-end management program established a series of intensive but unsuccessful Product X interworking sessions between the two divisions. RD would not consider a compromise to its market logic and adhered to its rule systems and beliefs, insisting that Product X should deliver its existing level of service: "*There is little of a lower standard that RD could actually live with*" (RD manager). RD was angry that DD refused to acknowledge the inadequacies of Product X from a market perspective, and actively policed and criticized DD's behavior. For their part, DD managers refused to consider modifications to the Product X spec. They adhered to the regulatory rule systems, asserting that as long as a product was delivered by the SID, DD would have met its requirements, which were separate from Utilco requirements.

Power plays between the two divisions ensued. RD began to create its own version of the regulatory logic, defining DD as an industry supplier and insisting that DD should upgrade the standard of supply. At the same time, RD realized that it would have to raise prices to meet rising costs from the regulatory change, which inflamed its embedded market values. For DD, these RD problems were based on an obsolete market logic. DD disrupted market-based assumptions, suggesting that a level playing field would reduce RD service because its previous service constituted an unfair advantage. The situation on Product X arrived at a stalemate.

As CC became aware of escalating contradictions between the logics, it attempted to balance the two by inducing a focus on overarching Utilco aims and prioritizing the SID. However, it also recognized the contradictions in that message: "*There is a problem with that because DD people are only allowed under the Framework to work to DD objectives, so it could constitute a breach to think of it that way for them, although the real breach will be if Utilco fails to meet the Framework*" (CC manager). Thus, by default, the CC maintained the regulatory logic without instituting work practices that would also enable the market logic.

Phase 4 (months 9–11): creating logics in relation to each other

In the ninth month, a meeting between key managers from RD, DD, and the Utilco CEO was held, at which RD asserted the importance of the market logic within Product X. The existing product from DD would enable them to meet the SID but in doing so would jeopardize customer service. The CEO insisted on adherence to both logics by declaring that the two sides must interwork on Product X. The CEO of Utilco and the CEOs of the two divisions began weekly meetings with the key Product X players to enable and police the maintenance of both logics in hopes that they could still meet the SID with an acceptable product.

Both divisions were motivated to accommodate the other's position, reconfiguring their own belief systems in order to create the other's logic in relation to their own. Thus RD advocated tolerance of the industry consultation delays: "*We've just got to learn that we've got to give DD headspace to develop things*" (RD manager); while DD tried to understand RD's service considerations with Product X: "*DD call-center people will go into RD call-centers to see what the problems will be*" (RD manager). However, as DD attempted to accommodate the market logic, problems emerged that required it to also actively maintain adherence to the regulatory logic by continuing to check that Product X modifications were important for all of industry, not solely RD.

RD also attempted to accommodate DD's need to consult industry by creating DD as an industry supplier and itself as an industry player. As all of industry would have to buy the same product, it could comply with both logics by lobbying industry and successfully gaining industry support for product specifications. RD was thus able to drive its market needs by defining the boundaries of the regulatory logic in relation to the market logic. DD was, however, worried about RD still having undue influence, believing that these additional Product X services were only relevant to RD, which differentiated on customer service. Hence, industry probably would not purchase these services, so that DD would be developing Product X primarily for RD. DD self-policed its regulatory rule systems by undertaking a legal appraisal, which suggested that it might constitute a competitive advantage for RD. RD strongly disagreed with this interpretation, asserting its market-based rule systems: "*This is something any scale operator would need of Product X*" (RD manager). RD engaged in its own policing, calling for arbitration from the CC. However, central arbitration was perceived as inappropriate, as DD adhered to its regulatory rules: "*The Center is not there to set commercial policy on DD products*" (DD manager).

Nonetheless, both sides attempted to accommodate the other, advocating tolerance of the other's position in relation to their own logic. RD accepted that DD was acting in good faith, while DD agreed it would not engage in a legal wrangle that could delay the LID, which was increasingly challenging. While both sides continued to interwork, the logics persistently remained incompatible due to "*the philosophical differences ... that we're working to*" (DD manager).

Utilco CC found itself in the difficult position of explaining to the Regulator that it would not meet the SID. It began to create a space for the market logic within the regulatory logic, explaining that this delay was necessary to ensure that the industry remained sound and intact, avoiding a collapse in customer service arising from an unacceptable

Product X. As a reasonable and responsive player, Utilco would prefer to pay the self-imposed fine than expose consumers to such risk. As RD was the largest industry player, the Regulator could be persuaded that it was important that Product X be serviceable for their large consumer base, especially as other industry players would also need to use the product at a later date. Utilco was thus able to maintain its commitment to the regulatory logic, whilst creating some room to adhere to their market logic of customer service, albeit at significant financial penalty.

Phase 5 (months 12–18): mutual adjustment between logics

Both divisions recognized the incompatibility between logics, as well as their operational interdependence in delivering Product X. Despite their interdependence, both sides continued to actively adhere to their own rule systems and assert their own beliefs. For example, enraged by delays to the DD release, RD responded by emphasizing the importance of customer service: "*It fundamentally changes the operating model of RD. That is quite a major strategic impact. That would effectively lose the customer service differentiation point of RD strategy*" (RD manager). DD disrupted the assumptions of market logic by suggesting a loss of customer experience to be the new norm: "*Isn't that the point of equivalence?*" (DD manager).

Nonetheless, both sides increasingly maintained their own logic in relation to potential impact from and upon the other logic. For example, DD acknowledged that its product did not meet RD's customer service expectations and tried to find alternative solutions, demonstrating a preparedness to police the incorporation of both logics within Product X. DD's willingness to acknowledge the market logic was made easier by RD's acknowledgment of the regulatory logic and its implications for its own work practices.

CC also actively began to enable the attainment of both logics within Product X, establishing specific work practices, including a weekly business-wide dashboard, at which differences could be dealt with quickly. This enabled the divisions to work around stalemates between the logics: "*There is less and less emphasis on artificial boundaries … a degree of pragmatism is breaking through*" (RD manager). However, interworking also represented threats, such that each logic had also to be maintained, involving conscious self-policing and active embedding of existing logics in day-to-day work practices. DD emphasized its independence, while RD emphasized that it would only meet the regulatory implications of Product X within the parameters of their market logic, i.e. by achieving satisfactory customer service.

As the LID loomed, RD further embedded the market logic within its work practices, flagging up its fears that they could not meet the LID because of customer impact. RD labeled this impact a *"service crisis,"* thereby preserving the norms of customer service but also engaging in political work, deterring others from overriding the market logic because of pragmatic concerns to meet the LID; *"The message 'a service crisis' is a political one. It sounds better to have a service crisis. No one will say 'just get on with it'"* (RD manager).

In the multiple interworking meetings that had been established, the CC actively supported mutual adjustment between logics. While pragmatic considerations about interworking had increased as the deadline approached, this did not entail relaxation of either logic. Rather, each was actively maintained in relation to the other. For example, RD reproduced its existing norms – *"I appreciate the need to protect the customer experience, which is the basic tenet in ... everything we do"* (RD manager) – whilst also acknowledging that it could not enforce a suitable product for its needs because of the regulatory norms shaping DD practices.

The CC continued to confirm that both logics needed to be maintained, even though it realized this meant mutual adjustment and potential compromise between logics: *"There can be no doubt where the CEO comes from. To reiterate – [the LID is] absolutely what we're aiming for, tempered by obviously continuing to look at the customer service position and ensuring that doesn't get any worse"* (RD manager).

At the LID, Product X was ready to use, albeit with reservations about how well it could cope with customer requirements in the short term. Utilco declared publicly that it had met the regulatory requirement of an equivalent Product X. However, at the same time in the external environment, it created a space for the market logic within its adherence to the regulatory logic by advocating the importance of customer service. For example, in its declaration it reserved the right to revert to its old, non-equivalent products temporarily, with financial penalties: *"To minimize customer disruption, we are carefully monitoring and slowly increasing our use of Product X ... [We] have the intention to use contingency systems if necessary to secure a high level of customer service. Given that Utilco reserves the right to use the existing fallback systems, we voluntarily prolong our payment to industry*" (CC manager).

Discussion

This chapter set out to address the exploratory research question: "How do organizations and the actors within them engage in different types of institutional work as they endeavor to cope with institutional pluralism over time?" Table 11.2 summarizes the five phases of institutional work we found within the different groups over an eighteen-month period at Utilco. We now discuss these findings in terms of their contributions to our understanding of institutional pluralism and institutional work. The discussion is centered on five key findings.

In phase 1, during the introduction of new regulatory measures, the divisions within Utilco actively engaged in all three types of institutional work. Disruption work was partially a facet of the strengthened regulatory framework, which created physical barriers between divisions that adhered to different logics. Such dramatic changes in work practices may be attributed to the state-conferred coercive power and legitimacy of regulatory institutions (Holm, 1995; Russo, 2001; Townley, 2002). Interestingly, these physical changes in the existing rule systems and rewards and sanctions also enabled DD to disrupt normative assumptions about the legitimacy and value of the market logic. By drawing on the legitimacy of the regulatory logic, they were able to make a virtue of their opposition to the market logic (Suchman, 1995). Similarly, CC, while not actively disrupting the market logic, also began to change normative assumptions by attributing regulatory rather than market-based meanings to RD's problems with the new order. Thus coercive mechanisms involved in disrupting the market logic were linked to more subtle disruptions to the moral foundations and assumptions underpinning that logic.

At the same time, DD engaged in creation work, defining the boundaries of what constituted "proper" behaviors for actors acting within a regulatory logic. While it was not necessary to actually "create" the regulatory logic, as it already had state and corporate parent legitimacy, political forms of creation work were part of the pluralistic context (Kraatz & Block, 2008). Creation work was a response to the embeddedness of the market logic, investing actions that opposed that logic with propriety. At the same time as creating the regulatory logic, both

Table 11.2. *Approaches to institutional pluralism in different phases (Key: RL = regulatory logic; ML = market logic)*

Phases	DD institutional work	RD institutional work	CC institutional work
1. Regulatory logic is asserted	*Disrupting ML:* Physical separation and information-sharing barriers disconnect rewards and sanctions, and require rerouting of existing patterns of interaction. This undermines assumptions and beliefs about the ML and disassociates from the taken-for-granted moral foundations of customer service. *Creating RL:* Engage in largely political creation work, defining to others the boundaries for what constitutes proper behavior from a regulatory perspective. *Maintaining RL:* Adherence to rule systems is predominant, particularly policing own behavior and embedding that in everyday practices, such as independent working.	*Maintaining ML:* Respond to attempted disruption by DD as threats to the ML. Engage in political acts of adherence, such as appealing for greater policing of potential threats from DD's behavior. Such acts also actively reconfirm and embed customer service beliefs within own activities.	*Maintaining RL:* Adhere to rule systems that support the RL, such as supporting non-engagement between the two divisions. This implicitly disrupts the ML by failing to advocate it. *Disrupting ML:* Undermine assumptions about work practices by suggesting that RD's problems with Product X require it to find different practices, rather than exercising dependence on or blaming DD.

2. Emerging incompatibility between logics	*Maintaining RL:* Establish practices for sharing information with industry and RD at the same time. This enables it to adhere to the norms and rules of its own logic, and embed them within everyday work practices.	*Maintaining ML:* Reinforce beliefs in the ML by emphasizing and insisting on customer-servicing work practices. Maintain own rule systems by policing DD behavior that is inappropriate to these systems. Attempt deterrence, by insisting that DD be accountable for the damage to customer service that might arise from its work practices.	*Maintaining RL:* Attempt to enable both logics by prioritizing regulatory objectives, whilst emphasizing deterrents for not achieving the SID. While this reinforces the RL at a high level, it does not pay attention to the complementary work practices between RD and DD necessary to achieve regulatory objectives.
3. Polarization of conflict between logics	*Maintaining RL:* Adhere to own rule systems and further embed them in independent work practices. Even where it considers the RD position, it does so only within the conscious adherence to its own rule systems, such as engaging with industry. *Disrupting ML:* Respond to RD's ML-based problems by suggesting that RD's beliefs in customer service no longer have legitimacy.	*Maintaining ML:* Engage in increasingly active maintenance work, including demonizing DD for destroying customer service levels in the entire industry. Police DD's anti-ML behavior and assert the rightness of its customer-service beliefs. *Creating RL in relation to ML:* Engage in political work, defining DD's position within the market as one of supplier, and hence defining those practices expected of a supplier from a market perspective. The RL is thus defined in relation to the ML.	*Maintaining RL:* Attempt to balance the two logics under a superordinate goal that, by default, adheres to the rule systems of the RL and, hence, does not actively maintain the ML.

Table 11.2. (*cont.*)

Phases	DD institutional work	RD institutional work	CC institutional work
4. Creating logics in relation to each other	*Creating ML in relation to RL:* Do some reconfiguring of belief systems in order to identify RD's ML-based problems as something DD may take into account, within necessary adherence to its own RL-based rule systems. *Maintaining RL:* Adhere to own rule systems by policing any potential ML-based threats to its belief in equivalence. Reinforce own belief systems by embedding separation of DD work practices from Utilco policing or coercion.	*Creating RL in relation to ML:* Do some reconfiguring of belief systems in order to identify barriers created by the RL as legitimate and requiring some changes in work practices within RD, such as new ways of communicating with DD through industry fora. *Maintaining ML:* Reinforce own belief systems by insisting that RD practices are the norm for large-scale operators within a market.	*Maintaining RL and ML:* Reinforce belief in both logics and insist on adherence to the rule systems and beliefs of both. Engage in greater policing and enabling of both logics by instituting weekly CEO meetings. *Creating RL in relation to ML:* Engage in political work of advocacy to external audiences in order to demonstrate that Utilco is committed to acting sensibly on the RL, accepting financial regulatory penalties in order to avoid destroying the ML.
5. Mutual adjustment between logics	*Maintaining RL in relation to ML:* Ongoing process of maintaining the RL in relation to the ML. This enables them to take account of and create some space to tolerate demands of the ML, whilst engaging in active countering, such as policing potential ML-based threats to the RL and embedding the RL within own work practices. This includes *some disrupting-type work*, such as invalidating ML practices where they are threatening.	*Maintaining ML in relation to RL:* Ongoing process of maintaining the ML in relation to the RL. This enables them to take account of and create some space to tolerate the RL, whilst engaging in active countering, such as asserting the "rightness" of their service differentiation, where threat to the RL is perceived.	*Creating RL in relation to ML:* Ongoing political work of advocacy to external audiences, in order to ensure that the RL can be met, with compromises that also enable Utilco to maintain the ML. *Maintaining RL and ML:* Engage in active reinforcing of and adherence to each logic, which involves mutual adjustment between divisions, until Product X is fully attained.

DD and CC engaged in active maintenance work, adhering to rule systems that ensured DD's independence and embedding those rules within the DD belief systems, norms, and work practices. DD was also active in self-policing, consciously adhering to its own rule systems whenever it felt compromised by its contact with actors working under market logic. RD was equally active in maintaining the market logic, as a response to the perceived threats of the regulatory logic, actively deterring regulatory influences upon its work and re-emphasizing its customer-service beliefs and norms. *Summary finding 1*: such conscious and active maintenance work by all parties, both in adhering to rule systems and also reproducing beliefs and norms, is associated with the perceived need to continuously fend off potential threat to an existing logic within a pluralistic context.

In phase 2, CC and DD ceased to actively disrupt the market logic or create the regulatory logic. However, they did not relax into taken-for-granted behavior but actively engaged in maintaining the regulatory logic, adhering to rule systems by self-policing and deterring perceived threats, as well as reinforcing the norms and beliefs embedded within independent work practices. At the same time, the RD actively maintained the market logic through emphasizing its norms and belief systems and actively deterring perceived regulatory threats. Thus, through the maintenance of their own logic within a pluralistic context, each side engaged in move and counter-move, perceiving maintenance acts by the other as oppositional and requiring active maintenance in response (Kraatz & Block, 2008; Lindblom, 1965). *Summary finding 2*: maintenance work within a pluralistic context may thus generate or at least support contradiction and conflict between opposing logics.

In phase 3, maintenance of each logic was associated with escalation of conflict between logics and increasingly political forms of institutional work. As the actors in each division adhered to their own logic, actively maintaining their own rules, controls, and work practice norms, they felt threatened by the ongoing active maintenance work of the other (Brown, Lawrence & Robinson, 2005). In particular, maintenance work became political for RD, as it demonized any actions that countered its market-based beliefs and insisted on the policing of regulatory behaviors that affected it (Bacharach & Lawler, 1980; Hardy & Clegg, 1996). For its part, DD felt that the regulatory logic was threatened by the ongoing maintenance of the market logic. As it had the legitimacy of the regulatory logic to protect its work practices and norms, it was able to resort to different political tactics (Bacharach & Lawler, 1980). It did not confront RD but rather engaged in further disruption work, invalidating RD's claims and norms from a regulatory perspective (Hardy & Clegg, 1996).

In the face of this disruption and unable to preserve its own logic through maintenance work, RD engaged in politically motivated creation work, attempting to minimize damage to its market logic by defining the appropriate supplier practices that it required of DD under the regulatory logic. This largely political attribution of meaning to the regulatory logic was a first attempt by actors working within the market logic to create the regulatory logic in relation to their own logic. *Summary finding 3*: we thus see how, in pluralistic contexts, maintenance work can not only escalate conflict between contradictory logics but also generate other forms of institutional work, as actors engage in the political work of disrupting or creating the opposing logic in relation to their own interests.

In phase 4, following stronger intervention from CC and the CEOs, and more opportunities for interworking, both sides began to actively create the other logic in relation to their own. In particular, they began to define the other logic as it impacted upon their own rule systems and, rather than dismissing or counteracting them, to consider how they might cope with these impacts within their own beliefs and practices. This was an important stage in shifting away from direct conflict, as it provided a basis for mutual adjustment between actors working within different logics (Kraatz & Block, 2008). However, the act of relating to another logic was also innately threatening, such that active maintenance work had to continue at the same time. During this phase, CC began to create the regulatory logic in relation to the market logic in its external relationships with the Regulator. This was politically necessary in order for it to advocate commitment to the regulatory logic whilst attempting to contain the extent of its potential damage to the market logic. *Summary finding 4*: we thus see that, in pluralistic contexts, institutional creation work may provide grounds for actors working within different logics to relate to each other. Such relational creation work will also entail further maintenance work, as actors police their own beliefs and practices to prevent consideration of the other from diluting their own logic.

In phase 5, creation of the other logic was increasingly absorbed into the work practices of each group as they maintained their own logic.

Thus, maintenance work included policing of the potential impacts that each side's beliefs and practices might have upon the other. This in no way entailed a blending of the two logics, which remained discrete and intact, but did involve some changes in work practices to accommodate the other, such as accepting greater lead times, acknowledging operational interdependence, and more rapidly escalating points of conflict for arbitration. These changes were accompanied by fierce maintenance of each side's own logic, policing beliefs, and norms, and actively re-embedding work practices in order to ensure that interaction did not damage either side's own logic. This process involved some compromises, not in the foundations of the logics but in their operationalization, as regulatory deadlines were delayed in order to ensure that minimum levels of customer service could be maintained, whilst volunteering financial penalties to support this compromise. These compromises may be seen as political acts of mutual adjustment in order to maintain pluralistic logics and continue to function within the principles of each (Lindblom, 1965). *Summary finding 5*: we thus see that, in pluralistic contexts, maintenance work entails both active maintenance of each side's own logic and also maintenance of its relationship with the other logic. In this way, actors can mutually adjust to each other, whilst reinforcing and maintaining their own beliefs and practices. Such mutual adjustments may entail political compromises over deadlines or other events to enable action without constituting a fundamental shift in either logic.

Conclusions and implications

The practice approach taken in this study has provided a lens for understanding how pluralistic institutional logics are realized within the interactions between organizational members. It is in these interactions that institutional work occurs, reproducing or modifying existing institutions, creating new institutions, and disrupting old ones. The findings discussed above have provided the following important insights into institutional work and institutional pluralism.

First, our findings illustrate that, in the context of institutional pluralism, institutional maintenance involves ongoing active work. Institutional maintenance has been a neglected topic of study because institutional persistence is taken-for-granted (Lawrence & Suddaby, 2006; Scott, 2001). The various types of agency, practical, discursive, iterative, and projective (Clegg, 1989; Emirbayer & Mische, 1998; Giddens, 1984), involved in the maintenance of institutions have thus been overlooked. Lawrence and Suddaby (2006) propose that agency and active maintenance work will be heightened during times of upheaval. Our study indicates that the continuous threat posed by other logics provokes active maintenance work as part of the ongoing practical-evaluative agency involved in coping with pluralistic logics (Emirbayer & Mische, 1998; Jarzabkowski, 2005). Our findings suggest that in pluralistic contexts institutional maintenance occurs as a pattern of move and countermove, as actors working within different logics respond to acts of maintenance by others. In order to maintain their own logics, different actors engaged in other forms of politically motivated institutional work, either disrupting the other logic or creating it in relation to their own interests. Thus, we elaborate Lawrence and Suddaby's (2006) concept of institutional maintenance by showing that, in pluralistic contexts, maintenance work is not an occasional activity but an ongoing, politicized activity of response and counter-response.

Second, our findings elaborate the concept of institutional maintenance by showing that, in pluralistic contexts, maintenance also involves acts of creation and disruption. That is, in order to maintain their own logics, different actors engaged in political acts of either disrupting the other logic or creating it in relation to their own interests. Active maintenance of coexisting logics within pluralistic contexts thus spills over into creative work and disruptive work.

Third, our findings on how actors create another logic in relation to their own further elaborate our understanding of institutional creation. While creation is typically an act in the emergence of a new institution (Lawrence & Suddaby, 2006), in the context of institutional pluralism, creation may be a political act used to establish a contradictory logic in relation to one's own interests, as shown by RD in phase 3. However, as shown by both divisions and CC in phase 4, creation may also be a pragmatic act that enables actors working within contradictory logics to find ways of considering the other within the principles of their own rule systems. Creation work may thus occur not only to generate a new institution but also to allow actors working within existing institutions to create "space" for other, contradictory logics to coexist with their own.

Fourth, our findings illuminate our understanding of institutional pluralism by showing how pluralistic institutions are realized within the actions and interactions of actors within organizations. The first pattern of institutional maintenance that we found in phases 2 and 3, involving move and countermove, indicates how actors can escalate conflict between institutions. Such moves lead to stalemate, as both institutions are legitimate such that neither side may "win" these direct conflict games (Hargrave & Van de Ven, 2006; Jarzabkowski & Fenton, 2006; Kraatz & Block, 2008; Seo, Putnam & Bartunek, 2004; Werner & Baxter, 1994). By contrast, the second pattern of creating and maintaining each side's logic in relation to the other, found in phases 4 and 5, provides the basis for mutual adjustment between logics. As Kraatz and Block (2008) suggest, this type of balancing of tensions in an ongoing and uneasy truce is one way that organizations and their actors may learn to cope with coexistent and competing logics (Werner & Baxter, 1994). Mutual adjustment between logics is a political means by which organizations and their actors may cope with institutional pluralism (Lindblom, 1965).

Fifth, we found that particular work practices that emerged in phases 4 and 5 enabled mutual adjustment, such as intensive and frequent interworking between actors working within different logics, active hierarchical intervention and arbitration by authority figures, such as CEOs, and clear escalation mechanisms for coping with conflict. These findings suggest that institutional pluralism may be managed through organizational governance mechanisms (Kraatz & Block, 2008; Lawrence & Lorsch, 1967; Selznick, 1949). Further research might elicit those governance mechanisms that best enable actors to cope with and negate the conflict occasioned by pluralistic logics.

Finally, our findings on the creation and maintenance of other logics in relation to each side's own logic indicates that pluralistic logics are interdependent and relational. That is, in order for one logic to exist, the other must also exist. In particular, the external advocacy work undertaken by CC to demonstrate the importance of attending to the regulatory logic whilst ensuring the maintenance of the market logic suggests an intriguing relationship. Without a market, there would be no need for a regulatory logic. The regulatory logic exists to enable a freely competitive market by curbing the competitive excesses of that market, such as monopoly. While our findings are too tentative to draw strong conclusions, they indicate grounds for future research into the relational and interdependent features of institutional pluralism, in which competing logics might be seen as part of a greater system of institutional interactions (Kraatz & Block, 2008; Selznick, 1949).

In summary, this chapter has shown that, under conditions of institutional pluralism, actors must continuously maintain opposing institutional logics, which also requires them to engage in the politicized work of creating their own institutional logic and disrupting the opposing logic. The practice approach taken here has illuminated the nature of different types of institutional work and the interdependencies between these types of work, in the context of pluralistic institutional logics. Our study shows the processes and practices through which organizations and the actors within them cope with tensions between pluralistic logics over time.

References

Archer, M. (1995) *Realist Social Theory: The Morphogenetic Approach.* Cambridge: Cambridge University Press.

Bacharach, S. B. & Lawler, E. J. (1980) *Power and Politics in Organizations: The Social Psychology of Conflict, Coalitions, and Bargaining.* San Francisco: Jossey-Bass.

Barley, S. (1986) Technology as an occasion for structuring: evidence from observations of CT scanners and the social order of radiography departments. *Administrative Science Quarterly*, 31(1): 78–109.

Barley, S. & Tolbert, P. (1997) Institutionalization and structuration: studying the links between action and institution. *Organization Studies*, 18(1): 93–117.

Benson, J. K. (1977) Organizations: a dialectical view. *Administrative Science Quarterly*, 22(1): 1–21.

Bohman, J. (1999) Practical reason and cultural constraint: agency in Bourdieu's theory of practice. In R. Shusterman (ed.), *Bourdieu: A Critical Reader*, pp. 128–152. Oxford: Blackwell.

Bourdieu, P. (1990) *The Logic of Practice.* Cambridge: Polity Press.

Brown, G., Lawrence, T. B. & Robinson, S. L. (2005) Territoriality in organizations. *Academy of Management Review*, 30(3): 577–594.

Child, J. (1997) Strategic choice in the analysis of action, structure, organizations and environment: retrospect and prospect. *Organization Studies*, 18(1): 43–76.

Clark, P. (2000) *Organisations in Action: Competition between Contexts.* London: Routledge.

Clegg, S. R. (1989) *Frameworks of Power.* London: Sage.

Cooper, D., Hinings, B., Greenwood, R. & Brown, J. (1996) Sedimentation and transformation in organization change: the case of Canadian law firms. *Organization Studies*, 17(4): 623–647.

Denis, J.-L., Langley, A. & Rouleau, L. (2007) Strategizing in pluralistic contexts: rethinking theoretical frames. *Human Relations*, 60(1): 179–215.

DiMaggio, P. J. & Powell, W. W. (1983) The iron cage revisited: institutional isomorphism and collective rationality in organizational fields. *American Sociological Review*, 48: 147–160.

Eisenhardt, K. (1989) Building theories from case study research. *Academy of Management Review*, 14(4): 532–550.

Emirbayer, M. & Mische, A. (1998) What is agency? *American Journal of Sociology*, 103(4): 962–1023.

Evered, R. & Louis, M. R. (1981) Alternative perspectives in the organizational sciences: "Inquiry from the inside" and "Inquiry from the outside." *Academy of Management Review*, 6(3): 385–396.

Friedland, R. & Alford, R. R. (1991) Bringing society back in: symbols, practices, and institutional contradictions. In W. W. Powell & P. J. DiMaggio (eds.), *The New Institutionalism in Organizational Analysis*, pp. 232–263. Chicago: University of Chicago Press.

Friedman, M. (1970) The social responsibility of business is to increase its profits. *New York Times Magazine*, September 1, 1970.

Geertz, C. (1973) *The Interpretation of Cultures*. New York: Basic Books.

Giddens, A. (1984) *The Constitution of Society*. Cambridge: Polity Press.

Glynn, M. & Lounsbury, M. (2005) From the critics' corner: logic blending, discursive change and authenticity in a cultural production system. *Journal of Management Studies*, 42(5): 1031–1055.

Greenwood, R. & Hinings, C. R. (1996) Understanding radical organizational change: bringing together the old and the new institutionalism. *Academy of Management Review*, 21: 1022–1054.

Greenwood, R., Suddaby, R. & Hinings, C. R. (2002) Theorizing change: the role of professional associations in the transformation of institutionalized fields. *Academy of Management Journal*, 45: 58–80.

Hardy, C. (1991) Pluralism, power and collegiality in universities. *Financial Accountability and Management*, 7(3): 127–142.

Hardy, C. & Clegg, S. R. (1996) Some dare call it power. In S. R. Clegg, C. Hardy & W. R. Nord (eds.), *Handbook of Organization Studies*, pp. 622–641. London: Sage.

Hargrave, T. & Van de Ven, A. (2006) A collective action model of institutional innovation. *Academy of Management Review*, 31(4): 864–888.

Holm, P. (1995) The dynamics of institutionalization: transformation processes in Norwegian fisheries. *Administrative Science Quarterly*, 40: 398–422.

Hopwood, A. & Miller, P. (eds.) (1994) *Accounting as Social and Institutional Practice*. Cambridge: Cambridge University Press.

Hung, S.-C. & Whittington, R. (1997) Strategy and institutions: a pluralistic account of strategies in the Taiwanese computing industry. *Organization Studies*, 18(4): 551–575.

Jarzabkowski, P. (2004) Strategy as practice: recursiveness, adaptation and practices-in-use. *Organization Studies*, 25(4): 529–560.

(2005) *Strategy as Practice: An Activity-Based View*. London: Sage.

Jarzabkowski, P., Balogun, J. & Seidl, D. (2007) Strategizing: the challenges of a practice perspective. *Human Relations*, 60(1): 5–27.

Jarzabkowski, P. & Fenton, E. (2006) Strategizing and organizing in pluralistic contexts. *Long Range Planning*, 39(6): 631–648.

Jarzabkowski, P., Matthiesen, J. & Van de Ven, A. (2008) Doing which work? A practice approach to institutional pluralism. *Aston Business School Working Paper*.

Jepperson, R. L. (1991) Institutions, institutional effects, and institutionalism. In W. W. Powell & P. J. DiMaggio (eds.), *The New Institutionalism in Organizational Analysis*, pp. 143–163. Chicago: University of Chicago Press.

Kay, J. (2000) Challenges of running a regulated business. *Mastering Strategy*, pp. 317–320. Harlow: Pearson Education Limited.

Kraatz, M. & Block, E. (2008) Organizational implications of institutional pluralism. In R. Greenwood, C. Oliver, K. Sahlin-Andersson & R. Suddaby (eds.), *Handbook of Organizational Institutionalism*, pp. 243–275. London: Sage.

Langley, A. (1999) Strategies for theorizing from process data. *Academy of Management Review*, 24(4): 691–710.

Lawrence, P. R. & Lorsch, J. W. (1967) *Organization and Environment: Managing Differentiation and Integration*. Cambridge, MA: Harvard University Press.

Lawrence, T. B. & Phillips, N. (2004) From Moby Dick to Free Willy: macrocultural discourse and institutional entrepreneurship in emerging institutional fields. *Organization*, 11(5): 689–711.

Lawrence, T. B. & Suddaby, R. (2006) Institutions and institutional work. In S. Clegg, C. Hardy, T. Lawrence & W. R. Nord (eds.), *Handbook of Organization Studies*, 2nd edn., pp. 215–254. Thousand Oaks, CA: Sage.

Lincoln, Y. S. & Guba, E. G. (1985) *Naturalistic Inquiry*. London: Sage.

Lindblom, C. E. (1965) *The Intelligence of Democracy: Decision Making through Mutual Adjustment*. New York: Free Press.

Lounsbury, M. (2007) A tale of two cities: competing logics and practice variation in the professionalizing of mutual funds. *Academy of Management Journal*, 50(2): 280–307.

Meyer, J. W. & Rowan, B. (1977) Institutionalized organizations: formal structure as myth and ceremony. *American Journal of Sociology*, 83: 340–363.

Miles, M. & Hubermann, A. (1994) *An Expanded Sourcebook: Qualitative Data Analysis*. London: Sage.

Oakes, L. S., Townley, B. & Cooper, D. J. (1998) Business planning as pedagogy: language and control in a changing institutional field. *Administrative Science Quarterly*, 43(2): 257–292.

Oliver, C. (1991) Strategic responses to institutional processes. *Academy of Management Review*, 16: 145–179.

Orlikowski, W. (1992) The duality of technology: rethinking the concept of technology in organizations. *Organization Science*, 3(3): 398–427.

  (2000) Using technology and constituting structures: a practice lens for studying technology in organizations. *Organization Science*, 11(4): 404–428.

  (2002) Knowing in practice: enacting a collective capability in distributive organizing. *Organization Science*, 13(3): 249–273.

Ortner, S. (1984) Theory in anthropology since the sixties. *Comparative Studies in Society and History*, 26: 126–166.

Pettigrew, A. (1990) Longitudinal field research on change: theory and practice. *Organization Science*, 1(3): 267–292.

Poole, M. S. & Van de Ven, A. H. (1989) Using paradox to build management and organization theories. *Academy of Management Review*, 14(4): 562–578.

Porter, M. E. (1980) *Competitive Strategy: Techniques for Analyzing Industries and Competitors*. New York: Free Press.

  (1985) *Competitive Advantage: Creating and Sustaining Superior Performance*. New York: Free Press.

Reay, T. & Hinings, C. R. (2005) The recomposition of an organizational field: health care in Alberta. *Organization Studies*, 26(3): 351–384.

Reckwitz, A. (2002) Towards a theory of social practice: a development in cultural theorizing. *European Journal of Social Theory*, 5(2): 243–263.

Russo, M. V. (2001) Institutions, exchange relations and the emergence of new fields: regulatory policies and independent power production in America, 1978–1992. *Administrative Science Quarterly*, 46: 57–86.

Schatzki, T. R., Knorr Cetina, K. and von Savigny, E. (2001) *The Practice Turn in Contemporary Theory*. London: Routledge.

Scott, W. R. (1995/2001) *Institutions and Organizations*. London: Sage.

Scott, W. R., Ruef, M., Mendel, P. J. & Caronna, C. A. (2000) *Institutional Change and Healthcare Organizations: From Professional Dominance to Managed Care*. Chicago: University of Chicago Press.

Selznick, P. (1949) *TVA and the Grass Roots*. Berkeley: University of California Press.

Seo, M. & Creed, W. E. D. (2002) Institutional contradictions, praxis, and institutional change: a dialectical perspective. *Academy of Management Review*, 27: 222–247.

Seo, M. G., Putnam, L. L. & Bartunek, J. M. (2004) Dualities and tensions of planned organizational change. In M. S. Poole & A. H. Van de Ven (eds.), *Handbook of Organizational Change and Innovation*, pp. 73–107. New York: Oxford University Press.

Sharratt, D., Brigham, B. H. & Brigham, M. (2007) The utility of social obligations in the UK energy industry. *Journal of Management Studies*, 44(8): 1503–1522.

Suchman, M. C. (1995) Managing legitimacy: strategic and institutional approaches. *Academy of Management Review*, 20(3): 571–611.

Suddaby, R. & Greenwood, R. (2005) Rhetorical strategies of legitimacy. *Administrative Science Quarterly*, 50: 35–67.

Sztompka, P. (1991) *Society in Action: The Theory of Social Becoming.* Cambridge: Polity Press.

Townley, B. (2002) The role of competing rationalities in institutional change. *Academy of Management Journal*, 45: 163–179.

Tsoukas, H. & Chia, R. (2002) On organizational becoming: rethinking organizational change. *Organization Science*, 13(5): 567–582.

Turner, S. (1994) *The Social Theory of Practices.* Cambridge: Polity Press.

Van de Ven, A. (1992) Suggestions for studying strategy process: a research note. *Strategic Management Journal*, 13: 169–188.

Van de Ven, A. H. & Hargrave, T. (2004) Social, technical, and institutional change: a literature review and synthesis. In M. S. Poole & A. H. Van de Ven (eds.), *Handbook of Organizational Change and Innovation*, pp. 259–303. New York: Oxford University Press.

Werner, C. M. & Baxter, L. A. (1994) Temporal qualities of relationships: organismic, transactional, and dialectical views. In M. Knapp & G. R. Miller (eds.), *Handbook of Interpersonal Communication*, 2nd edn., pp. 323–379. Thousand Oaks, CA: Sage.

Whittington, R. (1992) Putting Giddens into action: social systems and managerial agency. *Journal of Management Studies*, 29(6): 693–712.

(2006) Completing the practice turn in strategy research. *Organization Studies*, 27(5): 613–634.

Wilson, D. C. & Jarzabkowski, P. (2004) Thinking and acting strategically: new challenges for interrogating strategy. *European Management Review*, 1: 14–20.

Yin, R. K. (1994) *Case Study Research.* London: Sage.

Zilber, T. B. (2006) The work of the symbolic in institutional processes: translations of rational myths in Israel high tech. *Academy of Management Journal*, 49(2): 281–304.

Index

accomplishment 10
accountancy
  legitimacy 240
  multidivisional practices (MDPs) 128
accreditation 236–237, 239–240
  promoting accreditation 245–249
  reinforcing normative foundations
    243–245
ACT UP 132
action
  collective-action view 34
  and institutions 184
actor(s) 3, 4, 5, 31, 95–96
  agency and 32, 39
  alleviation of poverty and 98, 99–100
    marginal actors 103–105
  concept of an actor 3–5
  embedded 32, 42
  heroic 5
  individuals 41
  institutional entrepreneurship and 5
  marginal actors 96
  practical 6, 44
  rational actor model 34, 35
  state 4, 133, 243, 266, 269, 303
  subsidiary 106
actor network theory 185, 191, 194
agency 3, 4, 6, 31, 51, 93, 100, 121
  agency *versus* structure debate 32–35
    contribution of institutional theory
      to 35–36
  enabling conditions 38
    field-level 38–40
    individual-level 41–42
    organization-level 40–41
  institutional work and 3–6, 47–50, 100
  multidimensional view 12, 45–47
  paradox of embedded agency 32,
    36–38, 42, 43, 51, 92, 124

  relational view 12, 43–45
  Scandinavian institutionalism and
    190–193
aid programs 98
alleviation of poverty 97–99
  actors and 98, 99–100
  marginal actors 103–105
  enhancing institutions 105–107
  experimental institutional work
    101–103
  navigating across different
    institutional logics 111–112
  provisional institutions 109–111
  transforming and disrupting cultural
    beliefs, myths, and traditions
    107–109
Association to Advance Collegiate
  Schools of Business – International
  (AACSB) 237–240, 254–258
associations 16, 95, 106, 148, 153–155,
  165, 236, 263, 269, 270
athletic associations 148
authority 63, 121, 239, 296, 311

Bangladesh 101, 109, 112
  dispute resolution 104, 105
  education in 105
  health services 108
  microfinance 108, 112
  property rights 106
banking
  management of contradictions 126
  microfinance 107, 108, 112
  privatization and 269
bankruptcy 270
Boston College 252, 255, 256
bounded rationality 34
Bourdieu, Pierre 43, 44–45, 95
business education 237

Printed in Great Britain
by Amazon